INTERIOR DESIGN FUNDAMENTALS

INTERIOR DESIGN FUNDAMENTALS

Don Hepler
Executive Editor
Trade and Technical Occupations
McGraw-Hill Book Company

Cecil Jensen
Technical Director
The R. S. McLaughlin Collegiate
and Vocational Institute
Oshawa, Ontario, Canada

Paul Wallach
Fashion Institute of Design
and Merchandising
San Francisco, California

Gregg Division/McGraw-Hill Book Company
New York   Atlanta   Dallas   St. Louis   San Francisco
Auckland   Bogotá   Guatemala   Hamburg   Johannesburg   Lisbon
London   Madrid   Mexico   Montreal   New Delhi   Panama   Paris
San Juan   São Paulo   Singapore   Sydney   Tokyo   Toronto

Sponsoring Editor / Jeff McCartney
Editing Supervisor / Katharine Glynn
Design Supervisor / Caryl Valerie Spinka
Production Supervisor / Kathleen Morrissey
Art Supervisor / George T. Resch

Text Designer / Caliber Studios
Cover Designer / Dennis Sharkey
Cover Illustrator / Barbara Maslen
Technical Studio / Burmar Technical Studio, Inc.
Compositor / Monotype Composition Company
Color Separator / Ramapo Communications, Inc.

Library of Congress Cataloging in Publication Data

Hepler, Donald E.
    Interior design fundamentals.

    Includes index.
    1.   Interior decoration—Study and teaching—
United States.   I. Jensen, Cecil Howard,
(date)   joint author.   II. Wallach, Paul I.,
joint author.   III. Title
NK2116.5.H46   729   80-12529
ISBN 0-07-028296-X   AACR1

ISBN 0-07-028296-X

CONTENTS

PREFACE

Interior Design Fundamentals is a basal text designed to be used in a fundamentals course in interior design. Prerequisites are not presumed, however, fundamental courses in art or drafting may help the student proceed at a more rapid pace.

Interior Design Fundamentals is divided into five sections: Basic Design Principles, Area Planning, Surface Treatments, Furnishing and Equipment, Professional Services.

Section One, *Basic Design Principles,* covers the elements and principles of design, plus an introduction to architectural styles. Basic floor plan design including room planning is introduced as well as the principles and practices employed in drawing basic interior plans, in preparing pictorial drawings, and in the use of color in interiors.

Section Two, *Area Planning,* covers the basic elements of planning various areas of interiors and the process of combining these areas into functional and aesthetically pleasing living spaces.

Section Three, *Surface Treatments,* introduces the application of decorative and structural materials to floors, walls, and ceilings that contribute to the functional use of space as well as the enhancement of area aesthetic qualities.

Section Four, *Furnishing and Equipment,* treats the function selection and integration of major appliances, furniture, accessories and lighting systems into the total interior decor.

Section Five, *Professional Services,* is an introduction to the world of work in the field of interior design and covers the preparation of presentation drawings, models, and the use of samples, displays and manufacturers sources. This section also introduces basic financial and legal planning and the use of schedules and specifications in interior design work.

Interior Design is organized to be presented consecutively from Section One through Section Five. However, other sequences of study may be more suitable for classes with different backgrounds or emphases. Since each unit is prepared (to the degree possible) to stand alone, great sequential flexibility is possible.

All illustrations have been selected or were prepared to reinforce and amplify the principles and procedures described in the text. Wherever possible each principle and practice has been reduced to its most elementary form for easy comprehension.

Progression within each section and unit is from the simple to the complex, and from the familiar to the more abstract. The exercises that appear at the end of each unit are organized to provide the maximum amount of flexibility. Most units include problems that range from the simplest, which can be completed in a few minutes, to the more complex, which require considerable research and application of the principles and practices of interior design.

Since interior design is not only an art form but also a communication skill, communication in this field largely depends on the understanding of vocabulary. Therefore, new terms and symbols are defined when they first appear and are reinforced throughout the remainder of the text. A glossary in the appendix summarizes these terms.

The authors gratefully acknowledge the consultation services provided by Donna Goetzke, Sandra Poza, German Sonntag, Libby Hummel, and Harvey Rosenberg, whose reviews and recommendations served a key role in the development of this book. The illustrations prepared by Dana Helper also contributed immensely to the effective relationship between the text and illustrations which is so critical to the development of effective instructional materials. To the many companies who contributed technical data and illustrations, and especially to Wendy Talcott of Home Planners Inc., the authors offer particular thanks and appreciation.

Don Hepler
Cecil Jensen
Paul Wallach

viii

Celetex Corp.

INTRODUCTION

The practice of interior design began when the first cave dwellers made decisions concerning where to level and pad an area for sleeping, where to place and how to arrange facilities for cooking or fire making, and where and how to store tools, materials, and weapons. Centuries passed and civilizations developed, changing the form, function, and complexity of interiors. As materials, processes, and structures evolved; as human needs proliferated and lifestyles became more sophisticated; the role of the designer became more complex and critical in the development of environments for human growth and potential.

Using the elements of design (line, form, material, color, light, space, texture) and applying the principles of design (balance, variety, emphasis, unity, opposition, proportion, rhythm, subordination, transition, repetition) the modern designer creates aesthetically pleasing environments which enhance contemporary lifestyles and provide functional convenience. The following material is offered as an introduction to this new world of interior design.

1

SECTION ONE
BASIC DESIGN PRINCIPLES

DESIGN FACTORS

unit 1

Although every interior design may be different, the same elements of design are used to create each. Successfully combining these basic elements through the creative use of the principles of design is a hallmark of an effective designer. In addition to creating designs that are aesthetically pleasing, the successful interior designer must also create living spaces that are equally functional and consistent with the general architectural style of the building.

ELEMENTS OF DESIGN

The elements of design are the tools of the designer. They are the ingredients of every successful design. These basic elements are: line, form, color, space, light, texture, and material.

Line

The element of line is used to produce a sense of movement within an object or produce a greater sense of length or height. Lines enclose space and provide the outline or contour of forms. Straight lines are either vertical, horizontal, or diagonal; however, curved lines have an infinite number of directional variations. Curved lines

dominate the design shown in Fig. 1-1A, while the straight lines found in Fig. 1-1B create vertical emphasis.

A vertical line creates the illusion of an increase in height because the eye moves upward to follow the line. A horizontal line creates the illusion of an increase in width as the eye moves horizontally.

In duplicating the various positions of the human body, lines can create certain feelings. Vertical lines, for example, create a feeling of strength, simplicity, and alertness, while horizontal lines suggest relaxation and repose. Diagonal lines create a feeling of restlessness or transition, and curved lines are indicative of soft, graceful, and flowing movements.

As in any art form, the combination of straight and curved lines in patterns relate to the other elements of design to create the most pleasing total design configuration.

Form

Lines joined together produce form, or create the shape of an area. Straight lines joined together

Fig. 1-1 A. Curved stairs dominate this design. *Benjamin Moore Company*

Fig. 1-1 B. Vertical-line emphasis. *American Standard, Inc.*

Fig. 1-2. Open-form design. *Stanmar, Inc.*

produce rectangles, squares, and other geometric shapes. Curved lines form circles, ovals, and ellipses. The proportion of these forms or shapes is an important factor in design. Circles and ovals convey a feeling of completeness, while squares and rectangles produce a feeling of mathematical precision and should be used accordingly. The form of an object may be closed and solid or closed and volume-containing. It may also be open as shown in Fig. 1-2. The form of the structure, however, should always be determined by its function.

Color

Color is either an integral part of the material or must be added to create the desired effect. The use of color in interiors either distinguishes items, intensifies interest, or diminishes eye contact. For this reason color combinations are varied, depending on the purpose.

Color harmonies are groups of colors used in combination to create pleasing visual images. *Color hue* distinguishes one color from another. Color hue is the name of the color, such as red, yellow, and blue. The *value* of a color is the degree of darkness or lightness of the hue. A *tint* is a color on the lighter portion of the hue, a shade represents the darker portion of the *hue*. *Intensity,* or the saturation of color, refers to the degree of brightness or purity of the color.

Psychology of Color

Red is associated with warmth (Fig. 1-3) and action, while yellow, the color nearest to the sun, is related to cheer and exuberance. Yellow is the greatest attention-creating color, while orange is associated with light and heat. Violet, the color of shadows, creates a feeling of mystery, while green depicts coolness and restraint. Thus green is used in industrial applications to alleviate tension. Blue is associated with coolness, repose, and formality. It is associated with the sky, the ocean, and ice. It has been used throughout the ages as the symbol for truth, royalty, and purity.

Physical Effects of Color

Color is used to change the visual dimensions of a room. It is used to make rooms appear higher

Fig. 1-3. A warm color scheme. *Armstrong Cork Company*

Fig. 1-4 *A*. Bold green areas advance.
The Siesel Company

Fig. 1-4 *B*. Pale walls recede.

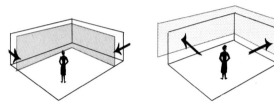

Fig. 1-4 *C*. Bold colors advance; pale colors recede.

Fig. 1-5. Blue creates a cool environment. *Scholz Homes, Inc.*

6 | or longer, lower or shorter. Bold colors, such as red, create the illusion of advancement, while pale colors (pastels) tend to recede. Notice how the bold green walls in Fig. 1-4*A* seem to advance and the pale walls in Fig. 1-4*B* tend to recede. Figure 1-4*C* shows the visual impression created. Color also affects the feeling of temperature within a room. Thus a blue room will feel colder at the same temperature than a red room. Notice how much cooler the blue room in Fig. 1-5 appears than the red room in Fig. 1-3.

Light and Shadow

Light reflects from the surfaces of forms. Shadows appear in the area that light cannot reach in varying degrees. Light and shadow both give a sense of depth to any structure. The effective designer plans the relationship of light and dark areas accordingly (Fig. 1-6). The designer must therefore consider which surfaces reflect particles instead of absorbing them and which surfaces refract (bend) light as it passes through the material. The designer must also remember that with continued exposure to light, visual sensitivity decreases. Thus we become adapted to degrees of darkness, or lightness, after extended exposure.

Fig. 1-6. Relationship of light and dark areas. *Armstrong Cork Company*

Fig. 1-7. Expansion of visual space through continuous ceilings. *Armstrong Cork Company*

Space

Space both surrounds form and is contained within it. The design can create the feeling of space. For example, the continuous ceiling shown in Fig. 1-7 creates a feeling of expanded space. Interior design is the art of handling space and space relationships in a manner that utilizes all other elements of design in a functional and aesthetic manner.

Materials

Materials are the raw substances with which interior designers create decors. Materials possess their own color, form, dimension, degree of hardness, and texture. The hardness of the material cannot be altered. However, to some degree, the color, form, and dimension of materials can be altered. Texture is the most significant factor in the selection of appropriate materials. *Texture* refers to the surface finish of an object—its roughness, smoothness, coarseness, or fineness. Surfaces such as concrete, stone, and brick have rough and dull surfaces and suggest strength and informality, while smoother surfaces, such as glass, aluminum, and plastics, create a feeling of luxury and formality. The designer must be careful not to include too many different textures of a similar nature. For this reason, masonries (brick and stone, for example) are not usually combined in close proximity. Contrasting textures, such as the wood texture shown in Fig. 1-8, are more pleasing when combined with contrasting surfaces.

Rough surfaces reduce the apparent height of the ceiling or distance of a wall and make colors appear darker. Smooth surfaces increase the apparent height of a ceiling or wall distances

Fig. 1-8. Contrasting textures and surfaces. *Redwood Shingle & Shake Bureau*

and reflect more light, thus making colors appear brighter.

PRINCIPLES OF DESIGN

The basic principles of design are the guidelines for applying the elements of design to create aesthetically functional interiors. The basic principles of design are: balance, variety, emphasis, unity, opposition, proportion, rhythm, subordination, transition, and repetition.

Balance

Balance is the achievement of equilibrium in design. An object or an arrangement of objects such as furniture is *formally balanced* if symmetrical or *informally balanced* if there is variety, yet harmony, in the distribution of space, form, line, color, light, and shade. The room shown in Fig. 1-9 is informally (asymmetrically) balanced.

Fig. 1-9. Asymmetrically balanced furnishings. *Scholz Homes, Inc.*

7

Fig. 1-10. Symmetrically balanced furnishings. *Scholz Homes, Inc.*

The room shown in Fig. 1-10 is formally (symmetrically) balanced.

Rhythm

When lines, planes, and surface treatments are repeated in a regular sequence, a sense of rhythm is achieved. The circular patterns in Fig. 1-11 give a sense of rhythm to the design. Rhythm is

Fig. 1-12. The pond creates the point of emphasis for this foyer. *Scholz Homes, Inc.*

used to create motion and carry the viewer's eyes to various parts of the space. This is accomplished by the repetition of lines, colors, and patterns. Placing accent colors strategically around a room, arranging pictures, and matching wall coverings and fabrics are a few of the methods used to create rhythm in interior design.

Emphasis

The principle of emphasis (or domination) is used by the designer to draw attention to an area or subject. Emphasis is achieved through the use of color, form, texture, or line. The pond in Fig. 1-12 creates a point of emphasis for this foyer. Although the design is consistent, color and form contrast with the remainder of the features.

In interior design, some emphasis or a focal point should be designed into each room. It may be a fireplace, a painting, a window treatment, or an art object. Directing attention to the point of emphasis (focal point) is accomplished by the arrangement of furnishings, the use of contrasting colors, line direction, light variations, space relationships, or material changes.

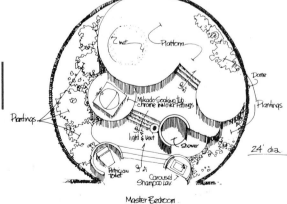

Fig. 1-11. Circular patterns provide a sense of rhythm. *Kohler*

8

Fig. 1-13. Well-proportioned relationship between mirror and dresser. *Filbar*

Proportion

The proportion (scale) of a room—its furniture and accessories—is important. Some proportions are more pleasing than others. The early Greeks found that rectangles with dimensions in the ratio of 2 to 3, 3 to 5, and 5 to 8 were more pleasing than others. A room 10′ × 15′ [3.1 × 4.6 m (meters)] or a rug 9′ × 12′ (2.7 × 3.7 m) have dimensions of this type. Likewise a 4′ (1.2 m) mirror over a 6′ (1.8 m) dresser is more pleasing than a 3′ (0.9 m) or 5′ (1.5 m) mirror (Fig. 1-13).

The scale between the room, furniture, and accessories should be harmonious, avoiding bulky furniture in a small room, small pictures in a large room, and vice versa. Figure 1-14 shows several proportional systems used in two-dimensional design.

Unity

Unity is the expression of the sense of wholeness in the design. Every room should appear complete. No parts should appear as appendages or

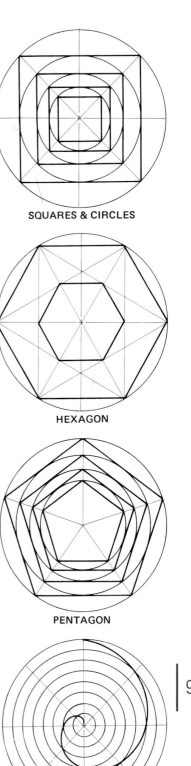

SQUARES & CIRCLES

HEXAGON

PENTAGON

SPIRAL

Fig. 1-14. Proportional systems.

9

Fig. 1-15. Example of line-and-color unity. *Armstrong Cork Company*

bringing together of the basic elements of good design to form one harmonious, unified whole. Before furnishings are added to a room, the designer must ensure that the line, form, texture, and color of the furnishings blend with these elements of the room in a harmonious manner. Unity (or harmony) is achieved through the utilization of any or all of these elements of design, for there is potential for unity within each.

Variety

Without variety, any area can become dull and tiresome to the eye of the observer. Too much rhythm, too much repetition, or too much unity ruin a sense of variety or contrast. Likewise, too little of any of the elements of design will also result in a lack of variety. Light, shadow, and color are used extensively to achieve variety. Light textured surfaces on walls, for example, are good contrast to the dark fireplace and furniture and provide variety to the room shown in Fig. 1-16.

afterthoughts. In the room shown in Fig. 1-15, the designer has achieved unity through the use of consistent line and color throughout the room. Unity, or harmony, as the name implies, is the

Fig. 1-16. Texture contrasts provide variety. *Olympic*

Fig. 1-17. Effective use of repetition of lines, spaces, and textures.

Repetition

Unity is often achieved through repetition. Vertical lines, spaces, and textures are repeated throughout the design to tie the structure together aesthetically and achieve unity, as shown in Fig. 1-17.

Opposition

Opposites in design add interest. Opposition involves contrasting elements such as short and long, thick and thin, straight and curved, or black and white. Opposite forms, colors, and lines in a design, when used effectively in conjunction with the other principles of design, are used to achieve balance, emphasis, and variety.

Subordination

When emphasis is achieved through some design feature, other features naturally become subordinate. Subordination can be related to either lines, shapes, or color in a design.

Transition

The change from one color to another, or from a curved to a straight line, if done while maintaining the unity of the design, is known as *transition*. Transition may involve the intersection of molding from one wall to another in the same room, or may apply to the transition of one floor surface to another in adjoining rooms. The interior designer's task in achieving successful transition in all aspects of the design makes for harmony of different elements of design without sacrificing unity.

CREATIVITY

Creativity in interior design involves the ability to create mental images of arrangements and forms not yet visible. Creative imagination is the ability to present new patterns, use new objects, and invent new configurations. Thus creativity and imagination are almost synonymous in interior design, for they relate to the forces that cause isolated and unrelated factors to come together into arrangements of cohesive unity and beauty.

FUNCTIONAL DESIGN

Any basic idea regardless of how creative or imaginative is useless unless the design can be successfully implemented and function as needed. Interior design involves not only how a room looks but how a room functions. Thus interior design begins with an assessment of human needs. Form follows function. However, functional success alone does not guarantee the design is aesthetically pleasing. The task of the interior designer is to combine functional efficiency and aesthetics into a unified design solution by successfully manipulating the elements of design through the effective application of the principles of design.

No design can exist in isolation. It must always be related to all situations influencing it.

11

Fig. 1-18. Contemporary living area. *Consoweld*

Fig. 1-19. Alternate design treatment of room shown in Fig. 1-18. *Consoweld*

This is why the modern interior designer must think in terms of the total interior design, not in terms of only the decorative aspects of design. Decoration suggests that something is merely added to the surface. A design, on the other hand, involves manipulating the entire environment in the creation process.

DESIGN PROCESS

The design process is the same regardless of the style. For example, the room shown in Fig. 1-18 represents the same space relationship of elements as the room shown in Fig. 1-19. The only difference is the style of furnishings.

Proceeding logically from a basic idea to a final design is often a long process. Rough ideas are recorded, sketches are refined and changed, and the basic form is established. Elements of line, texture, color, light, and shadow must be combined in the most appropriate relationships. The effects of unity and repetition, rhythm, variety, emphasis, and balance should be achieved without sacrificing the functional or technical aspects of the design.

Ideas in the creative stage may be recorded by sketching basic images. These sketches are then revised until the basic ideas are finally crystallized. First sketches rarely produce a finished design. Usually many revisions are necessary, as shown in Fig. 1-20. Many designers make a habit of never discarding a sketch. They resketch the problem on successive sheets of paper because often the fifth sketch may indeed reveal the solution to a problem in the tenth sketch. The ideas may not be combined in a functional design until perhaps 20 or 30 sketches have been made.

Design activities may be formal or informal. Informal designs occur when the designer works without a plan. Formal design involves preparing sketches and laying out drawings. These drawings are then used in the purchasing and/or building of interior design components. It is the latter approach that is used throughout the remainder of this text. It is through the medium of drawings and sketches that the designer also can best communicate to the client, for one of the key roles of the interior designer is to communicate effectively.

Changing Patterns and Tastes

Not only must the interior designer blend the basic elements of design with good functional design, but this must be done as styles and tastes change, for interior design literally changes with the times. There are periods when people prefer open planning, while at other times complete privacy is of primary concern. Individual and

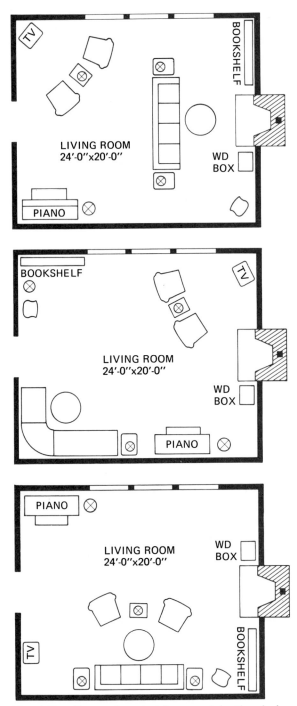

Fig. 1-20. Successive sketches used in the design process.

public tastes constantly change; but the designer must not be caught in a "fad trap." An effective, creative, well-grounded interior designer will recognize the difference between trends and fads, but the designer must constantly be on the alert,

examining, observing, preserving, constantly looking for the link between the present and the future. The contemporary designer must recall past experiences and apply old ideas to new situations in combinations of infinite variety.

ARCHITECTURAL STYLES

The total architectural style of the structure must be one of the first considerations in developing the interior design style. To be truly authentic, periods should be exactly matched internally and externally. This means that an Elizabethan-style home should be furnished only with English heritage furniture such as Queen Anne, a French Provincial–style home should accordingly be furnished with Louis XIV furniture, and so forth. Most designers are content, however, to match all European styles, early American styles, and modern styles of architecture with matching interiors. Figures 1-21 through 1-25 show the relationship between exterior and interior styles of architecture.

Although our architectural heritage is largely derived from European and early American architecture, specific architectural styles have evolved through the years as a result of technological developments and demands of the culture. Styles of the past reflect the culture of the past. Styles of the present reflect our current living habits and needs. Styles of the future will be largely determined by advancements in technology and changes in our living styles and patterns.

European Styles

The English, French, Italians, and Spanish have had the most significant influence on our architecture.

English Architecture
The English Tudor style of architecture originated in England during the fifteenth century. Tudor homes feature high-pitched gable roofs, small windows, shallow dormers, Norman towers, and tall chimneys which extended high above the roof line.

The Elizabethan, or half-timbered, style is an adaptation of the Tudor style. It is characterized by the use of mortar set between timbers.

Fig. 1-21 A. Elizabethan exterior design. *Scholz Homes, Inc.*

Fig. 1-21 B. Interior style compatible with European architecture. *Benjamin Moore Company*

Figures 1-21A and B show a modern adaptation of the Elizabethan style of architecture from which many of our modern styles are derived.

French Architecture

French Provincial architecture was brought to this continent when the French settled Quebec. French Provincial architecture can be identified by the mansard roof. This roof design was developed by the French architect François Mansard. On the French Provincial home this roof is high-pitched, with steep slopes and rounded dormer windows projecting from the sides.

Southern European Architecture

Spanish architecture was brought to this country by Spanish colonials who settled the Southwest. Spanish architecture is characterized by low-pitched roofs of ceramic tile and stucco exterior walls. A distinguishing feature of almost every Spanish home is a courtyard patio. Two-story Spanish homes contain open balconies enclosed in grillwork. One-story Spanish homes were the forerunners of the present ranch-style homes that first developed in southern California. (See Fig. 1-22.)

Italian architecture is very similar to Spanish architecture. One distinguishing feature is the use of columns and arches at a loggia entrance, and windows of balconies opening onto a loggia. A *loggia* is an open gallery covered by a roof. The use of classical mouldings around first-floor windows also helps to distinguish the Italian style from the Spanish.

Early American

Early colonists came to the New World from many different cultures and were familiar with many different styles of architecture.

New England Colonial

The colonists who settled the New England coastal areas were influenced largely by English styles of architecture. Lack of materials, time, and equipment greatly simplified their adaptation of these styles. One of the most popular of the New England styles was the *Cape Cod*. This is a one-and-one-half story gabled-roof house with dormers. It has a central front entrance, a large central chimney, and exterior walls of clapboard

Fig. 1-22. Spanish architectural style. *Scholz Homes, Inc.*

or bevel siding. Double-hung windows are fixed with shutters, and the floor plan is symmetrical. Cold New England winters influenced the development of many design features such as shutters, small window areas, double chimneys, and enclosed breezeways.

Mid-Atlantic Colonial

The availability of brick, a seasonal climate, and the influence of the architecture of Thomas Jefferson led to the development of the early American style of architecture illustrated in Figs. 1-23*A* and *B*. The style was formal, massive, and ornate. In colonial days, buildings from Virginia

Fig. 1-23 *A*. Mid-Atlantic colonial style. *Walt Disney Productions*

Fig. 1-23 *B*. Interior style compatible with colonial architecture. *Benjamin Moore Company*

15

Fig. 1-24 *A*. Western ranch style of architecture. *Potlatch Corp.*

to New Jersey were designed in this manner. It was an adaptation of many urban English designs.

Southern Colonial
When the early settlers migrated to the South, warmer climates and outdoor living activities led them to develop the Southern colonial style of architecture. As the house became the center of plantation living, the size was increased, and

often a second story was added. Two-story columns were used to support the front-roof overhang and the symmetrical gabled roof.

Ranch Style
As settlers moved West, architectural styles changed to meet their needs. The availability of space eliminated the need for second floors. This same amount of space could then be spread

Fig. 1-24 *B*. Interior of house shown in Fig. 1-24A. *Potlatch Corp.*

horizontally rather than vertically, resulting in a rambling plan (Fig. 1-24A). Figure 1-24B shows the interior of the right wing of the house shown in Fig. 1-24A. The Spanish and Mexican influence also led to the popularization of the Western ranch, which also utilized a U-shaped plan with a patio in the center.

VICTORIAN

The Industrial Revolution in this country provided architects and builders with machinery and equipment which could be used to construct very intricate millwork items. Since living habits had changed little, this new-found technology was used by adding decoration to a building. Intricate finials, lintels, parapets, balconies, and cornices were added to structures. Ornate aspects of Victorian architecture (gingerbread) were designed into homes until recent years.

CONTEMPORARY

The development of lighter, stronger building materials combined with the need to produce inexpensive structures in less time led to the evolution of simple functional designs, as shown in Fig. 1-25A. The matching interior shown in Fig. 1-25B is characterized by simpler lines and more open planning.

Fig. 1-25 A. Functional lines in contemporary design. *Scholz Homes, Inc.*

Fig. 1-25 B. Contemporary open style. *Scholz Homes, Inc.*

17

Review Questions

1. Define the following terms: informal, symmetrical, form, intensity, balance, texture, proportion, emphasis, rhythm, repetition, variety, unity, opposition, transition, Tudor, French Provincial, contemporary, Victorian.
2. Complete the exercises in the workbook, for Unit 1.
3. (*a*) Collect examples of architectural styles for your design scrapbook. Collect furniture styles that match these architectural styles. (*b*) Find examples of each element and principle of design from newspapers and magazines. Circle and label the specific application in each example.
4. In Unit 6 list the illustrations by figure numbers that represent the best example of the use of the following elements of design: horizontal line, curved line, bold color, abstract space, lines in transition, lines in opposition, two-dimensional form, three-dimensional form, rhythm, repetition, bisymmetrical balance, asymmetrical balance.
5. Find the focal point in Figs. 1-4*A*, 1-17, and 1-24*B*.
6. Refer to Fig. 6-11*A* and list which elements of design predominate and describe each element's contribution to the total design.
7. Resketch the room shown in Fig. 1-9 and improve the light and shadow patterns, provide more unity of texture and line, and select a basic color scheme.
8. Redesign Fig. 1-18 to provide more emphasis on light and shadow.
9. Redesign Fig. 1-25*A* and change the arrangement from symmetrical to asymmetrical.
10. Redesign Fig. 1-4*B* to provide more variety.
11. Redesign Fig. 1-9 to provide a major point of emphasis.
12. In Unit 6 list the figure numbers that represent the following styles of architecture: Tudor, Cape Cod, contemporary, Southern colonial, French Provincial, Spanish.

FLOOR-PLAN DESIGN unit 2

Before a designer can begin to create a floor-plan design, the requirements of each room in that design must first be considered. This includes analyzing the need for furniture and equipment and determining sizes to fulfill the basic function of each room. Only after the basic size has been established for each room, can the rooms be combined into a floor-plan layout.

ROOM PLANNING

Not long ago the outside of most homes was designed before the inside. A basic square, rectangle, or series of rectangles was established to a convenient overall size and then rooms were fitted into these forms.

Today the inside of most homes is designed before the outside, and the outside design is determined by the size and relationship of the inside areas. This is known as *designing from the inside out*.

Basic Requirements

In designing from the inside out, the designer evolves the plan from basic room requirements. By learning about the living habits and tastes of the occupants, the designer determines what facilities are required for each room. In this way the furniture, fixtures, and amount of space that will be appropriate for the activities are provided for.

Sequence of Design

When designing from the inside out, the designer first determines what furniture and fixtures are needed. Next the amount and size of furniture must be determined. The style selected will greatly affect the dimensions of the furniture.

After the furniture dimensions are established, furniture templates can be made and arranged in functional patterns. Room sizes are then established by drawing a perimeter around the furniture arrangements.

When the room sizes are determined, rooms can be combined into areas, and areas into the total floor plan. Finally the outside is designed by projecting the elevations from the floor plan. Figure 2-1 shows the importance of room planning in the overall sequence of planning a residence.

Furniture

Furniture styles vary greatly in size and proportion. Sizes of furniture therefore cannot be decided on until the style is chosen. The furniture style should be consistent with the style of architecture (Fig. 2-2).

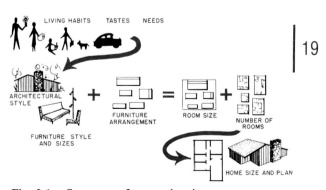

Fig. 2-1. Sequence of room planning.

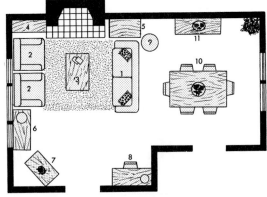

COMBINATION LIVING-DINING ROOM

1 - CHESTERFIELD   7 - TV CONSOLE
2 - LOUNGE CHAIR   8 - DESK
3 - COFFEE TABLE   9 - FLOOR LAMP
4 - BOOKCASE   10 - DINING ROOM TABLE
5 - END TABLE   AND 6 CHAIRS
6 - STEREO   11 - BUFFET

Fig. 2-3 A. Living needs determine the amount of furniture.

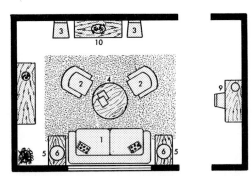

FURNITURE GROUPING AROUND COFFEE TABLE

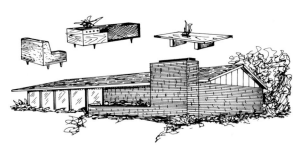

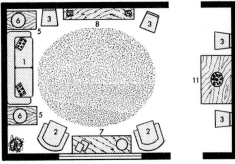

MULTIPURPOSE LIVING ROOM

1 - CHESTERFIELD   7 - STEREO
2 - LOUNGE CHAIR   8 - BUILT-IN CABINET
3 - CHAIR   9 - DESK AND CHAIR
4 - COFFEE TABLE   10 - BUFFET
5 - END TABLE   11 - FOLDING TABLE
6 - LAMP

Fig. 2-3 B. Lifestyle determines the furniture arrangement.

Fig. 2-2. Relationship of furniture style to architectural style.

Selection

Furniture should be selected according to the needs of the occupants (Figs. 2-3*A* and *B*). A piano should be provided for someone interested in music. A great amount of bookcase space must be provided for the avid reader. The artist, drafter, or engineer may require drafting equipment in the den or study. A good starting point in room planning is to list the uses to be made of each room. Then make a list of furniture needed for each of these activities.

From these requirements a rather comprehensive list of needed furniture can be compiled. When the exact style is determined, the width and length of each piece of furniture can also be added to the list, as shown below.

Living Room

1 couch 34″ × 100″ or 864 × 2540 mm
  (millimeters)
2 armchairs 30″ × 36″ (762 × 914 mm)
1 chaise 28″ × 60″ (711 × 1524 mm)
1 TV 26″ × 24″ (660 × 610 mm)
1 hi-fi 24″ × 56″ (610 × 1422 mm)
1 bookcase 15″ × 48″ (381 × 1219 mm)
1 floor lamp 6″ × 14″ (152 × 356 mm)
1 coffee table 18″ × 52″ (457 × 1321 mm)
2 end tables 14″ × 30″ (356 × 762 mm)
1 baby grand piano 60″ × 80″ (1524 ×2032
  mm)

Dining Room

1 dining table 44″ × 72″ (1118 × 1829 mm)
2 armchairs 28″ × 36″ (711 × 914 mm)
4 chairs 26″ × 36″ (660 × 914 mm)
1 china closet 18″ × 42″ (457 × 1067 mm)
1 buffet 26″ × 56″ (660 × 1422 mm)

Similar lists should be prepared for the kitchen, bedrooms, nursery, bath, and all other rooms where furniture is required. Figure 2-4 shows some typical furniture dimensions which can be included with the furniture lists.

Furniture Templates

Arranging and rearranging furniture in a room is heavy work. It is much easier to arrange furniture by the use of templates (Fig. 2-5). *Furniture templates* are thin pieces of paper, cardboard, plastic, or metal which represent the width and length of pieces of furniture. They are used to determine exactly how much floor space each piece of furniture will occupy. One template is made for each piece of furniture on the furniture list.

Templates are always prepared to the scale that will be used in the final drawing of the house. The scale most frequently used on floor plans is ¼″ = 1′-0″. Scales of ³/₁₆″ = 1′-0″ and ⅛″ = 1′-0″ are sometimes used.

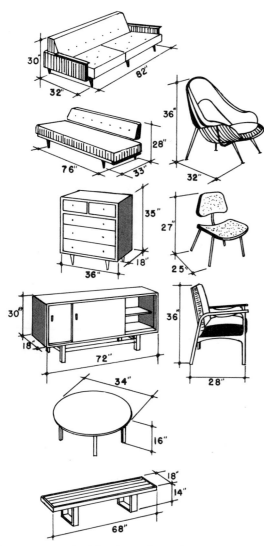

Fig. 2-4. Typical furniture dimensions.

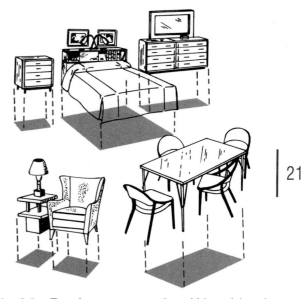

Fig. 2-5. Templates represent the width and length of each piece of furniture.

21

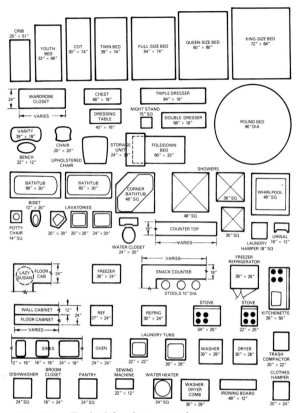

Fig. 2-6. Typical furniture templates.

Wall-hung furniture, or any projection from furniture, even though it does not touch the floor, should be included as a template because the floor space under this furniture is not usable for any other purpose.

Templates show only the width and length of furniture and the floor space covered (Fig. 2-6). Figure 2-7 shows common furniture sizes which can be used as a guide in constructing furniture templates.

Room Arrangements

Furniture templates are placed in the arrangement that will best fit the living pattern anticipated for the room. Space must be allowed for free flow of traffic and for opening and closing doors, drawers, and windows. Figure 2-8 shows furniture templates placed in several different arrangements before the room dimensions are established.

Determining Room Dimensions

After a suitable furniture arrangement has been established, the room dimensions can be deter-

COMMON FURNITURE SIZES

ITEM	LENGTH, INCHES (mm)	WIDTH, INCHES (mm)	HEIGHT, INCHES (mm)
COUCH	72(1829)	30(762)	30(762)
	84(2134)	30(762)	30(762)
	96(2438)	30(762)	30(762)
LOUNGE	28(711)	32(813)	29(737)
	34(864)	36(914)	37(940)
COFFEE TABLE	36(914)	20(508)	17(432)
	48(1219)	20(508)	17(432)
	54(1372)	20(508)	17(432)
DESK	50(1270)	21(533)	29(737)
	60(1524)	30(762)	29(737)
	72(1829)	36(914)	29(737)
STEREO CONSOLE	36(914)	16(406)	26(660)
	48(1219)	17(432)	26(660)
	62(1575)	17(432)	27(660)
END TABLE	22(559)	28(711)	21(533)
	26(660)	20(508)	21(533)
	28(711)	28(711)	20(508)
TV CONSOLE	38(965)	17(432)	29(737)
	40(1016)	18(457)	30(762)
	48(1219)	19(483)	30(762)
SHELF MODULES	18(457)	10(254)	60(1524)
	24(610)	10(254)	60(1524)
	36(914)	10(254)	60(1524)
	48(1219)	10(254)	60(1524)
DINING TABLE	48(1219)	30(762)	29(737)
	60(1524)	36(914)	29(737)
	72(1829)	42(1067)	28(711)
BUFFET	36(914)	16(406)	31(787)
	48(1219)	16(406)	31(787)
	52(1321)	18(457)	31(787)
DINING CHAIRS	20(508)	17(432)	36(914)
	22(559)	19(483)	29(737)
	24(610)	21(533)	31(787)

	DIAMETER, INCHES (mm)	HEIGHT, INCHES (mm)
DINING TABLE (ROUND)	36(914)	28(711)
	42(1067)	28(711)
	48(1219)	28(711)

Fig. 2-7. Common furniture sizes.

mined by drawing an outline around the furniture, as shown in Fig. 2-9.

Room templates are made by cutting around the outline of the room. Figure 2-10 shows some

WARDROBE CL

NIGHT STAND

TWIN BEDS

BOOKSHELF

DESK

BEDROOM
14'-9"x12'-6"

CHAIR

DRESSER   DRESSER

WARDROBE CLOSET

NIGHT STAND

QUEEN-SIZE BED

BEDROOM
16'-3"x12'-9"

CHAIR

NIGHT STAND

BOOKSHELF

DESK

DRESSER   DRESSER

Fig. 2-8. Alternative furniture arrangements.

typical room templates constructed by cutting around furniture template arrangements.

Common Room Sizes

Determining what room sizes are desirable is only one aspect of room planning. Since the cost of the home is largely determined by the size and the number of rooms, room sizes must be adjusted to conform to the acceptable price range. Figure 2-11 shows sizes for each room in large, medium, and small dwellings. These dimensions represent only average widths and lengths. Even in large homes where perhaps no financial restriction exists, a room can become too large to be functional for the purpose intended.

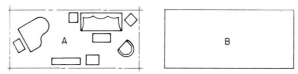

Fig. 2-9. Preferred method of showing room dimensions.

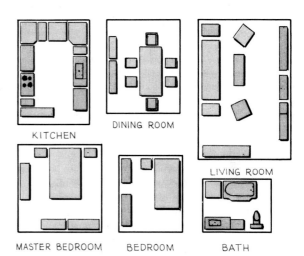

Fig. 2-10. Typical placement of furniture templates.

	LIVING ROOM, FT²/m²	DINING ROOM, FT²/m²	KITCHEN, FT²/m²	BEDROOMS, FT²/m²	BATH, FT²/m²
ROOM SIZES FOR SMALL, AVERAGE, AND LARGE HOMES					
SMALL HOME	200/18.6	155/14.4	110/10.2	140/13.0	40/3.7
AVERAGE HOME	250/24.2	175/16.3	135/12.5	170/15.8	70/6.5
LARGE HOME	300/27.9	195/18.1	165/15.3	190/17.7	100/9.3

Fig. 2-11. Room sizes for small, average, and large homes.

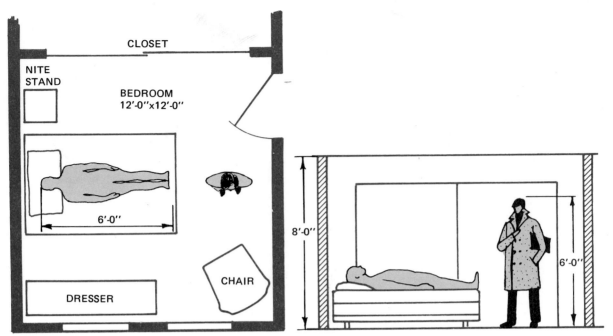

Fig. 2-12. Figures used to check room sizes.

Checking Methods

It is sometimes difficult to visualize the exact amount of real space that will be occupied by furniture or that should be allowed for traffic through a given room. One device used to give the layperson a point of reference is a template of a human figure, as shown in Fig. 2-12. With this template you can imagine yourself moving through the room to check the appropriateness of furniture placement and the adequacy of traffic allowances.

The experienced planner does not always go through the procedure of cutting out furniture templates and arranging them into patterns to arrive at room sizes. But the designer uses templates frequently to recheck designs. Until you are completely familiar with furniture dimensions and the sizes of building materials, the use of the procedures outlined here is recommended.

DESIGNING FLOOR PLANS

Designers develop and record ideas through preliminary sketches which are later transformed into final design sketches. These sketches may approximate the final design. Designers know through experience how large each room or area must be to perform a particular function. The experienced designer can mentally manipulate the relationships of areas and record design ideas through the use of sketches; however, this skill is attained after much experience.

Design Procedures

Until you have gained experience in designing floor plans, you may have difficulty in creating floor plans by the same methods used by professionals. In the beginning you should rely on more tangible methods of designing.

The information in this unit outlines the procedures you should use in developing floor-plan designs. These procedures represent real activities which relate to the mental activities of a professional designer. Figure 2-13 (pages 25–26) shows the sequence of these design activities in developing a floor plan. These room templates become the building blocks used in floor-plan designing. The room templates are arranged, rearranged, and moved into various patterns until the most desirable plan is achieved. Think of these room templates as pieces of a jigsaw puzzle which are manipulated to produce the final picture. Figure 2-14 shows a typical set of room templates prepared for use in floor-plan design.

24

1. Arrange furniture templates into groupings.

*Sleeping area

DRESSERS

TOILETS

LAVA-TORIES

NIGHT STANDS

DESK

CHAIRS

TUB

SHOWER

BEDS

*Living area

PIANO   BENCH   LARGE SOFA   SMALL SOFA   TV   STEREO   COFFEE TABLE   LAMP TABLES

CHAIRS   FIREPLACE   DINING TABLE   DESK   FOOT STOOL   UPHOLSTERED CHAIRS   BREAKFRONT

* Service Area

REF   RANGE   SINK   COUNTER   OVEN   BREAKFAST TABLE   COOK TOP   FRZ   DW   WH   LT   D   W

2. Group furniture template into rooms and add walls.

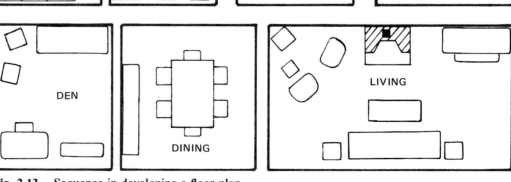

R   O

S

DW

KIT

B

BR

BR

UTILITY   WH

D   W   LT

B

DEN

DINING

LIVING

25

Fig. 2-13.   Sequence in developing a floor plan.

3. Arrange room templates

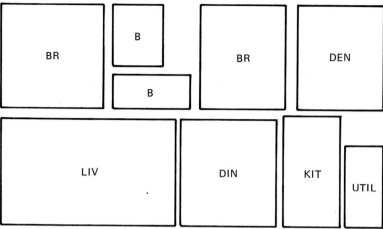

4. Add hall closets and storage.

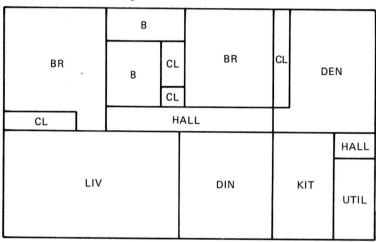

5. Complete preliminary sketch.

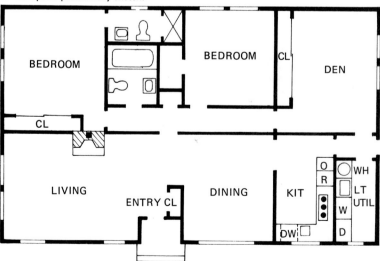

Fig. 2-13. Sequence in developing a floor plan.

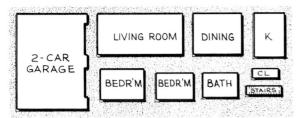

Fig. 2-14. Room templates prepared for floor-plan design use.

Planning with Room Templates

A residence or any other building is not a series of separate rooms, but a combination of several activity areas. In the design of floor plans, room templates are first divided into area classifications, as shown in Fig. 2-15. The templates are then arranged in the most desirable plan for each area (Fig. 2-16). Next the area arrangements are combined into one plan. The position of each room is then sketched and revised to achieve unity (Fig. 2-17).

As you combine areas, you will need to rearrange and readjust the position of individual rooms. At this time you should consider the traffic pattern, compass direction, street location, and relationship to landscape features. Space must be allowed for stairways and halls. Figure 2-18 shows some common arrangements for stairwells and halls on the floor plan. Unless closets have been incorporated into the room template, adequate space must also be provided for storage spaces.

Rooms and facilities such as the recreation room, laundry, workshop, and heating equipment are often placed in the basement. The designer must be sure that the floor plan developed provides sufficient space on the lower level for these facilities. In two-story houses, the sleeping area is usually placed on the level above the ground floor. Templates should also be developed for rooms on this level, but they must be adjusted to conform to the sizes established for the first level.

Floor-plan Sketching

Preparing a layout for a room template is only a preliminary step in designing the floor plan. The template layout shows only the desirable size, proportion, and relationship of each room to the entire plan.

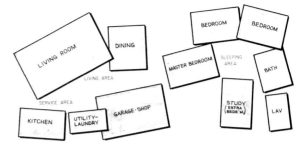

Fig. 2-15. Room templates divided into areas.

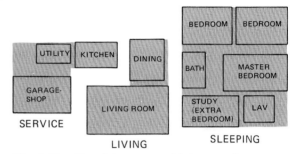

Fig. 2-16. Templates arranged into area plans.

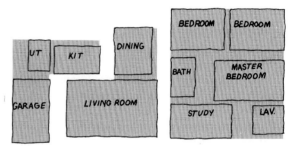

Fig. 2-17. Room templates combined into one plan.

Preliminary Sketching

Template layouts such as the one shown in Fig. 2-17 usually contain many irregularities and awkward corners because room dimensions were established before the overall plan was completed. These offsets and indentations can be smoothed out by increasing the dimensions of some rooms and changing slightly the arrangement of others. These alterations are usually made by sketching the template layout, as shown in Fig. 2-19A. At this time features such as fireplaces, closets, and divider walls can be added where appropriate.

Think of this first floor-plan sketch as only the beginning. Many sketches are usually necessary before the designer achieves an acceptable floor plan. In successive sketches such as the one

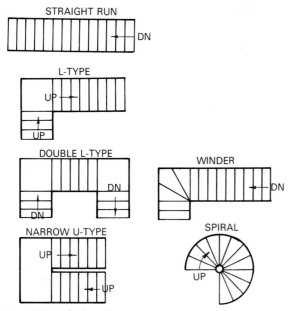

Fig. 2-18. Stairwell arrangements.

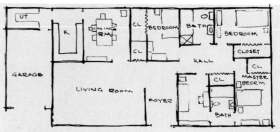

shown in Fig. 2-19B, the design should be refined further. Costly and unattractive offsets and indentations can be eliminated. Modular sizes can be established that will facilitate the maximum use of standard building materials and furnishings. The exact positions and sizes of doors, windows, closets, and halls can be determined.

Refinement of the design is done by re-sketching until a satisfactory sketch is reached, as shown in Fig 2-19C. Except for very minor changes, it is always better to make a series of sketches than to erase and change the original sketch. Many designers use tracing paper to trace the acceptable parts of the design and then change the poor features on the new sheet. This proce-

dure also provides the designer with a record of the total design process. Early sketches sometimes contain solutions to problems that develop later in the final design. Final sketches can still be improved as shown in Fig. 2-20.

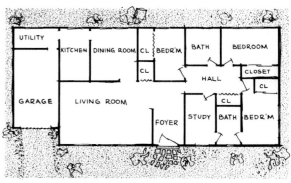

Fig. 2-19 B. A refined sketch.

28

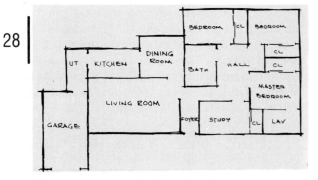

Fig. 2-19 A. A preliminary sketch.

Fig. 2-19 C. A final sketch.

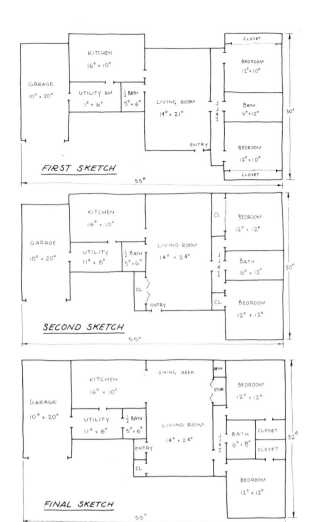

Fig. 2-20. Refinement of floor-plan sketches.

Fig. 2-21. Different arrangements from the same amount of space.

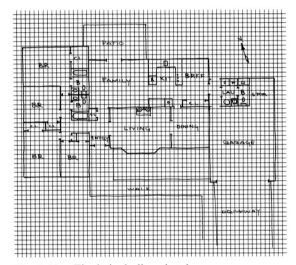

Fig. 2-22. Final single-line sketch.

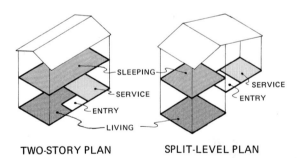

TWO-STORY PLAN   SPLIT-LEVEL PLAN

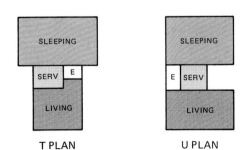

T PLAN   U PLAN

Fig. 2-23. Different plan variations.

Plan Variations

Many different room arrangements are possible within the same amount of space. Figure 2-21 shows two methods of rearranging and redistributing space to overcome poor design features.

Final Sketching

Single-line sketches are satisfactory for basic planning purposes. However, they are not adequate for establishing final sizes. A final sketch (Fig. 2-22) should be prepared on cross-sectional paper to provide a better description of wall thicknesses and to include property features. This sketch should include the exact position of doors, windows, and partitions. Figure 2-23 shows the many plan variations possible by

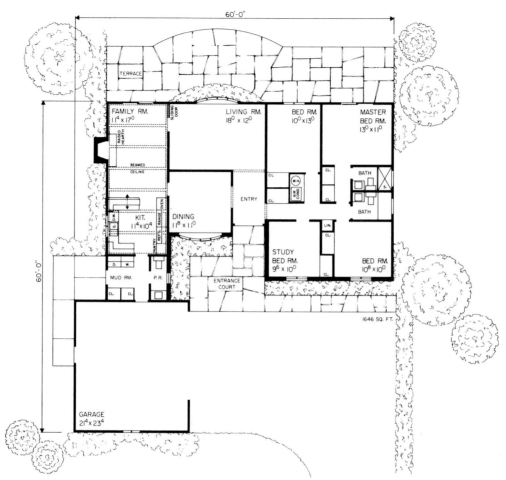

Fig. 2-24. A closed plan. *Home Planners, Inc.*

combining basic geometric shapes on different levels. Notice how the areas are arranged to achieve the most convenient plan.

Open Planning

When the rooms of a plan are divided by solid partitions, doors, or arches, the plan is known as a *closed plan*. A closed plan is shown in Fig. 2-24. If the partitions between the rooms of an area are eliminated, such as in Fig. 2-25, then the plan is known as an *open plan*.

The open plan is used mostly and to best advantage in the living area. Here the walls that separate the entrance foyer, living room, dining room, activities room, and recreation room can be removed or partially eliminated. These open areas are created to provide a sense of spacious-

ness, to aid lighting efficiency, and to increase the circulation of air through the areas.

Obviously not all the areas of a residence lend themselves well to open-planning techniques. For example, a closed plan is almost always used in the sleeping area.

The floor plan for an open plan is developed in the same manner as for a closed plan. However, in the open plan the partitions are often replaced by dividers, furniture, or by variations in level to set apart the various functions.

Review Questions

1. Define the following terms: open plan, closed plan, templates, furniture templates, room templates, floor plan.

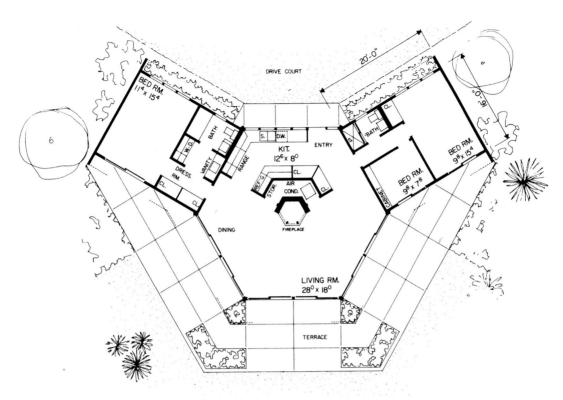

Fig. 2-25. An open plan. *Home Planners, Inc.*

2. Complete the exercises for Unit 2 in the workbook.

3. For your scrapbook, find examples of open and closed floor plans.

4. For your scrapbook, find pictures of rooms in magazines. Sketch the floor plan relating to each picture.

5. Refer to Fig. 2-25. List the good features of the floor-plan arrangement. List the poor features.

6. Prepare room templates and use them to make a functional arrangement for a living area, service area, and sleeping area.

7. Make a floor-plan sketch of the arrangement you completed in problem 6.

8. Prepare a final sketch complete with wall thicknesses and overall dimensions from the preliminary sketch developed in problem 7.

9. Make room templates of each room in your home. Redesign your home by rearranging these templates and make a remodeling sketch.

10. Rearrange the following steps in their proper order in room planning: (*a*) List the furniture needed. (*b*) Choose furniture styles. (*c*) Choose home style. (*d*) Determine living habits. (*e*) Make furniture templates. (*f*) Determine room dimensions. (*g*) Arrange furniture templates. (*h*) Determine sizes of furniture.

11. Convert the floor plan shown in Fig. 2-24 to an open plan. Sketch your solution.

12. Sketch your recommendations to improve the traffic pattern in Fig. 6-2.

13. Sketch the plan shown in Fig. 6-10 and determine the adequacy of room sizes by the use of furniture templates.

14. Compare Figs. 2-24 and 2-25. Choose which one you prefer. List the reasons.

15. Define your living needs and activities. List each piece of furniture needed for each room to fulfill these needs.

DRAWING BASIC PLANS unit 3

The total-interior designer must be able not only to create functional and aesthetically pleasing interiors, but also to communicate those designs to client, manufacturer, and construction personnel. The contemporary designer must develop skill in communicating ideas through the development of completely dimensioned floor plans and interior elevations that fully describe all elements and details of the design.

SKETCHING

Sketching is a communications medium used constantly by interior designers. In fact most interior designs begin with a preliminary rough sketch. Sketches are used to record room dimensions and record the placement of existing objects and room features prior to beginning the design. Sketches are used to show clients pos-

sibilities concerning the approach to the interior design problem (Fig. 3-1).

Sketching on graph paper helps increase speed and accuracy. Sketching also helps record ideas off the job and helps the designer remember unique features about a structure, so that the actual design activity can take place in a different location.

In sketching, use a soft pencil, hold the pencil comfortably, draw with the pencil, do not push it. Position the paper so your hand can move freely, as shown in Fig. 3-2. Sketch in short, rapid strokes. Long, continuous lines tend to bend on the arc line from elbow to fingers. A sketch, to be effective, must be readable by another person without additional explanations. If the sketch is not sufficiently complete, then notes must be added to ensure that the communication function is met.

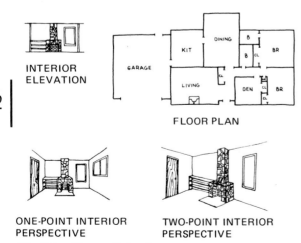

Fig. 3-1. Types of sketches.

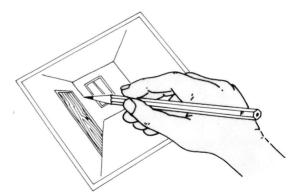

Fig. 3.2 Method of holding a pencil for sketching.

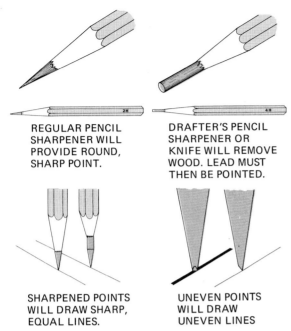

REGULAR PENCIL
SHARPENER WILL
PROVIDE ROUND,
SHARP POINT.

DRAFTER'S PENCIL
SHARPENER OR
KNIFE WILL REMOVE
WOOD. LEAD MUST
THEN BE POINTED.

SHARPENED POINTS
WILL DRAW SHARP,
EQUAL LINES.

UNEVEN POINTS
WILL DRAW
UNEVEN LINES

Fig. 3-3. Method of sharpening pencils

Sharpen the drawing pencil by exposing approximately one-half inch (10 mm) of lead, as shown in Fig. 3-3. Then form the lead into a sharp conical point on a sanding pad. Slowly rotate the pencil while you rub it over the sanding pad. A smooth single-cut file may also be used. Mechanical pencil-ejector sharpeners which eliminate sharpening and lead pointers are also available and convenient for this task.

The accuracy, effectiveness, and appearance of the finished drawing depends largely on the selection of the correct pencil and the pointing of that pencil. Figure 3-4 shows the degree of hardness of drawing pencils ranging from 9H, extremely hard, to 7B, extremely soft. Pencils in the hard range are used for layout work. Pencils in the soft range are used for sketching and rendering. Floor plans of the type prepared by interior designers are usually drawn with pencils in a medium range. When the pencil is too soft, it will produce a line that has a tendency to smudge the drawing. If the pencil is too hard, a groove will be left in the paper and the line will be very difficult to erase. Since the blackness of the line also depends on the hardness of the lead, it is necessary to select the correct degree of hardness for pencil tracings. Different degrees of hardness react differently, depending on the type of paper used.

EQUIPMENT

Interior designers need a large assortment of equipment, instruments, and supplies, including a large drawing table or drawing board capable of slight elevation to accommodate large architectural drawings. An overhead adjustable lamp is also needed in addition to general illumination. A variety of pens, pencils, and instruments used by designers are described in this unit.

T Square

The T square is used primarily as a guide for drawing horizontal lines and for guiding the triangle when drawing vertical and inclined lines. The T square is also the most useful instrument for drawing extremely long lines that deviate from the horizontal plane. Common T-square

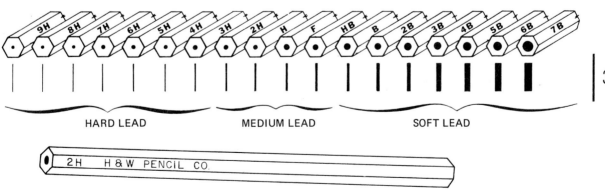

HARD LEAD   MEDIUM LEAD   SOFT LEAD

DRAFTING LEAD GRADE   SHARPEN THIS END

2H   H & W PENCIL CO.

Fig. 3-4. Pencil grades.

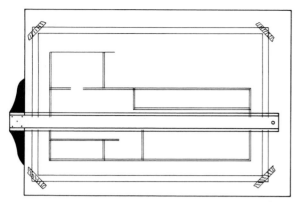

Fig. 3-5. Use of T square.

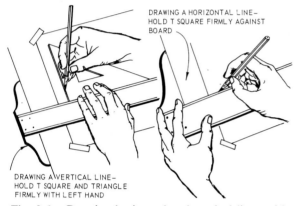

DRAWING A HORIZONTAL LINE—
HOLD T SQUARE FIRMLY AGAINST
BOARD

DRAWING A VERTICAL LINE—
HOLD T SQUARE AND TRIANGLE
FIRMLY WITH LEFT HAND

Fig. 3-6. Drawing horizontal and vertical lines with a T square and triangle.

lengths for use in architectural drafting are 18″ (457 mm), 24″ (610 mm), 30″ (762 mm), 36″ (914 mm), and 42″ (1067 mm).

T squares must be held tightly against the edge of the drawing board, and triangles must be held firmly against the T square to ensure accurate horizontal and vertical lines. Since only one end of the T square is held against the drawing board, considerable sag occurs when an extremely long T square is not held securely.

Horizontal Lines

Horizontal lines are always drawn with the aid of some instrument such as the T square, parallel slide, or drafting machine. In drawing horizontal lines with the T square, hold the head of the T square firmly against the left working edge of the drawing board (if you are righthanded). This procedure keeps the blade in a horizontal position to draw horizontal lines from left to right. Figure 3-5 shows the T square placed on the drawing board in the correct manner for drawing floor plans and elevations. Figure 3-6 shows the correct

34

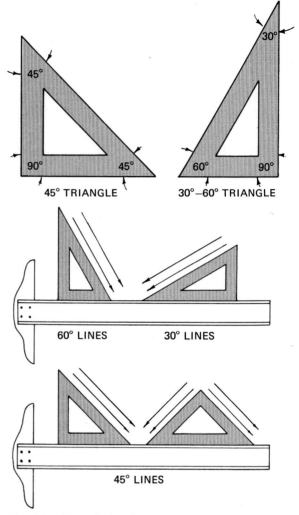

Fig. 3-7. Use of triangles.

method of drawing horizontal (and vertical) lines by the use of the T square.

Vertical Lines

Triangles are used with the T square for drawing vertical or inclined lines. The 8″ (203 mm), 45° triangle and the 10″ (254 mm), 30°–60° triangle are preferred for architectural work. Figure 3-7 shows the correct method of drawing vertical and inclined lines by the use of the T square and triangle.

Triangles

Triangles are used to draw vertical and inclined lines with either a T square or parallel slide. The 45° triangle is frequently used to draw miter lines

DRAWING HORIZONTAL LINES

DRAWING VERTICAL LINES

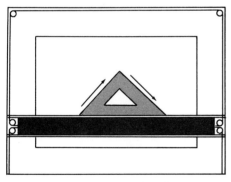

DRAWING SLOPING LINES

Fig. 3-8. Drawing with a parallel slide and triangle.

that are used to turn angles of buildings, as shown in Fig. 3-8. Triangles are used also to draw various symbols. Figure 3-9 shows the use of the 30°–60° triangle in drawing a door symbol.

Parallel Slide

The parallel slide performs the same function as the T square. It is used as a guide for drawing horizontal lines and as a base for aligning triangles in drawing vertical lines.

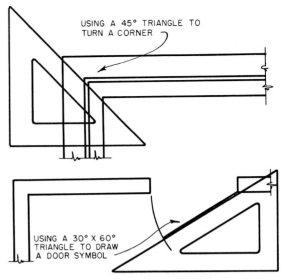

Fig. 3-9. Typical use of triangles.

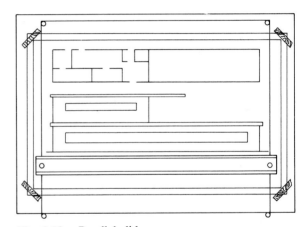

Fig. 3-10. Parallel slide.

Extremely long lines are common in many architectural drawings such as floor plans and elevations. Since most of these lines should be drawn continuously, the parallel slide is used extensively by architectural drafters.

The parallel slide is anchored at both sides of the drawing board, as shown in Figs. 3-8 and 3-10. This attachment eliminates the possibility of sag at one end, which is a common objection to the use of the T square.

In using the parallel slide the drawing board can be tilted to a very steep angle without causing the slide to fall to the bottom of the board. If the parallel slide is adjusted correctly, it will stay in the exact position in which it is placed.

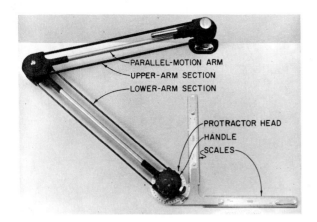

Fig. 3-11. Drafting machine.

Drafting Machine

Use of the drafting machine eliminates the need for the architect's scale, triangles, T square, or parallel slide. A drafting machine consists of a head to which two scales are attached (Fig. 3-11). These scales (arms) of the drafting machine are graduated like other architect's scales. They are usually made of aluminum or plastic. The two scales are attached to the head of the drafting machine perpendicular to each other. The horizontal scale performs the function of a T square or parallel slide in drawing horizontal lines. The vertical scale performs the function of a triangle in drawing vertical or inclined lines.

Dividers

Dividing an area into an equal number of parts is a common task performed by designers. In addition to the architect's scale, the dividers are used for this purpose. To divide an area equally, first adjust the dividers until they appear to represent the desired division of the area. Then place one point at the end of the area and step off the distance with the dividers. If the divisions turn out to be too short, increase the opening on the dividers by trial and error. Repeat the process until the line is equally divided. If the divisions are too long, decrease the setting. Figure 3-12 shows the use of dividers in dividing an area into an equal number of parts.

Dividers are frequently used to transfer dimensions and to enlarge or reduce the size of a drawing. Figure 3-13 shows the use of dividers also to double the size of a floor plan. This work is done by setting the dividers to the distances

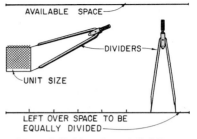

Fig. 3-12. Use of dividers in subdividing areas.

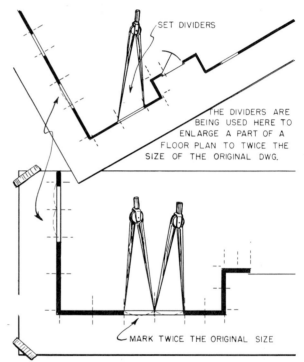

Fig. 3-13. Use of dividers to enlarge an area.

on the plan and then stepping off the distance twice on the new plan.

Compass

A compass is used on architectural drawings to draw circles, arcs, radii, and parts of many symbols. Small circles are drawn with a bow pencil compass (Fig. 3-14). The bow is set to the desired radius, holding the stem between the thumb and forefinger and rotating the compass with a clockwise forward motion and forward inclination.

Large circles on architectural drawings, such as those used to show the radius of drive-

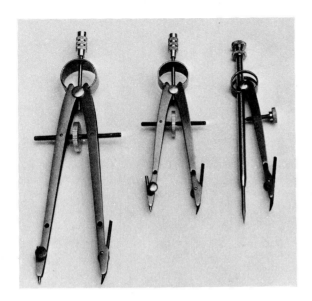

Fig. 3-14. Compasses.

ways, walks, patios, and stage outlines, are drawn with a large beam compass, as shown in Fig. 3-15.

Compasses cannot be used effectively to draw irregular curves. Curved lines that are not part of an arc are drawn with a French (irregular) curve as shown in Fig. 3-16.

Correction Equipment

A variety of erasers are used by the designer for various purposes. Basic erasers are used for general purposes. Gum erasers are used for light lines. Kneaded erasers will pick up loose graphite by dabbing, and dry-cleaner bags remove smudges. The powder is sprinkled on the drawing and enables drafting instruments to slide on the powder which keeps the drawing and instruments clean as they move.

Electric erasers are very fast and do not damage the surface of the drawing paper since a very light touch can be used to eradicate lines.

A drafting brush, which keeps particles from being redistributed into the paper, is used to remove eraser and graphite particles periodically.

Erasing shields are thin pieces of metal or plastic with a variety of openings which are used to erase lines without disturbing nearby lines or intersecting lines that are to remain on the drawing. See Fig. 3-17.

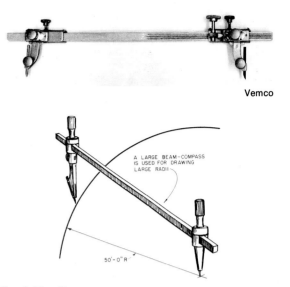

Vemco

Fig. 3-15. Beam compass.

① PLOT REQUIRED CURVE

② SKETCH CURVE LIGHTLY

③ FIT IRREGULAR CURVE OVER PART OF THE LINE. DO NOT DRAW THE EXTENT.

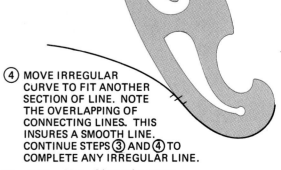

④ MOVE IRREGULAR CURVE TO FIT ANOTHER SECTION OF LINE. NOTE THE OVERLAPPING OF CONNECTING LINES. THIS INSURES A SMOOTH LINE. CONTINUE STEPS ③ AND ④ TO COMPLETE ANY IRREGULAR LINE.

Fig. 3-16. Use of irregular curve.

37

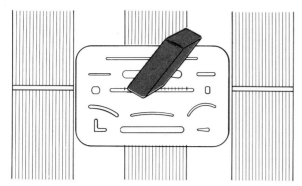

Fig. 3-17. Use of erasing shield.

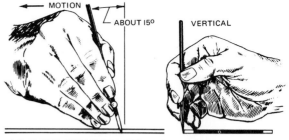

(A) INKING STRAIGHT LINES WITH A BLADE RULING PEN

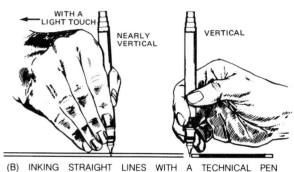

(B) INKING STRAIGHT LINES WITH A TECHNICAL PEN

Fig. 3-18. Drawing ink lines.

Inking Pens

Interior designers use ink drawings for much presentation work. Two basic types of inking pens are used. The ruling pen has an adjustable blade for drawing different width lines, and the technical fountain pen has a fixed-width line. A different technical pen is needed for each width line, as shown in Fig. 3-18.

TIME-SAVERS

Speed in the preparation of drawings is of utmost importance. For this reason many time-saving devices are employed by designers. The purpose of these time-saving devices is to eliminate unnecessary time on the drawing board without sacrificing the quality of the drawing.

Templates

Templates are pieces of paper, cardboard, metal, or plastic. Openings in the template are shaped to represent the outline of various symbols and fixtures. A symbol or fixture is traced on the drawing by following the outline with a pencil. This procedure eliminates the repetitive task of measuring and laying out the symbol each time it is to be used on the drawing.

Templates such as the one shown in Fig. 3-19 have openings that represent many different types of symbols and fixtures. This template is positioned to be used to outline a door symbol. Many templates are used to draw only one type of symbol. Special templates are available for doors, windows, electrical symbols, plumbing symbols, and furniture.

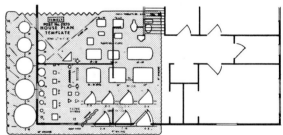

Fig. 3-19. Floor-plan symbols template. *Timely Products Company*

Overlays

An overlay is any sheet that is placed over an original drawing. The information placed on the overlay becomes part of the interpretation of the original drawing. Most overlays are made by drawing on transparent materials such as acetate, tracing cloth, or vellum. Overlays are used in the design process to add to or change features of the original drawing without marking the drawing.

Overlays are also used to add to a drawing features which would normally complicate the original drawing. Lines that would become hidden and many other details can be made clear by preparing this information on an overlay. Figure 3-20 shows the use of a temporary acetate overlay

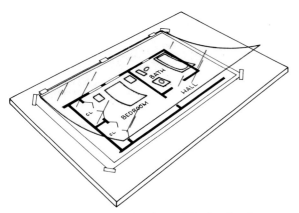

Fig. 3-20. Use of overlay in positioning furniture.

Fig. 3-21. Window and door underlays.

in locating furniture. The objects on the overlay can be moved as often as necessary to any position without changing the base drawing. Once the final locations are established the features are then added to the original drawing.

Permanent overlays which adhere to the surface of the drawing, save much drawing-board time. Attaching a preprinted symbol or fixture by this method is considerably faster than drawing it, even if a template is used.

Underlays

Underlays are drawings or parts of drawings which are placed under the original drawing and traced on the original.

Symbol Underlays

Many symbols and features of buildings are drawn more than once. The same style of door or window or the same type of tree or shrubbery may be drawn many times by the architectural drafter in the course of a day. It is a considerable waste of time to measure and lay out these features each time they are to be drawn. Therefore, many drafters prepare a series of underlays of the features repeated most often on their drawings. Figure 3-21 shows several underlays used in interior design work. Underlays are commonly prepared for doors, windows, fireplaces, furniture, major appliances, walls, and stairs.

Drawing paper preprinted with title blocks is also a considerable time-saver (Fig. 3-22).

HOME PLANNERS, INC. 16310 GRAND RIVER AVE. ● DETROIT 27, MICHIGAN	PLAN No.
	SHEET
	OF
	COPYRIGHT

Fig. 3-22. Title-block underlay.

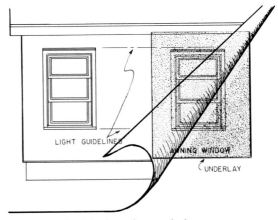

LIGHT GUIDELINES

AWNING WINDOW

UNDERLAY

Fig. 3-23. Positioning of an underlay.

When printed title blocks are not available, the title-block underlay is often used to save valuable layout time and to ensure the correct spacing of lettering.

Use of Underlays

Underlays are master drawings. To be effective, they must be prepared to the correct scale and carefully aligned. The underlay is first positioned under the drawing and aligned with light guidelines (Fig. 3-23); then it is traced on the drawing.

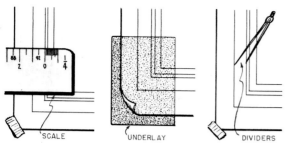

Fig. 3-24. Use of scale underlay and dividers to lay out wall thickness.

The underlay can now be removed or moved to a new location to trace the symbol or feature again if necessary. Drafters use master underlays many times.

Underlays do not necessarily replace the use of instruments or scales in original design work. They are most effective when symbols are continually repeated. Figure 3-24 shows a comparison of the use of the scale, dividers, and underlay in laying out wall thicknesses. The use of the underlay in this case is only possible after the original wall lengths have been established by the use of the scale.

Grids

Grid sheets are used under the tracing paper as underlays and are removed after the drawing is finished, or the drawing is prepared on nonreproducible grid paper. Nonreproducible grid paper does not reproduce when the original drawing is copied through photographic processes. Figure 3-25 shows an original drawing complete with nonreproducible grid lines and the print from this drawing without grid lines.

Squared Paper
Squared (graph) paper is available in graduations of 4, 8, 16, and 32 squares per inch. Squared paper is also available in decimal-divided increments of 5, 10, 20, and 30 or more squares per inch. Decimal-divided squared paper is used for the layout of survey and plot plants. Metric graph paper is ruled in millimeters.

Pictorial Grids
Grids prepared with isometric angles and preplotted to perspective vanishing points are used for pictorial illustrations. Perspective and iso-

40

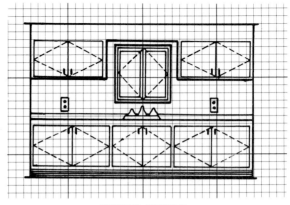

ORIGINAL DRAWING

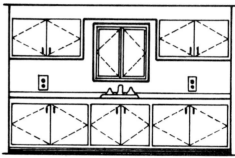

REPRODUCTION

Fig. 3-25. Use of cross-sectional grid.

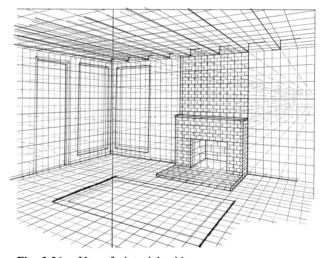

Fig. 3-26. Use of pictorial grid.

metric grid paper are available with many angles of projection (Fig. 3-26).

Perspective grids can be obtained with the vanishing point placed at various intervals from the station point and with the horizon placed in various locations.

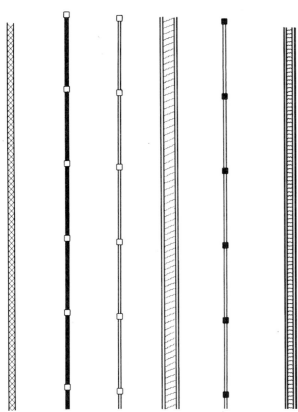

Fig. 3-27. Architectural-symbol tape. *Chart-pac, Inc.*

Fig. 3-28. Applying pressure-sensitive tape.

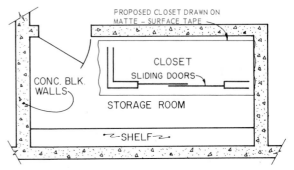

Fig. 3-29. Trial layout on matte-surface tape.

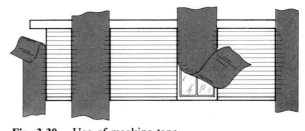

Fig. 3-30. Use of masking tape.

Tape

Many types of manufactured tape can be substituted for lines and symbols on architectural drawings.

Pressure-sensitive Tape

Tape with printed symbols and special lines is used to produce lines and symbols that otherwise would be difficult and time-consuming to construct. Figure 3-27 shows some of the various symbols and lines available in this kind of tape. A special roll-on applicator enables the drafter to draw lines by using tape, as shown in Fig. 3-28. This method is used extensively on overlays.

Matte-surface Tape

Temporary changes can be added to a drawing by drawing the symbol, note, or change on translucent matte-surface tape. If the drawing is changed, the tape can be removed and a new symbol added, or the symbol can be made per-

manent. The proposed closet wall in Fig. 3-29 was prepared on transparent tape. If the arrangement is unsatisfactory, the tape can be removed without destroying the drawing.

Masking Tape

Masking tape has other time-saving uses besides its use to attach the drawing to the drawing board. Strips of masking tape help ensure the equal length of lines when ruling many close lines. Strips of tape are placed on the drawing to mask the areas not to be lined. The lines are then drawn on the paper and extended on the tape. When the tape is removed, the ends of the lines are even and sharp, as shown in Fig. 3-30. This

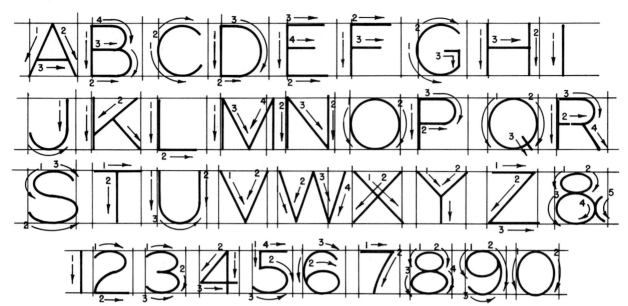

Fig. 3-31. The American Standard alphabet.

procedure eliminates the careful starting and stopping of the pencil stroke with each line.

Since masking tape will pull out some graphite, a piece of paper can be placed on drawings to perform the masking function for large areas. If a small area is to remain unlined, sometimes it is easier to line through the surface and erase the small area with an erasing shield (Fig. 3-17).

Abbreviations

Stenographers use shorthand to speed up and condense their work. Designers' shorthand consists of symbols and abbreviations. When a symbol does not describe an object completely, a word or phrase must be used. Words and phrases can occupy much space on a drawing. Abbreviations therefore should be used to minimize this space.

Rubber Stamps

For architectural symbols that are often repeated, the use of rubber stamps is effective and time-saving. Stamps can be used with any color ink, or stamps can be used in faint colors to provide an outline which may then be rendered with pencil or ink. Rubber stamps are used most often for symbols which do not require precise positioning on the drawing, such as landscape features, people, and cars. However, stamps may be used for furniture outlines and sometimes for labels.

Burnishing Plates

Burnishing plates are embossed sheets which have raised areas representing an outline of a symbol or texture lines. The plates are placed under a drawing; then a soft pencil is rubbed over the surface of the drawing. This creates lines on the drawing over the raised portions of the plate. The use of burnishing plates allows the drafter to create consistent texture lines throughout a series of drawings with a minimum use of time.

Photographic Reproduction

Often a section of a drawing needs to be changed, or a design element needs to be repeated on many drawings. The entire drawing need not be redrawn, nor must the design element be drawn repeatedly on each drawing. The section to be redrawn or repeated can be drawn once, attached to the drawing, and then the entire drawing can be reproduced through photographic processes.

Paper

Since the type of paper on which the line is drawn will greatly affect the line weight, different pencils

USE GUIDELINES FOR GREATER

ACCURACY IN LETTERING.

LETTERING WITHOUT GUIDELINES

LOOKS LIKE THIS.

Fig. 3-32. Always use guidelines for lettering.

IF YOU LETTER TOO

SLOWLY, YOUR LETTERS

WILL LOOK LIKE THIS.

MAKE QUICK RAPID

STROKES

Fig. 3-33. Make each stroke quickly.

may be necessary. Weather conditions, such as temperature and humidity, also greatly affect the line quality. During periods of high humidity, harder pencils must be employed.

LETTERING

A plan without any lettering does not communicate a complete description of the size and function of the various components. All labels, notes, dimensions, and descriptions must be legibly lettered on architectural drawings if they are to function as an effective means of graphic communication. Legible, well-formed letters and numerals do more for a drawing than merely aid in communication. Effective lettering helps give the drawing a finished and professional look. Poor lettering is the mark of an amateur.

Styles

Because architectural designs are somewhat personalized, many lettering styles have been developed by various designers. Nevertheless, these personalized styles are all based on the American National Standard alphabet shown in Fig. 3-31.

Rules for Lettering

Much practice is necessary to develop the skills necessary to letter effectively. Although lettering styles may be very different, all professionals follow certain basic rules of lettering. If you follow these rules you will develop accuracy, consistency, and speed in lettering your drawings.

1. Always use guidelines in lettering. Notice what a difference guidelines make in the lettering shown in Fig. 3-32.

2. Choose one style of lettering, and practice the formation of the letters of that style until you master it.
3. Make letters bold and distinctive. Avoid a delicate, fine touch.
4. Make each line quickly from the beginning to the end of the stroke. See the difference between letters drawn quickly and those drawn slowly in Fig. 3-33.
5. Practice with larger letters (about ¼″ or 6 mm), and gradually reduce the size until you can letter effectively at ¹/₁₆″, or 2 mm. Most lettering on interior design drawings is ¹/₈ to ³/₁₆″.
6. Practice spacing by lettering words and sentences, not alphabets. Figure 3-34 shows the effect of uniform and even spacing of letters.
7. Form the habit of lettering whenever possible—as you take notes, address envelopes, or write your name.
8. Practice only the capital alphabet. Lowercase letters are rarely used in architectural work.
9. Do not try to develop speed at first. Make each stroke quickly, but take your time between letters and between strokes until you have mastered each letter. Then gradually increase your speed.
10. If your lettering has a tendency to slant in one direction or the other, practice making a series of vertical and horizontal lines.
11. If slant lettering is desired, practice slanting the vertical strokes with guidelines.
12. Letter the drawing last to avoid smudges and overlapping with other areas of the drawing.

UNIFORM SPACING

UNEVEN SPACING

Fig. 3-34. Uniform spacing.

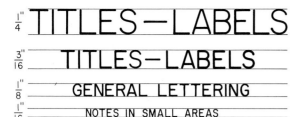

Fig. 3-35. Lettering height relates to importance.

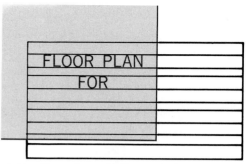

Fig. 3-36. Lettering guideline underlay.

Fig. 3-37. Lettering appliqués.

This procedure will enable you to space out your lettering and to avoid lettering through important details.

13. Use a soft pencil, preferably an HB or F. A soft pencil will glide and is more easily controlled than a hard pencil.

14. Numerals should be adapted to the style, just as the alphabet is adapted. Fractions also should be made consistent with the style. Fractions are twice the height of the whole number.

15. The size of the lettering should be related to the importance of the labeling (Fig. 3-35).

16. Lettering underlays should be used to trace labels that are used frequently. See Fig. 3-36.

17. Lettering appliqués can be used to reproduce complex lettering styles, as shown in Fig. 3-37.

18. Typeset letters, although more consistent in size and style than hand lettering, are much slower to apply.

SCALES AND MEASUREMENTS

In ancient times simple structures were built without detailed architectural plans and even without established dimensions. The outline of the structure and the position of each room could be determined experimentally by "pacing off" approximate distances. The builder could then erect the structure using existing materials by adjusting sizes and dimensions as necessary during the building process. In this case the builder played the role of the architect, designer, contractor, carpenter, mason, and, perhaps, the manufacturer of materials and components. Today, design requirements are so demanding and materials so diverse, that a complete dimensioned set of drawings is absolutely necessary to ensure proper execution of the design as conceived by the designer.

The modern interior designer must learn to read scaled drawings and use reduced-size scales. The ability to accurately use architect's scales is required not only in preparing drawings but in checking existing architectural plans and details before estimating an interior design project.

Size Description

Dimensions show the size of materials and exactly where they are to be located. Dimensions show the builder the width, height, length, and subdivisions of the building. They show the location of doors, windows, stairs, fireplace, and planters. The number of dimensions included on a plan depends largely on how much freedom of interpretation the designer wants to give the builder. If complete dimensions are shown on a plan, the builder cannot deviate greatly from the original design. However, if only a few dimensions are shown, then the builder must determine the sizes of many areas, fixtures, and details. When this occurs the builder must provide the dimensions and is placed in the position of designer.

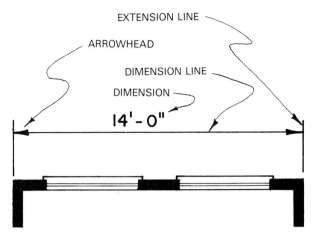

Fig. 3-38. Dimensions are shown as the distance between arrowheads.

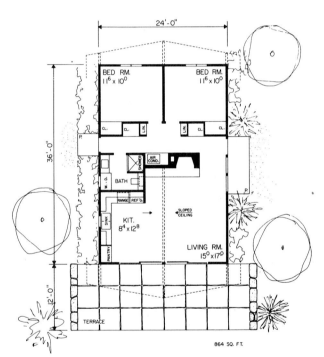

Fig. 3-39. Abbreviated dimensions are used on simple drawings. *Home Planners, Inc.*

Dimensions, or distances between points, are shown on architectural drawings by the use of dimension lines, extension lines, arrowheads, and numerals, as shown in Fig. 3-38. Dimensions are placed on a line that represents the distance between two arrowheads. All completely dimensioned architectural plans are shown in this manner. Abbreviated architectural plans such as the

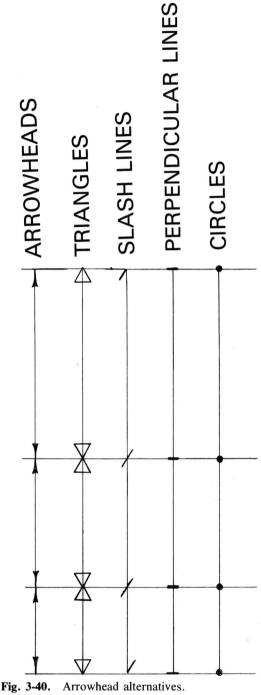

Fig. 3-40. Arrowhead alternatives.

one shown in Fig. 3-39 show only approximate dimensions of areas. In general, more detailed plans and complex designs include more detailed dimensioning. Although arrowheads, as shown in the left line in Fig. 3-40, are the accepted standard, many architectural drawings include

45

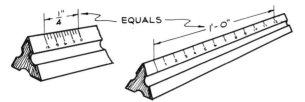

Fig. 3-41. On a drawing, ¼″ may represent 1′–0″.

alternative symbols to describe the length of an area, as shown in the remainder of Fig. 3-40.

Scales

When a drawing of an object is exactly the same scale (size) as the actual object, this is full-size scale (1:1). However, architectural structures are obviously too large to be drawn full size. They must, therefore, be reduced in scale to fit on sheets of paper. Three types of measuring scales are commonly used for scaled construction drawings: the architect's scale, the engineer's scale, and the metric scale.

The main function of any scale is to enable the designer to draw a building at a convenient size and to enable the builder to think in relation to the actual size of the structure as the drawing to construct the building is used. When a drawing is prepared to a reduced scale, 1′-0″ (12″) may actually be drawn ¼″ long. On the reduced scale, the builder does not think of this ¼″ line as

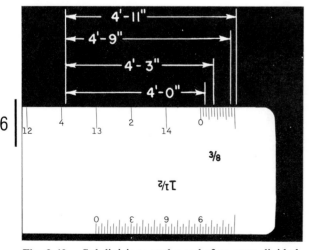

Fig. 3-42. Subdivisions at the end of an open-divided scale are used for inch measurements.

actually representing ¼″ but thinks of it as being 1′ long. If the area to be represented is very large, the reduction ratio will be very large. A very large plot plan may be reduced as much as 200 times, while a detailed drawing may be reduced only one or two times its actual size.

Architect's Scale

Architect's scales are either the bevel type or the triangular type. The triangular scale has 6 sides and 11 different scales: a full scale of 12″ graduated into 16 parts to an inch and 10 open-divided scales with ratios of ³/₃₂, ⅛, ³/₁₆, ¼, ⅜, ½, ¾, 1, 1½, and 3. Two scales are located on each face. One scale reads from left to right. The other scale, which is twice as large, reads from right to left. For example, the ¼ scale and half of this, the ⅛ scale, are placed on the same face. Similarly, the ¾ scale and the ⅜ scale are placed on the same face but are read from different directions. If the scale is read from the wrong direction, the measurement could be wrong, since the second row of numbers reads from the opposite side of the scale at half scale or twice the value.

The architect's scale is most commonly used to measure distances where the divisions of the scale equal 1′ or 1″. For example, in the ¼″ scale shown in Fig. 3-41, ¼″ can equal either 1″ or 1′. Since buildings are very large, most major architectural drawings use a scale which relates the parts of the scale to a foot. Architectural details such as cabinet construction and joints often use these same parts of the scale to represent 1″.

In reading an open-divided scale, the section at the end of the scale is not part of the numerical scale. When measuring with the scale, start with the zero line, *not* with the outside end line of the fully divided section. Always start with the number of feet or inches you wish to measure and then add the additional inches (or feet) in the subdivided area. For example, in Fig. 3-42 the distance 4′–11″ is derived by measuring from the line 4 to 0, then 11″ past zero, since each of the lines in the subdivision equals 1″. On smaller scales, the lines in the fully divided portion may equal 2″. On larger scales, they may equal ½″. Figure 3-43 shows this principle applied to a ½″ = 1′-0″ scale where ½″ equals 1′.

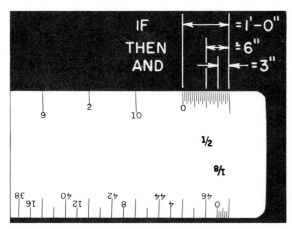

Fig. 3-43. If ½″ equals 1′ then ¼″ equals 6″ and ⅛″ equals 3″.

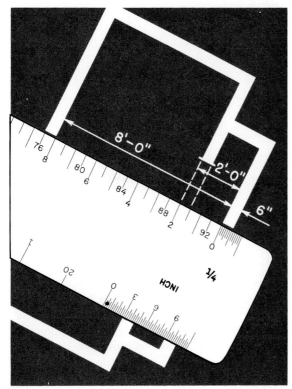

Fig. 3-44. Subdivisions of an architect's scale are used to indicate overall dimensions and subdimensions.

Figure 3-44 shows a further application of the use of the architect's scale. Notice the dimensioned distance of 8′-0″ extends from the 8 to the 0 on the scale and the 6″ wall is shown as ½′ on the subdivided foot on the end of the scale.

When the scale of the drawing changes, the length of each line increases or decreases and the width of various areas also increases or decreases. The actual appearance of a typical corner wall at a scale of ¹/₁₆″ = 1′-0″, ⅛″ = 1′-0″, ¼″ = 1′-0″, and ½″ = 1′-0″ is shown in Fig. 3-45. You can see that the wall drawn to the scale of ¹/₁₆″ = 1′-0″ is small and that a great amount of detail would be impossible. The ½″ = 1′-0″ wall would probably cover too large an area on a drawing if the building is very large. Therefore, the ¼″ = 1′-0″ and ⅛″ = 1′-0″ scales are the most popular for most basic architectural drawings.

Figure 3-46 shows the comparative distances used to measure 1′-9″ as it appears on various architect's scales. The colored bar on each of these scales represents 1′-9″. The same comparison would exist if the scales were related to 1″ rather than 1′. In this case, a distance of 1¾″ would have the same line length as 1′-9″ on the foot representation. The ³/₃₂″, ³/₁₆″, ⅛″, ¼″, ⅜″, ½″, and ¾″ scales represent a distance smaller than full size (1¾″).

Metric Measurement

The basic units of measure in the metric system are the meter (m) for distance, the gram (g) for mass (weight), and the liter (L) for volume. Since most measurements used on architectural drawings are linear distances, multiples or subdivisions of the meter are the metric units most commonly used. The meter, as shown in Fig. 3-47, represents a basic unit of one. All units of

47

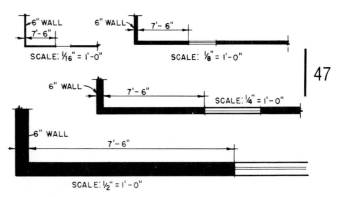

Fig. 3-45. Comparison of similar walls drawn to different scales.

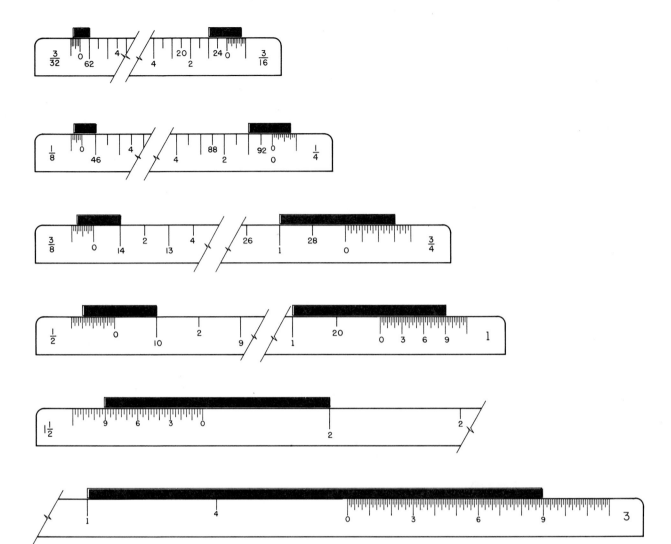

Fig. 3-46. A length of 1'–9" shown on different scales.

measure in architectural drawings can be written as an example 4.500 m or 4 500 mm.

Prefixes which represent multiples of meters are deka-, hecto-, and kilo-. A dekameter (dam) equals 10 meters. A hectometer (hm) equals 100 meters. A kilometer (km) equals 1000 meters.

Prefixes which represent subdivisions of meters are deci-, centi-, and milli-. A decimeter (dm) equals one-tenth (0.1) of a meter. A centimeter (cm) equals one-hundredth (0.01) of a meter. A millimeter (mm) equals one-thousandth (0.001) of a meter. The most useful subdivision of a meter for construction drawings is the millimeter. Figure 3-48 shows a portion of a meter scale in which the numbers on the scale denote millimeters and every tenth line represents a

centimeter. Each line on this scale represents a millimeter. Notice that there are 10 millimeters between each centimeter. Figure 3-49 shows the most useful metric prefixes and the relationship of these prefixes to the meter. This consistent use of prefixes makes the metric system much easier to use than customary units.

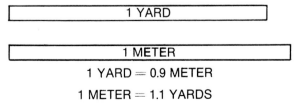

1 YARD = 0.9 METER
1 METER = 1.1 YARDS

Fig. 3-47. The meter is slightly longer than a yard.

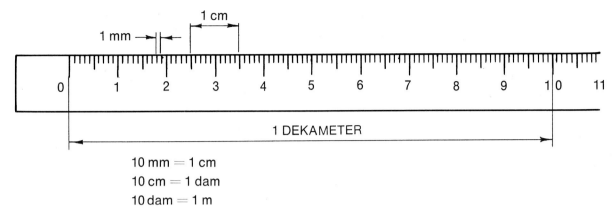

10 mm = 1 cm
10 cm = 1 dam
10 dam = 1 m

Fig. 3-48. A meter scale divided into millimeters.

Metric Dimensions

Linear metric sizes used on basic architectural drawings such as floor plans and elevations are shown in millimeters. Using millimeters exclusively is the preferred standard. When meter dimensions are used on plans, they are carried to three decimal points. If the decimal point is omitted the dimension will be in millimeters (Fig. 3-50). In detail drawings such as the one shown in Fig. 3-51, millimeters are used exclusively.

PREFIX		SYMBOL	+ METER =	
$1000 = 10^3$	kilo	k	kilometer	km
$100 = 10^2$	hecto	h	hectometer	hm
$10 = 10^1$	deka	da	dekameter	dam
$0.1 = 10^{-1}$	deci	d	decimeter	dm
$0.01 = 10^{-2}$	centi	c	centimeter	cm
$0.001 = 10^{-3}$	milli	m	millimeter	mm

Fig. 3-49. Prefixes change the base unit by increments of 10.

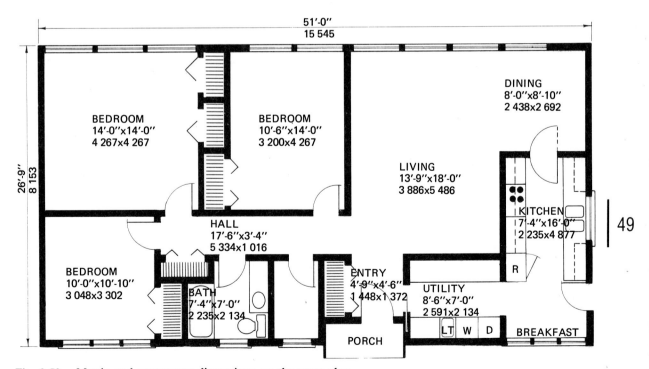

51'-0"
15 545

26'-9"
8 153

BEDROOM
14'-0"x14'-0"
4 267x4 267

BEDROOM
10'-6"x14'-0"
3 200x4 267

DINING
8'-0"x8'-10"
2 438x2 692

LIVING
13'-9"x18'-0"
3 886x5 486

KITCHEN
7'-4"x16'-0"
2 235x4 877

HALL
17'-6"x3'-4"
5 334x1 016

BEDROOM
10'-0"x10'-10"
3 048x3 302

BATH
7'-4"x7'-0"
2 235x2 134

ENTRY
4'-9"x4'-6"
1 448x1 372

UTILITY
8'-6"x7'-0"
2 591x2 134

R

LT   W   D

BREAKFAST

PORCH

49

Fig. 3-50. Metric and customary dimensions on the same plan.

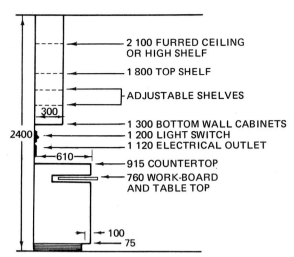

Fig. 3-51. Millimeters are used on metric detail drawings.

Metric scales such as those shown in Fig. 3-52 are used in the same manner as the architect's scale is used: to scale reduced-size drawings. Metric scales, however, use ratios in increments of 10 rather than fractional ratios of 12 used in architect's scales. Just as with fractional scales, the ratio chosen in a metric scale depends on the size of the drawing compared to the full size of the object.

Metric Conversion

Designers attempt to design exclusively in either U.S. customary units or in metric units. But often conversion is necessary because some components are not available in metric sizes, even though the basic design is prepared metrically. In renovation work, drawings of existing structures or structural components may be in customary units, and proposed additions may be prepared in metric units. When it is necessary to convert U.S. customary architectural dimensions and distances to metric dimensions and distances, the information found in Fig. 3-53 can be used for that purpose. These are approximate metric units compared to similar U.S. customary units.

As metrication becomes more widely accepted, more building materials will be manufactured in metric sizes, greatly simplifying the use of metric-prepared drawings.

When a drawing contains both metric and customary dimensions, two kinds of dimensions may be provided. Dual dimensions may be included in the drawing or conversion tables may be included with the drawing. Metric conversion tables are keyed to dimensions on the drawing that are either customary or metric. The equivalent is then read from the chart. Charts are sometimes master charts showing all equivalents or may include only the equivalents of the dimensions actually used on the drawing.

Knowing how to read the architect's, engineer's, and metric scales helps the designer read and understand scaled drawings. Use of scales can help find missing dimensions; however, be extremely careful in scaling prints of drawings. Print paper stretches in the process of printing,

Fig. 3-52. A metric scale showing two ratios.

50

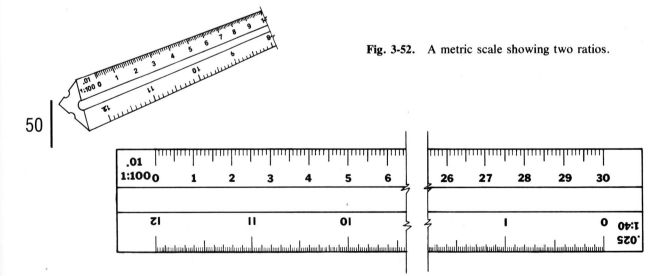

creating distances greater than those found on the original drawing. Measure several known dimensions on a print to determine the amount of stretch before using a scale to determine unknown dimensions.

DRAWING FLOOR PLANS

Multiview Interpretation

Although pictorial drawings are effective in showing at a glance the general design of an interior, they are not sufficiently precise to accurately describe all elements of the design. For this reason, multiview (several-view) drawings are used in the actual construction of buildings.

Multiview drawings are also called *orthographic* drawings. Orthographic drawings represent the exact form and size of each side of an object in two or more views (or planes) usually at right angles to each other. To visualize and understand multiview (orthographic) projection, imagine a structure surrounded by imaginary transparent planes, as shown in Fig. 3-54. If you draw the outline of the structure on the imaginary transparent planes, you create the various orthographic views: the front view on the front plane, the side view on the side plane, and the top view on the top plane. When the planes of the top, bottom, and sides are hinged (swung) out from the front plane, as shown in Fig. 3-55, the six views of an object are shown exactly as they are

APPROXIMATE METRIC UNITS COMPARED TO SIMILAR CUSTOMARY UNITS			
	WHEN YOU KNOW:	**YOU CAN FIND:**	**IF YOU MULTIPLY BY:**
LENGTH	inches	millimeters	25.4
	feet	centimeters	30.48
	yards	meters	0.9
	miles	kilometers	1.6
	millimeters	inches	0.04
	centimeters	inches	0.4
	meters	yards	1.1
	kilometers	miles	0.6
AREA	square inches	square centimeters	6.5
	square feet	square meters	0.09
	square yards	square meters	0.84
	square miles	square kilometers	2.6
	acres	square hectometers (hectares)	0.4
	square centimeters	square inches	0.16
	square meters	square yards	1.2
	square kilometers	square miles	0.4
MASS	ounces	grams	28.0
	pounds	kilograms	0.45
	short tons	megagrams (metric tons)	0.9
	grams	ounces	0.035
	kilograms	pounds	2.2
	megagrams (metric tons)	short tons	1.1
LIQUID VOLUME	ounces	milliliters	30.0
	pints	liters	0.47
	quarts	liters	0.95
	gallons	liters	3.8
	milliliters	ounces	0.034
	liters	pints	2.1
	liters	quarts	1.06
	liters	gallons	0.26
TEMPERATURE	degrees Fahrenheit	degrees Celsius	$5/9$ (after subtracting 32)
	degrees Celsius	degrees Fahrenheit	$9/5$ (then add 32)

Fig. 3-53. Approximate metric units compared to similar customary units.

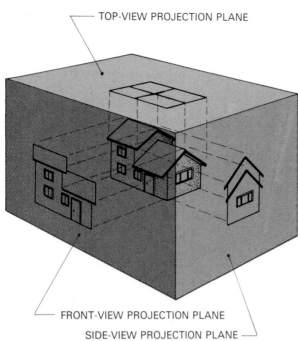

TOP-VIEW PROJECTION PLANE

FRONT-VIEW PROJECTION PLANE

SIDE-VIEW PROJECTION PLANE

Fig. 3-54. A projection box shows three planes of a building.

positioned on an orthographic drawing. Study the position of each view as it relates to the front view: the right side is to the right of the front view, the left side is to the left, the top (roof) view is on the top, the bottom view is on the bottom, and the rear view is to the left of the left-side view, since when this view hinges around to the back it would fall into this position.

COMPLETE FLOOR PLAN

A floor plan is a single-view orthographic drawing of the outline and partitions of a building as you would see them if the building were cut (sectioned) horizontally about 4' (1.2 m) above the floor line, as shown in Fig. 3-56. There are many types of floor plans, ranging from very simple sketches to completely dimensioned and detailed floor-plan working drawings.

Floor-plan Symbols

Designers substitute symbols for materials and fixtures. It is obviously more convenient and time-saving to draw a symbol of a feature than to repeat a description every time that material is used. There are alternative symbols for some

features depending on the style used on the drawing. For example, Fig. 3-57 shows several symbols designers use for representing walls.

Learning and remembering floor-plan symbols will be easier if you associate each symbol with the actual material or facility it represents.

Floor-plan symbols often represent the exact appearance of the floor-plan section as viewed from above, but sometimes this representation is not possible. Many floor-plan symbols are too intricate to be drawn to the scale $\frac{1}{4}'' = 1'-0''$ or $\frac{1}{8}'' = 1'-0''$. Therefore, many details are eliminated on the floor-plan symbol.

A thorough understanding of each symbol and the material, component, or feature it represents is absolutely vital to personnel involved in all phases and types of interior design. It is not necessary to develop total recall for each symbol, but it is important to recognize what material or component each symbol represents when reading construction drawings. The symbols in this unit represent materials or features which appear on drawings viewed from the top (plan view) and as they appear from the side (elevation view). Plan views are often sectional drawings. Therefore, the plan symbol represents materials in their sectioned (cut through) form.

Steps in Drawing Floor Plans

For maximum speed, accuracy, and clarity, the following steps, as illustrated in Fig. 3-58, should be observed in laying out and drawing floor plans:

1. Block in the overall dimensions of the house and add the thickness of the outside walls with a hard pencil (4H).
2. Lay out the position of interior partitions with a 4H pencil.
3. Locate the position of doors and windows by center line and by their widths.
4. Darken the object lines with an H pencil.
5. Add door and window symbols with an H pencil.
6. Add symbols for stairwells.
7. Erase extraneous layout lines if they are too heavy. If they are extremely light, they can remain.
8. Draw the outlines of kitchen and bathroom fixtures.
9. Add the symbols and sections for any ma-

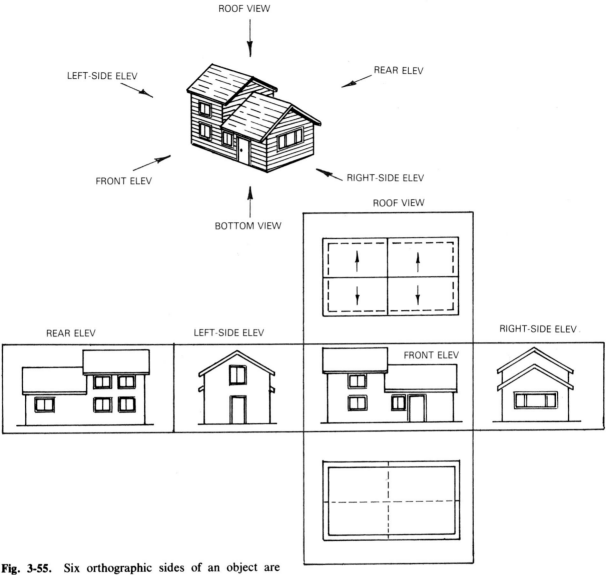

Fig. 3-55. Six orthographic sides of an object are shown when the projection box is opened and laid flat.

sonry work, such as fireplaces and planters.
10. Add positions of movable furniture and equipment if desired.
11. Dimension the drawing.

Second-floor Plan

Bilevel, two-story, one-and-one-half-story, and split-level homes require a separate floor plan for each additional level. This floor plan is prepared on tracing paper placed directly over the first-floor plan to ensure alignment of walls and bearing partitions. When the major outline has been

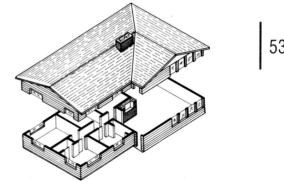

Fig. 3-56. A floor plan is a section cut through the building.

NAME	ABBREV	SYMBOL	ELEVATION	PICTORIAL
DOUBLE-HUNG WINDOW	DHW			
HORIZONTAL SLIDING WINDOW	SLD WDW			
AWNING WINDOW	AWN WDW			
HOPPER WINDOW	HOP WDW			
JALOUSIE WINDOW	JAL WDW			
DOUBLE DOUBLE-HUNG WINDOW	DDHW			
DOUBLE CASEMENT WINDOW	DBL CSMT WDW			

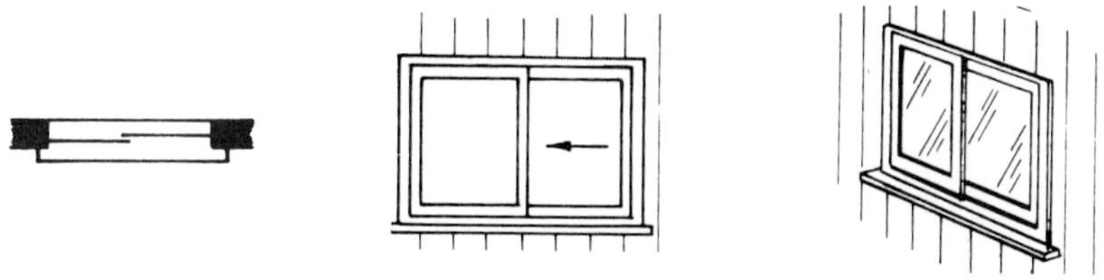

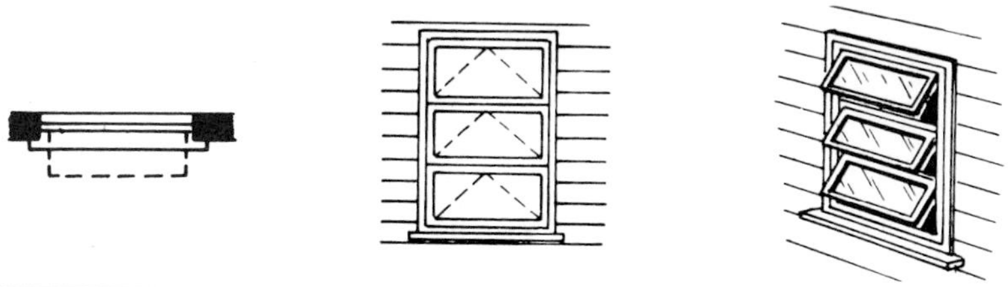

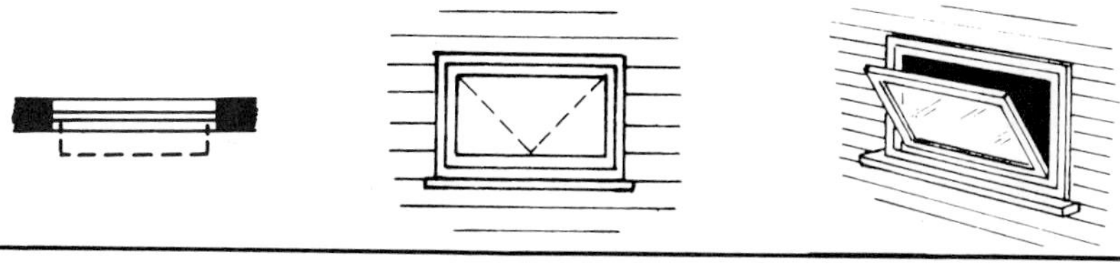

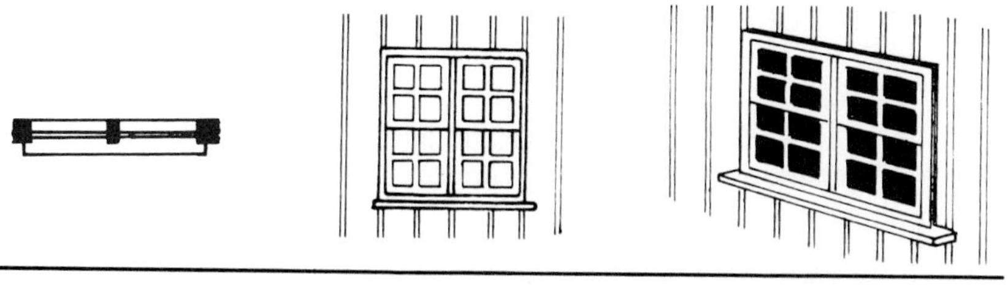

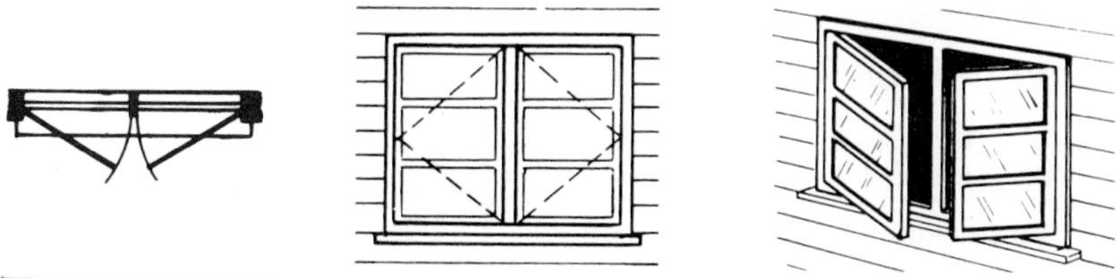

54

Fig. 3-57A. Floor-plan symbols.

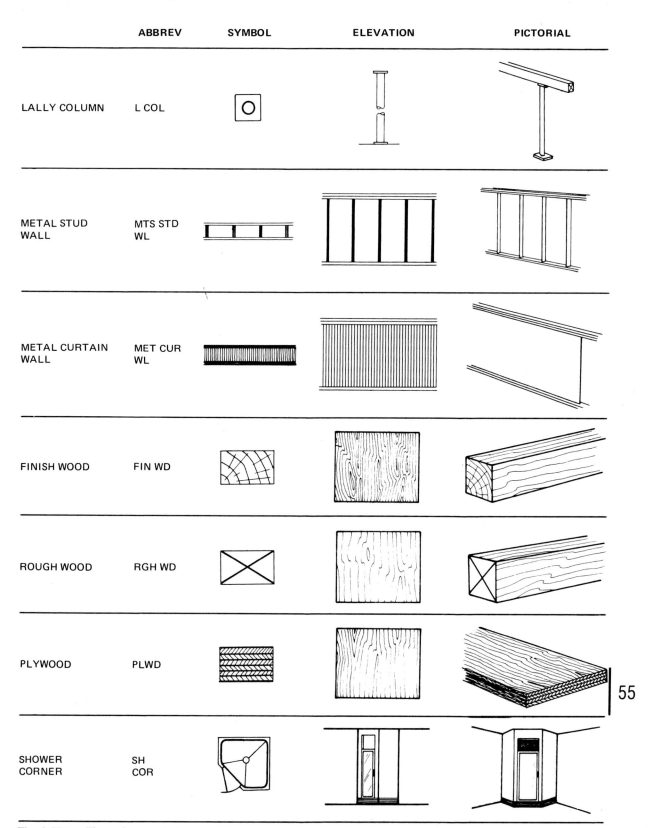

	ABBREV	SYMBOL	ELEVATION	PICTORIAL
LALLY COLUMN	L COL			
METAL STUD WALL	MTS STD WL			
METAL CURTAIN WALL	MET CUR WL			
FINISH WOOD	FIN WD			
ROUGH WOOD	RGH WD			
PLYWOOD	PLWD			
SHOWER CORNER	SH COR			

55

Fig. 3-57B. Floor-plan symbols.

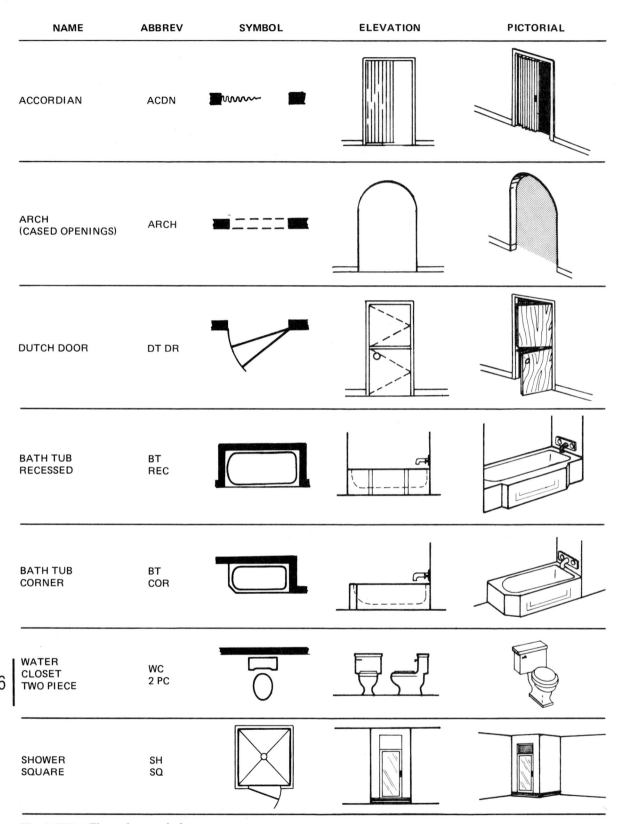

NAME	ABBREV	SYMBOL	ELEVATION	PICTORIAL
ACCORDIAN	ACDN			
ARCH (CASED OPENINGS)	ARCH			
DUTCH DOOR	DT DR			
BATH TUB RECESSED	BT REC			
BATH TUB CORNER	BT COR			
WATER CLOSET TWO PIECE	WC 2 PC			
SHOWER SQUARE	SH SQ			

56

Fig. 3-57C. Floor-plan symbols.

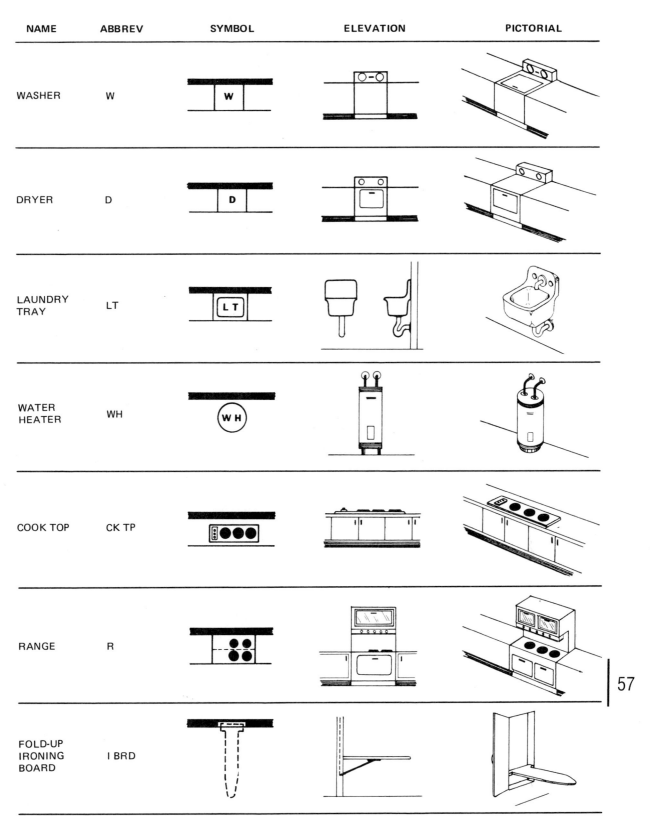

NAME	ABBREV	SYMBOL	ELEVATION	PICTORIAL
WASHER	W			
DRYER	D			
LAUNDRY TRAY	LT			
WATER HEATER	WH			
COOK TOP	CK TP			
RANGE	R			
FOLD-UP IRONING BOARD	I BRD			

57

Fig. 3-57D. Floor-plan symbols.

NAME	ABBREV	SYMBOL	ELEVATION	PICTORIAL
INTERIOR HINGED DOOR HOLLOW CORE	DR			
EXTERIOR HINGED DOOR SOLID CORE	DR			
DOUBLE ACTION DOOR	DBL AC DR			
BYPASSING SLIDING DOOR	BP SLDG DR			
DOUBLE FRENCH DOORS	DBL FR DR			
SLIDING POCKET DOOR	SLDG PK DR			
BIFOLDING DOORS	BI-FLD DR			

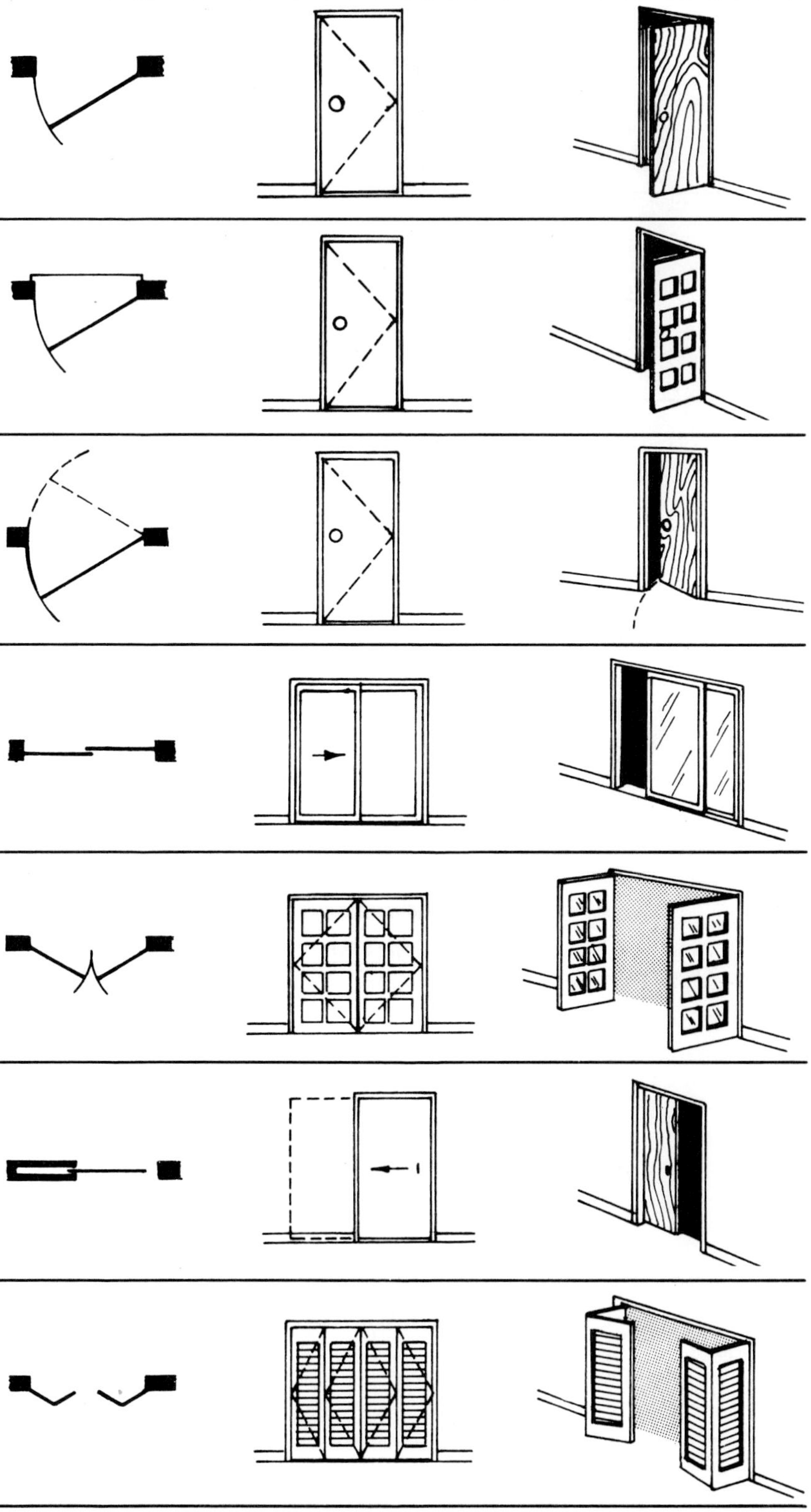

58

Fig. 3-57E. Floor-plan symbols.

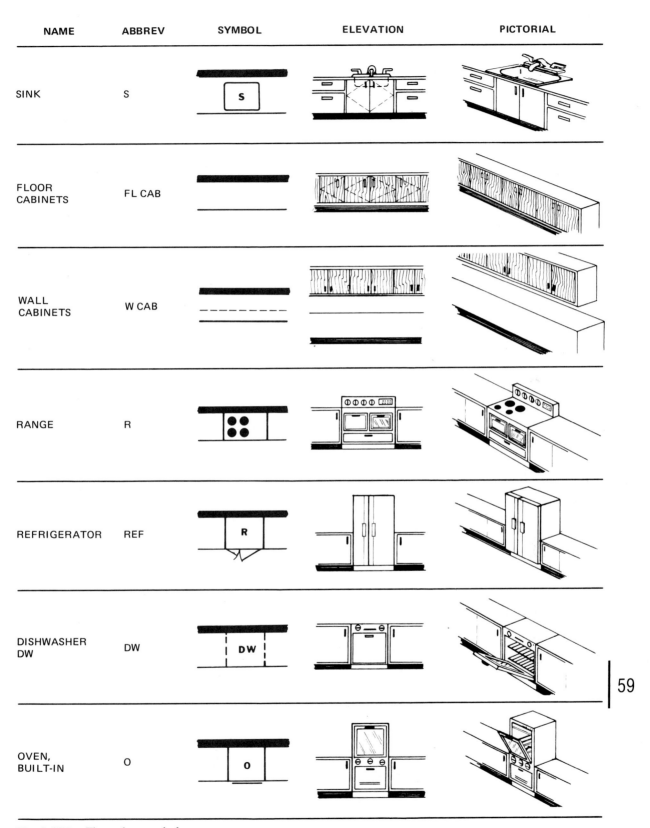

NAME	ABBREV	SYMBOL	ELEVATION	PICTORIAL
SINK	S			
FLOOR CABINETS	FL CAB			
WALL CABINETS	W CAB			
RANGE	R			
REFRIGERATOR	REF			
DISHWASHER DW	DW			
OVEN, BUILT-IN	O			

59

Fig. 3-57F. Floor-plan symbols.

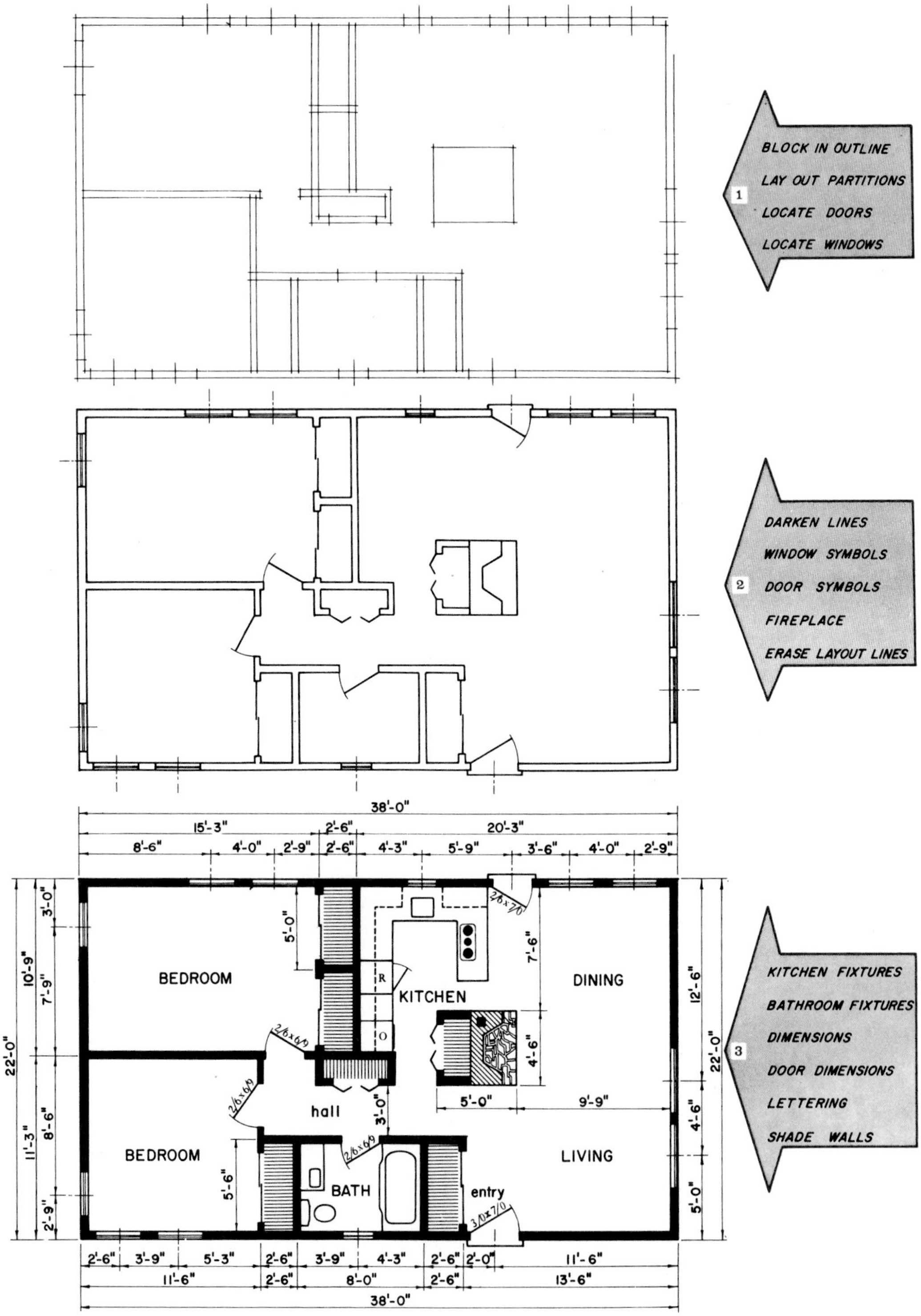

Fig. 3-58. Steps in drawing floor plans.

traced, the first-floor plan is removed. Figure 3-59 shows the method of projecting a second-floor plan from the first-floor plan. Alignment of features such as stairwell openings, outside walls,

FLOOR-PLAN DIMENSIONING

In colonial times, simple cabins could be built without detailed plans and without established dimensions.

Today, building materials are so varied, construction methods so complex, and design requirements so demanding that a completely dimensioned drawing is necessary to complete any project exactly as designed.

Size Description

Dimensions show the builder the width and length of the building. They show the location of doors, windows, stairs, fireplaces, and planters. Just as symbols and notes show exactly what materials are to be used in the building, dimensions show the sizes of materials and exactly where they are to be located.

Dimensioning practices often vary among designers. Several common methods of dimensioning floor plans are shown in Fig. 3-60. Because a large building must be drawn on a

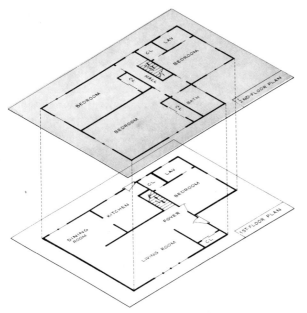

Fig. 3-59. Projection of second-floor plans.

plumbing walls, and chimneys is critical in preparing the second-floor plan.

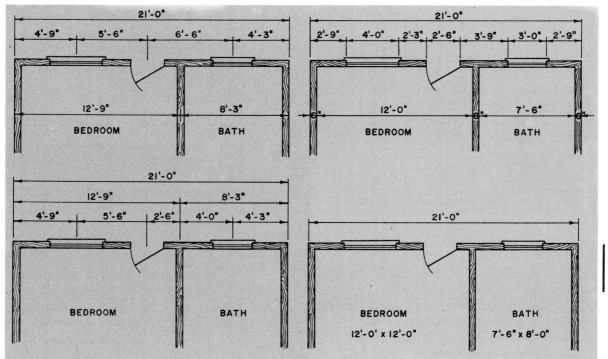

Fig. 3-60. Different methods of dimensioning floor plans.

relatively small sheet, a small scale ($\frac{1}{4}'' = 1'-0''$ or $\frac{1}{8}'' = 1'-0''$) must be used. The use of such small scale means that many dimensions must be crowded into a very small area. Therefore, only major dimensions such as the overall width and length of the building and of separate rooms, closets, halls, and wall thicknesses are shown on the floor plan. Dimensions too small to show directly on the floor plan are described either by a note on the floor plan or by separate, enlarged details. Enlarged details are sometimes merely enlargements of some portion of the floor plan. They may also be an allied section indexed to the floor plan. Separate details are usually necessary to interpret adequately the dimensioning of fireplaces, planters, built-in cabinets, door and window details, stair-framing details, or any unusual construction methods.

Complete Dimensions

The number of dimensions included on a floor plan depends largely on how much freedom of interpretation the architect wants to give to the builder. If complete dimensions are shown on the plan, a builder cannot deviate greatly from the original design. However, if only a few dimensions are shown, then the builder must determine many of the sizes of areas, fixtures, and details. When you rely on a builder to provide dimensions, you place the builder in the position of a designer. A good builder is not expected to be a good designer. Supplying adequate dimensions eliminates the need for unnecessary guesswork.

Limited Dimensions

This type of dimensioning, which shows only the overall building dimensions and the width and length of each room, is sufficient to summarize the relative sizes of the building and its rooms for the prospective owner. These dimensions are not sufficient for building purposes.

A floor plan must be completely dimensioned (Fig. 3-61) to ensure that the house will be constructed precisely as designed. These dimensions convey the exact wishes of the designer and owner to the builder, and little tolerance is allowed the contractor in interpreting the size and position of the various features of this plan. The exact size of each room, closet, partition, door, or window is given.

Rules for Dimensioning

Many construction mistakes result from errors in architectural drawings. Most errors in interior drawings result from mistakes in dimensioning. Dimensioning errors are therefore costly in time, efficiency, and money. Familiarization with the following rules for dimensioning floor plans will eliminate much confusion and error. These rules are illustrated by the numbered arrows in Fig. 3-61.

1. Architectural dimension lines are unbroken lines with dimensions placed above the line. Arrowheads of several styles are optional.
2. Foot and/or inch marks are used on all architectural dimensions.
3. Dimensions over $1'$ are expressed in feet and inches.
4. Dimensions less than $1'$ are shown in inches.
5. A slash is often used with fractional dimensions to conserve vertical space.
6. Dimensions should be placed to read from the right or from the bottom of the drawing.
7. Overall building dimensions are placed outside the other dimensions.
8. Line and arrowhead weights for architectural dimensioning are the same as those used in dimensioning mechanical drawings.
9. Room sizes may be shown by stating width and length.
10. When the area to be dimensioned is too small for the numerals, they are placed outside the extension lines.
11. Rooms are sometimes dimensioned from center lines of partitions; however, rule 13 is preferred.
12. Window and door sizes may be shown directly on the door or window symbol or may be indexed to a door or window schedule.
13. Rooms are dimensioned from finished wall to wall, exclusive of wall thickness.
14. Curved leaders are often used to eliminate confusion with other dimension lines.
15. When areas are too small for arrowheads, dots may be used to indicate dimension limits.
16. The dimensions of brick or stone veneer must be added to the framing dimension.
17. When the space is small, arrowheads may be placed outside the extension lines.
18. A dot with a leader refers to the large area noted.

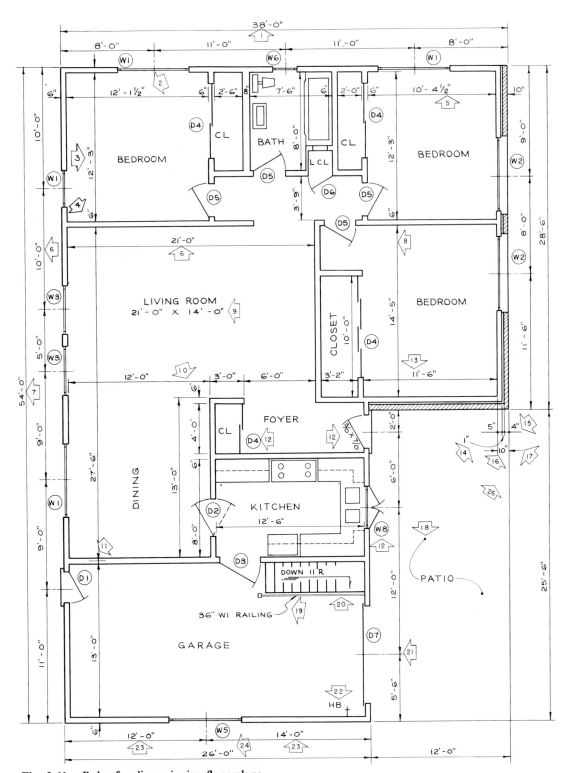

Fig. 3-61. Rules for dimensioning floor plans.

19. Dimensions that cannot be seen on the floor plan or those too small to place on the object are placed on leaders for easier reading.

20. In dimensioning stairs, the number of risers is placed on a line with an arrow indicating the direction (down or up).

63

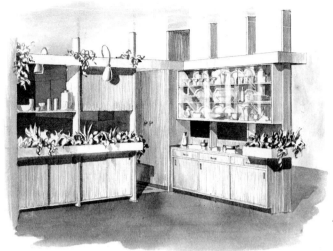

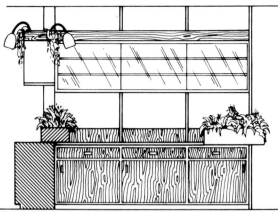

Fig. 3-62. An interior elevation drawing compared to a pictorial drawing of the same area.

21. Windows, doors, pilasters, beams, and areaways are dimensioned to their center lines.
22. Use abbreviations when symbols do not show clearly what is intended.
23. Subdimensions must add up to overall dimensions (14'-0" + 12'-0" = 26'-0").
24. Architectural dimensions always refer to the actual size of the building regardless of the scale of the drawing.
25. When framing dimensions are desirable, rooms are dimensioned by distances between studs in the partitions.
26. Since building materials vary somewhat in size, first establish the thickness of each component of the wall and partition, such as furring thickness, panel thickness, plaster thickness, stud thickness, brick and tile thicknesses. Add these thicknesses together to establish the total wall thickness.

INTERIOR ELEVATIONS

Floor plans show horizontal arrangements of partitions, fixtures, and appliances, but do not show the design of interior walls. Interior elevations, as shown in Fig. 3-62, are necessary to show the design of interior-vertical planes. Because of the need to show cabinet height and counter arrangements, interior wall elevations are often prepared for kitchen and bathroom walls. An interior wall elevation shows the appearance of the wall as viewed from the center of the room. Figure 3-63 shows four wall elevations of a kitchen. Imagine yourself in the center of the room looking north. You will see the north wall of the kitchen, which is drawn in the top of Fig. 3-63.

Now rotate the page so that you are facing east. You can now view the vertical height of the east wall and read the height dimensions from the base cabinet, wall cabinets, electrical outlets. Rotate the page upside down and you can read the south elevation as it appears from the center of the room. The same is true as you rotate the page so you are looking directly at the west wall.

The code symbol shows the direction of the view, the elevation detail number, and the page number to indicate where located.

The steps in drawing an interior elevation are outlined in Fig. 3-64.

Step 1. Outline the floor plan.
Step 2. Projections are made from the floor-plan outline perpendicular from each corner.
Step 3. Then ceiling lines are added to give each wall its specified height.
Step 4. Details are then projected directly from the floor plan to each elevation drawing. Projecting the interior elevations in this

64

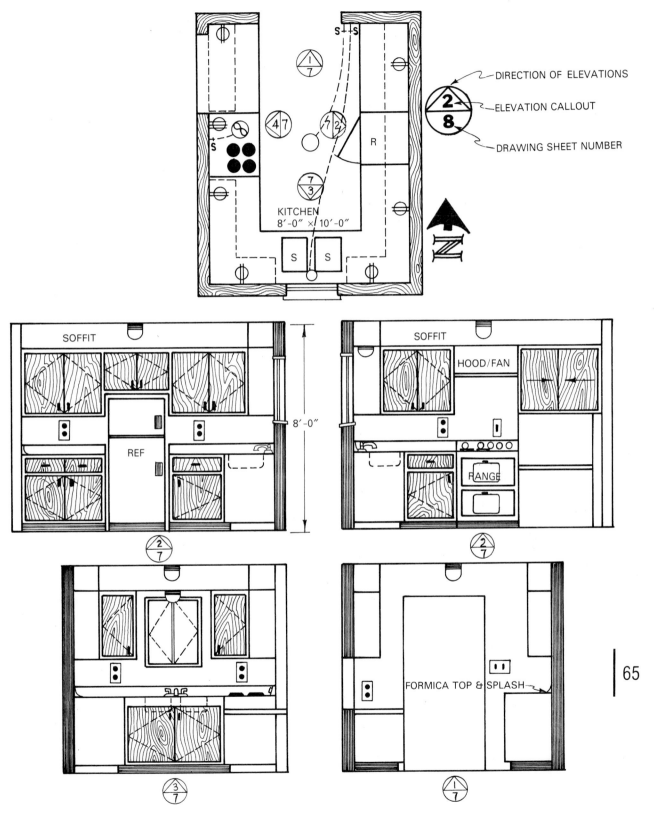

DIRECTION OF ELEVATIONS

ELEVATION CALLOUT

DRAWING SHEET NUMBER

KITCHEN
8'-0" × 10'-0"

SOFFIT

REF

SOFFIT

HOOD/FAN

RANGE

8'-0"

FORMICA TOP & SPLASH

Fig. 3-63. Coding used to identify interior wall elevations.

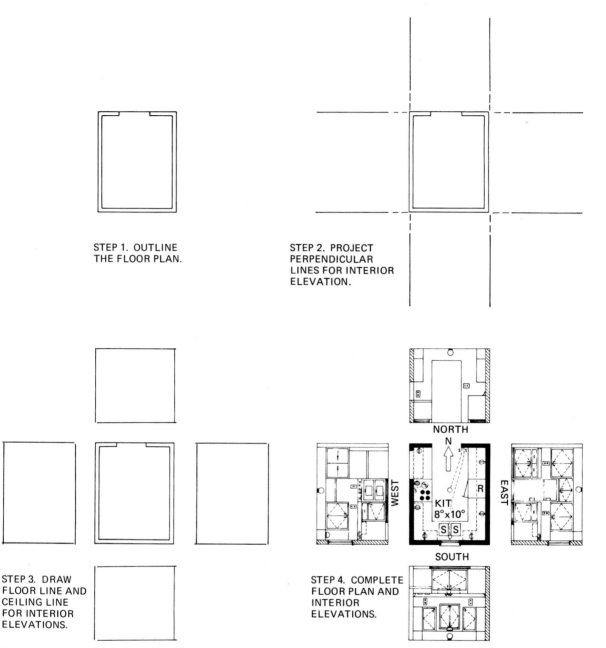

STEP 1. OUTLINE
THE FLOOR PLAN.

STEP 2. PROJECT
PERPENDICULAR
LINES FOR INTERIOR
ELEVATION.

STEP 3. DRAW
FLOOR LINE AND
CEILING LINE
FOR INTERIOR
ELEVATIONS.

STEP 4. COMPLETE
FLOOR PLAN AND
INTERIOR
ELEVATIONS.

NORTH

WEST

EAST

KIT
8°x10°

SOUTH

Fig. 3-64. Steps in drawing interior elevation.

manner results in an elevation drawn on its side or upside down. Interior elevation drawings, like exterior elevations, are not prepared in the original position as they are projected from the floor plans. Interior elevations are positioned with the floor line on the bottom as normally viewed. Once the features of the wall are added to the drawing projected from the floor plan symbols (Fig. 3-65), dimensions (Fig. 3-65), instructional notes (Fig. 3-66), and additional features can be added to the drawing.

A coding system is used to identify the walls on the floor plans for which interior elevations have been prepared.

NAME	ABBRV	SECTION SYMBOL	ELEVATION	NAME	ABBRV	SECTION SYMBOL	ELEVATION
EARTH	E			CUT STONE, ASHLAR	CT STN ASH		
ROCK	RK			CUT STONE, ROUGH	CT STN RGH		
SAND	SD			MARBLE	MARB		
GRAVEL	GV			FLAGSTONE	FLG ST		
CINDERS	CIN			CUT SLATE	CT SLT		
AGGREGATE	AGR			RANDOM RUBBLE	RND RUB		
CONCRETE	CONC			LIMESTONE	LM ST		
CEMENT	CEM			CERAMIC TILE	CER TL		
TERAZZO CONCRETE	TER CONC			TERRA-COTTA TILE	TC TL		
CONCRETE BLOCK	CONC BLK			STRUCTURAL CLAY TILE	ST CL TL		
CAST BLOCK	CST BLK			TILE SMALL SCALE	TL		
CINDER BLOCK	CIN BLK			GLAZED FACE HOLLOW TILE	GLZ FAC HOL TL		
TERRA-COTTA BLOCK LARGE SCALE	TC BLK			TERRA-COTTA BLOCK SMALL SCALE	TC BLK		

Fig. 3-65. Elevation symbols.

NAME	ABBRV	SECTION SYMBOL	ELEVATION	NAME	ABBRV	SECTION SYMBOL	ELEVATION
COMMON BRICK	COM BRK			WELDED WIRE MESH	WWM		
FACE BRICK	FC BRK			FABRIC	FAB		
FIREBRICK	FRB			LIQUID	LQD		
GLASS	GL			COMPOSITION SHINGLE	COMP SH		
GLASS BLOCK	GL BLK			RIDGID INSULATION SOLID	RDG INS		
STRUCTURAL GLASS	STRUC GL			LOOSE-FILL INSULATION	LF INS		
FROSTED GLASS	FRST GL			QUILT	QLT		
STEEL	STL			SOUND INSULATION	SND INS		
CAST IRON	CST IR			CORK INSULATION	CRK INS		
BRASS & BRONZE	BRS BRZ			PLASTER WALL	PLST WL		
ALUMINUM	AL			PLASTER BLOCK	PLST BLK		
SHEET METAL (FLASHING)	SHT MTL FLASH			PLASTER WALL AND METAL LATHE	PLST WL & MT LTH		
REINFORCING STEEL BARS	REBAR			PLASTER WALL AND CHANNEL STUDS	PLST WL & CHN STD		

Fig. 3-65. (*Cont.*)

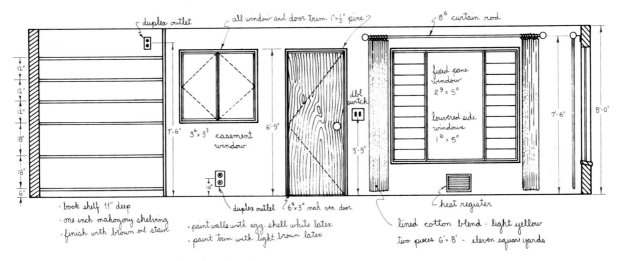

Fig. 3-66. Completely noted interior elevation.

Review Questions

1. Define the following terms: parallel slide, template, overlay, dimension line, extension line, metric, symbol, interior elevation.
2. Complete the exercises for Unit 3 in the workbook.
3. For your scrapbook, find examples of floor plans and interior elevations.
4. Refer to Fig. 2-24. (*a*) What is the overall length of the building? (*b*) What are the dimensions of bedroom 1? (*c*) What is the length of the stairwell opening? (*d*) What are the dimensions of bedroom 2? (*e*) What are the dimensions of the kitchen?
5. Draw a complete floor plan using a sketch of your own design as a guide. (Scale: ¼″ = 1′-0″.)
6. Draw a complete floor plan from the sketch shown in Fig. 2-20. (Scale: ¼″ = 1′-0″.)
7. Make a floor-plan sketch of your own home. Revise this sketch to show how you would propose to remodel the plan. Make a complete floor-plan drawing of the remodel design. (Scale: ¼″ = 1′-0″ or ⅛″ = 1′-0″.)
8. Draw a complete floor plan using the sketch shown in Fig. 2-22 as a guide.
9. Sketch or draw the dimensions on the floor plans shown in Fig. 2-21.
10. Arrange the following pencil grades from hard to soft: 3B, 3F, 2B, 2H, 4H.
11. Draw or sketch the front, rear, right, and left elevations of a room of a floor plan of your own design.
12. Project and sketch or draw an elevation from the pictorial drawing shown in Fig. 4-16.
13. Add dimensions to the elevation drawing shown in Fig. 4-4.
14. Complete an elevation projection for the back wall shown in Fig. 5-7.
15. Dimension an elevation drawing of a room in your own home.
16. Change the dimensions shown in Fig. 3-66 to metric units using meters and millimeters.

PICTORIAL DRAWINGS unit 4

Pictorial drawings are picture-like drawings. They show several sides of an object in one drawing. The perspective drawing is the most popular type of architectural pictorial drawing. Since the subject of most architectural pictorial drawings is extremely large, perspective techniques are necessary to eliminate distortion of the area.

LAYOUT

In perspective drawings, the parts of a building that are furthest from your view appear to recede. For example, as you look down a railroad track, the tracks appear to come together and vanish at a point on the distant horizon. Similarly, the lines of an interior seem to come together. The point at which these lines intersect on a perspective drawing is known as the *vanishing point*. (See Fig. 4-1.) Just as railroad tracks would appear to come together at the horizon, the vanishing points in a perspective drawing are always placed on a horizon line. In preparing perspective drawings, the horizon line is the same as your line of sight. If the horizon line is placed through the building, the building will appear at your eye level. If the horizon line is placed below the building, it will appear to be above your eye level. If the horizon line is placed above the object, it will appear to be below your line of sight. Applications of horizon-line placement are shown in Fig. 4-2. Because perspective drawings do not reveal the true size and shape of the building, perspective drawings are never used for working designs.

A pictorial drawing of the interior of a building may be an isometric drawing, a one-point-perspective drawing, or a two-point-perspective drawing (Fig. 4-3).

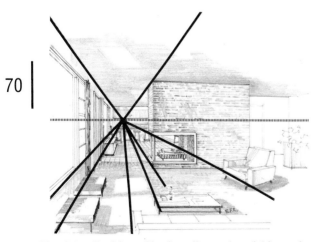

Fig. 4-1. Position of horizon line and vanishing point.

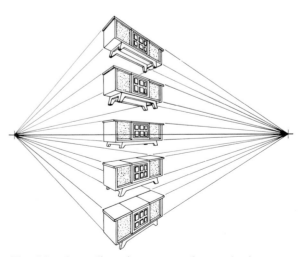

Fig. 4-2. Less distortion occurs close to horizon.

One-point Perspective

A one-point perspective of a room is a drawing in which all the intersections between walls, floors, ceilings, and furniture may be projected to one vanishing point. Drawing a one-point perspective of the interior of a room is similar to drawing the inside of a box with the front of the box removed. In a one-point interior perspective, walls perpendicular to the plane of projection, such as the back wall, are drawn to their proper scale and proportion. The vanishing point on the horizon line is then placed somewhere on this wall (actually behind this wall). The points of intersection where this wall meets the ceiling and floor are then projected from the vanishing point to form the intersection between the side walls and the ceiling and the side walls and the floor. Figure 4-4 shows the same interior drawn in both one- and two-point perspective.

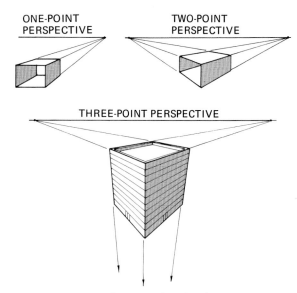

Fig. 4-3. Types of perspective drawings.

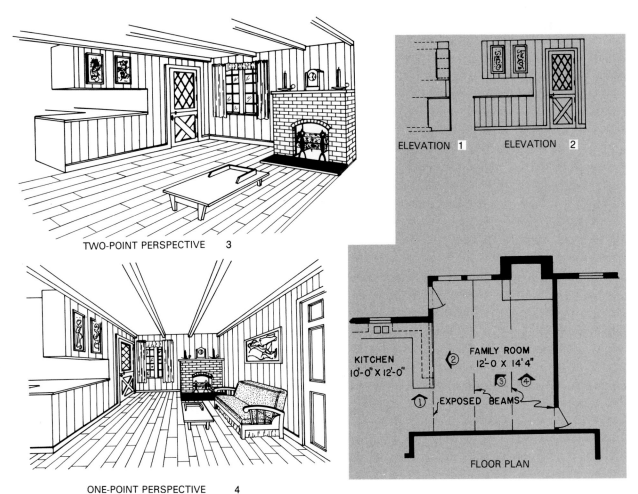

TWO-POINT PERSPECTIVE 3

ONE-POINT PERSPECTIVE 4

Fig. 4-4. Relationship of interior drawings.

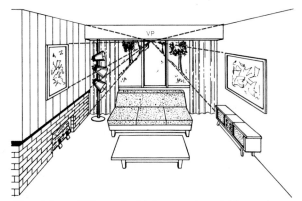

Fig. 4-5A. Effect of a high central vanishing point.

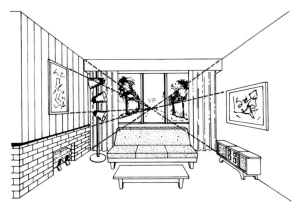

Fig. 4-5B. Effect of a centrally located vanishing point.

Fig. 4-5C. Effect of a low central vanishing point.

Vertical Placement

If the vanishing point is placed high, very little of the ceiling will show in the projection, but much of the floor area will be revealed (Fig.

4-5A). If the vanishing point is placed near the center of the back wall, an equal amount of ceiling and floor will show (Fig. 4-5B). If the vanishing point is placed low on the wall, much of the ceiling but very little of the floor will be shown (Fig. 4-5C). Since the horizon line and the vanishing point are at your eye level, you can see that the position of the vanishing point affects the angle from which you view the object.

Horizontal Placement

Moving the vanishing point from right to left on the back wall has an effect on the view of the side walls. If the vanishing point is placed to the left of the wall, more of the right wall will be revealed. Conversely, if the vanishing point is placed near the left side, more of the right wall will be revealed in the projection. If the vanishing point is placed in the center, an equal amount of right and left wall will be shown. When one wall should dominate, place the vanishing point on the extreme end of the opposite wall. Figure

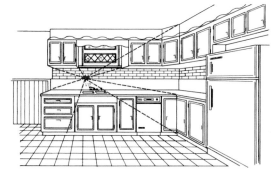

Fig. 4-6A. Effect of the horizontal placement of the vanishing point.

Fig. 4-6B. Effect of a right center vanishing point.

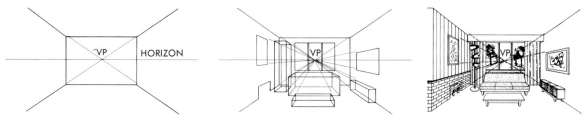

Fig. 4-7. Steps in developing an interior perspective.

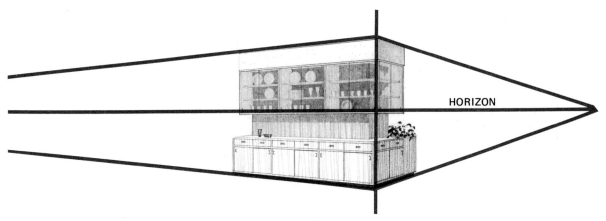

Fig. 4-8. Two-point perspective.

4-6A shows a vanishing point placed near the left side, revealing more of the right wall. The reverse is true in Fig. 4-6B.

When projecting wall offsets and furniture, always block in the overall size of the item to form a perspective view, as shown in Fig. 4-7. The details of furniture or closets or even of

persons can then be completed within this blocked-in cube or series of cubes.

Two-point Perspective

Two-point perspectives (Fig. 4-8) are normally prepared to show the final design and decor of

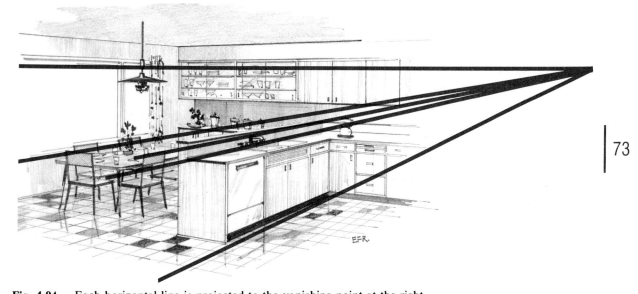

Fig. 4-9A. Each horizontal line is projected to the vanishing point at the right.

73

Fig. 4-9B. Each horizontal line is projected to the central vanishing point.

two walls of a room. The horizon on an interior two-point perspective is similar to the horizon on an exterior two-point perspective. The base line in the drawing shown in Fig. 4-8 is the corner of the fireplace. Two rooms or an L-shaped room can then be shown projected to each vanishing point.

Once the walls are projected to the vanishing points in the two-point perspective, each object in the room can also be projected to the vanishing point as shown in Figs. 4-9A and B.

The sequence of steps in drawing two-point interior perspectives is shown in Fig. 4-10.

RENDERING

To render a pictorial drawing is to make the drawing appear more realistic. This may be done through the media of pencil, pen and ink, water colors, pastels, color overlaps, screentones, or airbrush. Drawings are rendered by adding re-

alistic texture to the materials and establishing shade and shadow patterns.

Media

Soft pencils are one of the most effective media for rendering architectural drawings because tones can be greatly varied by the weight of the line used. Smudge blending can be accomplished by rubbing a finger over penciled areas to add tone.

Pen-and-ink renderings of architectural drawings vary greatly. Strokes must be placed further apart to create light effects and closer together to produce darker effects. Water colors are also used especially when the color scheme is to be emphasized. Figure 4-11A shows a sample of pencil rendering technique. Figure 4-11B is a pen-and-ink drawing with a wash over the line work to create color and depth impressions. Figure 4-11C utilizes a black-and-white wash technique with major lines reinforced with light ink lines.

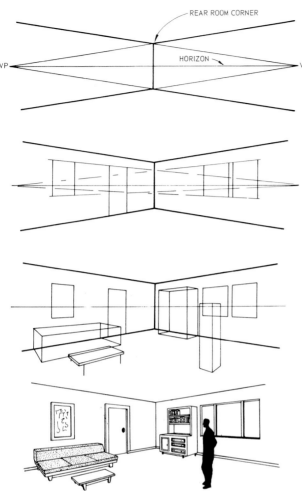

Fig. 4-10. Sequence in drawing a two-point interior perspective.

Fig. 4-11B. Pen-and-ink rendering with wash. *Georgia Pacific*

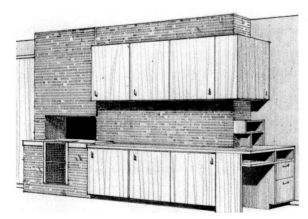

Fig. 4-11 A. Pencil rendering technique. *Home Planners, Inc.*

Fig. 4-11C. Black-and-white wash technique. *Home Planners, Inc.*

75

SHADOWING AND RENDERING

Fig. 4-12. Use of shading to show sunlight on areas.

Shade

When you shade an object you lighten the part of the object exposed to the sun or other light sources and darken the part of the object not exposed to the sun or light source (Fig. 4-12). Notice how the different parts of Fig. 4-13 are shaded darker and the top shaded lighter to show the different exposure to the light. Likewise the right portion of Fig. 4-14 is shaded darker to denote distance and lack of direct sunlight. When objects with sharp corners are exposed to strong sunlight, one area may be extremely light and the other side of the object extremely dark. However, when objects and buildings have areas that are round (cylindrical), so that their parts move gradually from dark to light areas, a gradual shading from extremely dark to extremely light must be made.

Shadow

In order to determine what areas of the building will be drawn darker to indicate shadowing, the angle of the light source or sources must be established. When the angle of the light is established (Fig. 4-15), all shading should be consistent with the direction and angle of the shadow. On buildings that are drawn considerably below the horizon line, shadow patterns will often reveal

Fig. 4-13. Use of shading to show sun exposures.

Fig. 4-14. Use of shading to show distances.

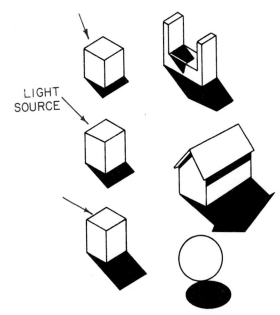

LIGHT SOURCE

Fig. 4-15. Shadow the area opposite the light source.

Fig. 4-16. Shadow patterns reveal surface shapes. *Home Planners, Inc.*

more than the actual outline can reveal. Notice how the shadow patterns in Fig. 4-16 reveal the shape and depth of the fireplace opening.

Texture

Giving texture to an architectural drawing means making building materials appear as rough or as smooth as they actually are. Smooth surfaces are no problem since they are very reflective and hence are very light. Only a few reflection lines are usually necessary to illustrate smoothness of surfaces such as aluminum, glass, and painted surfaces. On rough surfaces, the thickness or roughness of the material can often be shown by shading.

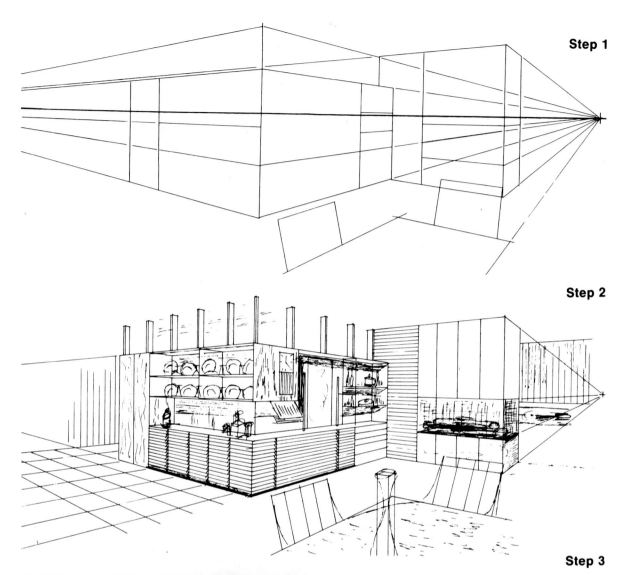

Step 1

Step 2

Step 3

Fig. 4-17 Steps in preparing interior rendering.

SIDING

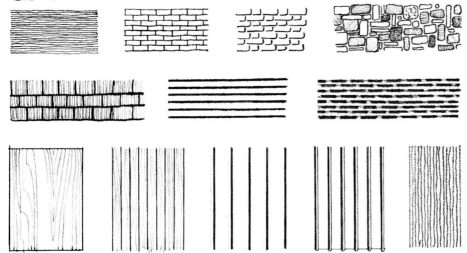

Fig. 4-18. Rendering of architectural materials.

Sequence

In preparing pictorial renderings, proceed in the following sequence, as shown in Fig. 4-17.

1. Block in with single lines the projection of the perspective (Step 1).
2. Sketch the detail outline of building materials in preparation for rendering (Step 2). This work can be done with a soft pencil, a ruling pen, or a crow-quill pen. Establish and sketch shadows and shading.
3. Add texture to the building materials. For example, show the position of each brick with a chisel-point pencil. Leave the mortar space white and lighten the pressure for the areas

that are in direct sunlight (Step 3). Complete the rendering by emphasizing light and dark areas and establishing more visible contrasts of light and dark shadow patterns.

Material Rendering Techniques

Figure 4-18 shows the application of various rendering techniques to architectural materials. Figure 4-19 shows depth and shadows in rendering windows. Notice that some windows are rendered to show reflected light, and others are drawn to reveal the room behind, as though the window were open. Figure 4-20 shows various techniques used by designers and illustrators to

WINDOWS

79

Fig. 4-19. Window rendering techniques.

DOORS

Fig. 4-20. Door rendering techniques.

render different types of interior doors. Renderings require a combination of shade, shadow, and texture techniques.

Sketches of people are often necessary to show the relative size of an area and to put the total design in proper perspective. Since people should not interfere with the view of the building, designers frequently draw people in outline or in an extremely simple form. People are also used to show traffic patterns, size differences (Fig. 4-21), and to provide a feeling of perspective and depth. Notice that most of this is done by light shading and also by variation of the pencil-stroke widths.

One popular technique that can be used to convert a perspective line drawing into a rendering is to apply screen tones. The drawings shown in Fig. 4-22 are simple line drawings with various shades of screens added to denote texture and shadow.

Review Questions

1. Define the following terms: pictorial, one-point perspective, two-point perspective,

Fig. 4-21. Use of people to show traffic patterns.

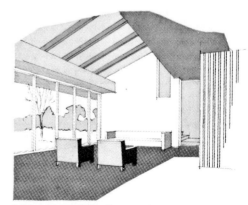

Fig. 4-22. Use of shading to show texture.

80

vanishing point, horizon, render, shade, texture.

2. Complete the exercises for Unit 4 in the workbook.

3. Find examples of one- and two-point-perspective drawings for your scrapbook. Add and label horizon and vanishing points.

4. Project a two-point-perspective drawing for the living area from the floor plan shown in Fig. 1-20.

5. Develop a one-point perspective of the living room shown in Fig. 1-16.

6. Trace the photographs shown in Fig. 1-18. Find the position of the vanishing point and the horizon.

7. Draw a one-point-perspective drawing of your own living room.

8. Draw a two-point-perspective drawing of your own living room.

9. Trace the drawings shown in Fig. 4-13. Project a ceiling and floor line to find a vanishing point and horizon line.

10. Trace the perspective drawing shown in Fig. 4-16. Find the position of the vanishing points. Extend the drawing to include the right wall of the living area.

11. Render a perspective drawing of the living area shown in Fig. 3-39.

12. Render a perspective drawing of your own design.

81

Color is a vital element to the designer. Its qualities are inherent and transcend seasons and trends. Each color has its own personality and psychology. These are altered by their color group.

Each color is characterized by its *hue* which is constant. Value is the degree of darkness or lightness of hue. *Tint* is a color on the lighter side of a hue. *Shade* is a color on the darker side of a hue. *Intensity,* or the saturation of color, refers to the degree of brightness or purity of the color.

Nothing distinguishes an interior design more than the effective use of color. Rooms are often referred to not by their function but by their color: The Rose Room, the Blue Room, and so forth. The interior designer must combine the elements of the color spectrum in the appropriate relationship to produce the desired color harmony. Paints and finishes can be mixed to a precise formula, but many furnishings and equipment are available only in a limited range of color. Consequently the interior designer must be most skillful in working around such problems. To do this a thorough understanding of the relationship of colors and potential color harmonies is essential. The color wheel shown in Fig. 5-1 is the basis for all color planning. Colors are classified by spectrum, quality, and harmony. The circumference of the color wheel represents the entire spectrum of color. The quality of color refers to the hue, value, and intensity of each color, and color harmony relates to the combination of colors.

82

THE COLOR SPECTRUM

Colors in the spectrum are divided into primary, secondary, and tertiary colors. *Primary* colors are those colors that cannot be made from any other color. Primary colors are red, yellow, and blue, as shown in Fig. 5-2. Figure 5-3 shows a color scheme composed essentially from primary colors.

A *secondary* color is made from equal mixtures of two primaries, as shown in Fig. 5-4. Green is a combination of yellow and blue. Violet is a combination of blue and red; orange is a combination of red and yellow. The color scheme in Fig. 5-5 utilizes mostly secondary colors.

A *tertiary* color is the combination of a primary color and a neighboring secondary color as shown on the color wheel in Fig. 5-6. The tertiary colors are *red-orange, yellow-orange, yellow-green, blue-green, blue-violet* and *red-violet.* Figure 5-7A shows a color scheme using this combination. Notice the difference color makes when compared to the black-and-white photograph of the same room shown in Fig. 5-7B. *Yellow-Orange* is a combination of primary yellow and secondary orange. Figure 5-8 utilizes this combination. *Yellow-green* is a combination of primary yellow and secondary green, as shown in Fig. 5-9. *Blue-green* is a combination of primary blue and secondary green. Figure 5-10 shows one application of this combination, and Fig. 5-11 shows another. Although both examples utilize blue-green, the combinations and intensities make the color schemes appear drastically different. *Blue-violet* is a combination of primary blue and secondary violet, as exemplified in Fig. 5-12.

There are many other colors which fall between any of these adjacent colors. However, these examples illustrate the principles of effective use of color in planning interior color schemes. Many degrees or gradations of a color can be obtained, for example. Green is a mixture of equal parts of blue and yellow, but if one part blue and nine parts yellow is mixed, the resultant color would be much closer to yellow than to blue. If the amount of blue is increased and the amount of yellow decreased, many degrees of green can be obtained.

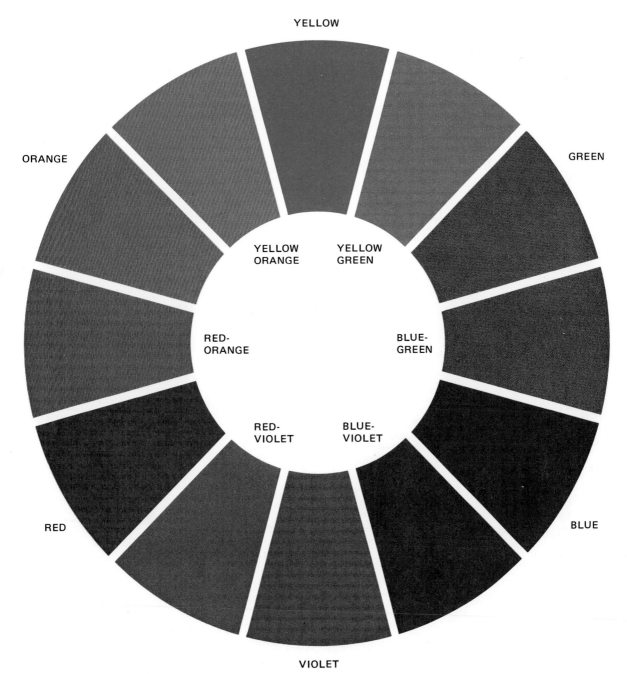

Fig. 5-1. The color wheel.

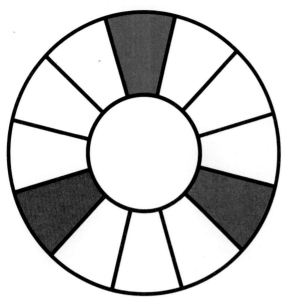

Fig. 5-2. Primary colors—yellow, blue, and red.

Fig. 5-4. Secondary colors—green, violet, and orange.

Fig. 5-3. A primary color scheme. *United States Plywood Corporation*

84

Fig. 5-5. Color scheme using secondary colors. *National Decorative Products Assn.*

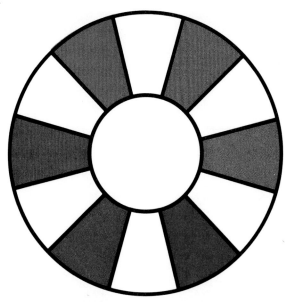

Fig. 5-6. Tertiary colors—yellow-green, blue-green, blue-violet, red-violet, red-orange, and yellow-orange.

Fig. 5-7A. Yellow-orange color scheme. *Sol Vista Homes*

Fig. 5-7B. Room shown in Fig. 5-7A without color. *Fred Farish*

Fig. 5-8. Orange-yellow scheme. *National Decorative Products Assn.*

Fig. 5-9. Yellow-green color scheme. *National Decorative Products Assn.*

Fig. 5-10. Blue-green combination. *National Decorative Products Assn.*

Fig. 5-11. Blue-green combination. *Kohler*

Fig. 5-12. Blue-violet combination. *PPG Industries*

Fig. 5-13. Nearly neutral color scheme. *PPG Industries*

A *neutral* shows no color in the ordinary sense of the word. Neutrals are white, gray, and black. The three primary colors, if mixed in equal strengths, will produce black. When colors cancel each other out in this manner, they are neutralized. Figure 5-13 shows a color scheme which is nearly neutral, except for the slight dash of yellow.

COLOR QUALITY

For greater accuracy in describing a color's exact appearance, colorists distinguish three qualities: hue, value, and intensity.

The *hue* of a color is its basic consistent identity. A color hue may be identified as being yellow, yellow-green, blue, blue-green, and so forth. Even when a color is made lighter or darker, the hue remains the same. Such names as pink, crimson, vermilion, all refer to the color whose hue is red. These colors are derived by adding white, gray, or black to primary red. To change one hue to another its fundamental nature must be altered as when blue is made into green by adding yellow.

The *value* of a color refers to the lightness or darkness of the hue. A *tint* is lighter (or higher) in value than the normal value of a color. A tint of a hue will make a room look larger in area. Varying the value properties can dramatically change the mood of a room. For example, a light yellow room will be cheerful, bright and exuberant; but a light violet room will look mysterious and soft. And a light green room will look restful and organic.

A *shade* is darker (or lower) in value than the normal value of the color. A great many

degrees of value can be obtained as shown in Fig. 5-14. A tint is produced by adding white to the normal color. A shade is produced by adding black to the normal color. A dark shade will make a room smaller and fuller. Again, the individual colors have strong specific personalities. Red adds drama, passion, action; with a little blue added, it becomes royal purple. A dark blue room will be elegant, formal.

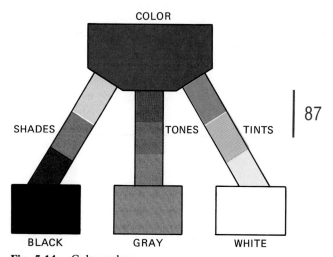

Fig. 5-14. Color values.

87

Fig. 5-15. High-intensity color scheme. *Imperial Wallpaper Mills, Inc.*

Fig. 5-16. Muted color scheme. *Steelcase, Inc.*

A *tone* is produced by adding gray or some value to the normal color. Each normal color on a color wheel has a value that can be expressed as equivalent to the degree of gray included.

The *intensity* (or strength) of a color is its degree of purity (or brightness); that is, its freedom from neutralizing factors. This quality is also referred to in color terminology as *chroma*. A color entirely free of neutral elements is called *saturated*. The intensity of a color can be changed without changing the value of a color by mixing the color with a gray of the same value. As more gray is added, the intensity of the mixture becomes lower, but the value stays constant if the gray is the same value as the color. Decorators refer to grayed colors as muted. Figure 5-15 shows a high-intensity color scheme which is contrasted with the muted color scheme shown in Fig. 5-16, both using the primary color red as the base.

COLOR HARMONIES

Harmonies are groups of colors which relate to each other in a predictable manner. The basic harmonies are complementary, analogous, split-complementary, monochromatic, and triadic.

Complementary Harmonies

A color's complement is that color directly across from it on the color wheel. Observing the color wheel, note the complement of red is green, the complement of blue is orange, the complement of blue-green is red-orange, and so forth. When a color is added to its complement, the effect will be neutralization. Complementaries can be mixed, but it must be done with great care, for often the results will be a muddy brown and not the desired gray. Because there are differences in the chemical composition of pigments of commercial paints and in tinting colors, it is very difficult to find paint colors that are absolute true complements (Fig. 5-17).

Adjacent or Analogous Color Harmony

If blue is selected as the basic color (Fig. 5-18), the colors adjacent to blue, on either side, are

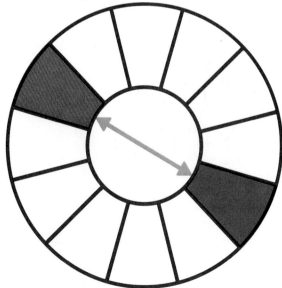

Fig. 5-17. An example of complementary colors—blue and orange.

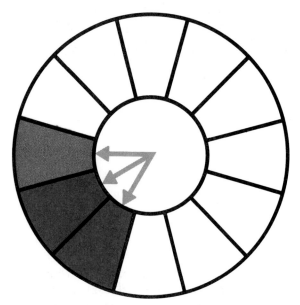

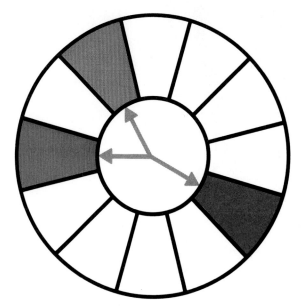

Fig. 5-18. An example of the analogous colors to blue —blue-green and blue-violet.

Fig. 5-20. The split-complementary colors for blue are red-orange and yellow-orange.

blue-green and blue-violet. These are also referred to by decorators as *close harmonies*.

Colors that fall side by side on the color wheel are easy to combine harmoniously because they are similar hues in the spectrum, i.e., they have a single color in common. Blue, for example, is the common factor of blue-green, blue-violet, and violet. Blue and violet alone might clash, but with the blue-violet to unite or blend them,

harmony can be established, as shown in Fig. 5-19.

In an analogous color scheme, as in any color scheme, one color should be dominant.

Split-complementary Harmony

Split-complementary color harmonies are shown in the example in Fig. 5-20. Using blue as the

Fig. 5-19. Blue-violet harmony. *Kohler*

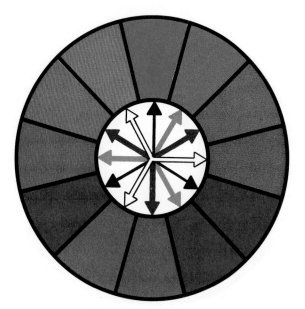

Fig. 5-21. Triadic color scheme.

example, notice that orange is its direct complement, that is, orange is directly across the color wheel from blue. On either side of the true complement orange, are red-orange and yellow-orange. These two colors make up a *split-complementary harmony,* sometimes called *contrasting harmonies.*

Monochromatic Color Harmony

A color scheme based on this harmony uses one underlying color as the base. Variety is obtained by the blending and contrasting of only the values and intensities of one color. Also differences in texture add variety to this scheme. Neutrals, white, gray, and black, are often added to the monochromatic color scheme for relief without altering the basic color plan. Occasionally an accenting accessory or different hue is introduced into the monochromatic color scheme, but the scheme is then no longer purely monochromatic.

Triadic Color Harmony

Figure 5-21 shows examples of a triadic color scheme, in which any three colors, each of which is approximately the same distance apart on the color wheel from the other, is involved. The three primaries, red, yellow, and blue, form the most conspicuous triad. Another triad, for example, would be orange, green, and violet. A triadic

scheme is adaptable to a friendly, informal room. This can be a very striking color effect, but to avoid disagreeing contrasts, one color must dominate, and each color altered in value and intensity.

Harmony of Shades

In addition to harmonies produced by combining hues and shade, harmonies are a device that can be used effectively by the designer. Grayed shades can be produced by adding gray to shades of color with the same degree of variability. Or different shades can be produced with the use of variegated colors with the same color value. The use of harmonies of equal and different shades can also be used to create a balanced dramatic effect.

COLOR EFFECTS

Temperature

The impression of coolness is produced by blue, and colors containing more blue than any other color. A feeling of warmth is created by the colors red and yellow and colors containing red and yellow, such as orange. Warm colors include all red and yellow shades, including mixed browns. They will raise the temperature of a room and make it seem cozier and smaller. Cold colors include all blue and green shades. These will lower the temperature in a room and make it seem airy and bright.

Figure 5-22 contains all warm colors. Green and violet are not considered either warm or

Fig. 5-22. Use of warm interior and exterior colors. *California Redwood Association*

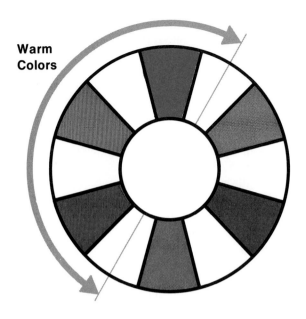

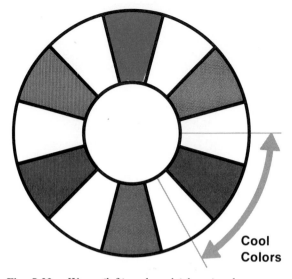

Fig. 5-23. Warm (left) and cool (above) colors.

cold. Green contains equal amounts of yellow, a warm color, and blue, a cool color. Violet is similar in this respect in that it has equal parts of a warm color (red) and a cool color (blue). Colors vary in warmness and coolness. As the green and violet go to warm colors, they gain warmth. They become cooler as they approach blue. The more yellow a green contains, the more warmth it expresses, and the more blue that is added to the blue-green, the cooler it becomes (see Fig. 5-23).

Effective Light

In choosing colors, the type of light used in a room must be considered. It is best to choose the color under the kind of light in which it will be seen. If a common incandescent bulb is used, select the color under it. If the room has fluorescent lighting, examine the color under the exact type of fluorescent tube that will be used. Incandescent lighting is inclined to emphasize reds and yellows but tones down blues and greens. On the other hand, some types of fluorescent lighting emphasizes blues and gives a cool effect.

The exposure during the day should be considered in choosing a color. Look at the color both in daylight and under artificial light. Choose the color that looks best at the time the room is most frequently used, either evenings or days. Different rooms of course receive different

amounts of sunlight during different parts of the day. A room with northern exposure, such as the one shown in Fig. 5-24, can be made more cheerful with a warm color. Yellows are usually avoided in rooms that have a great deal of sunshine. The use of cool blues will make a room with a southern exposure or western exposure seem cooler. If the room doesn't have much natural light, light tints rather than dark shades are usually preferable. It is only in very light rooms that dark shades can be used without seriously reducing the amount of natural light.

Fig. 5-24. Northern exposure requires warmer colors.

91

Fig. 5-25. Warm colors advance. *National Decorative Products Assn.*

ATMOSPHERE

Colors have a strong effect on the atmosphere of a room. Colors can be used to make a room more cheerful and comfortable or to establish a more formal and luxurious atmosphere. Warm, bright colors tend to make a room informal. Cool colors provide a soothing and quiet air for the room but do not necessarily create formality, since the furnishings, texture, and upholstery all contribute to the feel of a room.

The physical features of a room must be considered in deciding between light and dark colors, but personal color preference is also an important factor, because only the people using the area know the colors they like best and can live with them happily. The choice of colors for a home can be an expression of lifestyle.

Colors can affect the apparent proportions of a room. Bold colors such as bright blues, greens, and reds will make walls advance. Their skillful use can make a room appear lower, shorter etc. Pastel colors such as light blue, yellow, etc. will make a room appear higher or longer.

Warm colors tend to make objects advance, as shown in Fig. 5-25. Deep colors can have the same effect on bringing a wall or object nearer. A warm color on a high ceiling has the effect of lowering it. If a room is too long and narrow, the end walls advance thus creating an illusion of making the room more square. Or a square room can be made more pleasing by having one wall a different color than the other three, thereby avoiding a boxy appearance. Pastels have been used a great deal because they help make a room seem light and airy and because they provide an opportunity for using dark color fabrics, draperies, etc., to create more interesting, contrasting, and dramatic effects.

The following basic list gives a general explanation of color psychology.

White—innocence, purity, coldness
Black—night, mourning, death, evil
Blue—faithfulness, depth, formality, royalty, chastity
Green—hope, growth, immaturity
Yellow—envy, hate, shame
Gold—sun, riches, joy
Red—blood, passion, man
Purple—ruler, majesty
Violet—mourning, mystery, shadow, dignity
Gray—inferiority, age

Fig. 5-26. Intense colors are reserved for accents for small areas. *United States Plywood Corporation*

Fig. 5-27. Warm colors are suitable for entrances. *Kohler*

Fig. 5-28. Use of bright colors in the dining areas. *PPG Industries*

Distribution of Color

The stronger the intensity of a color, the smaller the area this color should occupy. It also follows that the weaker the intensity of the color, the greater area it may occupy. Also extremeness in value of the color, either very high or low, should be avoided in large areas. One dominant color in a color scheme gives unity and harmony to a room. In selecting the amount of different colors to use, avoid precise obvious divisions of areas two colors occupy. Use divisions in the ratios of 2 to 3, 3 to 5, and so forth. In other words, don't use equal amounts of two colors, or of three colors. Sometimes four colors are used, but more

than four will make the room look color confused, and you may lose any actual scheme. Make one color dominant, use a second color in a lesser amount, and a third still less. The most intense colors are usually reserved for accents and are used in smaller amounts. The room in Fig. 5-26 used brown as the basic color with orange as the secondary color used in a lesser mass of area.

Color schemes should also be built around such items as drapery, wallpaper, paintings, and so forth by matching the wall, ceiling, and trim colors to the color proportions found in the drapery, wallpaper, or paintings. But remember to balance the color distribution by repeating colors throughout the room.

In planning the color schemes of connecting rooms, color linking is very important, especially when you can see easily from one room to another. The colors you select should blend, or the walls can be the same color. If the rooms are small, this gives the illusion of space and at the same time gives unity.

Treatment of the various residential areas usually differ somewhat colorwise, and there are some general preferences for various rooms. For example, warm, interesting, inviting colors are suitable for the entrance hall (Fig. 5-27), which is a welcome area for guests. Conservative color treatment is generally preferred for the living room because it should appeal to all who gather there. Dining rooms can be brighter, because shorter periods of time are spent there. Notice how the use of mirrors expands the effect of color in Fig. 5-28. Vivid colors can be used in

Fig. 5-29. Vivid colors used in the kitchen. *Frigidaire*

the kitchen (Fig. 5-29) since stimulating colors make routine chores less boring. Children's rooms are usually decorated in warm, lively colors. However, bedrooms should be restful and relaxing, thus subdued values are usually used here. Bathrooms and dressing rooms should contain colors and lighting that are most realistic. Notice the difference color makes in the bathrooms shown in Figs. 5-30A, B, and C. These three rooms are exactly the same except for the application of color. Figure 5-30A is shown without color, Fig. 5-30B uses a green-yellow scheme, and Fig. 5-30C uses a blue-brown combination of colors.

COLOR SCHEMES

Although there are no absolute rules governing color combinations, most interior decorators combine colors in harmonies mentioned in the guidelines above. Figure 5-31 shows recommended relationships between dominant color hue, harmonizing colors, and contrasting colors for each major hue.

Fig. 5-30A. Bath without color. *Eljer*

Fig. 5-30B. Bath in green-yellow scheme. *Eljer*

Fig. 5-30C. Bath in blue-brown scheme. *Eljer*

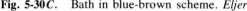

DOMINANT COLOR (HUE)	NAVY	BLUE	LIGHT BLUE	LAVENDER (BLUE-RED)	PURPLE
HARMONIZING COLORS	Light blue Blue Myrtle green Light green Green Heliotrope Purple Lavender Gray	Light blue Navy Light green Green Heliotrope Purple Lavender Gray	Blue Navy Myrtle Light green Lavender Gray	Light blue Blue Navy Light green Green Pink Purple Gray Brown Dark brown	Blue Navy Myrtle green Light green Green Pink Maroon Heliotrope Lavender Gray Brown Dark brown
CONTRASTING COLORS	Yellow Orange Red Maroon Heliotrope Cream Tan Brown Dark brown	Olive Yellow Orange Cream Tan Brown Dark brown	Olive Pink Cream Tan	Olive Yellow Cream Tan	Yellow Orange Cream Tan

DOMINANT COLOR (HUE)	CREAM	TAN	BROWN	DARK BROWN	MYRTLE GREEN
HARMONIZING COLORS	Yellow Orange Pink Gray Tan Brown Dark brown	Olive Yellow Cream Brown Dark brown	Olive Yellow Orange Red Maroon Heliotrope Purple Lavender Cream Tan Dark brown	Lavender Cream Tan Brown Olive Yellow Orange Red Maroon Heliotrope Purple	Navy Green Yellow Purple Gray
CONTRASTING COLORS	Blue Light blue Navy Myrtle green Green Light green Olive Red Heliotrope Purple Lavender	Light blue Blue Navy Myrtle green Light green Green Maroon Heliotrope Purple Lavender	Blue Navy Light green Green	Blue Navy Light green Green	Red Heliotrope Cream Tan

Fig. 5-31. Color planning schedule. (Read across.)

HELIOTROPE (RED-PURPLE)	MAROON OR WINE	RED	PINK	ORANGE	YELLOW
Blue	Pink	Orange	Red	Olive	Light green
Pink	Red	Pink	Maroon	Yellow	Green
Red	Heliotrope	Maroon	Heliotrope	Red	Olive
Maroon	Purple	Heliotrope	Purple	Cream	Orange
Purple	Brown	Brown	Lavender	Tan	Cream
Gray	Dark brown	Dark brown	Cream	Brown	Tan
Brown				Dark brown	Brown
Dark brown					Dark brown

Navy	Navy	Navy	Light blue	Blue	Blue
Myrtle green	Light green	Myrtle green	Light green	Navy	Navy
Light green	Green	Light green	Green	Light green	Myrtle green
Green	Olive	Green	Olive	Green	Red
Yellow	Yellow	Olive	Gray	Heliotrope	Maroon
Orange	Gray	Yellow		Purple	Purple
Cream	Cream	Gray			Heliotrope
Tan	Tan	Cream			Lavender
					Gray

LIGHT GREEN	GREEN	OLIVE	GRAY	BLACK WHITE	NEUTRAL
Light blue	Blue	Myrtle green	Light blue	Use grayed medium tones of any color.	Useful additions to any scheme. Goes with all colors.
Blue	Navy	Light green	Blue		
Navy	Myrtle green	Green	Navy		
Myrtle green	Light green	Yellow	Myrtle green		
Green	Olive	Orange	Light green		
Olive	Yellow	Tan	Green		
Yellow	Lavender	Brown	Heliotrope		
Lavender	Gray	Dark brown	Purple		
Gray			Lavender		
			Cream		

Orange	Orange	Light blue	Yellow	Use bright gay tones of any color.	They are:
Pink	Pink	Blue	Orange		White
Red	Red	Pink	Pink		Black
Maroon	Maroon	Red	Red		Ivory
Heliotrope	Heliotrope	Maroon	Maroon		Beige
Purple	Purple	Lavender			Gray
Cream	Cream	Cream			Cream
Tan	Tan				
Brown	Brown				
Dark brown	Dark brown				

Fig. 5-31. (Cont.)

Review Questions

1. Define the following terms: primary, secondary, tertiary, spectrum, neutral, hue, intensity, tint, shade, muted, harmony, scheme, complementary, analogous, split complementary, monochromatic, triadic, pastel, linking.
2. Complete the exercises for Unit 5 in the workbook.
3. For your scrapbook, find newspaper and magazine examples of each color harmony covered in this unit.
4. Create a color scheme for an interior of your own design.
5. Trace the pictorial drawing in Fig. 6-12. Add color to develop (a) an analogous color scheme, (b) a monochromatic color scheme, and (c) a triadic color scheme.
6. In Unit 6 identify the figure numbers which show a monochromatic, triadic, and split-complementary color scheme.
7. Refer to Fig. 1-5. Blue is the dominant color. Give other colors you would choose to develop the following: (a) a split-complementary scheme, (b) a triadic color scheme, and (c) an analogous color scheme.
8. Name three factors used to classify colors.
9. Name three major parts of the color spectrum.
10. List the illustrations in Unit 1 that represent muted color emphasis.
11. Find the figure numbers in Unit 1 that represent the warmest color scheme.
12. Find the illustrations in Unit 1 that represent the coolest color schemes.

SECTION TWO
AREA PLANNING

LIVING AREA

The first impression of most homes is probably the image retained of the living area. In fact, this is the only area of the home that most guests observe. The living area is just what the name implies, the area where most of the living occurs. It is here the occupants entertain, relax, dine, listen to music, watch television, enjoy hobbies, and participate in other recreational activities.

The total living area is divided into smaller areas (rooms) which are designed to perform specific living functions. The subdivisions of most living areas may include the living room, dining room, recreation or game room, family room, patio, entrance foyer, den or study, and guest lavatories. Other specialized rooms, such as the library, music room, or sewing room, are often included as part of the living area of large houses that have the space to devote to such specialized functions. In smaller homes, many of the standard rooms combine two or more rooms. For example, the living room and dining room are often combined. In extremely small homes, the living room constitutes the entire living area and provides all the facilities normally assigned to other rooms in the living area. Although the subdivisions of the living area are called *rooms,* they are not always separated by a partition or a wall. Nevertheless, they perform the function of a room, whether there is a complete separation, a partial separation, or no separation.

When rooms are completely separated by partitions and doors, the plan is known as a *closed plan.* When partitions do not divide the rooms of an area, the arrangement is called an *open plan.*

In most two-story dwellings the living area is normally located on the first floor. However, in split-level homes or one-story homes with functional basements, part of the living area may be located on the lower level.

THE LIVING ROOM

The living room is the center of the living area in most homes. In small homes the living room may represent the entire living area. Hence, the function, location, decor, size, and shape of the living room are extremely important and affect the design, functioning, and appearance of the other living-area rooms.

Function

The living room is designed to perform many functions. The exact function depends on the living habits of the occupants. In the home it is often the entertainment center, the recreation center, the library, the music room, the TV center, the reception room, the social room, the study, and occasionally the dining center. In small dwellings the living room often becomes a guest bedroom. If the living room is to perform all or some of these functions, then it should be designed accordingly. The shape, size, location,

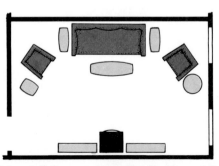

Fig. 6-1. A living room specifically planned for television viewing.

100

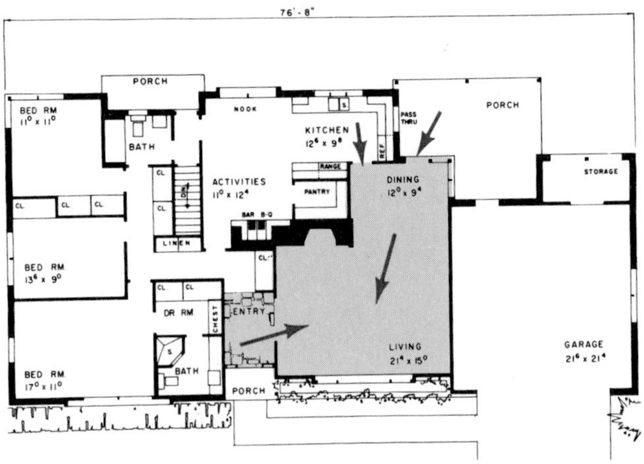

Fig. 6-2. A centrally located living room. *Home Planners, Inc.*

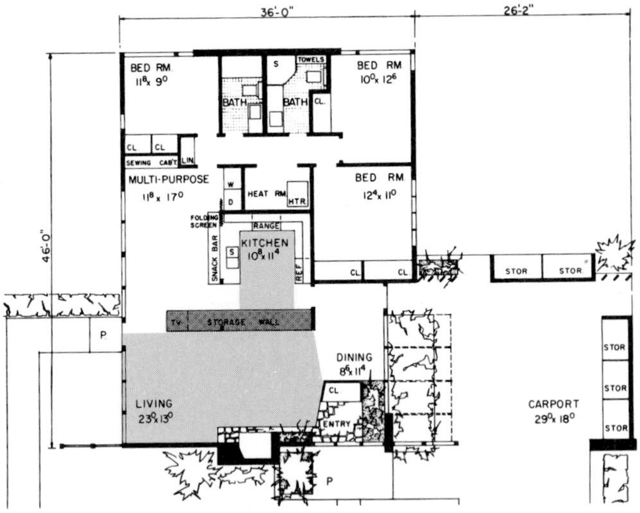

Fig. 6-4. The storage wall separates the living room from the kitchen without enclosing the room. *Home Planners, Inc.*

decor, and facilities of the room should be planned to provide for each activity. For example, if the living room is to be used for television viewing, it will be planned differently from a living room without television. Figure 6-1 shows some of the considerations in planning a room for TV viewing.

Many of the facilities normally associated with the living room can be eliminated if a separate, special-purpose room exists for that activity. For example, if television viewing is restricted to a recreation room, then planning for TV in the living room can be eliminated. If a den or study is provided for reading and for storing books, facilities for the use of large numbers of books in the living room can be eliminated. Regardless of the exact activities anticipated, the living room should always be planned as a functional, integral part of the home. The living room is planned for the comfort and convenience of the family and guests.

Location

The living room should be centrally located. It should be adjacent to the outside entrance, but the entrance should not lead directly into the living room. In smaller residences the entrance may open into the living room, but whenever possible this arrangement is to be avoided. The living room should not be a traffic access to the sleeping and service area of the house. Since the living room and dining room function together, the living room should also be adjacent to the dining room. Figure 6-2 shows the central location of a living room and its proximity to other rooms of the living area.

Open Plan

In an open-plan living area, the living room, dining room, and entrance may be part of one open area, as shown in Fig. 6-3. The living room may be separated from other rooms by means of a divider without doors, such as the storage wall shown in Fig. 6-4. In Fig. 6-5, the living room is

101

Fig. 6-3. An open-plan living room. *Bethlehem Steel Corp.*

Fig. 6-5. A fireplace can be used to separate the living room from the dining room without isolation. *Rittling Corporation*

Fig. 6-6. A living room separated from the foyer by a wrought-iron screen. *Weyerhaeuser Company*

Fig. 6-7. A living room separated from adjacent rooms by level. *Potlatch Corp.*

102

Fig. 6-8. A living room separated by furniture clusters and area-defining rugs. *Thomas Industries, Inc.*

Fig. 6-9. In the open plan, folding doors provide privacy when needed. *Rolscreen Company*

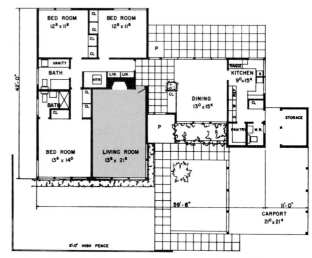

Fig. 6-10. A closed-plan living room. *Home Planners, Inc.*

separated from the dining room by a fireplace. In Fig. 6-6 the wrought-iron grill provides partial separation of the living room and foyer. Often a separation is accomplished by placing the living room on a different level (Fig. 6-7). Separation may also be achieved by the use of area rugs and furniture placement, as shown in Fig. 6-8. Of course, these features do not separate the rooms visually, but they do effect a functional separation.

When an open plan is desired and yet the designer wants to provide some means of closing off the room completely, sliding doors or folding doors can be used (Fig. 6-9).

Closed Plan

In a closed plan, the living room would be completely closed from the other rooms by means of walls. Access would be through doors, arches, or relatively small openings in partitions (Fig. 6-10).

Fig. 6-11A. A contemporary-style living room. *Armstrong Cork Company*

Decor

There is no one way to design and decorate a room. The decor depends primarily on the tastes, habits, and personalities of the people who will use the room. If the residents' tastes are modern, the wall, ceiling, and floor treatments should be consistent with the clean, functional lines of modern architecture and modern furniture, as shown in Fig. 6-11A. If colonial (Fig. 6-11B) or

Fig. 6-11B. Colonial decor.

103

Fig. 6-11C. Period-style decor.

period-style (Fig. 6-11C) architecture is preferred, then this theme should be reflected in the decor of the room.

The living room should appear inviting, comfortable, and spacious. This appearance can be accomplished by an effective use of color and lighting techniques and by the tasteful selection of wall, ceiling, and floor-covering materials. The selection and placement of functional, well-designed furniture also helps the appearance. All these techniques have been combined to create a most desirable total impression in the living room shown in Fig. 6-12. Decorating a room is much like selecting clothing. The color, style, and materials should be selected to minimize faults and to emphasize good points. Figure 6-13 shows that the use of mirrors and floor-to-ceiling drapes along with proper furniture placement can create a spacious effect in a relatively small room.

104

Walls

The design and placement of doors, windows, and chimneys along the walls of the living room

can change the entire appearance of the room. The kind of wall-covering material used can also affect the appearance. Wall coverings are selected from a variety of materials, including plaster, gypsum wallboard, wood paneling, brick, stone, and glass. Sometimes furniture is built into the

Fig. 6-12. The living room should appear inviting, comfortable, and spacious. *Weyerhaeuser Company*

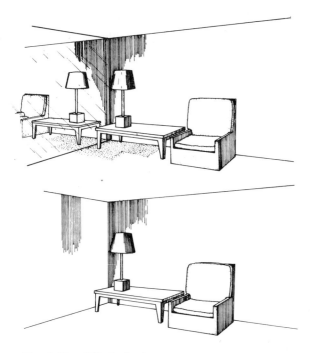

Fig. 6-13. Effect of mirror on space.

Fig. 6-14A. A functionally designed open-plan living-room wall.

Fig. 6-14B. A closed-plan living room.

walls. Fireplaces, windows, doors, or openings to other areas should be designed as integral parts of the room. They should not appear as afterthoughts. Notice the difference between the two designs in Figs. 6-14A and B. Figure 6-14A shows a wall, fireplace, and opening designed as a functional part of the room. Figure 6-14B shows the same room with door openings, fireplaces, and wall treatments placed on the wall without reference to other parts of the room.

Orientation

The living room should be oriented to take full advantage of the position of the sun and the most attractive view. Since the living room is used primarily in the afternoon and evening, it should be located to take advantage of the afternoon sun by facing Southwest.

Windows

When a window is placed in a living-room wall it should become an integral part of that wall. The view from the window or windows becomes part of the living-room decor, especially when landscape features are near and are readily observable, as in Fig. 6-15. When planning win-

Fig. 6-15. The outdoors can become part of the living-room decor. *Scholz Homes, Inc.*

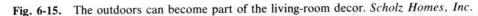

Fig. 6-16. Translucent glass admits light while it subdues images. *PPG Industries*

Fig. 6-17. The use of translucent drapes for semiprivacy. *Hedrich-Blessing*

Fig. 6-18. The view from an apartment must be considered in planning the placement and orientation of the living room. *Hedrich-Blessing*

dows, consider also the various seasonal changes in landscape features.

Although the primary function of a window is twofold, to admit light and to provide a pleasant view of the landscape, there are many conditions under which only the admission of light is desirable. If the view from the window is unpleasant

or is restricted by other buildings, translucent glass, which primarily admits light, as shown in Fig. 6-16, can be incorporated into the plan.

Translucent drapes, as shown in Fig. 6-17, can also be used to admit light while providing a semivisual separation. Window placement in apartment buildings cannot always be altered. However, the location and orientation of the living room must be planned to provide the most desirable furniture arrangement in designing apartment buildings (Fig. 6-18).

Fig. 6-19. This fireplace design is an integral part of the room. *Potlatch Corp.*

Fig. 6-20. The size and placement of the fireplace and chimney determine the type of foundation needed to support its weight. *Home Planners, Inc.*

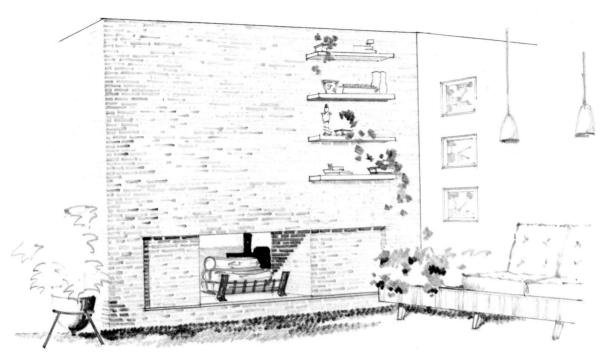

Fig. 6-21. Fireplace used as room divider. *Home Planners, Inc.*

Fireplace

The primary function of a fireplace is to provide heat, but it is also a permanent decorative feature. The fireplace and accompanying masonry should maintain a clean, simple line consistent with the decor of the room and of the wall where they are placed. In Fig. 6-19, the fireplace and chimney masonry becomes the focal point of the room. The corner fireplace shown in Fig. 6-20 is used to divide the library area of the living room from the conversation area. The fireplace shown in Fig. 6-21 is used as the major separation between the living room and the dining room.

The external appearance of the house must be considered in locating the fireplace, because the location of the fireplace in the room determines the position of the chimney on the roof. This does not mean that the outside of the house should be designed first. But it does mean that the outside appearance must be considered in designing and locating features of the house that appear inside and outside. Examples to be considered are fireplaces, doors, and windows.

Floors

The living-room floor should reinforce and blend with the color scheme, textures, and overall style of the living room. Exposed hardwood flooring, room-size carpeting, wall-to-wall carpeting, throw rugs, and sometimes polished flagstone are appropriate for living-room use.

Ceilings

Most conventional or gypsum board ceilings are flat surfaces covered with plaster. New building materials, such as laminated beams and arches, and new construction methods now enable architects to design ceilings that conserve building materials and utilize previously wasted space. An example of an open-beam ceiling is shown in

Fig. 6-22. Open-beam ceiling. *Red Shingle & Shake Bureau*

Fig. 6-23A. Cathedral ceilings help make the room look more spacious.

Fig. 6-23B. A conventional ceiling.

Fig. 6-22. Figure 6-23A shows two optional methods of producing cathedral ceilings either in double-pitch or in single-pitch style. The cathedral ceiling makes a room appear more spacious, through the addition of more area. Compare the space provided by the cathedral ceilings shown in Fig. 6-23A with the space available in the conventional ceiling shown in Fig. 6-23B.

Lighting

Living-room lighting is divided into two types, general lighting and local lighting. General lighting is designed to illuminate the entire room through the use of ceiling fixtures, wall spots, or cove lighting. Local lighting is provided for a specific purpose, such as reading, drawing, or sewing. Local lighting can be supplied by table lamps, wall lamps, pole lamps, or floor lamps. Note the two types of lighting in Fig. 6-24.

Furniture

Furniture for the living room should reflect the motif and architectural style of the home. If the architectural style of the home is modern, the furniture should be modern. If the home is colonial, the furniture should be colonial. If the home is of some period style, the furniture should reflect the furniture style of that period. Figure 6-25 shows the relationship between the various furniture styles and architectural styles. The mixing of modern and period furniture styles should be avoided.

Furniture should not only be consistent in period and style but should also be related in texture and design. All the furniture in the living room should be of same kind of wood. If walnut is used for built-in furniture, in the paneling, and in the trim, walnut should be repeated in the other furniture in the room. Avoid mixing furniture of different kinds of wood, such as oak, walnut, and mahogany. Wood furniture should be finished in the same type of finish throughout the room, such as all glossy, all semiglossy, all flat, or all satin.

A special effort should be made to have built-in furniture maintain lines consistent with the remaining wall treatment. Notice how the built-in shelves and storage cabinets in Fig. 6-26 and the built-in book shelves in Fig. 6-27 eliminate the need for other pieces of furniture in the room. Each blends functionally into the total decor of

Fig. 6-24. Two types of living-room lighting. *General Electric*

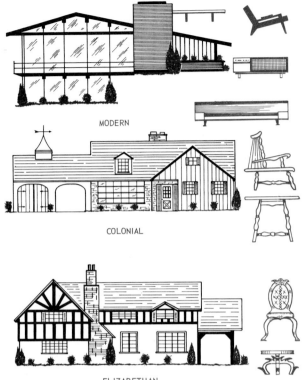

MODERN

COLONIAL

ELIZABETHAN

Fig. 6-25. Furniture styles should be related to the type of architecture.

Fig. 6-27. Built-ins eliminate need for other furniture. *American Plywood Association*

Fig. 6-26. Built-in units must be consistent with wall treatment. *Home Planners, Inc.*

109

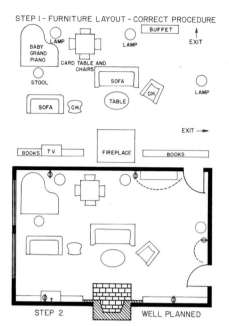

Fig. 6-28A. A living room planned to accommodate the necessary furniture.

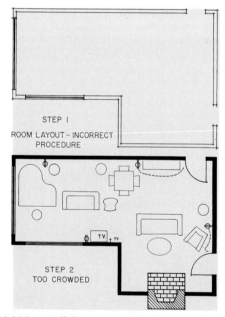

Fig. 6-28B. A living room of inadequate size for the furniture needed.

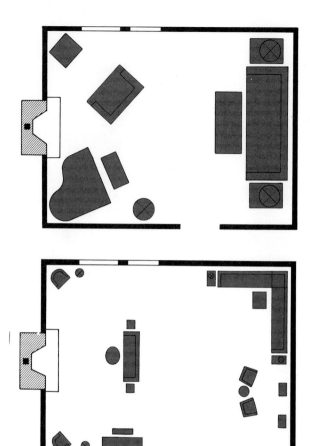

Fig. 6-29A. Furniture scale too large (above) and too small (below).

the room. The furniture for the living room is chosen to fit the living needs of the residents. The size, shape, and layout of the room should be designed to accommodate the furniture. Figure 6-28A shows a living room of adequate size which functions well with the necessary furniture. Figure 6-28B shows a room with a size and shape

not adequate for the furniture. This latter design is a result of establishing the size and shape of the room without considering the size and number of pieces of furniture to be used. However if the room size is fixed the designer must obviously work within these constraints.

Size and Shape

One of the most difficult aspects of planning the size and shape of a living room, or any other room, is to provide sufficient wall space for the effective placement of furniture. Continuous wall space is needed for the placement of many articles of furniture, especially musical equipment, bookcases, chairs, and couches. The placement of fireplaces, doors, or openings to other rooms should be planned to conserve as much wall space for furniture placement as possible. Figure 6-29A shows a living room with furniture of too large and too small scale. Figure 6-29B shows

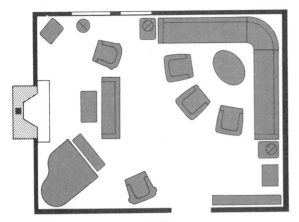

FURNITURE TOO CROWDED

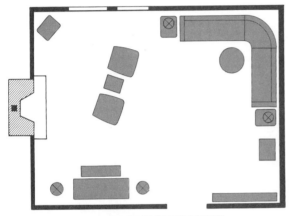

FURNITURE PLACEMENT APPROPRIATE

Fig. 6-29B. Too much furniture for area (above) and correct scale (below).

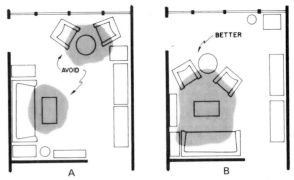

Fig. 6-30A and B. Avoid breaking the room into several isolated conversation areas.

Fig. 6-31. A dining alcove in the living area. *California Redwood Association*

the same room with the correct scale furniture but too crowded a room with correct scale and furniture placement.

Rectangular rooms are generally easier to plan and to place furniture in than are square rooms. However, the designer must be careful not to establish a proportion that will break the living room into several conversation areas, as shown in Fig. 6-30A. This design has actually resulted in the merging of two separate rooms into one. The arrangement shown in Fig. 6-30B is much more desirable, since it integrates the total activities of the room without separation.

Living rooms vary greatly in size. A room 12′ by 18′ (3.7 × 5.5 m) would be considered a small or minimum-sized living room. A living room of average size would be approximately 16′ × 20′ (4.9 × 6.1 m), and a very large or optimum-sized living room would be 20′ × 26′ (6.1 × 7.9 m) or more.

THE DINING ROOM

The dining facilities designed for a residence depend greatly on the dining habits of the occupants. The dining room may be large and formal, or the dining area may consist of a dining alcove, as shown in Fig. 6-31. It may also be a breakfast nook in the kitchen. Large homes may contain dining facilities in all these areas.

Function

The function of a dining area is to provide a place for the family to gather for breakfast, lunch, or dinner in both casual and formal situations. When possible, a separate dining area potentially ca-

Fig. 6-32. An informal dining area. *Scholz Homes, Inc.*

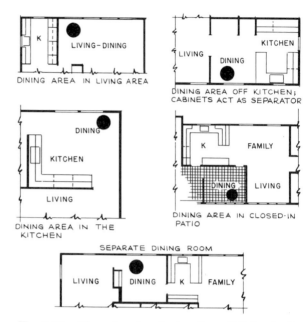

Fig. 6-33. Plans showing the location of dining facilities in many different areas.

pable of seating from eight to twelve persons for dinner should be provided in addition to breakfast or dinette facilities. Contrast the formal dining area shown in Fig. 6-31 with the informal dining facilities shown in the dining area in Fig. 6-32.

Location

Dining facilities can be located in many different areas, depending on the capacity needed and the type of plan. In the closed plan, a separate dining room is usually provided. In an open plan, many different dining locations are possible (Fig. 6-33). Open-area dining facilities are provided in the kitchen shown in Fig. 6-34. In Fig. 6-35 the living room houses the dining area.

Relation to Kitchen

Regardless of the exact position of the dining area, it must be placed adjacent to the kitchen. The ideal dining location is one that requires few steps from the kitchen to the dining table. However, the preparation of food and other kitchen activities should be baffled from direct view from the dining area (Fig. 6-35).

Relation to Living Room

If dining facilities are not located in the living room, they should be located next to it. Family and guests normally enter the dining room from the living room and use both rooms jointly.

The nearness of the dining room to the kitchen, and to the living room, requires that it

Fig. 6-34. A dining area located in the kitchen. *Potlatch Corp.*

Fig. 6-35. A dining area located in a living room. *California Redwood Association, James D. Morton Architect*

112

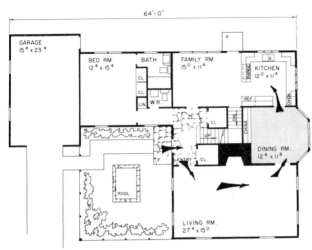

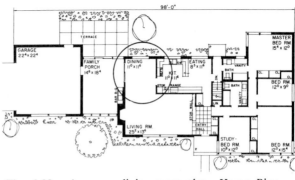

Fig. 6-39. An open dining-room plan. *Home Planners, Inc.*

Fig. 6-36. The dining room is located between the living room and the kitchen. *Home Planners, Inc.*

be placed between the kitchen and the living area. The dining room in the closed plan shown in Fig. 6-36 is located in this manner.

Separation

Complete separation should be possible between the kitchen and the dining room. The area between the living room and the dining room may be entirely open, partially baffled, or completely closed off. Sometimes the separation of the dining room and the living room is accomplished by level or by dividing the rooms with a common fireplace. Figure 6-37 shows a direct access designed into the relationship between the kitchen and living area. Another method of separating the dining area in an open plan is through the use of partial partitions, as shown in Fig. 6-38. Compare these semi-isolated arrangements with the completely open dining areas shown in Figs. 6-39 and 6-40.

Fig. 6-37. The dining room should have direct access to kitchen and living room. *Home Planners, Inc.*

Fig. 6-40. An open dining area. *Armstrong Cork Company*

Fig. 6-38. A partial wall without a door makes this an open plan. *Masonite Corporation*

Fig. 6-41. Dining facilities located adjacent to the patio. *Home Planners, Inc.*

Fig. 6-42. Dining facilities may be moved to a porch in fair weather. *Western Wood Products Association*

Outside Dining Facilities

There is often a need for dining facilities on or adjacent to the patio, as shown in Fig. 6-41. The porch or patio should be near the kitchen and directly accessible to it. Locating the patio or dining porch directly outside the dining room or kitchen wall provides maximum use of the facilities. This minimizes the inconvenience of using outside dining facilities (Fig. 6-42).

Decor

The decor of the dining room should be consistent with the rest of the house and specifically relate in style to the other parts of the living area. This relationship is especially desirable in the open plan, in which the dining area is integrated with the rest of the living area. Floor, wall, and ceiling treatment should be the same in the dining area as in the living area.

If a dining porch or a dining patio is used, its decor must also be considered part of the dining-room decor. This is because the outside dining area is viewed from the inside. Notice how the view of the courtyard in Fig. 6-43 is brought to the inside by the use of window walls directly next to the dining area.

Dividers

If semi-isolation is desired, partial divider walls can be used effectively. These dividers may be planter walls, glass walls, half walls of brick or stone, paneled walls, fireplaces, or grillwork. Figure 6-44 shows the effective use of arches to provide semi-isolation for the dining area. The

Fig. 6-43. Consider the view when locating the dining area. *American-Saint Gobain Corp.*

Fig. 6-44. The use of arches to provide semi-isolation. *Scholz Homes, Inc.*

Fig. 6-45. The use of levels to separate the dining area. *Julius Shulman*

dining area shown in Fig. 6-45 is separated by level.

Lighting
Controlled lighting can greatly enhance the decor of the dining room. General illumination which can be subdued or intensified can provide the right atmosphere for almost any occasion. Lighting is controlled by a rheostat which is commonly known as a *dimmer switch*.

In addition to general illumination, local lighting should be provided for the table either by a direct ceiling spot light or by a hanging lamp (Fig. 6-46). A hanging lamp can be adjusted down for local dining lighting and up for general illumination when the dining facilities are not in use.

Size and Shape

The size and shape of the dining area are determined by the size of the family, the size and number of pieces of furniture, and the clearances and traffic areas between furniture.

Maximum Planning
The dining area should be planned for the largest group that will dine in it regularly. There is little advantage in having a dining-room table that expands, if the room is not large enough to accommodate the expansion. One advantage of

115

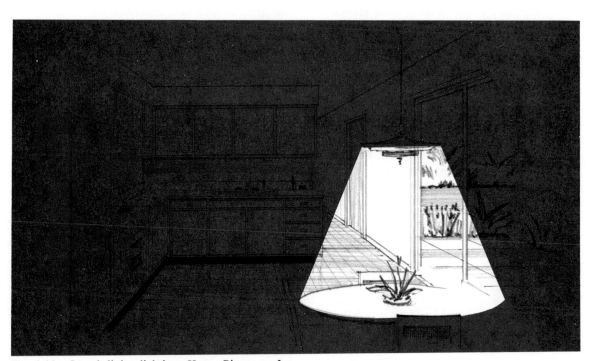

Fig. 6-46. Local dining lighting. *Home Planners, Inc.*

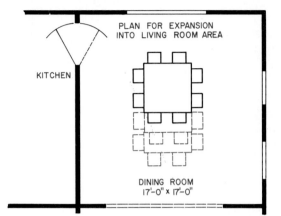

Fig. 6-47. A dining area planned for maximum expansion.

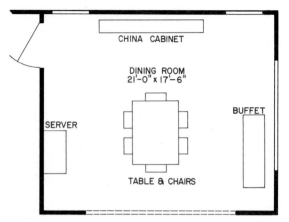

Fig. 6-48. Typical furniture placement in a dining room.

the open plan is that the dining facilities can be expanded in an unlimited manner into the living area, as shown in Fig. 6-47. Thus, the living area temporarily becomes part of the dining area.

Furniture

The dining room should be planned to accommodate the furniture. Dining-room furniture may include an expandable table, side chairs, armchairs, buffet, server or serving cart, china closet, and serving bar. In most situations a rectangular dining room will accommodate the furniture better than a square room. Figure 6-48 shows a typical furniture placement for a dining room.

Clearance

Regardless of the furniture arrangement, a minimum space of 24″ (610 mm) should be allowed between the chair and the wall or furniture when the chair is pulled to the "out" position. This allowance will permit serving traffic behind chairs and will permit entrance to and exit from the table without difficulty. A distance of 27″ (690 mm) per person should be allowed at the table. This spacing is accomplished by allowing 27″ (690 mm) from the center line of one chair to the center line of another, as shown in Fig. 6-49.

Recommended Sizes

A dining room that would accommodate the *minimum* amount of furniture—a table, four chairs, and a buffet—would be approximately 10′ × 12′ (3.1 × 3.7 m). An average-sized dining room which would accommodate a dining table, six or eight persons, a buffet, a china closet, and a server would be approximately 12′ × 15′ (3.7

× 4.6 m). A more nearly *optimum*-sized dining room would be 14′ × 18′ (4.3 × 5.5 m) or larger. A room of this size would accommodate practically any size gathering.

THE FAMILY ROOM

Several years ago the term *family room* did not exist in the designer's vocabulary. The trend toward more informal living because of more leisure time has influenced the popularity of the family room. Today the majority of homes are designed to include a family room.

Function

The purpose of the family room is to provide facilities for family-centered activities. It is designed for the entire family, children and adults alike.

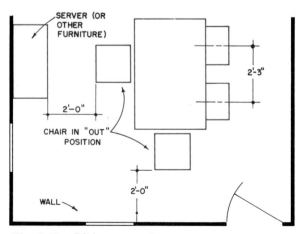

Fig. 6-49. Dining room clearances.

116

Fig. 6-50. A children's area in the family room. *Lisanti*

Fig. 6-51: A family room designed for television viewing and chess. *Armstrong Cork Company*

Only in extremely large residences is there sufficient space for a separate sewing room, children's playroom, hobby room, or music room. The modern family room often performs the functions of all these rooms. The children's area in the family room in Fig. 6-50 provides facilities for a variety of children's activities. The area of the family room in Fig. 6-51 is designed primarily for watching television and pursuing chess as a hobby.

Location

Activities in the family room often result in the accumulation of hobby materials and clutter. Thus, the family room is often located in an area accessible from, but not visible from, the rest of the living area.

It is quite common to locate the family room adjacent to the kitchen, as shown in Fig. 6-52. This location revives the idea of the old country kitchen in which most family activities were centered.

When the family room is located adjacent to the living room or dining room, it becomes an extension of these rooms for social affairs. In this location, the family room is often separated from the other rooms by folding doors, screens, or sliding doors. The family room shown in Fig. 6-53 is located next to the kitchen and yet is accessible from the living room when the folding door is open.

Another popular location for the family room is between the service area and the living

Fig. 6-52. A family room located adjacent to the kitchen. *Olson-Spencer & Associates*

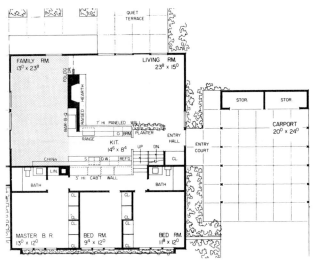

Fig. 6-53. A family room accessible from the kitchen and living room. *Home Planners, Inc.*

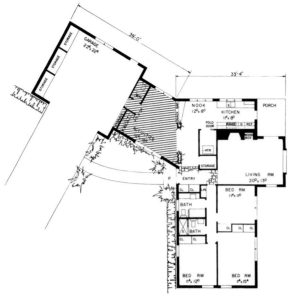

Fig. 6-54. A family room located near the service area. *Home Planners, Inc.*

area. The family room shown in Fig. 6-54 is located between the garage, the kitchen, and the entrance. This location is especially appropriate when some service functions are assigned to the family room.

Decor

The family room is also known as the *activities room* or *multiactivities room*. Decoration of this room should provide a vibrant atmosphere. Ease of maintenance should be one of the chief considerations in decorating the family room.

Furniture

Family-room furniture should be informal and suited to all members of the family. The use of plastics, leather, and wood provides great flexibility in color and style and promotes easy maintenance.

Floors

Floors should be resilient. Linoleum or tile made of asphalt, rubber, or vinyl will best resist the abuse normally given a family-room floor. If rugs are used, they should be the kind that will stand up under rough treatment. They should also be washable.

Walls

Soft, easily damaged materials such as wallpaper and plaster should be avoided for the family room. Materials such as tile and paneling are most functional. Chalkboards, bulletin boards, built-in cupboards, and toy-storage cabinets should be used when appropriate. Work areas that fold into the wall when not in use conserve space and may perform a dual function if the cover wall can also be used as a chalkboard or a bulletin board.

Storage

Since a variety of hobby and game materials will be used in the family room, sufficient space must be provided for the storage of these materials. Figure 6-55 shows the use of built-in storage facilities, including cabinets, closets, and drawer storage.

Fig. 6-55. Plan for adequate storage in the family room.

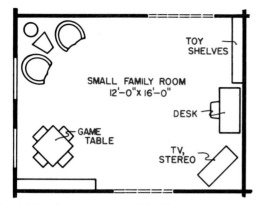

Fig. 6-56. An average-sized family room

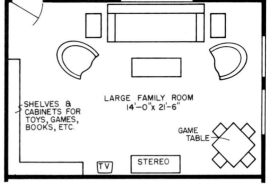

Fig. 6-57. An optimum-sized family room.

Ceilings

Acoustical ceilings are recommended to keep the noise of the various activities from spreading to other parts of the house. This feature is especially important if the family room is located on a lower level.

Size and Shape

The size and shape of the family room depends directly on the equipment needed for the activities the family will pursue in this room. The room may vary from an average-sized room, as shown in Fig. 6-56, to the more optimum-sized family room shown in Fig. 6-57. This room contains practically all the equipment almost any family would need in the family room. Included are a sewing machine, a hobby table, bulletin boards, drawing boards, easels, a television set, a studio couch, chalkboards, a bookcase, a desk, a children's desk, a children's play table, a children's

toy box, storage cabinets, a motion-picture screen, and a serving bar. Most family-room requirements lie somewhere between the two rooms shown.

THE RECREATION ROOM

The recreation room (game room, playroom) is exactly what the name implies. It is a room for play and recreation. It includes facilities for participation in recreational activities.

Function

The design of the recreation room depends on the number and arrangement of the facilities needed for the various pursuits. Activities for which many recreation rooms are designed include billiards, chess, checkers, Ping-Pong, darts, television watching, eating, and dancing. For example, the recreation room shown in Fig. 6-58

Fig. 6-58. The design of the recreation room depends on the number of activities planned. *Armstrong Cork Company*

119

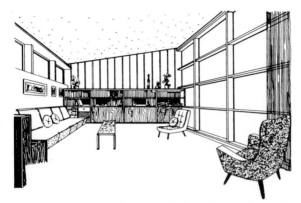

Fig. 6-59. A recreation room designed around a music center. *American Plywood Association*

Fig. 6-61 A. A typical basement before conversion. *Armstrong Cork Company*

has been designed around three activity areas: the Ping-Pong area, the chess area, and the television and conversation area. Designing the recreation room around a music center, as shown in Fig. 6-59, is also very practical.

The function of the recreation room often overlaps that of the family room. Overlapping occurs when a multipurpose room is designed to provide for recreational activities such as Ping-Pong and billiards and also includes facilities for more sedentary family activities such as sewing, knitting, model-building, and other hobbies.

Location

The recreation room is frequently located in the basement in order to use space that would otherwise be wasted. Basement recreation rooms often provide more space for the use of large equip-

ment, such as Ping-Pong tables, billiard tables, and shuffleboard. Figure 6-60 shows a basement recreation room with a fireplace located directly beneath the living-room fireplace on the upper level. The most important reason why recreation rooms are often located in the basement of older homes, however, is because the basement is the only available space which can be converted into a recreation room. An example of the conversion of the basement of an older home into a well-planned recreation room is shown in Figs. 6-61A and 6-61B.

When the recreation room is located on the ground level, its function can be expanded to the patio or terrace, as shown in Fig. 6-62. Regardless of the level, the recreation room should be located away from the quiet areas of the house.

Often the recreation room can actually be separated from the main part of the house. This separation is possible when the recreation room

Fig. 6-60. This recreation-room fireplace is located directly below the living-room fireplace. *Armstrong Cork Company*

Fig. 6-61 B. A basement converted to a recreation room. *Armstrong Cork Company*

Fig. 6-62. Whenever possible, the recreation room should be located adjacent to the patio. *Julius Shulman*

is included as part of the garage or carport design, as shown in Fig. 6-63. When a separate location such as this is selected, some sheltered access should be provided from the house to the recreation area.

Decor

Designers take more liberties in decorating the recreation room than any other room. They do so primarily because the active, informal atmosphere which characterizes the recreation room lends itself readily to unconventional furniture, fixtures, and color schemes. Bright warm colors can reflect a party mood. Furnishings and accessories can accent a dramatic central theme. The designer of the recreation room shown in Fig. 6-64 has developed a restful, quietly dignified atmosphere through the use of an oriental decor.

Fig. 6-63. Recreation room included in separate garage.

The designer of the recreation room shown in Fig. 6-65 has created a festive yet casual atmosphere using a winter sports theme.

Regardless of the central theme, recreation-room furniture should be comfortable and easy to maintain. The same rules apply to recreation-room walls, floors, and ceilings as apply to those of the family room. Floors should be hard-surfaced and easy to maintain. Walls should be paneled or covered with some easily maintained material. Acoustical (soundproofed) ceilings are recommended if the recreation room is located in the basement or on a lower level.

Fig. 6-64. A quiet, restful recreation room. *Condon-King Company*

Fig. 6-65. A recreation room decorated in a winter sports theme. *Armstrong Cork Company*

121

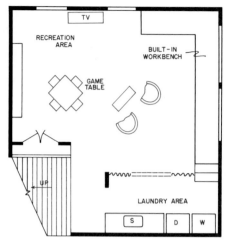

Fig. 6-66. A recreation room occupying a large area.

Fig. 6-68. This porch extends into a perimeter balcony. *California Redwood Association*

Size and Shape

The size and shape of the recreation room depend on whether the room occupies an area on the main level or whether it occupies basement space. If basement space is used, the only restrictions on the size are the other facilities that will also occupy space in the basement, such as the laundry, the workshop, or the garage. Figure 6-66 shows a recreation room which occupies a rather large basement area which would otherwise be wasted space. Figure 6-67 shows a relatively small recreation room located in the basement of the house. The size of most recreation rooms ranges between these two extremes.

PORCHES

A porch is a covered platform leading into an entrance of a building. Porches are commonly enclosed by glass, screen, or post and railings.

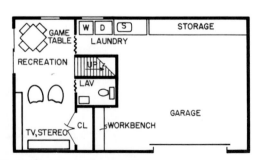

Fig. 6-67. A small recreation room.

A porch is not the same as a patio. The porch is attached structurally to the house, whereas a patio is placed directly on the ground. The porch on the house shown in Fig. 6-68 is connected to a balcony that extends around the perimeter of the house and covers the patio below. Balconies and decks are actually elevated porches.

Function

Porches serve a variety of functions. Some are used for dining and some for entertaining and relaxing. Others are furnished and function like patios for outdoor living. Still others provide an additional shelter for the entrance to a house or patio. The primary function of a porch depends on the structure and purpose of the building to which it is attached. For example, the porch in Fig. 6-69 provides outdoor living facilities and

Fig. 6-69. A porch used to connect motel units. *Western Wood Products Association*

Fig. 6-70. An apartment porch designed for privacy. *Western Wood Products Association*

Fig. 6-72. A Southern colonial home with a veranda. *Oil by Margaret de Loo*

access to motel rooms. The condominium porch shown in Fig. 6-70 is designed as an outdoor private extension to the living room. The porch in Fig. 6-71 is planned to provide maximum appreciation of an ocean view.

Verandas

Southern colonial homes such as the one in Fig. 6-72 were designed with large porches, or verandas, extending around several sides of the home. Outdoor plantation life centered on the veranda, which was very large.

Fig. 6-71. A porch designed with a view. *Potlatch Corp.*

Balconies

A balcony is a porch suspended from an upper level of a structure. It usually has no access from the outside. Balconies often provide an extension to the living area or a private extension to a bedroom.

The house shown in Fig. 6-73 is distinguished by several types of balconies. The upper balcony is supported by cantilevered beams and provides an extension which covers the porch below. The porch in turn shelters a patio below it. Hillside lots lend themselves to vertical plans and provide maximum flexibility in using outdoor living facilities.

Fig. 6-73. The upper balcony of this house provides protection for the porch and patio below. *Western Wood Products Association*

123

Fig. 6-74. A cantilevered porch (left). *Western Wood Products Association*

Fig. 6-75. Steel members make large cantilevered distances possible.

Spanish- and Italian-style architecture is characterized by numerous balconies. The return of the balcony to popularity has been influenced and accelerated by new developments in building materials. These materials permit large areas to be suspended. The balcony in the house shown in Fig. 6-74 is cantilevered (supported only at one end) on wood joists that extend beyond the exterior wall.

The principle of cantileverage, or suspension in space, can also be used to a greater extent with steel construction. An example is shown in the balcony which overhangs the patio in Fig. 6-75.

Stoop
The stoop is a projection from a building, similar to a porch. However, a stoop does not provide sufficient space for any activities. It provides only shelter and an access to the entrance of the building.

124

The Modern Porch
Only in the last several years has the porch been functionally designed and effectively utilized for outdoor living. The classic front porch and back porch which characterized most homes built in this country during the 1920s and 1930s were designed and used merely as places in which to sit. Little effort was made to use the porch for

any other activities. A porch for a modern home should be designed for the specific activities anticipated for it. The form of the porch should be determined by its function.

Location
Since the porch is an integral part of the total house design, it must be located where it will function best. The porch in Fig. 6-76 becomes a functional extension of the living area when in use. A porch can be made consistent with the rest of the house by extending the lines of the

Fig. 6-76. This porch is an extension of the living room located on the right.

Fig. 6-77. This porch is an integral part of the exterior design. *Rocky Mountain National Park*

roof to provide sufficient *overhang*, or projection (Fig. 6-77).

A dining porch should be located adjacent to either the dining room or the kitchen. The dining porch shown in Fig. 6-78 can be approached from the dining room through the terrace. This arrangement makes possible the use of the nook, dining room, patio, or porch for dining purposes with little traffic difficulty. Locating the porch between two walls of the house in this manner is also economical, since only two sides must be enclosed.

The porch should be located to provide the maximum in flexibility. A porch which can function for dining and other living activities is desirable. The primary functions of the porch should be considered when orienting the porch with the sun. If much daytime use is anticipated and direct sunlight is desirable, a southern exposure should be planned. If little sun is wanted during the day, a northern exposure would be preferable. If morning sun is desirable, an eastern exposure would be best, and for the afternoon sun, a western exposure.

Decor

The porch should be designed as an integral and functional part of the total structure. A blending of roof styles and major lines of the porch roof and house roof is especially important (Fig. 6-79). A similar consistency should characterize the vertical columns or support members of the porch. This illustration shows some relationships that can be established to prevent the tacked-on look and to ensure uniformity in design.

Various materials and methods can be used as deck railing, depending on the degree of

privacy or sun and wind protection needed. For example, the sides of the porch shown in Fig. 6-70 (on page 123) provide complete privacy but also block out ventilation. The sides of the porch shown in Fig. 6-80 provide adequate ventilation

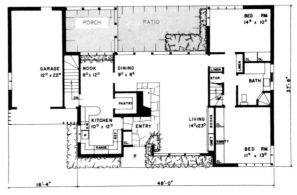

Fig. 6-78. Location of a dining porch. *Home Planners, Inc.*

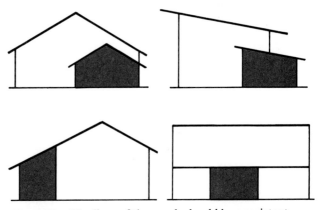

Fig. 6-79. The lines of the porch should be consistent with the major lines of the house.

Fig. 6-80. The use of vertical strips to provide semi-privacy, safety, and wind baffling. *Western Wood Products Association*

125

Fig. 6-81. Glass windscreens protect this porch from wind and sand. *PPG Industries*

but also offer semiprivacy and safety. Railings on elevated porches such as this should be designed at a height above 3′ (915 mm) to discourage the use of the top rail as a place to sit.

Porch furniture should withstand deterioration in any kind of weather. Covering material should be waterproof, stain-resistant, and washable. Protection from wind and rain should be planned. Note how the use of glass on the porch shown in Fig. 6-81 blocks out wind-driven sand and yet allows maximum sun exposure.

Size and Shape

Porches range in size from the very large veranda to rather modest-sized stoops, which provide only shelter and a landing surface for the main entrance. Figure 6-82 shows a large porch which extends across the entire front of the house. Figure 6-83 shows the effective use of a small porch at ground level, and Fig. 6-84 shows how an elevated porch can be designed to extend the living area outdoors. A porch approximately 6′ × 8′ (1.8 × 2.4 m) is considered a minimum size. An 8′ × 12′ (2.4 × 3.7 m) porch is about average. Porches larger than 12′ × 18′ (3.7 × 5.5 m) are considered rather large.

The shape of the porch depends greatly upon how the porch can be integrated into the overall design of the house.

PATIOS

A *patio* is a covered surface adjacent or directly accessible to the house. The word *patio* comes from the Spanish word for courtyard. Courtyard living was an important aspect of Spanish culture, and courtyard design was an important part of early Spanish architecture.

Function

The patio at various times may perform outdoors all the functions that the living room, dining room, recreation room, kitchen, and family room perform indoors.

The patio is often referred to by other names, such as *loggia, breezeway,* and *terrace.*

Patios can be divided into three main types according to function: living patios, play patios, and quiet patios. The home shown in Fig. 6-85 contains all three kinds of patios.

Location

Patios should be located adjacent to the area of the home to which they relate. They should also be somewhat secluded from the street and from neighboring residences.

Fig. 6-82. A large porch. *Frank Lotz Miller*

Fig. 6-83. A small porch at ground level. *Western Wood Products Association*

Fig. 6-85. This plan includes three types of patios. *Home Planners, Inc.*

Living Patio

Living patios should be located close to the living room or the dining room. When dining is anticipated on the patio, access should be provided from the kitchen or dining room.

Play Patio

It is often advantageous to provide a play patio for use by children and for physical activities not normally associated with the living patio. The play patio sometimes doubles as the service patio and can conveniently be placed adjacent to the service area. Notice the location of the play patio in Fig. 6-85. It is related directly to the service area and also to the family room in the living area.

Fig. 6-84. Elevated porches. *California Redwood Association*

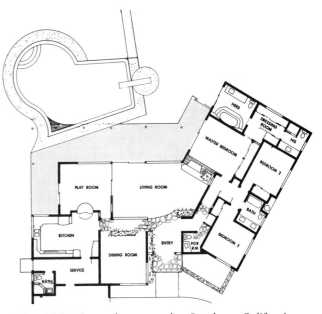

Fig. 6-86. A continuous patio. *Southern California Gas Company*

Quiet Patio

The quiet patio can actually become an extension of the bedroom. It can be used for relaxation or even sleeping. The quiet patio shown in Fig. 6-85 can be entered from the bedrooms or the living area. This type of patio should be secluded from the normal traffic of the home. Often the design of the house will allow these separately functioning patios to be combined in one large, continuous patio. This kind of patio is shown in Fig. 6-86. Here the play room, living room, master bedroom, and kitchen all have access to the patio.

127

Fig. 6-87A. A living-area patio viewed from the interior. *PPG Industries*

Placement

Patios can be conveniently placed at the end of a building, as the living patio is placed in Fig. 6-85 and Figs. 6-87A and B. They may be placed between corners of a house as in the play and quiet terraces in Fig. 6-85. Patios may be wrapped around the side of the house, as shown in Fig. 6-86, or they may be placed in the center of a U-shaped house or in a courtyard. The

Fig. 6-87B. The living-area patio viewed from the exterior. *PPG Industries*

courtyard patio shown in Fig. 6-88 offers complete privacy from all sides.

Separate Patios

In addition to the preceding locations, the patio is often located completely apart from the house. When a wooded area, a particular view, or a terrain feature is of interest, the patio can be placed away from the house. When it is located in this manner, it should be readily accessible, as shown in Fig. 6-89.

Orientation

When the patio is placed on the north side of the house, the house itself can be used to shade the patio. If sunlight is desired, the patio should be located on the south side of the house. The planner should take full advantage of the most pleasing view and should restrict the view of undesirable sights.

Fig. 6-88. A courtyard patio. *Shakertown*

Fig. 6-89. A separated patio. *California Redwood Association*

Fig. 6-90. A wood-slat patio deck. *Julius Shulman*

Fig. 6-91. A brick-surface patio. *Olympic Stains*

Decor

The materials used in the deck, cover, baffles, and furniture of the patio should be consistent with the lines and materials used in the rest of the home. Patios should not appear to be designed as an afterthought but should appear and function as an integral part of the total design.

Patio Deck

The deck (floor) of the patio should be constructed from materials that are permanent and maintenance-free. Flagstone, redwood, concrete, and brick are among the best materials for use on patio decks. Wood slats such as those shown in Fig. 6-90 provide for drainage between the slats and also create a warm appearance. However, they do require some maintenance.

Brick-surface patio decks are very popular because bricks can be placed in a variety of arrangements to adapt to practically any shape or space. The area between the bricks may be filled with concrete, gravel, sand, or grass (Fig. 6-91).

A concrete deck is effective when a smooth, unbroken surface is desired. Patios where bouncing-ball games are played, or where pool-side cover is desired, can use concrete advantageously (Fig. 6-92).

Fig. 6-92. A concrete-deck patio. *Scholz Homes, Inc.*

Patio Cover

Patios need not be covered if the house is oriented to shade the patio during the times of the day when shade is normally desired. Since a patio is designed to provide outdoor living, too much cover can defeat the purpose of the patio. Coverings can be an extension of the roof structure, as shown in Fig. 6-93. They may be graded or

Fig. 6-93. A roof extension used as a pool and patio cover. *PPG Industries*

129

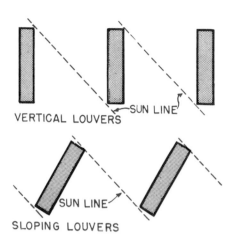

VERTICAL LOUVERS

SUN LINE

SUN LINE

SLOPING LOUVERS

Fig. 6-94. The angle and spacing of louvers is important in sunscreening.

Fig. 6-96. A translucent overhang helps protect this patio. *California Redwood Association*

tilted to allow light to enter when the sun is high and to block the sun's rays when the sun is lower. The graded effect can be obtained by placing louvers spaced straight or slanted to admit the high sun and block the low sun, as shown in Fig. 6-94. Figure 6-95 shows a louvered patio supported by posts which rest in a garden area. The center portion of the cover is solid, and the outer part is slotted.

Plastic, glass fiber, and other translucent materials used to cover patios admit sunlight and yet provide protection from the direct rays of the sun. Translucent covers also provide shelter from rain. When translucent covering is used, it is often desirable to have only part of the patio covered. This arrangement provides sun for part of the patio and shade for other parts (Fig. 6-96).

Fig. 6-97. A balcony used to provide patio shelter. *PPG Industries*

Balconies may also be used effectively to provide shelter for a patio, as shown in Fig. 6-97.

Walls and Baffles
Patios are designed for outdoor living, but outdoor living need not be public living. Some privacy is always desirable. Solid walls can often be used effectively to baffle the patio from a street view, from wind, and from the low rays of the sun (Fig. 6-98). Baffling devices include solid

Fig. 6-95. A louvered patio cover. *California Redwood Association*

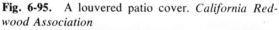

Fig. 6-98. A patio with a fence used as a wall. *Julius Shulman*

Fig. 6-99. A slatted baffle wall provides privacy but admits light and air. *California Redwood Association*

Fig. 6-100. A battle wall used to separate the patio from the service entrance. *New Homes Guide*

Fig. 6-101A. A semi-isolated patio. *Home Planners, Inc.*

fences, slatted fences, concrete blocks, post and rails, brick or stone walls, and hedges or other shrubbery.

A solid baffle wall is often undesirable because it restricts the view, eliminates the circulation of air, and makes the patio appear

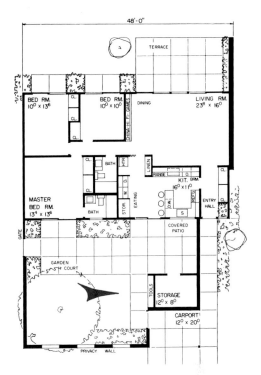

Fig. 6-101B. Plan of the semi-isolated patio.

smaller. Figure 6-99 shows a baffle wall used to provide privacy for the patio without restricting circulation of air. The baffle wall in Fig. 6-100 is used to separate the patio from the service entrance without restricting the view.

In mild climates, completely enclosing a patio by solid walls can help make the patio function as another room. In such an enclosed patio, some opening should be provided to allow light and air to enter. The grillwork openings on the wall shown in Figs. 6-101A and 6-101B provide an effective and aesthetically pleasing solution to this problem.

Occasionally nature provides its own baffle through a rise in the landscape, as shown in Fig. 6-102. This condition is highly desirable and should be taken advantage of, if sufficient drain-

Fig. 6-102. A natural patio baffle. *Paul J. Peart, Landscape Architect*

Fig. 6-103. The patio at midday. *Julius Shulman*

Fig. 6-105. Examples of types of patio lighting. *Western Wood Products Association*

age away from the house and patio can be maintained.

Day and Night Decor

To be totally effective, the patio should be designed for both daytime and nighttime use. Figure 6-103 shows a typical midday use of the patio. Figure 6-104 shows some of the possibilities for nighttime utilization. Correct use of general and local lighting can make the patio useful for many hours each day. If the walls between the inside areas of the house and the patio are designed as in Fig. 6-104, much light from the inside can be utilized on the patio. Figure 6-105 shows some of the specific types of lights and lighting that can be used to illuminate patios at night.

Size and Shape

Patios may be as small as the garden patio shown in Fig. 6-106 or as spacious as the courtyard patio

shown in Fig. 6-107. The primary function will largely determine the size. The Japanese garden has no furniture and is designed primarily to provide a baffle and a beautiful view. The courtyard patio is designed for many uses.

Activities should be governed by the amount of space needed for equipment. Equipment and furnishings normally used on patios include picnic tables and benches, lounge chairs, serving carts, game apparatus, and barbecue pits (Fig. 6-108). The placement of these items and the storage of games, apparatus, and fixtures should determine the size of the patio. Patios vary more in length than in width since patios may extend over the entire length of the house. A patio 12′ × 12′ (3.7 × 3.7 m) is considered a minimum-sized patio. Patios with dimensions of 20′ × 30′ (6.1 × 9.1 m) or more are not uncommon but are considered large. When a pool is designed for a home, it becomes an integral part of the patio. The pool-side and the entire area around

Fig. 6-104. The patio should also be designed for nighttime use. *Western Wood Products Association*

Fig. 6-106. A small garden patio. *California Redwood Association*

Fig. 6-109*B*. The patio and pool design can be blended together. *PPG Industries*

Fig. 6-107. A spacious courtyard patio. *Home Planners, Inc.*

Fig. 6-108. Barbecue equipment incorporated into a patio design. *Frigidaire Division, General Motors Corporation*

the pool function as a patio (Fig. 6-109).

Many pool shapes now available allow the designer to blend the pool into the size and shape of the patio. Figure 6-110 shows standard pool shapes available from most construction companies.

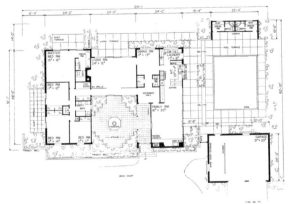

Fig. 6-109*A*. A pool integrated into the patio design. *Libbey-Owens-Ford Company*

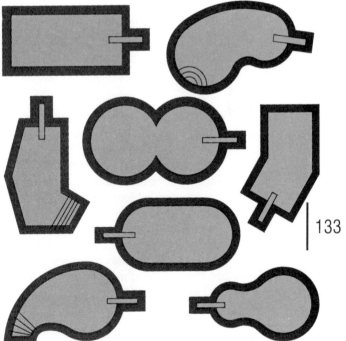

Fig. 6-110. Pool shapes.

133

Fig. 6-111. Extended roof overhang creates this lanai. *Home Planners, Inc.*

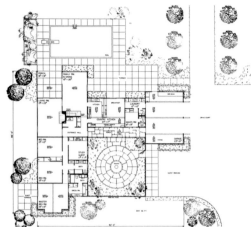

Fig. 6-112A. A typical lanai plan. *Home Planners, Inc.*

When designing and locating a pool, the location of the filter, heater (if used), electrical, plumbing, and filter lines must be planned. Since the filter runs continuously it should be located as far from the patio as possible without the use of excessively long plumbing, electrical, and filter supply lines.

LANAIS

Lanai is the Hawaiian word for porch. However, the word *lanai* is now used to refer to a covered exterior passageway.

Function

Large lanais are often used as patios, although their main function is to provide shelter for the traffic accesses on the exterior of a building. Lanais are actually exterior hallways.

Lanais which are located parallel to exterior walls are usually created by extending the roof overhang to cover a traffic area, as shown in Fig. 6-111. Figures 6-112A and 6-112B show a typical lanai plan which eliminates the need for more costly interior halls. Lanais are used extensively in commercial buildings, especially in warmer climates, as shown in Fig. 6-113.

Location

In residence planning, a lanai can be used most effectively to connect opposite areas of a home.

Fig. 6-112B. View of the lanai shown in A. *Home Planners, Inc.*

Fig. 6-113. Commercial use of a lanai. *Western Wood Products Association*

Lanais are commonly located between the garage and the kitchen, the patio and the kitchen or the living area, and the living area and the service

Fig. 6-114. A semi-enclosed lanai. *California Redwood Association*

Fig. 6-115. A lanai porch created with roof overhang. *Western Wood Products Association*

area. U-shaped houses are especially suitable for using lanais because of the natural connection of the extremities of the U.

When lanais are carefully located they can also function as sheltered access from inside areas to outside facilities such as patios, pools, or outdoor cooking areas. A covered or partially covered patio is also considered a lanai when it doubles as a major access from one area of a structure to another. A lanai can also be semi-enclosed, and provide not only traffic access but also privacy and sun and wind shielding. When lanais are used to connect the building with the street, they actually function as marquees (Fig. 6-114).

Decor

The lanai should be a consistent, integral part of the design of the structure. The lanai cover may be an extension of the roof overhang (Fig. 6-115) or may be supported by columns, as shown in Fig. 6-116. If glass is placed between the columns, the lanai becomes an interior hallway rather than an exterior one. This separation is sometimes the only difference between a lanai and an interior hall. It is often desirable to design and locate the lanai to provide access from one end of an extremely long building to the other. The lines of this kind of lanai strengthen and reinforce the

basic lines of the building. If a lanai is to be utilized extensively at night, effective lighting must be provided. Light from within is used when drapes are open, but additional lighting fixtures are used when drapes are closed.

Size and Shape

Lanais may extend the full length of a building and may be designed for maximum traffic loads,

135

Fig. 6-116. A lanai supported by columns. *Bethlehem Steel Corp.*

Fig. 6-117. A large residential lanai. *Julius Shulman*

Fig. 6-118. A long lanai connecting several buildings. *California Redwood Association*

as shown in Fig. 6-117. They may be as narrow as the area under a 2' or 3' (610 or 915 mm) roof overhang. However, a lanai at least 4' (1220 mm) wide is desirable. The length and type of cover is limited only by the location of areas to be covered. For example, the lanai shown in Fig. 6-118 extends a very long distance between buildings.

TRAFFIC AREAS

Traffic both inside and outside the building must be considered. Traffic areas for employees, visitors, and deliveries into and out of the building must be allocated using a minimum amount of space for commercial buildings. Planning the traffic areas of a residence is not as complex because of the small number of people involved. Nevertheless, the same basic principles of efficient space allocation prevail. The traffic areas of the home provide passage from one room or area to another. The main traffic areas of a residence include the halls, entrance foyers, stairs, lanais, and areas of rooms that are part of the traffic pattern.

Traffic Patterns

Traffic patterns of a residence should be carefully considered in the design of the room layout. A minimum amount of space should be devoted to traffic areas. Extremely long halls and corridors

136

should be avoided. They are difficult to light and actually provide no living space. Traffic patterns that require passage through one room to get to another should also be avoided, especially in the sleeping area.

The traffic pattern shown in the plan in Fig. 6-119 is efficient and functional. It contains a

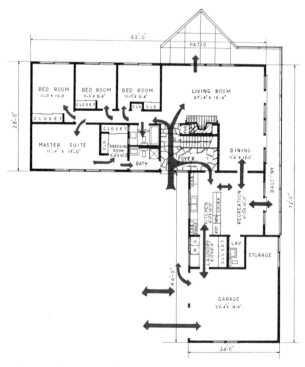

Fig. 6-119. An efficient traffic pattern. *Home Planners, Inc.*

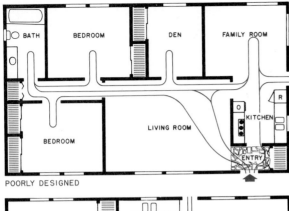

POORLY DESIGNED

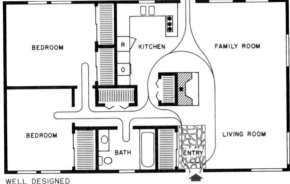

WELL DESIGNED

Fig. 6-120. The difference between a poorly designed and a well-designed traffic pattern.

Fig. 6-121. A traffic area with light and level variations.

Fig. 6-122. The use of furniture components in separating traffic areas. *United States Plywood Corporation*

through other areas. In this plan the service entrance provides access to the kitchen from the carport and other parts of the service area.

One method of determining the effectiveness of the traffic pattern of a house is to imagine yourself moving through the house by placing your pencil on the floor plan and tracing your route through the house as you perform your daily routine. If you trace through a whole day's activities, including those of other members of the household, you will be able to see graphically where the heaviest traffic occurs and whether the traffic areas have been planned effectively. Figure 6-120 shows the difference between a poorly designed traffic pattern and a well-designed traffic pattern.

Halls

Halls are the highways and streets of the home. They provide a controlled path which connects the various areas of the house. Halls should be planned to keep to a minimum or eliminate the passage of traffic through rooms. Long, dark, tunnel-like halls should be avoided. Halls should be well lighted, light in color and texture, and planned with the decor of the whole house in mind. The hall shown in Fig. 6-121 is extremely long; however, it is broken by level, by open partitions, and by light variations.

One method of channeling hall traffic without the use of solid walls is with the use of dividers. Planters, half-walls, louvered walls, and even furniture can be used as dividers. Figure 6-122 shows the use of furniture components in dividing the living area from the hall. This arrangement enables both the hall and the living room to share ventilation, light, and heat.

minimum amount of wasted hall space without creating a boxed-in appearance. It provides access to each of the areas without passing through other areas. The arrows clearly show that the sleeping area, living area, and service area are accessible from the entrance without passage

Fig. 6-123. The use of movable partitions to separate traffic areas.

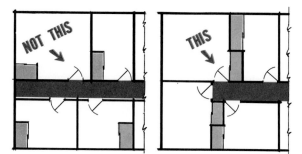

Fig. 6-124. Principles of efficient hall design.

Fig. 6-126. An exposed stair system. *Armstrong Cork Company*

Another method of designing halls and corridors as an integral part of the area design is with the use of movable partitions. The Japanese scheme of placing these partitions between the living area and a hall is shown in Fig. 6-123. In some Japanese homes this hall actually becomes a lanai when the partition between the living area and the hall is closed and the outside wall is opened. Figure 6-124 shows some of the basic principles of efficient hall design.

Stairs

Stairs are inclined hallways. They provide access from one level to another. Stairs may lead directly from one area to another without a change of direction, they may turn 90° by means of a landing, or they may turn 180° by means of landings. Figure 6-125 shows four basic types of stairs and the amount of space utilized by each type.

With the use of newer, stronger building materials and new techniques, there is no longer any reason for enclosing stairs in walls that restrict light and ventilation (Fig. 6-126). Stairs can now be supported by many different devices. The stairs in Fig. 6-127 are center-supported and

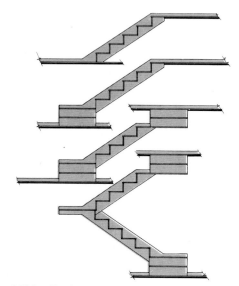

Fig. 6-125. Basic types of stairs. *National Lumber Manufacturers Association*

Fig. 6-127. Center-supported stairs.

Fig. 6-128. Stairs hung from steel rods. *Armstrong Cork Company*

Fig. 6-129A. When possible, use natural light to illuminate stairwells. *Rohm & Haas Company*

Fig. 6-129B. Circular stairs are used where space is restricted. *Scholz Homes, Inc.*

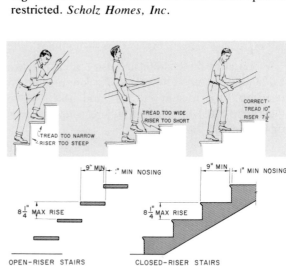

Fig. 6-130. Correct tread and riser design is important.

therefore do not need side walls or other supports. Even when vertical supports are necessary or desirable, completely closing in the wall is not mandatory. Figure 6-128 shows stairs supported by exposed steel rods which maintain the open plan without sacrificing support or safety. These stairs are supported by hanging one side of the tread from steel rods. Combining open-stair assemblies with windows provides the maximum amount of light, especially when the windows in the open area extend through several levels, as shown in Fig. 6-129A. Where space is extremely restricted or to be used for other purposes, circular stairs, as shown in Fig. 6-129B, offer an effective solution.

Space Requirements

There are many variables to consider in designing stairs. The *tread* width, the *riser* height, the width of the stair opening, and the headroom all help to determine the total length of the stairwell.

The *tread* is the horizontal part of the stair, the part upon which you walk. The average width of the tread is 10″ (254 mm). The riser is the vertical part of the stair. The average riser height is 7¼″ (184 mm). Figure 6-130 shows the importance of correct tread and riser design.

The overall width of the stairs is the length or distance across the treads. A minimum of 3′ (914 mm) should be allowed for the total stair

139

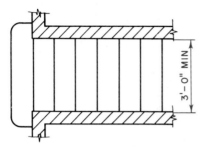

Fig. 6-131. Minimum width of stairs.

width. However, a width of 3'-6" (1067 mm) or even 4' (1220 mm) is preferred (Fig. 6-131).

Headroom is the vertical distance between the top of each tread and the top of the stairwell ceiling. A minimum headroom distance of 6'-6" (1981 mm) should be allowed. However, distances of 7' (2134 mm) are more desirable (Fig. 6-132).

Landing dimensions are also critical. Figure 6-133 shows some allowances for landings when used to turn a stairway 90° and 180°. More clearance must be allowed where a door opens on a landing.

ENTRANCES

Entrances are divided into several different types: the main entrance, the service entrance, and the special-purpose entrance. The entrance is composed of an outside waiting area (porch, marquee, lanai), a separation (door), and an inside waiting area (foyer, entrance hall).

Function

Entrances provide for and control the flow of traffic into and out of a building. Different types of entrances have somewhat different functions.

Main Entrance

The main entrance provides access to the house, through which guests are welcomed and from which all major traffic patterns radiate. The main entrance should be readily identifiable by a stranger. It should provide shelter to anyone awaiting entrance. The entrance of the house shown in Fig. 6-134 has two walkways. The one on the right leads to the street; the one on the left leads to the driveway and garage.

Some provision should be made in the main-entrance wall for the viewing of callers from the

Fig. 6-132. Minimum headroom clearance.

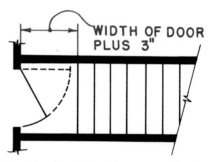

Fig. 6-133. Landing dimensions are critical.

Fig. 6-134. A main entrance with a walk leading to the street and to the driveway. *California Redwood Association*

inside. This can be accomplished through the use of side panels, lights (panes) in the door, or

Fig. 6-137. Undesirable areas (parking) should be baffled visually from the entrance. *Western Wood Products Association*

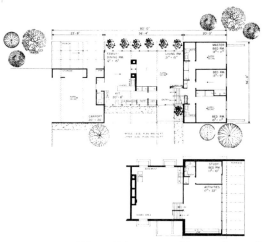

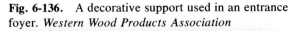

Fig. 6-135. Side windows provide a view of the entrance from the inside. *Home Planners, Inc.*

windows (Fig. 6-135) which face the side of the entrance.

The main entrance should be planned to create a desirable first impression (Fig. 6-136). A direct view of other areas of the house from the foyer should be baffled but not sealed off. This result is often accomplished by placing the access to the other rooms at the rear or to one side of the entrance foyer. Also, a direct view of exterior parking areas should be baffled from view as shown in Fig. 6-137.

The entrance foyer should include a closet for the storage of outside clothing and bad-

weather gear. This foyer closet should have a capacity which will accommodate both family and guests. The foyer closet shown in Fig. 6-138A is located at a convenient distance from the entrance door.

Service Entrance

The service entrance provides access to the house through which supplies can be delivered to the service areas without going through other parts of the house. It should also provide access to parts of the service area (garage, laundry, workshop) for which the main entrance is inappropriate and inconvenient.

Special-purpose Entrances

Special-purpose entrances and exits do not provide for outside traffic. Instead they provide for movement from the inside living area of the house

Fig. 6-136. A decorative support used in an entrance foyer. *Western Wood Products Association*

Fig. 6-138A. The foyer should include storage facilities.

Fig. 6-138B. Emphasis on wood texture. *Western Wood Products Association*

Fig. 6-140. The entrance adjacent to a quiet patio. *PPG Industries*

to the outside living areas (Fig. 6-138B). A sliding door from the living area to the patio is a special-purpose entrance. It is not an entrance through which street, drive, or sidewalk traffic would have access. Figure 6-139 shows the difference between special-purpose entrances, main entrance, and service entrances.

Location

The main entrance should be centrally located to provide easy access to each area. It should be conveniently accessible from driveways, sidewalks, or street.

The service entrance should be located close to the drive and garage. It should be placed near the kitchen or food-storage areas.

Special-purpose entrances and exits are often located between the bedroom and the quiet

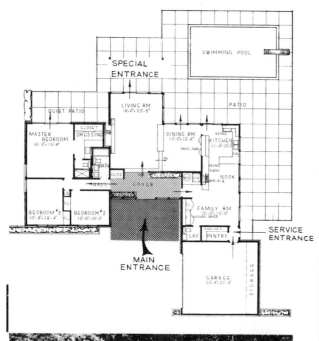

Fig. 6-139. The basic types of entrances. *Scholz Homes, Inc.*

142

Fig. 6-141. A first impression is an important feature of an entrance. *Western Wood Products Association*

Fig. 6-142. Left: an entrance with lines related to the lines of the structure. Right: an entrance with lines unrelated to the lines of the structure.

patio, between the living room and the living patio (Fig. 6-140), and between the dining room or kitchen and the dining patio.

Decor

The entrance should create a desirable first impression. It should be easily identifiable yet an integral part of the architectural style (Fig. 6-141).

Consistency of Style

The total design of the entrance should be consistent with the overall design of the house. The design of the door, the side panel, and the deck and cover should be directly related to the lines of the house. The lines of the entrances shown at the left in Fig. 6-142 are designed as integral parts of the exterior. The lines of the entrance shown at the right in Fig. 6-142 are unrelated to the major building lines of the structure.

The entrance shown in Figs. 6-143*A, B,* and *C* is a good example of entrance design involving all the principles of location, style consistency, lighting utilization, and size and shape effectiveness. Figure 6-143*A* shows a close view of the entrance, Fig. 6-143*C* shows the location of the entrance in reference to the entire front of the house, and Fig. 6-143*B* shows an interior view of the entrance foyer.

Fig. 6-143A. A close view of related entrance lines.

Fig. 6-143B. Entrance lines related to the remainder of the home.

Fig. 6-143C. The foyer side of the entrance shown in *A* and *B* is consistent with the outside. *Scholz Homes, Inc.*

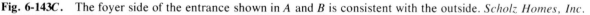

Fig. 6-144. An elevated entrance. *PPG Industries*

Open Planning

The view from the main entrance to the living area should be baffled without creating a boxed-in appearance. The foyer should not appear as a dead end. The extensive use of glass, effective lighting, and carefully placed baffle walls can create an open and inviting impression. Open planning between the entrance foyer and the living areas can also be accomplished by the use of louvered walls or planter walls. These provide a break in the line of sight but not a complete separation. Sinking or elevating the foyer or entrance approach as shown in Fig. 6-144 also provides the desired separation without isolation.

Flooring

The outside portion of the entrance should be weather-resistant stone, brick, or concrete. If a porch is used outside the entrance, a wood deck will suffice. The foyer deck should be easily maintained and be resistant to mud, water, and dirt brought in from the outside. Asphalt, vinyl or rubber tile, stone, flagstone, marble, and terrazzo are most frequently used for the foyer deck. The use of a different material in the foyer area helps to define the area when no other separation exists.

Foyer Walls

Paneling, masonry, planters, murals, and glass are used extensively for entrance foyer walls. The walls of the exterior portion of the entrance should be consistent with the other materials used on the exterior of the house.

Lighting

An entrance must be designed to function day and night. General lighting, spot lighting, and all-night lighting (Fig. 6-145) are effective for this purpose. Lighting can be used to accent distinguishing features or to illuminate the pattern of a wall, which actually provides more light by reflection and helps to identify and accentuate the entrance at night.

Fig. 6-145. Effective use of outside-entrance lighting. *PPG Industries*

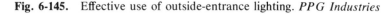

Fig. 6-146. Natural lighting used in a foyer. *Western Wood Products Association*

Natural lighting as shown in Fig. 6-146 is also effective in lighting entrance areas during daylight hours.

Size and Shape

The size and shape of the areas inside and outside the entrance depend on the budget and the type of plan. Foyers are not bounded by solid walls in the open plan.

The Outside

The outside, covered portion of the entrance should be large enough to shelter several people at one time. Sufficient space should be allowed

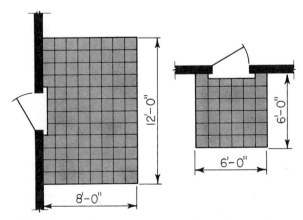

Fig. 6-147. The entrance area on the left has optimum dimensions. The entrance on the right has minimum dimensions.

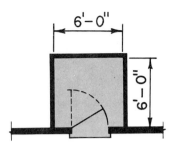

Fig. 6-148. A minimum-sized foyer.

on all sides, exclusive of the amount of space needed to open storm doors which open to the outside. Outside shelter areas range in size from the minimum arrangement shown at the right in Fig. 6-147 to the more generous size shown at the left in Fig. 6-147.

The Inside

The inside of the entrance foyer should be sufficiently large to allow several people to enter at the same time, remove their coats, and store them in the closet. A 6′ × 6′ (1.8 × 1.8 m) foyer, as shown in Fig. 6-148, is considered minimum for this function. A foyer 8′ × 10′ (2.4 × 3.0 m) is average, but a more desirable size is 8′ × 15′ (2.4 × 4.6 m), as shown in Fig. 6-149.

Figure 6-149 also shows a foyer arrangement which allows for the swing of the door, something which must be taken into consideration in determining the size of the foyer. If the foyer is too shallow, passage will be blocked when the door is open, and only one person may enter at a time. Figure 6-143C (on page 143) shows a foyer that is near the optimum size. It is not extremely deep, but it does extend a great distance on either side. This allows sufficient traffic to pass. It also allows sufficient movement around the doors when they are opened.

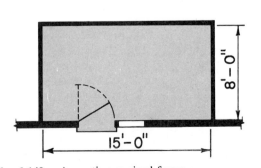

Fig. 6-149. An optimum-sized foyer.

Foyers are normally rectangular because they lead to several areas of the home. They do not need much depth in any one direction. The ideal entry includes:

1. Adequate room to handle traffic flow
2. Access to all three areas of a home
3. A closet
4. Bath access for guests
5. Consistent decor
6. Outside weather protection
7. Effective lighting day and night

THE DEN

The den or study can be designed for many different purposes, depending on the living habits of its occupants.

Function

The den may function basically as a reading room, writing room, hobby room, or professional office. For the teacher, writer, or cleric, the study may be basically a reading room. For the engineer, architect, drafter, or artist, the den or study may function primarily as a studio and may include such facilities as those shown in the study in Fig. 6-150.

The den or study often doubles as a guest room. Quite often the children's bedroom must provide facilities normally included in a study such as desk, bookcase, and typewriter.

The den is often considered part of the sleeping area since it may require placement in a quiet part of the house. It also may function primarily in the living area, especially if the study is used as a professional office by a physician or an insurance agent whose clients call at home. Figure 6-151 shows a professional study or office located near the main entrance hall and accessible from the main entrance and also from a side entrance directly from the garage.

Fig. 6-150. This study was planned for drawing and designing activities. *Louis Rens Photo:* Interiors Magazine

Location

If a study doubles as an office, it should be located in an accessible area. However, if it is to serve a private use, then it can be located in the basement or attic, utilizing otherwise wasted space.

Decor and Lighting

The decor of the study should reflect the main activity and should allow for well-diffused general lighting and glareproof local lighting. Notice the open effect achieved in Fig. 6-152 by the row of windows above eye level. They admit the max-

Fig. 6-151. A study used as a professional office. *Home Planners, Inc.*

Fig. 6-152. High windows admit light but block the view. *Bethlehem Steel Corp.*

146

imum amount of light without exposing distracting eye-level images from the outside.

As in the recreation room, a central theme may be used in the decoration of the study. The people who used the study shown in Fig. 6-153 obviously enjoyed reading. Notice how the architect has created an inviting atmosphere for reading by providing the warmth of a fireplace, adequate bookshelf space, and the natural light from a skylight.

Size and Shape

The size and shape of the den, study, or office will vary greatly with its function. Size and shape will depend on whether one or two persons expect to use the room privately or whether it should provide a meeting place for business clients. Studies range in size from just enough space for a desk and chair in a small corner to a large amount of space with a diversity of furnishings. A study with the maximum number of furnishings would include a desk and chair, lounge chair, studio couch, file cabinets, bookcases, storage space, and coffee table.

Review Questions

1. Define the following terms: cantilever, closed plan, open plan, orientation, lanai, traffic pattern, tread, riser.
2. Complete the workbook exercises for Unit 6.
3. List the furniture you would include in your living room. Cut out samples from catalogs, magazines, and newspapers for your scrapbook.
4. Sketch an open-plan living room. Indicate the position of windows, fireplace, foyer, entrance, and dining room.
5. Sketch a closed-plan living room. Show the position of adjacent rooms.
6. Determine the best size of a living room to accommodate the following pieces of furniture: couch, television, stereo system, grand piano, bookcase, chaise lounge, coffee table, fireplace, two club chairs.
7. Convert the living room shown in Fig. 6-151 to an open-plan living area.

Fig. 6-153. A quiet, restful study.

8. Determine the size and shape of a family room to accommodate the following activities: television viewing, sewing, knitting, model building, slide viewing, dancing, eating.
9. Add a lanai to the plan shown in Fig. 6-151.
10. Design a family room that doubles as a guest bedroom.
11. Add a patio design to the floor-plan layout shown in Fig. 6-36.
12. Sketch the floor plan shown in Fig. 6-78. Redesign the traffic pattern. Eliminate passage through the living room to get to the sleeping area.
13. Sketch the plan shown in Fig. 6-78. Move the entrance to another location to provide a more efficient traffic pattern.
14. Sketch the plans shown in Fig. 2-13. Shorten the long hall in the bedroom area.
15. Sketch a baffle wall for the exposed patio shown in Fig. 2-22.
16. Plan and sketch a foyer for the living area shown in Fig. 2-20.
17. Sketch a plan for a recreation room including facilities for billiards, chess, shuffleboard, and television watching.
18. Sketch a recreation room of your own design.
19. Determine the size and shape of a recreation room to accommodate television set, stereo, chaise lounge, studio couch, lounge chair, bar and stools, bookcase, and billiard table.
20. Add an outdoor dining porch to the plan shown in Fig. 2-19.
21. Add a porch to the floor plan shown in Fig. 3-50. Show exact width and length and list materials you recommend for the deck, roof, and enclosure.

SERVICE AREA

unit 7

The service area includes the kitchen, laundry, garage, workshops, storage centers, and utility room. Since a great number of different activities take place in the service area, it should be designed for the greatest efficiency. The service area includes facilities for the maintenance and servicing of the other areas of the home. The functioning of the living and the sleeping areas is greatly dependent upon the efficiency of the service area.

THE KITCHEN

A well-planned kitchen is efficient, attractive, and easy to maintain. To design an efficient kitchen, the designer must consider the function, basic shape, decor, size, and location of equipment (Fig. 7-1).

Function

The preparation of food is the basic function of the kitchen. However, the kitchen may also be used as a dining area (Fig. 7-2) and as a laundry. The proper placement of appliances, storage cabinets, and furniture is important in planning efficient kitchens. Locating appliances in an efficient pattern eliminates much wasted motion

Fig. 7-1. An efficient, attractive, and easily maintained kitchen. *Tappan Company*

148

Fig. 7-2. A family kitchen designed for a variety of activities. *Frigidaire*

(Fig. 7-3). An efficient kitchen is divided into three areas: the storage and mixing center, the cleaning and preparation center, and the cooking center. Figure 7-3 also shows the division of these areas.

Storage and Mixing Center
The refrigerator is the major appliance in the storage and mixing center. The refrigerator may be freestanding, built-in, or suspended from a wall. The storage and mixing center also includes

Fig. 7-3. Efficiency depends on the placement of appliances, storage cabinets, and furniture. *Hotpoint*

149

Fig. 7-4. The sink is a major fixture in the preparation and cleaning area. *Formica Corporation*

cabinets for the storage of utensils and ingredients used in cooking and baking, as well as a countertop work area.

Preparation and Cleaning Center

The sink is the major fixture in the preparation and cleaning center (Fig. 7-4). Sinks are available in one- and two-bowl models with a variety of cabinet arrangements and countertop and drainboard areas. The preparation and cleaning center may also include a waste-disposal unit, an automatic dishwasher, a waste compactor, and cabinets for storing brushes, towels, and cleaning supplies.

Cooking Center

The range and oven are the major appliances in the cooking center. The range and oven may be combined into one appliance, or the burners may be installed in the countertop and the oven built into the wall. The cooking center should also include countertop work space, as well as storage space for minor appliances and cooking utensils that will be used in the area. The cooking center must have an adequate supply of electrical outlets for the many minor appliances used in cooking.

Figure 7-5 shows the size requirements for the storage or installation of many minor appliances that may be located in the various centers.

150

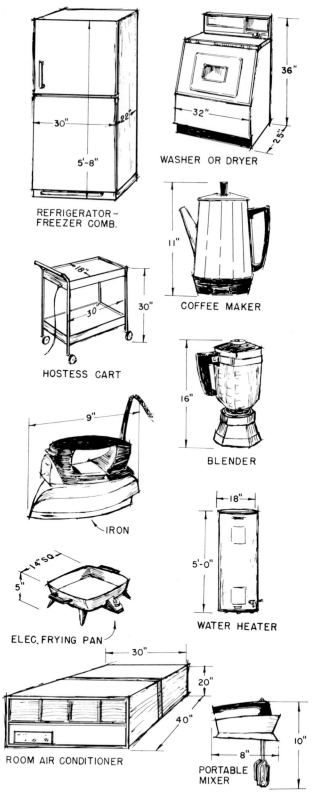

Fig. 7-5. Sizes of common appliances.

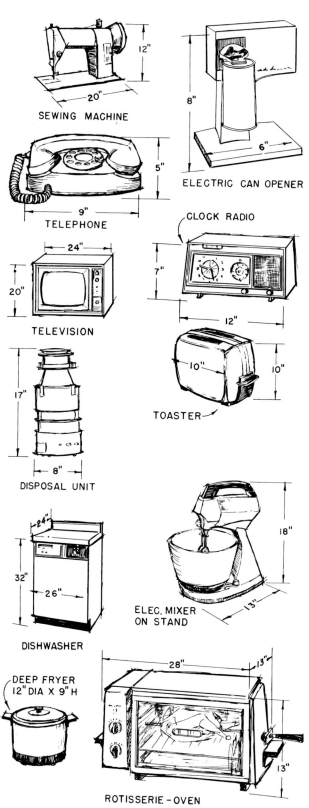

SEWING MACHINE

12"

20"

ELECTRIC CAN OPENER

8"

6"

TELEPHONE

5"

9"

CLOCK RADIO

7"

12"

TELEVISION

24"

20"

TOASTER

10"

10"

DISPOSAL UNIT

17"

8"

ELEC. MIXER ON STAND

18"

13"

DISHWASHER

24"

32"

26"

DEEP FRYER
12" DIA X 9" H

ROTISSERIE - OVEN

28"

13"

13"

Fig. 7-5. Sizes of common appliances.

Fig. 7-6. The work triangle should be between 12′ and 22′ (3.7 and 6.7 m). *Superior Kitchens, Inc.*

Work Triangle

If you draw a line connecting the three centers of the kitchen, a triangle is formed (Fig. 7-6). This is called the *work triangle*. The perimeter of an efficient kitchen work triangle should be between 12′ and 22′ (3.7 and 6.7 m).

Basic Shapes

The position of the three areas on the work triangle may vary greatly. However, the most efficient arrangements usually fall into the following categories.

Peninsula Kitchen

The peninsula kitchen (Fig. 7-7*A* is similar to the U kitchen. However, one end of the U is not enclosed with a wall. The cooking center is often located in this peninsula, and the peninsula is often used to join the kitchen to the dining or

Fig. 7-7A. A peninsula kitchen. *General Electric Corporation*

Fig. 7-7B. The peninsula kitchen work station. *Karpy Custom Kitchens*

Fig. 7-9B. An L kitchen with an eating area. *General Electric*

family room. Figure 7-7B shows a peninsula used as a work station. Figure 7-8 shows various arrangements of peninsula kitchens and the resulting work triangles.

L-shaped Kitchen

The L-shaped kitchen (Fig. 7-9A) has continuous counters and appliances and equipment on two adjoining walls. The work triangle is not in the traffic pattern. The remaining space is often used for other kitchen facilities, such as dining or laundry facilities. If the walls of an L-shaped kitchen are too long, the compact efficiency of the kitchen is destroyed. Figure 7-9B shows an L kitchen with an eating area designed into the L. Figure 7-10 shows several L-shaped kitchens and the work triangles that result from these arrangements.

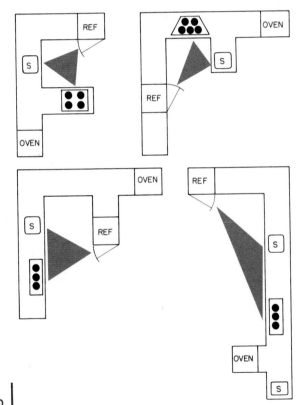

152 | **Fig. 7-8.** Four arrangements for a peninsula kitchen.

Fig. 7-9A. Basic L-shaped kitchen. *Tappan Company*

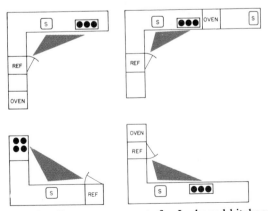

Fig. 7-10. Four arrangements for L-shaped kitchens.

Fig. 7-11. One-wall kitchen. *Frigidaire*

Fig. 7-13. U-shaped kitchen. *Hotpoint*

One-wall Kitchen

A one-wall kitchen is an excellent plan for small apartments, cabins, or houses in which little space is available. The work centers are located in one line and produce a very efficient arrangement (Fig. 7-11). However, in planning the one-wall kitchen, the designer must be careful to avoid having the wall too long and must provide adequate storage facilities. Figure 7-12 shows several one-wall-kitchen arrangements.

U-shaped Kitchen

The U-shaped kitchen, as shown in Fig. 7-13*A*, is a very efficient arrangement. The sink is located at the bottom of the U, and the range and the refrigerator are at the opposite ends. In this arrangement, traffic passing through the kitchen is completely separated from the work triangle. The open space in the U between the sides may be 4′ or 5′ (1.2 or 1.5 m). This arrangement produces a very efficient but small kitchen. Figure

7-14 shows various U-shaped-kitchen layouts and the resulting work triangles.

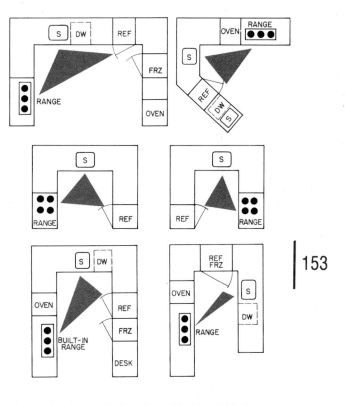

153

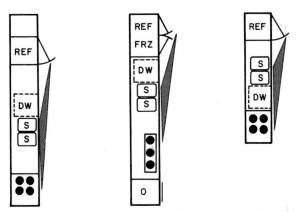

Fig. 7-12. Three arrangements for one-wall kitchens.

Fig. 7-14. Six variations for a U-shaped kitchen.

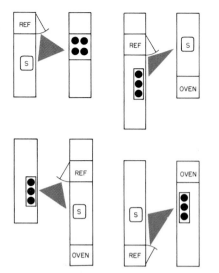

Fig. 7-15.   Four arrangements for corridor kitchens.

Island Kitchen

The island, which serves as a separator for the different parts of the kitchen, usually has a range top or sink, or both, and is accessible on all sides. Other facilities that are sometimes located in the island are the mixing center, work table,

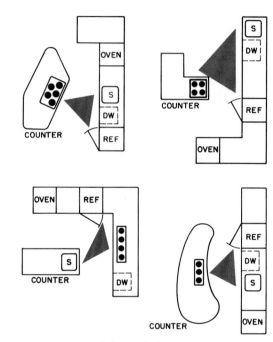

Fig. 7-17A.   Four island-kitchen arrangements.

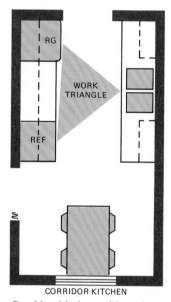

Fig. 7-16.   Corridor kitchen with eating area.

154 | ## Corridor Kitchen

The two-wall corridor kitchens shown in Fig. 7-15 are very efficient arrangements for long, narrow rooms. A corridor kitchen is unsatisfactory, however, if considerable traffic passes through the work triangle. A corridor kitchen produces one of the most efficient work triangles of all the arrangements. Figure 7-16 shows a corridor kitchen designed to include an eating area.

Fig. 7-17B.   An island kitchen with a sink in the island. *Quaker Maid Kitchens*

Fig. 7-17C. An auxiliary-sink island. *General Electric*

buffet counter, extra sink, and snack center. See Fig. 7-17A. Figures 7-17B and C show an unusual arrangement of an island with a combination sink and counter in the island.

Family Kitchen

The family kitchen is an open kitchen using any of the basic plans. Its function is to provide a meeting place for the entire family in addition to providing for the normal kitchen functions. Family kitchens are normally divided into two sections. One section is for food preparation, which includes the three work centers; the other section includes a dining area and family-room facilities, as shown in Fig. 7-18.

Family kitchens must be rather large to accommodate these facilities. An average size for a family kitchen is 15' × 15' (4.6 × 4.6m). Figure 7-19 shows several possible arrangements for family kitchens.

Kitchen Sink Locations

Because much time is spent at the kitchen sink, this equipment should be carefully located.

There are five basic locations for the sink, one of which should suit your kitchen plan. The proper model selection will enhance the beauty of the kitchen and add to its purpose and function.

Fig. 7-18. A family kitchen. *General Electric Company*

155

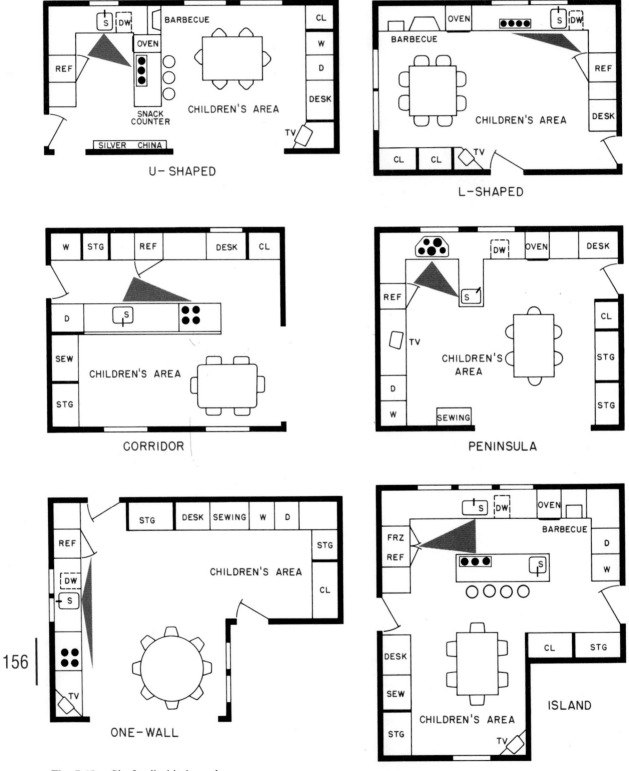

Fig. 7-19. Six family-kitchen plans.

156

Fig. 7-21. Sink away from window. *Elkay Manufacturing Company*

Fig. 7-22. Sink in island. *Elkay Manufacturing Company*

try a location that may save many steps and add convenience (Fig. 7-21).

As an Island Putting your sink on an island-type counter near the middle of the kitchen activity makes it easier to reach and saves many countless steps (Fig. 7-22).

In a Corner While some sinks are installed in corners to utilize *dead-corner* cabinet space, this is the least practical of the five basic locations. You should consider the merits of all other

Fig. 7-20. Sink under window. *Elkay Manufacturing Company*

Under a Window Most sinks, in this plan, are placed under the window to take advantage of the natural light and view. Locate the sink first, then the other kitchen appliances (Fig. 7-20).

Away from Window When an under-a-window location does not allow for an efficient layout,

157

Fig. 7-23. Sink in corner. *Elkay Manufacturing Company*

Fig. 7-24. Sink on peninsula. *Elkay Manufacturing Company*

Fig. 7-25. Base and wall cabinet storage. *Rubbermaid, Incorporated*

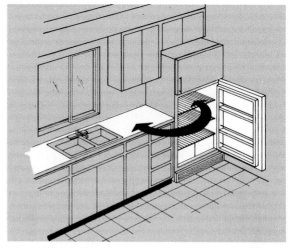

Fig. 7-26. Refrigerator storage. *Southern California Gas Company*

locations before deciding on an *around-the-corner* type of location (Fig. 7-23).

On a Peninsula One of the handiest locations for your sink is on a peninsula-type counter. This type may also serve as a room divider separating kitchen and dining area (Fig. 7-24).

Storage

Nowhere is storage more critical than in the kitchen. Since stored items may be in almost constant use in the kitchen, storage location is critical to the efficient functioning of the kitchen. Figure 7-25 shows the normal storage use of kitchen base and wall cabinets. Figures 7-26 to 7-55 shows some effective ideas for making maximum use of all usable kitchen storage possibilities.

Local Area Storage

The Right Hinged Door The right hinged door refrigerator is located to the right of the preparation counter for easy loading and unloading (Fig. 7-26).

Clean-up Center with Raised Dishwasher If space permits, you may wish to raise the dishwasher 6″ to 12″ (152 to 305 mm) above the floor. This places the racks at a more convenient height. The pantry-style dish cabinet is lower than the

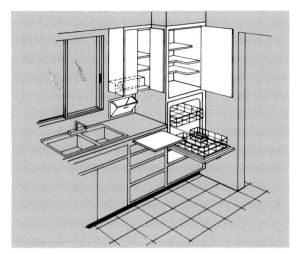

Fig. 7-27. Wall cabinet storage. *Southern California Gas Company*

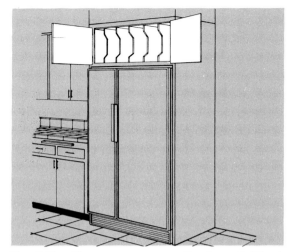

Fig. 7-29. Top pantry storage. *Southern California Gas Company*

usual wall cabinet and offers more convenient storage (Fig. 7-27).

Dishwasher-Clean-up Center An extra large sink section can be used for bulky items that will not fit in the dishwasher. Other conveniences include built-in automatic can opener, trash chute, pull-out board, towel-drying bars, pull-out shelf, and door-mounted wastebaskets (Fig. 7-28).

Above-refrigerator Storage Take advantage of that high and deep space above the refrigerator. Vertical dividers spaced 4″ to 6″ (102 to 152 mm)

apart provide convenient storage for baking tins such as cake and muffin pans, cookie sheets, etc. (Fig. 7-29).

Range-top Center Specialized storage can be planned at the range center, such as a divided drawer, slide-out pan shelves, lid racks, slotted drawer, and spice shelves. Full-extension roller hardware gives easy access to these deep drawers and pan shelves (Fig. 7-30).

Oven Center This built-in oven is located so that its door does not open into the doorway or

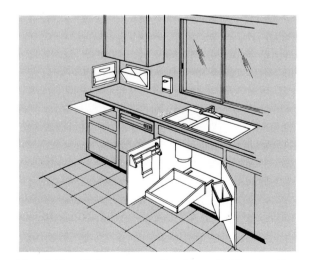

Fig. 7-28. Sink storage. *Southern California Gas Company*

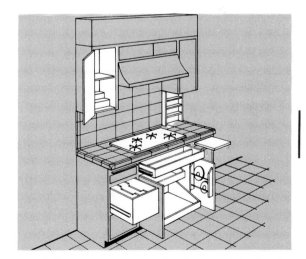

Fig. 7-30. Range storage. *Southern California Gas Company*

159

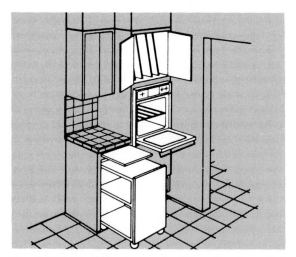

Fig. 7-31. Movable storage facilities. *Southern California Gas Company*

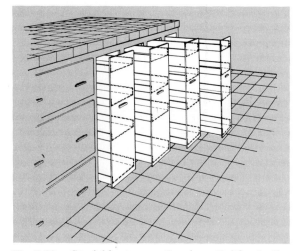

Fig. 7-33. Stack bin storage. *Southern California Gas Company*

narrow passage. Divided cabinet above oven, heatproof counter, pull-out board, and a cart that stores under the counter make good use of this corner space (Fig. 7-31).

Under-counter Cart This storage cabinet on wheels is designed to match the kitchen cabinets so it is concealed when in place. The laminated hardwood top is an ideal counter for food preparation and serving wherever needed (Fig. 7-32).

Vertical Roll-out Shelves This compact under-counter pantry is made possible with easy-access roll-out shelves. A variety of shelf heights ac-

commodates large and small items. Be sure to use heavy-duty hardware that will support a heavy supply of canned and packaged foods (Fig. 7-33).

Corner Center-revolving Shelves Revolving shelves above and below the counter to increase the convenience of corner storage. A small under-cabinet light brightens this corner. The built-in countertop mixer-blender is a convenient feature (Fig. 7-34).

Cabinet Features Wall cabinets with adjustable shelves, half-shelves, step shelves, and shelves

Fig. 7-32. Movable work-station storage. *Southern California Gas Company*

Fig. 7-34. Corner center-revolving storage. *Southern California Gas Company*

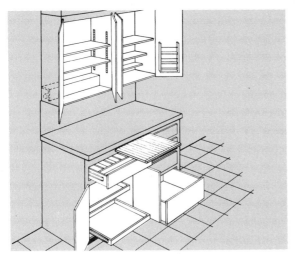

Fig. 7-35. Utensil storage. *Southern California Gas Company*

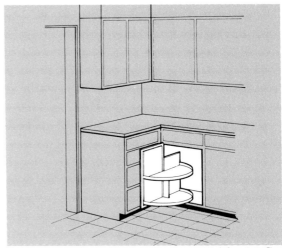

Fig. 7-37. Door storage. *Southern California Gas Company*

on doors accommodate different types of storage. Hardwood pull-out board provides added counter. Base cabinets have roll-out shelves and shallow divided drawers (Fig. 7-35).

Place-mat Storage Wide, shallow slide-out shelves for linens and place mats prevent unnecessary folds and wrinkles. Also notice the divided drawers for orderly storage of small utensils near the cooking center. Spices are within handy reach in shallow shelves (Fig. 7-36).

Corner Storage—Swing-out Shelves Half-circle shelves attached to the cabinet door swing out

and make use of dead-corner storage space. Heavy-duty hinges will take the added load on the cabinet door. Raised lip on shelves will hold stored items in place (Fig. 7-37).

Towel Bar and Deep-drawer Storage Pull-out towel bars are a practical and compact solution to this aspect of kitchen storage. The deep drawers will easily take care of the larger sacks of sugar or flour and large loaves of bread (Fig. 7-38).

Bread Box Near the breadboard it's a good idea to size one drawer to fit the metal bread drawer

161

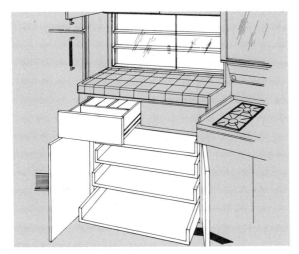

Fig. 7-36. Drawer storage. *Southern California Gas Company*

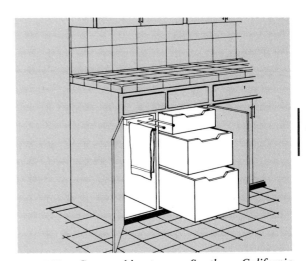

Fig. 7-38. Counter bin storage. *Southern California Gas Company*

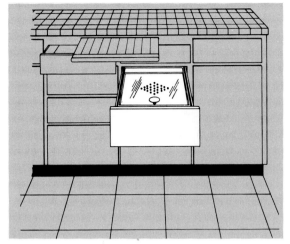

Fig. 7-39. Bread storage. *Southern California Gas Company*

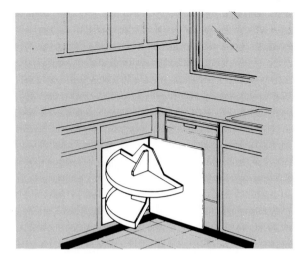

Fig. 7-41. Corner rotating shelves. *Southern California Gas Company*

bins available. This frees counter area usually required for a bread box. Drawer bins are also available for sugar, flour, rice, etc. (Fig. 7-39).

Tilt-out Sink Storage For hideaway storage of small clean-up items, these shallow, tilt-out, and waterproof bins are ideal to hold plate scrapers, cleansing pads, and sponges (Fig. 7-40).

Corner Storage—Half-round Shelves Hard-to-reach corner storage next to the dishwasher has been made useful with these half-round, swing-out shelves. Pivots are attached to the cabinet

frame so each shelf swings out independent of the cabinet door (Fig. 7-41).

Tray and Produce Storage Divided storage for trays and platters makes these items so much easier to handle. The pull-out, open-air bins are ideal to store produce such as potatoes and onions. They are available in a variety of shapes and sizes (Fig. 7-42).

Corner and Spice Storage The notch-type revolving shelves allow you to stand closer to the corner to reach the lazy Susan shelves in the

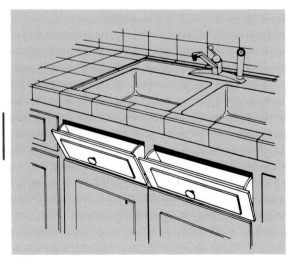

Fig. 7-40. Tilt-out storage. *Southern California Gas Company*

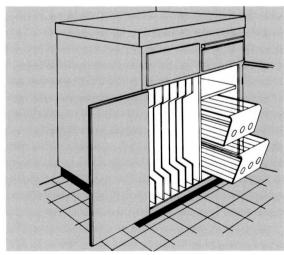

Fig. 7-42. Vertical storage. *Southern California Gas Company*

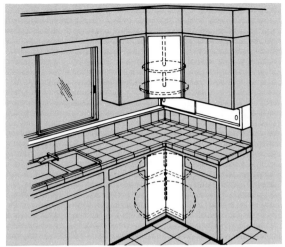

Fig. 7-43. Rotating-shelf corner storage. *Southern California Gas Company*

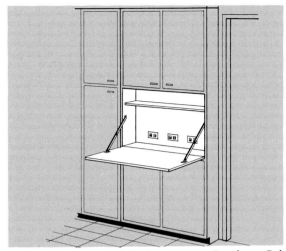

Fig. 7-45. Desk combination storage. *Southern California Gas Company*

upper cabinet. Floor cabinet below the wall cabinet adds convenient storage for small items such as spices (Fig. 7-43).

Roll-out Shelves   A pantry cabinet filled with roll-out shelves provides convenient storage for many kinds of foods: canned, packaged, dry, etc. This pull-out type of storage is also convenient for pans, utensils, and small appliances (Fig. 7-44).

Drop-down Counter   This handy center can be used even where aisle space is limited. It may be used as a planning desk, small appliance center,

gift-wrapping center, sewing center, study center, etc. (Fig. 7-45).

Central Large Storage

Wall Pantry for Dining Service   A floor-to-ceiling wall pantry with adjustable shelves provides storage for a myriad of company's-coming crystal, linens, and silver (Fig. 7-46).

Corner Small-appliance Center   This cabinet is particularly useful for storing small appliances frequently used on the counter such as a mixer,

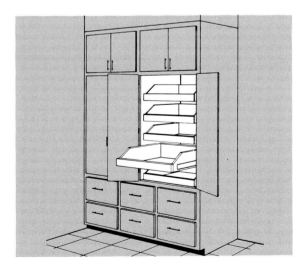

Fig. 7-44. Bin cabinet storage. *Southern California Gas Company*

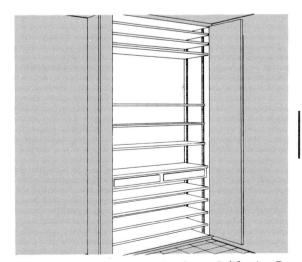

Fig. 7-46. Shelf storage. *Southern California Gas Company*

163

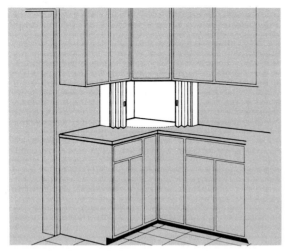

Fig. 7-47. Corner ledge storage. *Southern California Gas Company*

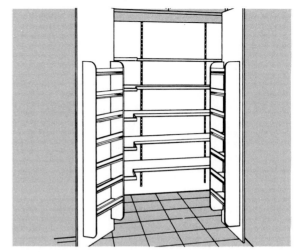

Fig. 7-49. Pantry storage. *Southern California Gas Company*

blender, toaster, coffee pot, etc. Cabinet is fitted with folding doors to keep appliances hidden, but handy (Fig. 7-47).

Small-appliance Storage Center   Space between counter and upper cabinets may be enclosed to house small appliances such as mixers, toasters, coffee pots, can openers, etc. Tambour door rolls down to hide appliances when they are not in use (Fig. 7-48).

Walk-in Pantry   Convert a closet or build a small room and line with shallow shelves. Add doors

with shelves and a light and you have a walk-in pantry. Make some or all of the shelves adjustable to accommodate odd-sized items (Fig. 7-49).

A Superpantry   This pantry provides storage in abundance. Secret to large storage volume is the swing-out unit, which has storage shelves on both sides. Raised lip on shelves holds objects in place when the unit is pivoting (Fig. 7-50).

Hanging Linens   Between the kitchen and dining area might be just the place to plan this floor-to-ceiling cabinet for hanging table linens to avoid

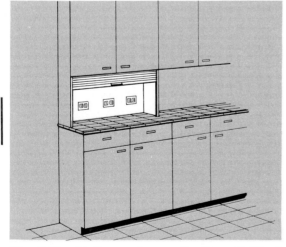

Fig. 7-48. Appliance storage. *Southern California Gas Company*

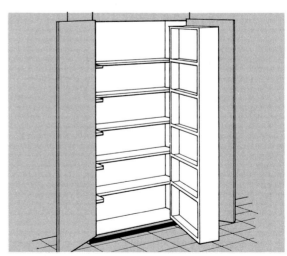

Fig. 7-50. Closet storage. *Southern California Gas Company*

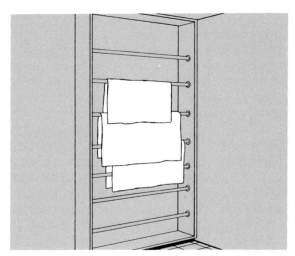

Fig. 7-51. Dryer storage area. *Southern California Gas Company*

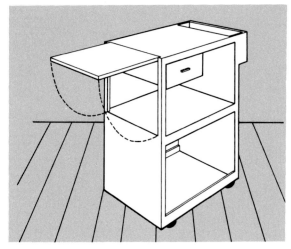

Fig. 7-53. Movable work-center storage area. *Southern California Gas Company*

creases and wrinkles. Use large diameter closet poles in a 6″ to 12″ (152 to 305 mm) deep cabinet (Fig. 7-51).

Desk Center A planning center can be anything from a small drop-leaf desk to a complete kitchen office. The telephone should be here with a bulletin board for notes and reminders (Fig. 7-52).

Serving Cart A serving cart provides extra counter space at any one of the kitchen centers or laundry and sewing centers. It also becomes

a mobile serving center in the dining room, living room, den, or patio areas. A swing-up shelf extends the surface area (Fig. 7-53).

Beverage Storage Planned beverage storage, such as this, is a wonderful convenience. It can be simple, inexpensive, and designed to hold favorite family beverages in quantities. Various types of clay and cement pipes and decorative blocks may be used (Fig. 7-54).

Barbecue Center Another cooking appliance that many people are bringing indoors is the

165

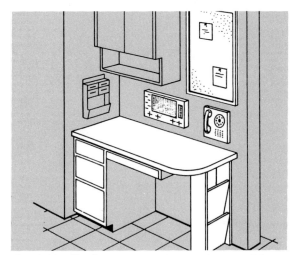

Fig. 7-52. Desk storage area. *Southern California Gas Company*

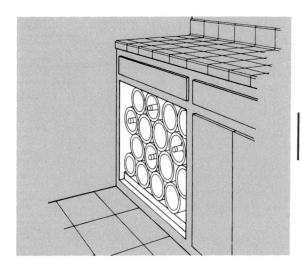

Fig. 7-54. Beverage storage area. *Southern California Gas Company*

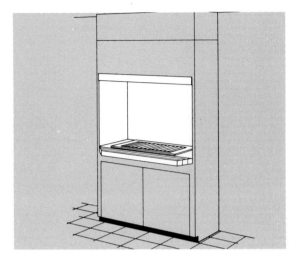

Fig. 7-55. Grill storage area. *Southern California Gas Company*

countertop grill. It is best to locate the grill against a wall and enclose it on one or both sides. An efficient exhaust system will remove the smoke from barbecuing meats (Fig. 7-55).

Decor

Even though kitchen appliances are of contemporary design, some homemakers prefer to decorate kitchens with a period or colonial motif. The design of the cabinets, floors, walls, and accessory furniture must therefore be accented to give the desired effect. Compare the colonial kitchen shown in Fig. 7-56 with the modern kitchen shown in Fig. 7-57. You will notice that it is somewhat easier to design the lines of the modern kitchen in harmony with the lines of the major appliances. However, front panels can be added to some appliances to make them conform to the style and color scheme of the kitchen. The kitchen shown in Fig. 7-56 is a colonial version of the kitchen shown in Fig. 7-57.

Regardless of the style, kitchen walls, floors, countertops, and cabinets should require a minimum amount of maintenance. Materials that are relatively maintenance-free include stainless steel, stain-resistant plastic. ceramic tile, washable wall coverings, washable paint, asphalt vinyl tile, and laminated plastic countertops.

Location

Since the kitchen is the core of the service area, it should be located near the service entrance and near the waste-disposal area. The children's play area should also be visible from the kitchen, and the kitchen must be adjacent to the dining area and outdoor eating areas.

Kitchen Planning Guides

The following guides for kitchen planning provide a review of the more important factors to consider in designing efficent and functional kitchens:

1. The traffic lane is clear of the work triangle.
2. The work areas include all necessary appliances and facilities.

Fig. 7-56. Colonial kitchen decor. *Consoweld*

Fig. 7-57. Contemporary kitchen decor. *Consoweld*

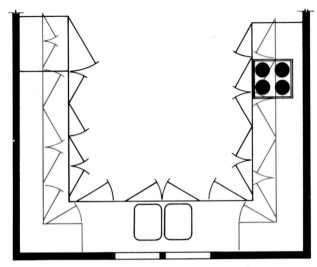

Fig. 7-58. Cabinet doors should open away from the work triangle.

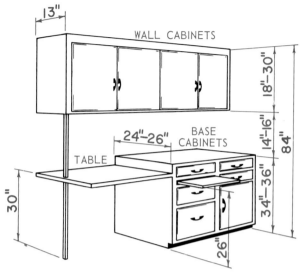

Fig. 7-59. Heights of kitchen working surfaces.

3. The kitchen is located adjacent to the dining area.
4. The kitchen is located near the children's play area.
5. The view from the kitchen is cheerful and pleasant.
6. The centers include (*a*) the storage center, (*b*) the preparation and cleaning center, and (*c*) the cooking center.
7. The work triangle measures between 12′ and 22′ (3.7 and 6.7 m).
8. Electrical outlets are provided for each work center.
9. Adequate storage facilities are available in each work center.
10. Shadowless and glareless light is provided and is concentrated on each work center.

11. Adequate counter space is provided for meal preparation.
12. Ventilation is adequate.
13. The oven and range are separated from the refrigerator by at least one cabinet.
14. Doors on appliances swing away from the work triangle (Fig. 7-58).
15. Lapboard heights are 26″ (660 mm) (Fig. 7-59).
16. Working heights for counters are 36″ (915 mm) (Fig. 7-60).
17. Working heights for tables are usually 30″ (760 mm).
18. The combination of base cabinets, wall cabinets, and appliances provides a consistent standard unit without gaps or awkward depressions or extensions.

167

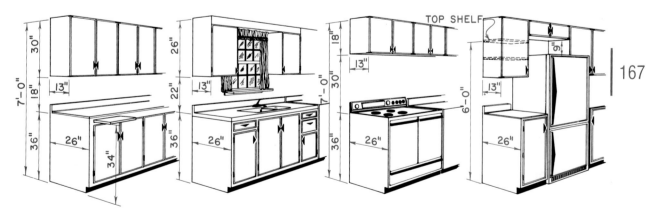

Fig. 7-60. Heights of kitchen cabinets.

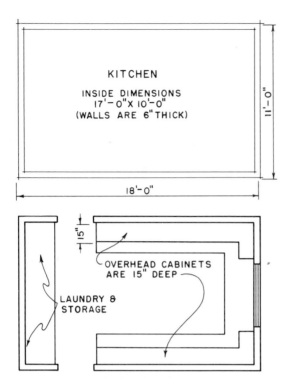

KITCHEN

INSIDE DIMENSIONS
17'-0" X 10'-0"
(WALLS ARE 6" THICK)

11'-0"

18'-0"

15"

OVERHEAD CABINETS
ARE 15" DEEP

LAUNDRY &
STORAGE

Fig. 7-61. Steps in drawing kitchen plans.

19. In planning and drawing kitchen floor plans, use template planning techniques and procedures. However, once basic dimensions are established or if room dimensions are predetermined, follow the steps outlined in Fig. 7-61 in drawing a kitchen floor plan.

THE UTILITY ROOM

The utility room may include facilities for washing, drying, ironing, sewing, and storing household cleaning equipment. It may contain heating and air-conditioning equipment or even a pantry for storing foods. Other names for this room are service room, all-purpose room, and laundry room (Fig. 7-62).

168

If the utility room is used for heating and air conditioning, space must be planned for the furnace, heating, and air-conditioning ducts, hot-water heater, and any related equipment such as humidifiers or air purifiers.

Shape and Size

The shapes and sizes of utility rooms differ, as shown in Figs. 7-63 and 7-64. The average floor

Fig. 7-62. Washing and drying are the two basic functions of a utility room. *Frigidaire*

VERY SMALL
70 SQUARE FEET

SMALL
90 SQUARE FEET

AVERAGE
100 SQUARE FEET

LARGE
120 SQUARE FEET

Fig. 7-63. Size of the utility room varies according to the budget and needs of the occupant.

space required for appliances, counter, and storage area is 108 ft^2 (10 m^2). However, the size may vary according to the budget or needs of the household.

Style and Decor

Style and decor in a utility room depend on the function of the appliances, which are themselves

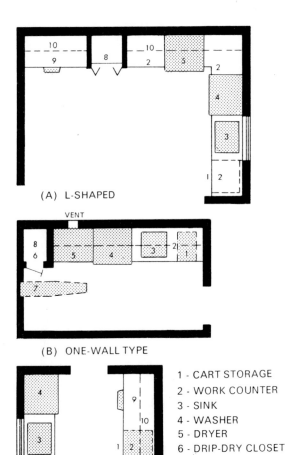

(A) L-SHAPED

VENT

(B) ONE-WALL TYPE

1 - CART STORAGE
2 - WORK COUNTER
3 - SINK
4 - WASHER
5 - DRYER
6 - DRIP-DRY CLOSET
7 - IRONING BOARD
8 - LINEN CLOSET
9 - SEWING CENTER
10 - STORAGE

(C) CORRIDOR TYPE

Fig. 7-64. Types of laundry arrangements.

An important part of the decor is the color of the paint used for walls and cabinet finishes. Colors should harmonize with the colors used on the appliances. All finishes should be washable. The walls may be lined with sound-absorbing tiles or wood paneling.

The lighting in a utility room should be carefully planned so that it will be 48″ (1220 mm) above the equipment used for washing, ironing, and sewing (Fig. 7-65). However, the lighting fixtures placed above the preparation area and laundry sinks can be further from the work-top area.

The Laundry Area

The laundry area is only one part of the utility room, but it is usually the most important center. To make laundry work as easy as possible, the appliances and working spaces in a laundry area should be located in the order in which they will be used. Such an arrangement will save time and effort. There are four steps in the process of laundering. The equipment needed for each of these steps should be grouped so that the person doing the laundry can proceed from one stage to the next in an orderly and efficient way (Fig. 7-66).

Receiving and Preparing Laundry

The first step in laundering—receiving and preparing the items—requires hampers or bins, as well as counters on which to collect and sort the articles. Near this equipment there should be storage facilities for laundry products such as detergents, bleaches, and stain removers.

Washing

The next step, the actual washing, takes place in the area containing the washing machine and laundry tubs or sink.

an important factor in the appearance of the room. Simplicity, straight lines, and continuous counter spaces produce an orderly effect and permit work to progress easily. Such features also make the room easy to clean.

169

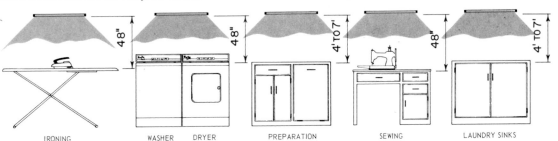

IRONING   WASHER   DRYER   PREPARATION   SEWING   LAUNDRY SINKS

Fig. 7-65. Utility-room lighting.

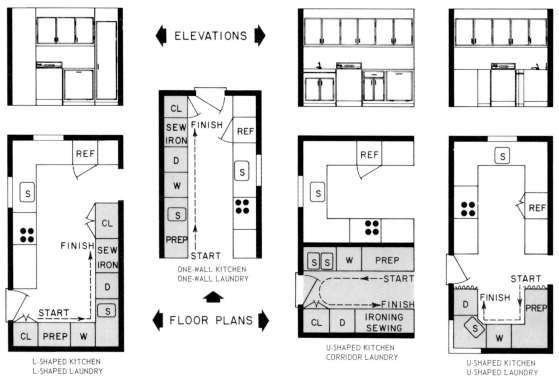

ELEVATIONS

FLOOR PLANS

ONE-WALL KITCHEN
ONE-WALL LAUNDRY

L-SHAPED KITCHEN
L-SHAPED LAUNDRY

U-SHAPED KITCHEN
CORRIDOR LAUNDRY

U-SHAPED KITCHEN
U-SHAPED LAUNDRY

Fig. 7-66. Appliances and work spaces should be arranged in the order in which they are used.

Fig. 7-67. Compact laundry center combines a cabinet, a shoulder-high dryer, and an automatic washer. *Frigidaire*

Drying
The equipment needed for this stage of the work includes a dryer, indoor drying lines, and space to store clothespins. Figure 7-67 shows a compact but complete washing and drying center.

Ironing and Storage
For the last part of the process, the required equipment consists of an iron and a board or an automatic ironer, a counter for sprinkling and folding, a rack on which to hang finished ironing, and facilities for sewing and mending. If a sewing machine is included, it may be portable, or it may fold into a counter or wall.

Location

Separate Laundry Area
The location of the laundry area in a utility room is desirable because all laundry functions, including repairs, are centered in one place. A further advantage of the separate room is that laundering is kept well apart from the preparation of foods.

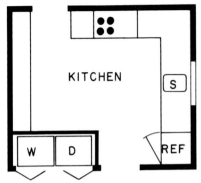

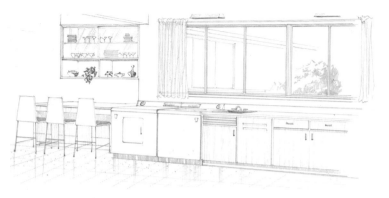

Fig. 7-68. Laundry located adjacent to the kitchen.

Fig. 7-69. Laundry area in a family room. *Westinghouse*

Space is not always available for a utility room, however, the laundry appliances and space for washing and drying may need to be located in some other area. Wherever it is placed, the equipment in the laundry unit should be arranged in the order in which the work must be done.

The Kitchen

Placing the laundry unit in or near the kitchen as shown in Fig. 7-68 has some advantages. The unit is in a central location and is near a service entrance. In Fig. 7-69 the laundry is located adjacent to the kitchen and family room. Plumbing facilities are near. The sink may be used as a laundry tub, and the drainboards may be used as counters for sprinkling and folding.

Other Locations

Laundry appliances may be located in a closet (Fig. 7-70), on a service porch, in a basement, or in a garage or carport. The service porch, basement, garage or carport provides less expensive floor space than other parts of the house. Even bedrooms are sometimes used, as shown in Fig. 7-71. The advantage to this arrangement is the elimination of transportation of soiled clothing to another area. The disadvantage is the noise and humidity caused by the operation of the washer and dryer. This problem, however, can be overcome by operating the units when the bedroom is not normally occupied.

Garages and Carports

Storage of the automobile occupies a large percentage of the available space of the house or property. Garages and carports must therefore be

Fig. 7-70. Laundry facilities located in a closet. *General Electric*

Fig. 7-71. Concealed bedroom laundry area. *Maytag Company*

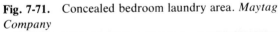

Fig. 7-72. An attached carport. *Home Planners, Inc.*

Fig. 7-73. Garage style must be integrated with the house style. *Home Planners, Inc.*

designed with the greatest care to ensure maximum utilization of space.

Garage

A *garage* is a structure designed primarily to shelter an automobile. It may be used for many secondary purposes such as a workshop or for storage space. A garage may be connected with the house (integral) or it may be a separate building.

Carport

A *carport* is a garage with one or more of the exterior walls removed. It may consist of a freestanding roof completely separate from the

Fig. 7-74. An integrated breezeway.

house, or it may be built against the existing walls of the house (Fig. 7-72.) Carports are most acceptable in mild climates where complete protection from cold weather is not needed. A carport offers protection primarily from sun and precipitation.

The garage and the carport both have distinct advantages. The garage is more secure and provides more shelter. However, carports lend themselves to open-planning techniques and are less expensive than garages.

Design

The lines of the garage or carport should be consistent with the major building lines of the house. The style of the garage should be consistent with the style of architecture used in the house (Fig. 7-73).

The garage or carport must never appear as an afterthought. Often a patio, porch, or breezeway is planned between the garage and the house to integrate a detached garage with the house (Fig. 7-74). A covered walkway from the garage or carport to the house should be provided if the garage is detached.

The garage floor must be solid and easily maintained. A concrete slab 3″ or 4″ (76 or 102 mm) thick provides the best floor for a garage or carport. The garage floor must have adequate drainage either to the outside or through drains located inside the garage. A vapor barrier consisting of waterproof materials under the slab should be provided. The driveway should be of asphalt or concrete construction, preferably with welded-wire fabric to maintain rigidity.

The design of the garage door greatly affects the appearance of the garage. Several types of garage doors are available. These include the

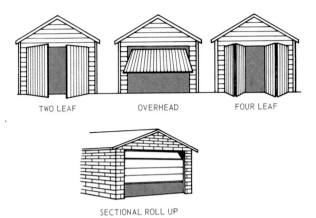

TWO LEAF   OVERHEAD   FOUR LEAF

SECTIONAL ROLL UP

Fig. 7-75. Common types of garage doors.

two-leaf swinging, overhead, four-leaf swinging, and sectional roll-up doors (Fig. 7-75). Several electronic devices are available for opening the door of the garage for the car.

Size

The size and number of automobiles and the additional facilities needed for storage or work-shop use should determine the size of the garage (Fig. 7-76).

The dimensions of a single-car garage range between 11' × 19' (3.4 × 5.8 m) and 13' × 25' (4.0 × 7.6 m). A 16' × 25' (4.9 × 7.6 m) garage is more desirable if space is needed for benches, mowers, tools, and the storage of children's vehicles. A full double garage is 25' × 25' (7.6 × 7.6 m).

A two-car garage does not cost twice as much as a one-car garage. However, if the second half is added at a later date, the cost will more than double.

Storage

Storage is often an additional function of most garages. The storage space over the hood of the car should be utilized effectively (Fig. 7-77A). Cabinets should be elevated from the floor several inches to eliminate moisture and to facilitate cleaning the garage floor. Garden-tool cabinets can be designed to open from the outside of the garage (Fig. 7-77B).

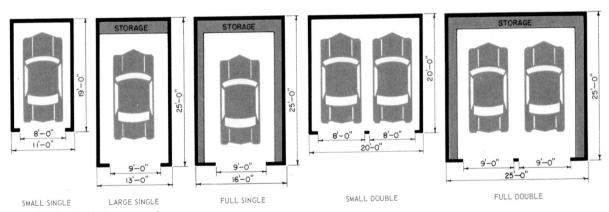

SMALL SINGLE   LARGE SINGLE   FULL SINGLE   SMALL DOUBLE   FULL DOUBLE

Fig. 7-76. Typical garage sizes.

173

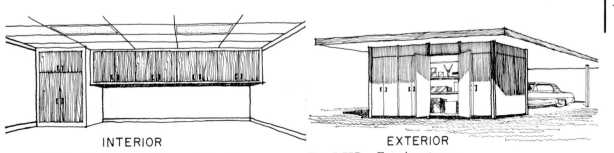

INTERIOR

Fig. 7-77 A. Storage over the car's hood.

EXTERIOR

Fig. 7-77B. Exterior storage.

Fig. 7-78. The home work area is used for a variety of activities. *Lisanti*

HOME WORK AREA

The home work area is designed for activities ranging from hobbies to home-maintenance work (Fig. 7-78). The home work area may be located in part of the garage, in the basement, in a separate room, or in an adjacent building (Fig. 7-79).

Layout

Power tools, hand tools, workbench space, and storage should be systematically planned. A workbench complete with vise is needed in every home work area. The average workbench is 36″ (915 mm) high. A movable workbench is appropriate when large projects are to be constructed. A peninsula workbench provides three working sides and storage compartments on three sides. A drop-leaf workbench is excellent for work areas where a minimum amount of space is available.

Hand Tools

Some hand tools are basic to all types of hobbies or home-maintenance work. These basic tools

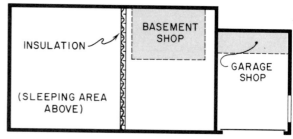

Fig. 7-79. The home workshop may be located in the garage, basement, or in a separate building.

include a claw hammer, carpenter's square, files, hand drills, screwdrivers, planes, pliers, chisels, scales, wrenches, saws, a brace and bit, mallets, and clamps.

Power Tools

Although power tools are not absolutely necessary for the performance of most home workshop activities, they do make the performance of many tasks easier and quicker. Some of the more common power tools used in home workshops include electric drills, jigsaws, routers, band saws, circular saws, radial-arm saws, jointers, belt sanders, lathes, and drill presses. Placement of equipment should be planned to provide the maximum amount of work space. Figure 7-80 suggests clearances necessary for safe and efficient machine operation.

174

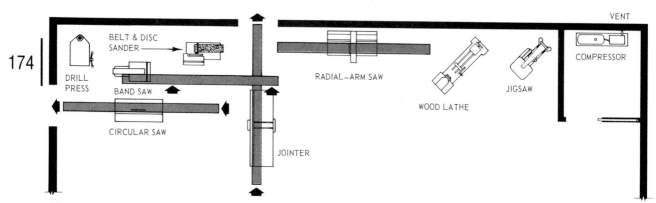

Fig. 7-80. Machinery must be spaced for proper clearance.

Fig. 7-81. Facilities must be planned for storing tools. *Better Homes and Gardens*

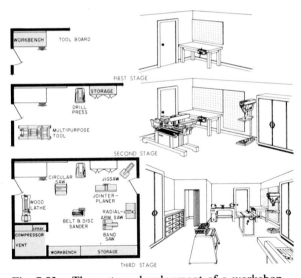

Fig. 7-82. Three-stage development of a workshop.

Storage Facilities

Maximum storage facilities in the home work area are essential. Hand tools may be stored in cabinets which keep them dust-free and safe or hung on perforated hardboard, as shown in Fig. 7-81. Tools too small to be hung should be kept in special-purpose drawers, and any inflammable finishing material, such as turpentine or oil paint, should be stored in metal cabinets.

Size and Shape

The size of the work area depends on the size and number of power tools and equipment, the amount of workbench area, and the amount of tool and material storage facilities provided. The size of the work area should be planned for maximum expansion, even though only a workbench or a few tools may be available when the area is first occupied. Therefore, space for the maximum amount of facilities should be planned and located when the area is designed. As new equipment is added, it will fit appropriately into the basic plan (Fig. 7-82).

The designer must anticipate the type and number of materials requiring storage and design the storage space accordingly.

Decor

The work area should be as maintenance-free as possible. Glossy paint or tile retards an accumulation of shop dust on the walls. Exhaust fans eliminate much of the dust and the gasses produced in the shop. The shop floor should be of concrete or linoleum for easy maintenance. Abrasive strips around machines will eliminate the possibility of slipping. Do not locate noisy equipment near the children's sleeping area. Interior walls and ceilings should be soundproofed by offsetting studs and adding adequate insulation to produce a sound barrier.

Light and color are most important factors in designing the work area. Pastel colors, which reduce eye strain, should be used for the general color scheme of the shop. Extremely light colors that produce glare, and extremely dark colors that reduce effective illumination, should be avoided. Adopting one of the major paint manufacturers' color systems for color coding will help to create a pleasant atmosphere in the shop and will also help to provide the most efficient and safest working conditions.

General lighting should be provided in the shop to a level of 100 fc (footcandles) [1076 lux (lx)] on machines and worktable tops.

STORAGE

Storage areas should be provided for general storage and for specific storage within each room

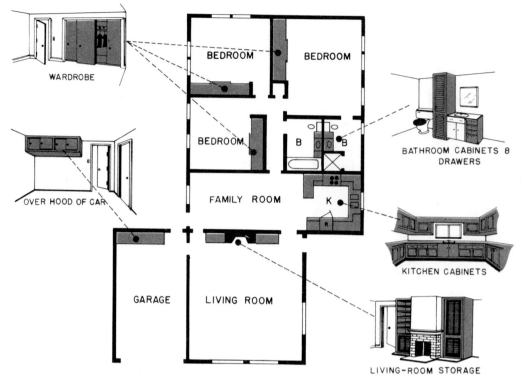

Fig. 7-83. Location of common storage areas.

(Fig 7-83). Areas that would otherwise be considered wasted space should be used as general storage areas. Parts of the basement, attic, or garage often fall into this category (Fig. 7-84). Effective storage planning is necessary to provide storage facilities within each room that will create the least amount of inconvenience in securing the stored articles. Articles that are used daily or weekly should be stored in or near the room where they will be used. Articles that are used only seasonally should be placed in more permanent general storage areas.

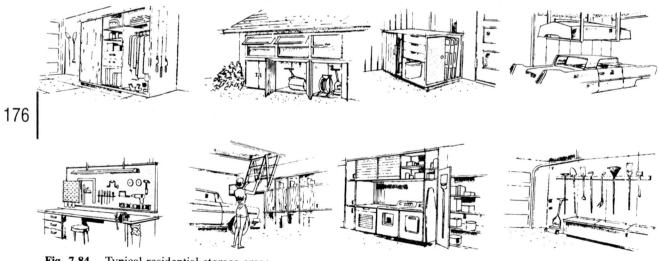

176

Fig. 7-84. Typical residential storage areas.

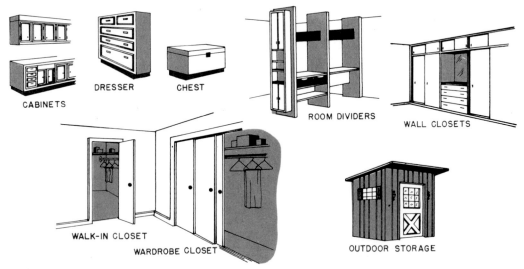

Fig. 7-85. Types of storage facilities.

Storage Facilities

Storage facilities, equipment, and furniture used for storage within the various rooms of the house are divided into the following categories (Fig 7-85):

Wardrobe Closets

A *wardrobe closet* is a shallow clothes closet built into the wall. The minimum depth for the wardrobe is 24″ (610 mm). If this closet is more than 30″ (760 mm) deep, you will be unable to reach the back of the closet. Swinging or sliding doors should expose all parts of the closet to your reach. A disadvantage of the wardrobe closet is the amount of wall space needed for the doors (Fig 7-86).

Walk-in Closets

Walk-in closets are closets large enough to walk into. The area needed for this type of closet is an area equal to the amount of space needed to hang clothes plus enough space to walk and turn. Although some area is wasted in the passage, the use of the walk-in closet does provide more wall area for furniture placement, since only one door is needed (Fig. 7-87).

Fig. 7-86. Wardrobe closet dimensions.

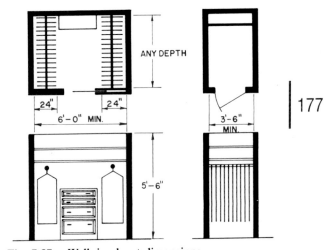

Fig. 7-87. Walk-in closet dimensions.

177

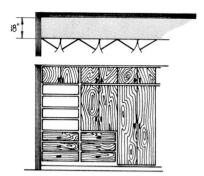

Fig. 7-88. Wall storage uses a minimum of floor space.

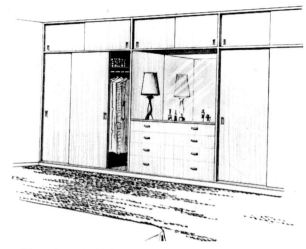

Fig. 7-89. Built-in closets and drawer storage. *Home Planners, Inc.*

Wall Closets

A *wall closet* is a shallow closet in the wall holding cupboards, shelves, and drawers. Wall closets are normally 18″ (460 mm) deep, since this size provides access to all stored items without using an excessive amount of floor area (Fig. 7-88). Figure 7-89 shows an example of wall storage with wardrobe closets on each side.

Protruding closets that create an offset in a room should be avoided. Often by filling the entire wall between two bedrooms with closet space it is possible to design a square or rectangular room without the use of offsets (Fig. 7-90). Doors on closets should be sufficiently wide to allow easy accessibility. Swing-out doors have the advantage of providing extra storage space on the back of the door. However, space must be allowed for the swing. For this reason, sliding doors are usually preferred. All closets, except very shallow linen closets, should be provided with lighting.

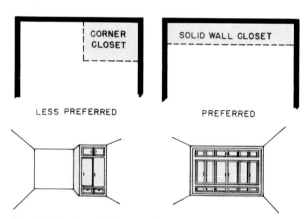

Fig. 7-90. Avoid closets that create offsets.

Chests and Dressers

Chests and dressers are freestanding pieces of furniture used for storage, generally in the bedroom. They are available in a variety of sizes, usually with shelves and drawers.

Room Dividers

A room divider often doubles as a storage area, especially when a protruding closet divides several areas. Room dividers often extend from the floor to the ceiling or may only be several feet high. Many room dividers include shelves and drawers that open from both sides (Fig. 7-91).

Location

Different types of storage facilities are necessary for areas of the home, depending on the type of

Fig. 7-91. Room dividers can double as storage area. *Home Planners, Inc.*

Fig. 7-92. Living area built-in wall cabinets.

Fig. 7-94. Family room storage. *Home Planners, Inc.*

article to be stored. The most appropriate types of storage facilities for each room in the house are as follows:

> *Living room:* room divider, built-in wall cabinets (Fig. 7-92), bookcases, window seats
>
> *Dining area:* room divider, built-in wall closet (Fig. 7-93)
>
> *Family room:* built-in wall storage, window seats
>
> *Recreation room:* built-in wall storage (Fig. 7-94)
>
> *Porches:* under porch stairs, walk-in closet
>
> *Patios:* sides of barbecue, separate building
>
> *Outside:* closets built into the side of the house
>
> *Halls:* solid built-in wall closets, ends of blind halls (Fig. 7-95)
>
> *Entrance:* room divider, wardrobe, walk-in closet
>
> *Den:* built-in wall closet, window seats, bookcases
>
> *Kitchen:* wall and floor cabinets, room divider, wall closets (Fig. 7-96)

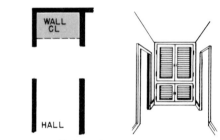

Fig. 7-95. Built-in hall storage.

179

Fig. 7-96. Effective kitchen storage facilities. *Abbott Hall*

Fig. 7-93. Dining room storage facilities.

Fig. 7-97. Bedroom built-in storage. *Home Planners, Inc.*

Utility room: cabinets on floor and walls

Garage: cabinets over hood of car, wall closets along sides, added construction on the outside of the garage

Work area: open tool board, wall closets, cabinets

Bedroom: walk-in closet, wardrobe closet, under bed, foot of bed, head of bed, built-in cabinets and shelves, dressers, chests (Fig. 7-97)

Bathroom: cabinets on floor and ceiling, room dividers

Review Questions

1. Define the following terms: work triangle, U-shape, peninsula, L-shape, island.
2. Complete the workbook exercises for Unit 7.
3. For your scrapbook, find examples of each type of kitchen found in this unit.
4. Sketch a floor plan of a kitchen of your own design.
5. Sketch the floor plan of a kitchen shown in Fig. 7-1.
6. Sketch two elevation drawings of the two walls of the kitchen shown in Fig. 7-3.
7. Redesign the kitchen shown in Fig. 7-16 to include a laundry area.
9. Sketch a complete laundry of your own design.
10. Sketch a two-car garage plan to show the following storage facilities: storage wall, outside storage, laundry area, gardening equipment, storage over hood of car.
11. Design a home work area in a double-car garage.
12. Add additional storage facilities to the floor plan shown in Fig. 2-25.
13. Enlarge the kitchen shown in Fig. 7-17A and convert it into a family kitchen.

SLEEPING AREA

unit **8**

One-third of our time is spent in sleeping. Because of its importance, the sleeping area
should be planned to provide facilities for maximum comfort and relaxation. The sleeping area
is usually located in a quiet part of the house
and contains bedrooms, baths, dressing areas,
and nurseries.

Fig. 8-1. Master-bedroom suite. *Scholz Homes, Inc.*

BEDROOMS

Houses are usually classified by size according
to the number of bedrooms; for example, a three-
bedroom home, or a four-bedroom home. In a
home there are bedrooms, master bedrooms, and
nursery rooms, according to the size of the family.

Function

The primary function of a bedroom is to provide
facilities for sleeping. Some bedrooms may also
provide facilities for writing, reading, sewing,
listening to music, or generally relaxing. Figure
8-1 shows a master bedroom with adjacent bath.

Number of Bedrooms

Ideally, each occupant should have his or her
own private bedroom. A family with no children
may require only one bedroom. However, two
bedrooms are usually desirable, in order to pro-

181

Fig. 8-2. Minimum bedroom furniture. *Filbar*

Fig. 8-3. Complete bedroom components. *Filbar*

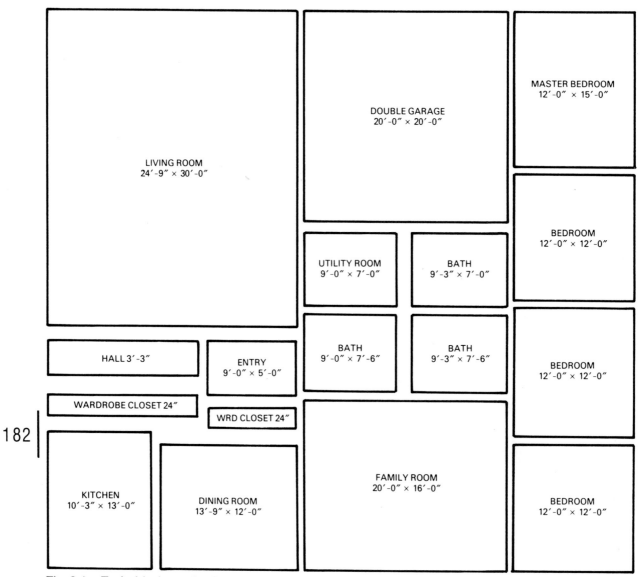

LIVING ROOM
24'-9" × 30'-0"

DOUBLE GARAGE
20'-0" × 20'-0"

MASTER BEDROOM
12'-0" × 15'-0"

BEDROOM
12'-0" × 12'-0"

UTILITY ROOM
9'-0" × 7'-0"

BATH
9'-3" × 7'-0"

HALL 3'-3"

ENTRY
9'-0" × 5'-0"

BATH
9'-0" × 7'-6"

BATH
9'-3" × 7'-6"

BEDROOM
12'-0" × 12'-0"

WARDROBE CLOSET 24"

WRD CLOSET 24"

182

KITCHEN
10'-3" × 13'-0"

DINING ROOM
13'-9" × 12'-0"

FAMILY ROOM
20'-0" × 16'-0"

BEDROOM
12'-0" × 12'-0"

Fig. 8-4. Typical bedroom furniture sizes.

vide one for guest use (Fig. 8-1). Three-bedroom homes are most popular because they provide a minimum of accommodation for a family with one boy and one girl. As a family enlarges, boys can share one bedroom and girls can share the other. With only two bedrooms, this is not possible.

Sizes and Shapes

The size and shape of a bedroom depend upon the amount of furniture needed. A minimum-sized bedroom (Fig. 8-2) would accommodate a single bed, bedside table, and dresser. In contrast, a complete bedroom (Fig. 8-3) might include a double bed or twin beds, bedside stands, dresser, chest of drawers, lounge chair, dressing area, and adjacent master bath.

Space Requirements

The type and style of furniture included in the bedroom should be chosen before the size of the bedroom is established. The size of the furniture should determine the size of the room, not the reverse. Although, if room sizes are fixed, the selection process is reversed. Average bedroom furniture sizes are shown in Fig. 8-4. Since the bed is the largest item in the bedroom, furniture sizes (Fig. 8-5), and spacing (Fig. 8-6), are extremely critical. Figure 8-7 shows different shapes of beds.

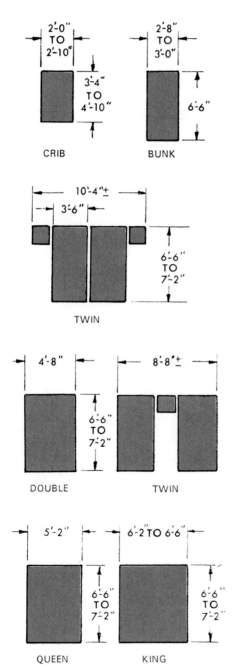

Fig. 8-5. Bed sizes.

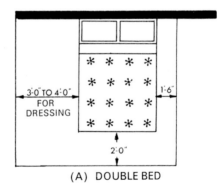

(A) DOUBLE BED

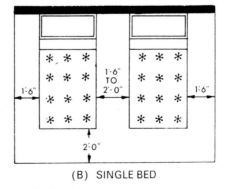

(B) SINGLE BED

Fig. 8-6. Bed spacing.

183

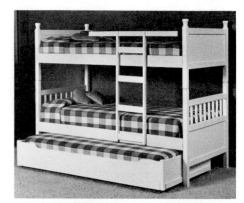

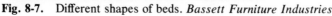

Fig. 8-7. Different shapes of beds. *Bassett Furniture Industries*

The wall space needed for twin beds is 8'-6" (2.6 m). A full bed with a nightstand requires 6' (1.8 m) of wall space.

A small bedroom would average from 90 to 100 ft² (8.36 to 9.29 m²), an average bedroom from 100 to 150 ft² (9.29 to 13.9 m²), and a large bedroom over 200 ft² (18.6 m⁶). Since wall space is critical in the placement of furniture in the bedroom, the designer must plan for maximum wall space. One method of conserving wall space

for bedroom furniture placement is by using high windows. High, shallow windows allow furniture to be placed underneath, and they also provide some privacy for the bedroom.

Dressing Areas

Dressing areas are sometimes separate rooms or an alcove or a part of the room separated by a

Fig. 8-8. Master-bedroom dressing area. *Crane Company*

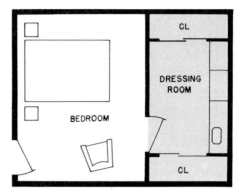

Fig. 8-9. Dressing-area floor plan.

divider. Figure 8-8 shows a typical dressing room–master bedroom relationship and Fig. 8-9 shows a common floor-plan arrangement.

Bedroom Doors

Unless it has doors leading to a patio, the bedroom will normally have only one access door from the inside. Entrance doors, closet doors, and windows should be grouped to conserve wall space whenever possible. Separating these doors slightly will spread out the amount of unusable wall space by eliminating long stretches of unused wall space. Sliding doors for closets and for entrance doors help to conserve valuable wall space in bedrooms. If swinging doors are used, the door should always swing into the bedroom and not into the hall (Fig. 8-10).

Noise Control

Since noise contributes to fatigue, it is important to plan for the elimination of as much noise as possible from the bedroom area (Fig. 8-11A). The following guides for noise control will help you design bedrooms that are quiet and restful:

1. The bedroom should be in the quiet part of the house, away from major street noises and away from the living area, as shown in Fig. 8-11B.
2. Carpeting or soft-cork wall panels helps to absorb many noises.
3. Rooms above a bedroom should be carpeted.
4. Floor-to-ceiling draperies help to reduce noise.

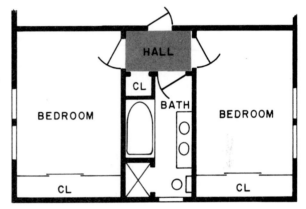

Fig. 8-10. Bedroom doors should not open into halls.

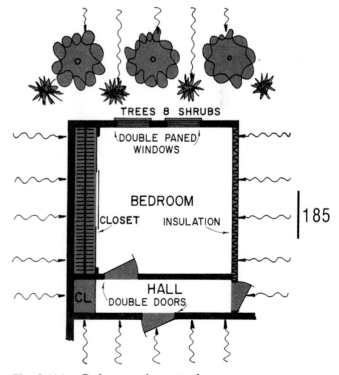

185

Fig. 8-11A. Bedroom noise control.

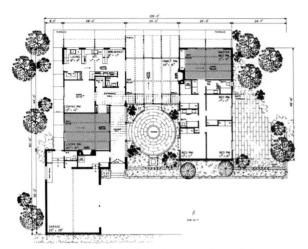

Fig. 8-11*B*. Bedroom location away from living area. *Home Planners, Inc.*

5. Acoustical tile in the ceiling is effective in reducing noise.
6. Trees and shrubbery outside the bedroom help deaden sounds.
7. The use of insulating glass in windows and sliding doors helps to seal off the bedroom.
8. The windows of an air-conditioned room should be kept closed during hot weather. Air conditioning eliminates much noise and aids in keeping the bedroom free from dust and pollen.
9. Air is a good insulator; therefore, closets provide additional buffers which eliminate much noise coming from other rooms.
10. In extreme cases when complete soundproofing is desired, fibrous materials in the walls may be used, and studs may be offset to provide a sound buffer.
11. Placing rubber pads under appliances such as refrigerators, dishwashers, washers, and dryers often eliminates much vibration and noise throughout the house.

186 | Storage Space

Storage space in the bedroom is needed primarily for clothing and personal accessories. Storage areas should be easy to reach, easy to maintain, and large. Walk-in closets or wardrobe closets should be built in for hanging clothes (Fig. 8-12). Care should be taken to eliminate offset closets. Balancing offset closets from one room to an adjacent bedroom helps solve this problem. Providing built-in storage facilities also helps in overcoming awkward offsets, as shown in Fig.

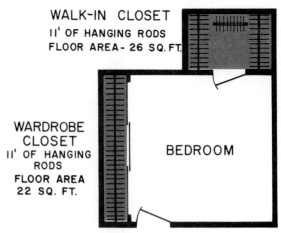

Fig. 8-12. Walk-in and wardrobe closets.

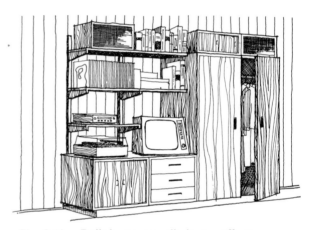

Fig. 8-13. Built-in storage eliminates offsets.

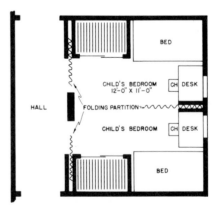

Fig. 8-14. Convertible double bedroom.

8-13. Except for the storage space provided in dressers, chests, vanities, and dressing tables, most storage space should be provided in the closet. Double rooms (Fig. 8-14) allow for maximum storage, yet provide flexibility and privacy as the family expands.

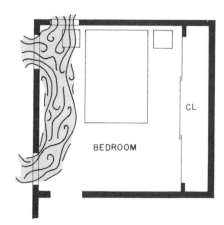

Fig. 8-15. Cross ventilation should not pass over the bed.

Ventilation

Proper ventilation is necessary and is conducive to sound rest and sleep. Central air conditioning and humidity control provide constant levels of temperature and humidity and are an efficient method of providing ventilation and air circulation. When air conditioning is available, the windows and doors may remain closed. Without air conditioning, windows and doors must pro-

Fig. 8-16. A few changes convert this child's room into a teenager's bedroom. *Armstrong Cork Company*

Fig. 8-17. A child's room converted for teenager's use. *Armstrong Cork Company*

vide the ventilation. Bedrooms should have cross-ventilation. However, the draft must not pass over the bed (Fig. 8-15). High ribbon windows provide light, privacy, and cross-ventilation without causing a draft on the bed. Jalousie windows are also very effective, since they direct the air flow upward.

Nurseries

Children's bedrooms and nurseries need special facilities. They must be planned to be comfortable, quiet, and sufficiently flexible to change as the child grows and matures (Figs. 8-16 and 8-17). Storage shelves and rods in closets should be adjustable so that they may be raised as the child becomes taller. Light switches should be placed low, with a delay switch which allows the light to stay on for some time after the switch has been thrown.

Chalkboards and bulletin boards help make the child's room usable. Adequate facilities for study and some hobby activities should be provided, such as a desk and worktable. Storage space for books, models, and athletic equipment is also desirable.

Decor

Bedrooms should be decorated in quiet, restful tones. Matching or contrasting bedspreads, draperies, and carpets help accent the color scheme. Uncluttered furniture with simple lines also helps to develop a restful atmosphere in the bedroom.

BATHS

The design of the bathroom requires careful planning, as does every other room in the house. The bath must be planned to be functional, attractive, and easily maintained (Fig. 8-18).

Fig. 8-18. A functional, attractive, and easily maintained bath. *Armstrong Cork Company*

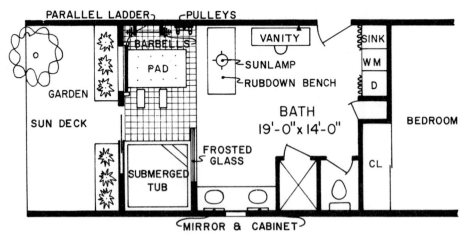

Fig. 8-19. A multifunctional bath.

Function

In addition to the normal functions of the bath, facilities may also be included for dressing, exercising, sunning, and laundering (Fig 8-19). Designing the bath involves the appropriate placing of fixtures; providing for adequate ventilation, lighting, and heating; and planning efficient runs for plumbing pipes.

Ideally it would be advisable to provide a bath for each bedroom, as in Fig. 8-20. Usually this provision is not possible, and a central bath is designed to meet the needs of the entire family (Fig. 8-21). A bath for general use and a bath adjacent to the master bedroom are a desirable compromise (Fig. 8-22). When it is impossible to have a bath with the master bedroom (Fig. 8-23), the general bath should be accessible from all bedrooms in the sleeping area. A bath may also function as a dressing room (Fig. 8-24). In this case, a combination bath and dressing room with

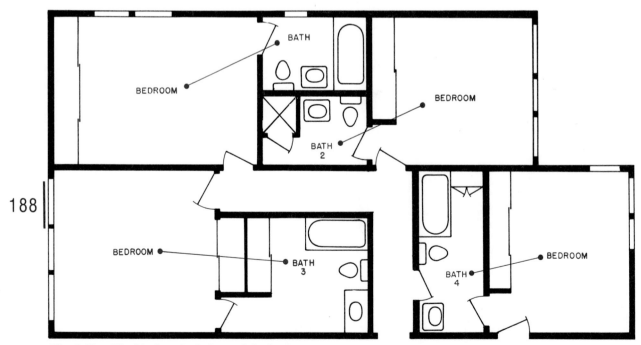

188

Fig. 8-20. The ideal—a bath for each bedroom.

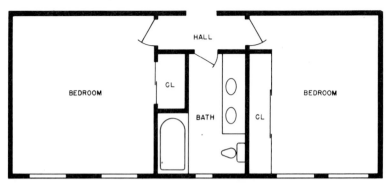

Fig. 8-21. Central bath serving several bedrooms.

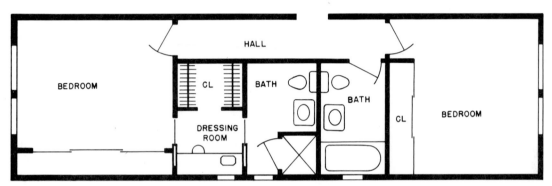

Fig. 8-22. A bath for the master bedroom and another bath for all other bedrooms is a convenient compromise.

Fig. 8-23. A master-bedroom bath. *Southern California Edison Company*

space for clothing storage can be placed between the bathroom and the bedroom.

Fixtures
The three basic fixtures included in most bathrooms are a lavatory, water closet, and tub or shower. The efficiency of the bath is greatly

189

Fig. 8-24. Bedroom with a compartment bath and dressing area.

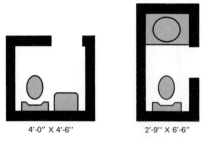

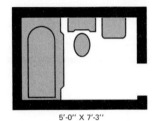

4'-0'' X 4'-6''   2'-9'' X 6'-6''

(A) AUXILIARY BATHROOMS

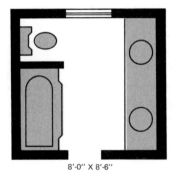

5'-0'' X 7'-3''

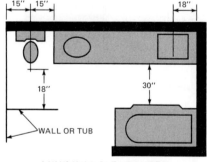

8'-0'' X 8'-6''

(B) MAIN BATHROOMS

BATHROOM LAYOUTS

15'' 15''   18''

18''   30''

WALL OR TUB

MINIMUM CLEARANCES
FOR BATHROOM FIXTURES

Fig. 8-25. Clearances for bathroom fixtures.

dependent upon the effectiveness of the arrangement of these three fixtures. Mirrors should be located a distance from the tub to prevent fogging. Sinks should be well lighted and free from traffic. If sinks are placed 18" (460 mm) from other fixtures, they need no separate plumbing lines.

Fig. 8-26. Skylights used for bath illumination. *Consoweld*

See Fig. 8-25 for fixture clearances. The water closet needs a minimum of 15" (380 mm) from the center to the side wall or other fixtures. Tubs and showers are available in a great variety of sizes and shapes. Square, rectangular, or sunken-pool tubs allow flexibility in fixture arrangement.

Ventilation

Baths should have either natural ventilation from a window or forced ventilation from an exhaust fan. Care should be taken to place windows in a position where they will not cause a draft on the tub or interfere with privacy.

Lighting

Lighting should be relatively shadowless in the area used for grooming. Shadowless general lighting can be achieved by the use of fluorescent tubes on the ceiling, covered with glass or plastic panels. Skylights as shown in Fig. 8-26, can also be used for general illumination if the bath is without outside walls.

Heating

Heating in the bath is most important to prevent chills. In addition to the conventional heating outlets, an electric heater or heat lamp is often used to provide instant heat. It is advisable to have the source of heat under the window to eliminate drafts. All gas heaters should be properly ventilated. All electric heaters should be properly grounded.

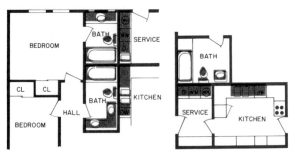

Fig. 8-27. Fixture arrangements that compact plumbing lines.

Plumbing Lines

The plumbing lines that carry water to and from the fixtures should be concealed and minimized as much as possible. When two bathrooms are placed side by side, placing the fixtures back to back on opposite sides of the plumbing wall results in a reduction of the length of plumbing lines (Fig. 8-27). In multiple-story dwellings, the length of plumbing lines can be reduced and a common plumbing wall used if the baths are placed directly above each other. When a bath is placed on a second floor, a plumbing wall must be provided through the first floor for the soil and water pipes.

Layout

There are two basic types of bathroom layout, the compartment and the open plan. In the *compartment plan,* partitions (sliding doors, glass dividers, louvers, or even plants) are used to divide the bath into several compartments, one housing the water closet, another the lavatory area, and the third the bathing area (Fig. 8-28). In the *open plan,* all bath fixtures are completely visible. A bath designed for, or used partially by, children should include a low or tilt-down mirror, benches for reaching the lavatory, low towel racks, and shelves for personal items and toys.

Size and Shape

The size and shape of the bath are influenced by the spacing of basic fixtures, the number of auxiliary functions requiring additional equipment, the arrangement or compartmentalization of areas, and the relationship to other rooms in the house.

Furniture

Typical fixture sizes, as shown in Fig. 8-29, greatly influence the ultimate size of the bath.

Fig. 8-28. A compartment bath. *Consoweld*

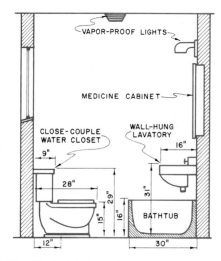

Fig. 8-29. Typical fixture sizes.

Fig. 8-30. Minimum-sized baths.

191

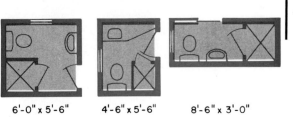

6'-0" x 5'-6"   4'-6" x 5'-6"   8'-6" x 3'-0"

Fig. 8-31. Small baths.

Figure 8-30 shows minimum-sized baths. Figure 8-31 shows small baths. Figure 8-32. shows av-

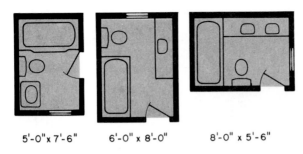

5'-0"x 7'-6"   6'-0" x 8'-0"   8'-0" x 5'-6"

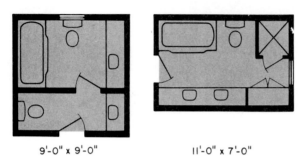

9'-0" x 9'-0"   11'-0" x 7'-0"

Fig. 8-33A. Large baths.

erage baths, and Fig. 8-33A shows large baths. Regardless of the size, these baths contain the three basic fixtures: lavatory, tub or shower, and water closet.

The sizes given here refer to complete baths and not to half-baths, which include only a lavatory and water closet. Half-baths are used in conjunction with the living area and therefore are not designed for bathing.

Accessories

In addition to the three basic fixtures, the following accessories are often included in a bath designed for optimum use:

> exhaust fan
> sunlamp
> heat lamp
> instant wall heater
> medicine cabinet
> extra mirrors
> magnifying mirror
> hot tub (Fig. 8-33B)
> extra counter space
> dressing table
> whirlpool bath
> foot-pedal control for water
> single-mixing, one-control faucets
> facility for linen storage
> clothes hamper
> bidet

Figure 8-34 shows a bath with many of these extra features.

Fig. 8-33B. Hot tub. *Georgia Pacific*

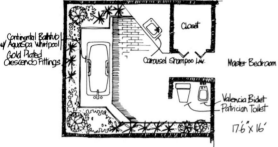

Fig. 8-34. A bath with many extra features. *Kohler*

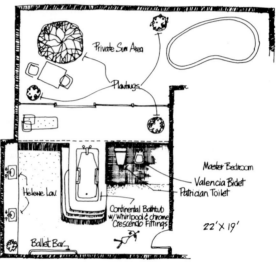

Fig. 8-36. A bath designed with unusual space relationships. (Top) *Photo by Hedrick-Blessing, reprinted with permission from Professional Builder, Feb. 1979.*

Fig. 8-35. Waterproof materials must be used in the bath. *Kohler*

Decor

The bath should be decorated and designed to provide the maximum amount of light and color. Materials used in the bath should be water-re-

sistant, easily maintained, and easily sanitized (Fig. 8-35). Tiles, linoleum, marble, plastic laminate, and glass are excellent materials for bathroom use. If wallpaper or wood paneling is used, it should be waterproof. If plastered or dry-wall construction is exposed, a gloss or semigloss paint should be used on the surface.

Fixtures and accessories should match in color. Fixtures are now available in a variety of colors. Matching countertops and cabinets are also available.

Baths need not be small boxes with plumbing fixtures. With new building materials and products, bathrooms can be designed in an infinite number of arrangements and decors, as shown in Fig. 8-36.

New materials and components are now available which enable the designer to plan bath-

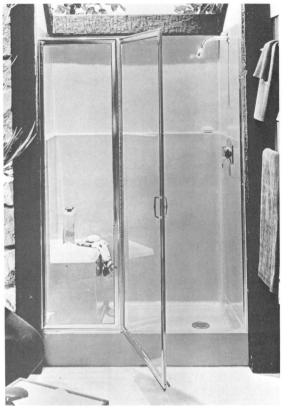

Fig. 8-37. Precast shower unit. *American Standard, Inc.*

rooms with modular units that range from one-piece molded showers and tubs, as shown in Fig. 8-37, to entire bath modules. In these units, plumbing and electrical wiring are connected after the unit is installed.

Today's bathroom need not be strictly functional and sterile in decor. Bathrooms can be planned and furnished in a variety of styles. Figures 8-38 to 8-43 show examples of a variety

Fig. 8-38. Roman decor. *American Standard, Inc.*

Fig. 8-39. Oriental decor. *American Standard, Inc.*

of bathroom decors and motifs. Figure 8-38 utilizes a Roman motif while Fig. 8-39 incorporates Oriental design influences to create the desired impression. In contrast, Fig. 8-40 uses open space and architectural impediments to create a classical decor. A rather unique "gay nineties" effect is achieved in Fig. 8-41 by the use of period fixtures, while Figs. 8-42 and 8-43 use a more modern approach with island placement of fixtures used to create an open feeling.

Fig. 8-40. Classical decor. *American Standard, Inc.*

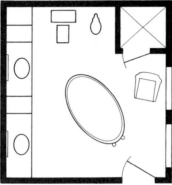

11'-0" x 11'-3"

Fig. 8-41. Gay nineties decor. *Kohler*

Fig. 8-42. Sink island arrangement. *American Standard, Inc.*

195

Review Questions

1. Define the following terms: alcove, cross-ventilation, acoustical tile, master suite, lavatory, compartmentalized.
2. Complete the problems in the workbook on pp. 51 and 52.
3. For your scrapbook, find examples of different master bedrooms with bath arrangements.
4. Design a master-bedroom suite of your own design.
5. Design a 120 ft² (11.15 m²) bedroom for a very young child to be converted in later years to a teenager's bedroom.
6. Design a master-bedroom suite in 200 ft² (18.6 m²).
7. Redesign the sleeping area in Fig. 8-24 to include an additional bedroom.

Fig. 8-43. Tub island arangement. *Kohler*

8. Design two bedrooms and a bath in an area of 13' × 34' (4 × 10 m).
9. Draw a remodeling plan for the sleeping area shown in Fig. 8-21. Add a bath to accompany bedroom #2.

SECTION THREE
SURFACE TREATMENTS

FABRICS

From the earliest days of recorded history, people have twisted plant and animal fibers into crude yarn for baskets, nets, and crude fabrics. The spinning of wool into yarn probably predated the use of cotton, flax, or silk as fabric raw material. In ancient India people spun yarn from cotton they called vegetable lamb and wove cloth from it even before the time of the Egyptians. For thousands of years flax was cultivated in Mesopotamia, Syria, and Egypt, and its fibers spun into yarn. In ancient China silk manufacture began some time between 2700 B.C. and 2640 B.C.

But regardless of the material used, the spinning process is applicable to all fibers today as it was in ancient times. Fibers, whether natural or manufactured, are cleaned, separated, and laid parallel. Then these loosely gathered strands are drawn out to the desired thickness and twisted into yarn.

Today fabrics are used to tie together many elements of interior design, and a wide variety is used in furniture, carpets, drapes, bed coverings, table coverings, and in tapestry. Thus it is possible to design an entire interior using nothing but fabrics as surface treatments.

198

Fabrics soften the look of a room and can be replaced more easily than another surface treatment. Fabrics are available in a wide variety of sizes and can be manipulated by folding, pleating, draping, or stretching. And they can be attached by stapling, nailing, gluing, or sewing. Thus the fibers of today are a most flexible resource for the interior designer. Consequently the interior designer must be acutely aware of the characteristics and common uses of modern fabrics.

FIBERS

There are two basic types of fibers: natural fibers and synthetic fibers. Each fiber possesses different characteristics such as absorbent qualities, strength, shrinkage resistance, temperature stability, flammability, and so forth. Consequently the use for which the fibers are designed must be considered in conjunction with their characteristics, as shown in Fig. 9-1.

Natural Fibers

Natural fibers are fibers that are derived from animal or vegetable sources. Animal sources such as camel, goat, and horse are used to produce fleece. Sheep are used to produce wool. Vegetable sources of fibers include corn, cotton, flax, hemp, and jute.

Wool is the oldest natural fiber known to humans. It is resilient, lustrous, warm, and soil-resistant. Wool yarn also holds color extremely well. The main disadvantage in using wool is that some unnatural stains require professional help for removal.

Cotton is the most popular natural vegetable fiber which can be processed into yarn at a fairly low cost. Since it is white, cotton can be dyed a complete range of colors with resulting excellent fastness. Cotton has a lower resistance to soiling than wool, and as a result requires more regular cleaning.

GROUP	GENERIC NAME	CHARACTERISTICS	COMMON USES
CELLULOSE	Rayon	Absorbent, dyes readily, moth resistant; special finishes will give properties of crease resistance and water repellency.	Used alone or in blends with natural or other synthetic fibers for all kinds of woven or knitted fabrics for all manner of apparel and household uses.
	Acetate	Adequate strength, moderate absorbency, drapes well, little or no shrinkage, moth resistant; can be solution-dyed; melts at high temperatures.	Used alone or in blends with natural or other synthetic fibers for all kinds of woven or knitted fabrics for all manner of apparel and household uses.
	Triacetate	Higher wet strength than regular acetate; withstands higher temperatures, dyes readily; resists shrinkage, moths, takes durable pleats.	Used alone or in blends with natural or other synthetic fibers for all kinds of woven or knitted fabrics for apparel and household uses.
CHEMICAL COMPOUNDS	Nylon	Superior strength and abrasion resistance. Lightweight and thermoplastic (can be heat-set for stretch or texture—fabrics for smooth finish resistance to shrinkage).	Most widely used synthetic fiber in fabrics for all kinds of apparel and household use; textured yarns in sweaters, stretch fabrics, carpets.
	Polyester	Shares strength, lightweight and abrasion resistance with other thermoplastic fibers. Resilient and versatile for blending with natural and other synthetic fibers.	Widely used in blends with natural fibers for all kinds of fabrics, particularly those given durable press finishes. Also used alone in apparel and household fabrics.
	Acrylic	Has great bulking power for soft, warm and lightweight fabrics; takes brilliant, fast colors.	Knits of all types, sweaters, half hose, dresses; also wool-like woven fabrics, deep pile fabrics and carpets.
	Modacrylic	Resilient and resistant to chemicals. Lightweight, soft and wrinkle resistant.	Mainly used in carpets, synthetic furs and chemically resistant work clothing.
	Olefin	Lightweight, strong and resilient. Resists sunlight and chemical deterioration.	Carpeting, sweaters, hosiery, knitting yarns, cordage and upholstery.
PROTEIN	Azion	Warm, resilient, soft; keeps whiteness, dyes readily.	Used mostly in blends with wool, sometimes with rayon.
POLYMER	Rubber	Will stretch to many times its original length. Damaged by light, heat and bleach.	Used mainly as the core around which yarns of other fibers are spun for foundation garments.
	Spandex	Exceptionally strong, durable, excellent restraining power, yet lightweight; high elasticity and recovery ability.	Foundation garments, swimsuit fabrics, support hosiery and all kinds of core-spun knits, stretch fabrics and apparel.
	Anidex	Elastic fiber with superior resistance to heat, sunlight and chemicals.	Used to provide stretch qualities for fabrics and apparel.

199

Fig. 9-1. Characteristics of fibers. *Canadian Textile Institute*

GROUP	GENERIC NAME	CHARACTERISTICS	COMMON USES
GLASS	Glass	Good tensile strength. Unaffected by moisture and sunlight. Non-inflammable.	Draperies, sheer curtains, and industrial fabrics.
METALLIC	Metallic	Non-tarnishable. Washable when protected by film. Can be produced in colors as well as silver, gold.	Decorative fabrics and trimmings; solid lamé or glitter effects added to other fabrics.

NATURAL FIBERS

GROUP	GENERIC NAME	CHARACTERISTICS	COMMON USES
VEGETABLE (CELLULOSE)	Cotton	Medium strong, durable, absorbent, easily dyed, excellent launderability. Wrinkles readily unless protected by finish; can be damaged by mildew.	Most widely used fiber alone or in blends with synthetic fibers for all types of apparel and household fabrics; all weights from sheet to heavy-duty.
	Linen	Same as cotton except has superior strength especially when wet; very absorbent.	Warm weather apparel; blends with other fibers; table linens.
ANIMAL (PROTEIN)	Wool and (other animal hair fibers) Angora, Alpaca, Camel, Cashmere, Mohair, Vicuna	Warmth, resilience, medium strength, absorbent, dyes readily, flame resistant, dries slowly, felts in hot water with agitation.	Suitings, coatings, dress fabrics, felts, sweaters, socks and other woven and knitted cloths of all weights; carpets, blankets, etc.
	Silk	Fine, strong fiber with lustrous finish, drapes well, absorbent, dyes readily; damaged by chlorine bleaches, perspiration and sunlight.	Fine fabrics, both woven and knitted for many types of apparel and household uses.

Fig. 9-1. (*Cont.*)

Synthetic or Manufactured Fibers

Most synthetic fibers are produced by chemical means involving extreme heat or pressure. The range of synthetic fibers available has mushroomed in recent years.

Cellulosic fibers are partly synthetic because they are produced from cellulose, a natural fiber substance derived from plants. Usually the cellulose is derived from spruce and other soft woods. Rayon, also partly synthetic, is composed of almost pure cellulose and is one of the most absorbent and versatile of all textile fibers, natural or synthetic. Other important cellulose fibers are acetate and triacetate.

Synthetic polymer fibers are called noncellulosic. Some of the most common of the noncellulosic fibers include acrylic, modacrylic, olefin, nylon, and polyester. The chemicals for the making of these fibers are derived from elements obtained from coal, air, water, limestone, petroleum, natural gas, and salt.

Other synthetic fibers are manufactured from glass and metallic elements.

FORMING FABRICS

Weaving is the most usual means used to interlace yarn upon a loom to make cloth. The warp yarns

200

are the yarns that are fixed and taut on the loom while the filling yarns are the yarns that run across the warp and are the action (moving) threads. There are three basic types of weaves:

PLAIN WEAVE

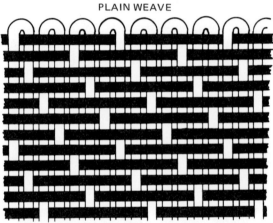

SATIN WEAVE

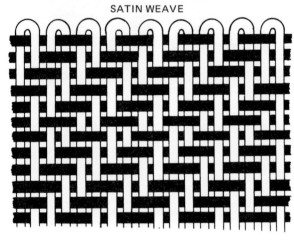

TWILL WEAVE

Fig. 9-2. Three basic types of weaves.

plain, satin, and *twill,* as shown in Fig. 9-2. *Plain weaves* are either basket, cord, rep rib, or tabby. *Twill weaves* are either broken, figure, herringbone, or regular.

Knitting is the second most used process of producing fabrics. One string of yarn can be used to form the entire fabric. By means of a series of loops, the yarn is hooked together. Knitting is the fastest-growing fabric-making method today and is likely to continue to be for some time.

Other fabrics are formed by a process called bonding. Short, loose fibers are placed together and heat and pressure applied to force the fibers together. Felt is an early example of a bonded fabric. For some uses, bonded nonwoven fabrics are superior to knit or woven fabrics. They have a greater porosity, better shape, high bulk, and non-raveling edges. For other uses they have less strength, are stiffer for handling, and poorer for draping.

Needle-punch fabrics are formed by a device with tiny hooked needles that punch, tangle, and intertwine a web of fiber to form a fabric that is becoming increasingly used for blankets.

Tufting is a process which began as a cottage industry in Georgia. Tufting is now popular for carpets and bedspreads, but new developments in machinery and fibers will expand the market for many uses.

One of the new textiles is a fabric called laminate. It consists of two fabrics or a fabric and a material like urethane foam that have been bonded together by use of heat or chemicals.

DESIGNER CATEGORIES

Fabrics must be chosen by the designer not only for their physical characteristics as they relate to use, heat, condensation, and so forth; but they must also be chosen on the basis of color and compatibility with the remainder of the decor. The following categories represent families which possess somewhat the same physical characteristics and can be used in similar decors depending on the exact color desired and environment situation.

Coarse, Simple Fabrics

Fabrics that possess a rough, strong beauty include burlap, chintz, linen, homespun, tweeds,

BURLAP CHINTZ LINEN HOMESPUN

TWEED SAILCLOTH NEEDLEPOINT SUEDECLOTH

Fig. 9-3. Coarse, simple fabrics. *Nettlecreek Industries*

sailcloth, needlepoint, or suede cloth. These fabrics can be dyed to brilliant colors (Fig. 9-3).

Greater Intricacy of Weave

Fabrics such as antique silk, silk taffeta, sateen, moiré, strie, and velveteen fit into the listing of weaves that are slightly more intricate than the above category and include pattern work especially suitable for traditional decors (Fig. 9-4).

Elaborate and Elegant Fabrics

Brocade, damask, matelassé, satin, cut velvet, and taffeta are the elaborate and elegant fabrics

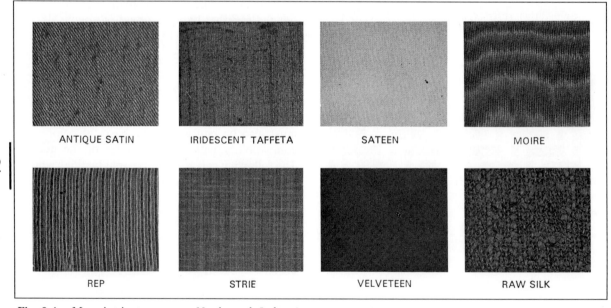

ANTIQUE SATIN IRIDESCENT TAFFETA SATEEN MOIRE

REP STRIE VELVETEEN RAW SILK

Fig. 9-4. More intricate weaves. *Nettlecreek Industries*

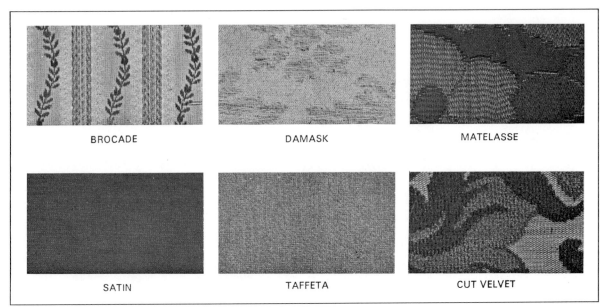

Fig. 9-5. Elaborate and elegant fabrics. *Nettlecreek Industries*

that are most often used in classical settings (Fig. 9-5).

Curtain Fabrics

These fabrics, which are also clothing fabrics, include casement cloth, marquisette, ninon, voile, batiste, and printed nylon (Fig. 9-6).

Canvas

Sturdy cotton canvas has the body and handling ease that make it an ideal decorator fabric for many interior uses. It can be draped loosely or lashed tautly to lightweight supporting structures. Its colors can be coordinated in solids and stripes, to blend subtly or contrast dramatically with any

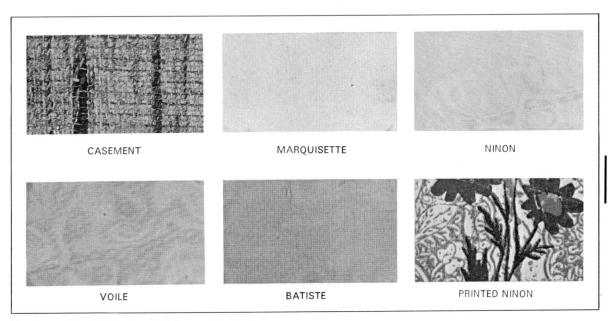

Fig. 9-6. Curtain fabrics. *Nettlecreek Industries*

Fig. 9-7. Interior canvas applications. *American Canvas Institute*

decor. Figure 9-7 shows the application of canvas to residential interior design.

Review Questions

1. Define the following terms: twill, bonded, tufted, laminate, weave, knit, natural.
2. Complete the exercises in the workbook on page 53.
3. For your scrapbook, collect and mount swatches of fabrics you would use for the following types of furnishings: early American, contemporary, French Provincial.
4. List fabrics you would select for an interior of your own design.
5. List the fabrics you would specify for the rooms shown in Fig. 6-2. Indicate where the fabrics would be used and indicate color.
6. Pick upholstery for the furniture shown in Figs. 5-16, 10-5, 10-6, and 10-8.
7. Indicate whether each of the following fabrics are natural or synthetic: cotton, acrylic, cellulose, flax, polyester, hemp, jute, nylon, wool.

FLOOR COVERINGS unit 10

Floors are one of the most difficult areas with which an interior designer must work. Floors must be capable of withstanding extremely heavy traffic and yet maintain an attractive and well-groomed appearance. Selecting floors that are attractive, practical, and economical both in the short run and in the long run requires a knowledge of the characteristics, advantages, and disadvantages of many different systems.

HARD-SURFACE FLOOR COVERINGS

The beautiful and varied patterns available in today's hard-surface floor coverings provide unlimited decorating possibilities. They are both practical and glamorous. You may choose a random plank design to harmonize with early American furnishings, or a pebble design which compliments open-beam ceilings, natural stone walls, and rustic furniture. Design and color of hard-surface floor coverings may set the mood for traditional, modern, Mediterranean, East Indian, Scandinavian, Western, or Pennsylvania Dutch decor. (See Fig. 10-1A.) The pattern of flooring also significantly affects the size and proportion appearance of a room, as shown in Fig. 10-1B.

Resilient Flooring

Luxury, practicality, convenience, and long wear are a few of the reasons resilient flooring continues to be a popular choice for high-traffic areas such as foyers, halls, kitchens, and laundries.

HARD-SURFACE FLOOR COVERINGS	
FLOORS	**CHARACTERISTICS**
WOOD	Hardwood (oak and maple); soft wood (white pine and fir). Rich natural beauty, durable.
LINOLEUM	Inlaid (printed through) or printed (surface print only). Comes in rolls, units and tiles in wide range of colors and patterns.
VINYL	Four types: Roto-print; Calendered; Vinyl Asbestos; Homogenous Tile. Very durable and resistant to grease, alkali, acid, abrasions. Non-porous.
ASPHALT	Color and design printed through. Damaged by grease and oil. Colors run when solvent products come in contact.
RUBBER	Comes in square or oblong tiles. Extra resilient, resistant to soil, and easy to maintain.
SEALED CORK	Resilient, muffles noise, warm in winter, cool in summer.
CERAMIC	Unglazed or glazed tile.
CONCRETE	Rough.
BRICK	Usually glazed.
SLATE	Rugged.
TERRAZZO	70% marble chips on concrete base.

Fig. 10-1A. Hard-surface floor covering characteristics. *Armstrong Cork Company*

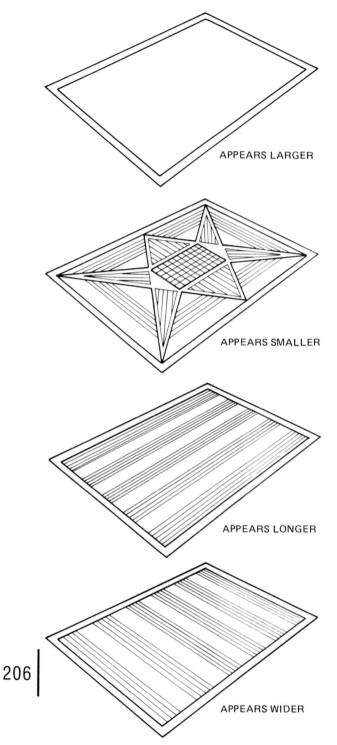

APPEARS LARGER

APPEARS SMALLER

APPEARS LONGER

206

APPEARS WIDER

Fig. 10-1 B. Hard-surface floor patterns.

For all its delicate beauty, today's resilient flooring is remarkably tough and resistant to wear. It's made to last for years with little care.

Resilient flooring is sanitary and easy to keep clean. Dusting or a quick once-over with a damp mop is the only regular maintenance required. Beyond this, an occasional washing and waxing will keep the floor bright and shiny for years. In addition, some recently developed floors don't need waxing. Considering its long service life, resilient flooring is an economical flooring material available for the home.

In the final analysis, it's current fashion that gives resilient floors their chief appeal. With the tremendous variety of materials, it's possible to create just about any floor scheme that the design dictates.

Sheet or Tile

Resilient floors are manufactured in two basic types: tiles (Fig. 10-2A) and sheet materials (Fig. 10-2B). Tiles are intended to be cemented in

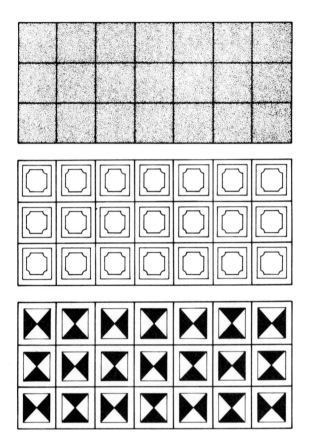

Fig. 10-3. Several available tile patterns.

place to serve as a permanent floor. Sheet materials are also intended to be cemented, but in some cases can be installed loosely like rugs. Tiles are generally available in nine- or twelve-inch (229 or 305 mm) squares and in a variety of patterns (Fig. 10-3); sheet materials are available in continuous rolls up to twelve-feet (3.7 m) wide.

Economical Floor Coverings
Economical floor coverings, materials which are loose-laid, are also available. These products are designed for areas where an attractive floor is desired, and are especially popular with persons living in rented housing or apartments, since they represent a modest cost investment and can be taken up if desired.

Selection
Selecting resilient flooring is first a matter of designating the proper type with respect to subfloor, traffic, and the type of installation desired. Once these factors are accounted for, color, pattern, and cost should then be considered.

It is best to approach the job on a room-by-room basis, since flooring requirements vary according to area. The right floor for a given room is the one that best satisfies the functional and decorative needs of the space.

Location and type of subfloor is the first consideration because, obviously, the material must be *installable*. Some resilient products cannot be used in basements or on concrete subfloors in direct contact with the ground. Still others cannot be used over existing resilient flooring, which necessitates removal of the old floor before a new installation can begin. Therefore, always determine subfloor condition before deciding on the type of floor you should install.

Once the subfloor problem has been solved, the next step is to determine the traffic load of the floor and the maintenance features desired. If the floor is subject to very heavy traffic and wear, you'll need a floor that will withstand considerable abuse. On the other hand, if the floor will not be subject to much foot traffic, then you can safely choose a material designed for moderate-to-light traffic.

Wear
It is very seldom that a properly installed and maintained resilient floor wears out. If replacement is necessary, it usually is to create a change in interior decor rather than to replace a worn-out floor.

This is not to say that all resilient floors wear the same. Products whose designs extend completely through the wear thickness can be expected to last longer than materials which rely solely on a surface effect.

Flooring Options
Having made the initial decision, the various options available in resilient flooring can now be considered.

A popular option in sheet flooring is cushioning. This feature produces a quiet, comfortable floor that is ideal for all home areas.

You also have a choice of widths. You can choose 6′ or 12′ (1.8 or 3.7 m) wide sheet materials; the wider products produce the fewest seams in the completed installation. In areas where surface moisture is likely to be a problem, the feature of seamlessness becomes especially important.

Fig. 10-4. Marble floors are moisture-resistant and extremely hard. *Armstrong Cork Company*

Fig. 10-5. Strip oak flooring. *Harris Manufacturing Company*

A popular option in vinyl-asbestos tile is the self-adhering capacity of some products. These tiles come with the adhesive already on the back of the tile and reduce flooring replacement to just simply peeling off the protective paper and fitting in place.

Cost

Cost is always a factor in any purchase, including a new resilient floor. However, in the case of flooring, selection should never be based on cost alone. The lowest-cost material does not necessarily represent the best flooring value any more than the highest-priced floor does. Your selection should, first and foremost, satisfy the functional requirements of the job as previously outlined and should satisfy personal taste, design, and color requirements.

The hard-surface flooring materials mentioned so far are classified as resilient. There are other smooth floors available.

Ceramic Tile, Brick, Slate

By using tiles with geometric or floral motifs, strikingly handsome durable floors can be achieved. Glazed ceramic tile is highly stain-resistant, but unglazed tile, brick, and slate must be sealed with special stain-resisting materials.

Marble and Terrazzo

These floors, as shown in Fig. 10-4, are durable, moisture-resistant, hard underfoot, and noisy.

Marble makes a handsome floor but is porous, making stain removal a problem. Terrazzo flooring consists of marble chips combined with cement and polished to a smooth finish. Because of its moisture resistance and ease of maintenance, it is popular in damp climates and in rooms designed for indoor-outdoor living.

Wood

Wood will always be one of the most popular hard floorings. Although oak is perhaps the most popular wood, over a hundred different kinds of wood are used for floors. Wood has natural beauty, durability, and resilience. It can be refinished repeatedly, if necessary, to restore its appearance. Wood flooring is available in strips, random-width planks, and parquet.

The random widths and walnut pegs of plank oak floors provide the authentic flavor of colonial decor. Modern floor manufacturing and finishing methods magnify oak's warm, mellow beauty, reduce cost, and make floor care very easy.

Strip

Distinctive appearance and low cost have made this the most widely used of all residential flooring materials. Strip oak floors (Fig. 10-5) harmonize well with all types of architectural design and interior decorating schemes.

Parquet

Many interesting floor patterns—block, basket-weave, herringbone—can be achieved with par-

Fig. 10-6. Parquet flooring. *Harris Manufacturing Company*

Fig. 10-7. Wall-to-wall carpeting. *Bigelow-Sanford, Incorporated*

quet oak flooring made of short strips in geometric designs. Factory-assembled blocks can be installed over wood subfloors or concrete. See Fig. 10-6.

CARPETING

Carpets add warmth, graciousness, color, and serenity to any living area. They bring together many different elements, creating a harmonious whole. Carpeted floors give a finished look to a room. They add decorative color, texture, warmth, a feeling of luxury, and quietness. And today they have the additional qualities of durability and cleanability.

Carpeting is available in three forms: wall-to-wall (Fig. 10-7), large rugs ("room-size" or "room-fit") (Fig. 10-8), and area rugs, as shown

Fig. 10-8. Large room-size rug. *Kohler*

209

Fig. 10-9A. Large area rug. *Armstrong Cork Company*

Fig. 10-9B. Fur rug. *Georgia Pacific*

in Fig. 10-9A. Area fur rugs, as shown in Fig. 10-9B, are often used to reinforce natural or rustic decors. Figure 10-10 shows the application of different styles to the same situation. Figure 10-11 compares the basic types of carpets.

Wall-to-wall carpeting covers the floor completely and makes a room seem more spacious because of the unbroken area of color and texture.

It provides one surface for easy cleaning and serves as a finished floor covering.

Large rugs are available in prefinished standard sizes, such as 9′ × 12′, (2.7 × 3.7 m) or 12′ × 15′ (3.7 × 4.6 m), or they can be cut to desired size from rolls of carpet. Room-size rugs generally leave a "border" around the room—about 8″ (200 mm) from the wall in a small room; 10″ to 12″ (250

210

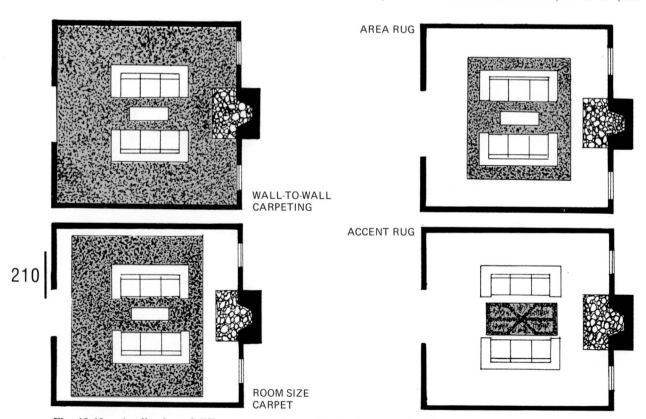

WALL-TO-WALL CARPETING

AREA RUG

ACCENT RUG

ROOM SIZE CARPET

Fig. 10-10. Application of different types of carpeting to the same situation.

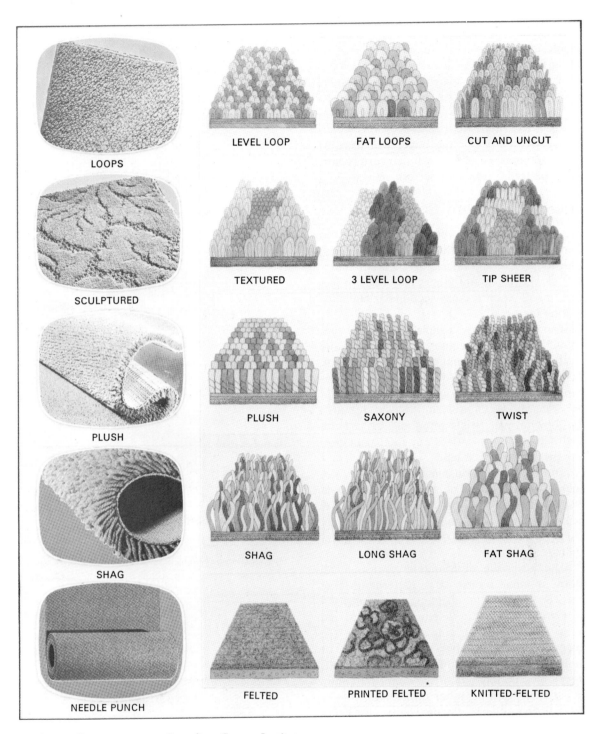

Fig. 10-11. Carpet textures. *Canadian Carpet Institute*

to 300 mm) in a larger room. Room-fit rugs can extend to the walls and follow room contours for the effect of a wall-to-wall carpet without its complete installation.

Rugs can be turned to distribute wear evenly and can be moved easily to another location. They offer good value especially for families who move often, or anyone in a temporary home.

Area rugs range in size from 3' × 5' (1 × 1.5 m) to 12' × 15' (3.6 × 4.5 m) and are also available in varied shapes—round, oval, rectangular, or free-form. They define an area of a room and accent this area with color and design. Consider room proportions in selecting size to avoid the "postage-stamp" look of a skimpy rug in a large area. There are several decisions which a prospective carpet or rug buyer will have to make and some of these will concern color, texture, pattern, price, and performance.

Texture and Pattern

There are many textures of carpet available on the market today and these include plushes, twists, loops, cut and uncut, tip-sheared, sculptured, carved, shag and others (see Fig. 10-11). Figure 10-12 shows cross-sectional details of carpeting textures.

You might choose a definite texture type, such as thick loops, because it complements the smooth finish of the furniture, or the sleek look of contemporary design. You might like the graceful appearance of curved lines, as seen in sculptured or carved textures. Plain, "plush" textures often look formal, twists often suggest a more rugged feeling in a room—at any rate, your own preference is your best guide.

The period of furnishings may or may not influence your choice of texture, but it will certainly influence your choice of a definite style. Since patterns contain several colors in distinct designs, decorating with them requires a bit of planning.

The best rule of thumb is to use small patterns in small rooms, large patterns in large rooms, or for dramatic effect.

Carpet patterns are practical underfoot and offer a "built-in" decorating scheme. Since the homeowner will probably change drapery or upholstery fabrics more often than the carpet, you can pick up any one of the dominant colors in a carpet pattern for other furnishings to vary the decorating scheme. Carpet is also now being used on walls and ceilings, which in turn opens a new dimension.

Color

There are two very good reasons for starting with color when shopping for a carpet or rug. First,

CARPETING

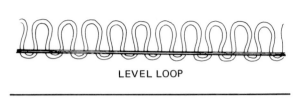

LEVEL LOOP

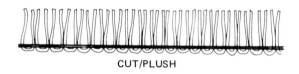

CUT/PLUSH

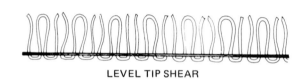

LEVEL TIP SHEAR

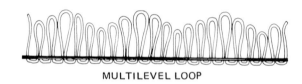

MULTILEVEL LOOP

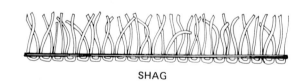

SHAG

RANDOM SHEAR

Fig. 10-12. Cross section of carpeting textures.

until you've found a carpet that you really like, you're still just looking! Color is always important in the home, but never more so than when it's seen in a big area, such as the floor. And, of course, you want color to do "the most" for each room, decoratively speaking.

Second, the color of the carpet should be practical. No other item of home furnishings gets walked on every day—and you don't want the quick appearance of soil to mar the beauty of the carpet or rug. But that doesn't mean that you have to resign yourself to dull, nondescript colors!

Within each color family there are many variations, from light to dark, in both solid colors or subtle mixtures. This wide variety makes it easy to choose the exact color desired—and the version that would be most practical.

Be bold with color! You can plan a variety of wonderful decorating schemes with carpet as your starting point. Color can make a room appear larger or smaller, warmer or cooler—and add to the constant enjoyment.

There are three basic color families—warms, neutrals, and cools.

Warms

Warm colors (red, yellow, orange) are lively, exciting, and friendly. They are especially suitable for rooms which get little direct sunlight and might otherwise appear cold and dreary. They can be overpowering if used too profusely in a small space but can do a great deal to make a large room seem cozier.

Neutrals

The "neutrals" (white, gray, black) are the colors that go well with both warm and cool colors. In some cases, however, the "neutrals" have definite color leanings! So you'll often choose "neutrals" for the same reasons that you choose the pronounced warm or cool colors—to suggest the mood of a room, or to achieve a new feeling of space.

Cools

Cool colors are quiet and relaxing. The various shades of blues and greens remind us of the restful beauty of nature and make us feel cool even on the warmest days. They are especially suited for sunny rooms with lots of windows, such as those on southern exposures. These colors suggest space and can be used to make a small room seem larger.

Performance and Quality

Beauty is important—but so is durability. You want to be sure that the carpet or rug selected is the "best buy" for the home.

It's time to select quality and judge performance—how well the carpet will hold its appearance and how long the surface and backing will last.

Actually, you've already considered one aspect of performance—choosing color and texture. The style of a carpet does play a role in appearance-retention. Medium colors, color mixtures, and patterns are best at disguising signs of use between cleanings and tightly textured surfaces don't readily "show every footprint." Consider the most practical version of the color family and texture type desired.

To make a wise decision on durability—the other aspect of performance—ask these questions: How long should carpets last? How much use will this carpet get? Where will the carpet or rug be used? And what kind and frequency of maintenance can be expected?

In selecting the quality of carpeting remember that stairs, living rooms, foyers, family rooms, kitchens, and hallways are high-traffic areas. Dining rooms and studies or dens are medium-traffic areas, and bedrooms or guest rooms are relatively low-traffic areas.

Density and Depth

In selecting a carpet or rug on the appearance value alone, it is necessary to be conscious of the importance of depth and density of the pile.

A carpet with a low pile height but high density may be equally comparable to another carpet of high pile and low density. The correct balancing of many factors must be considered in your selection.

Padding

Padding (also called "underlay" or "cushion") adds comfort, quiet, and insulation to the carpet on your floor. It acts as a shock-absorber and thereby extends the life of rugs or wall-to-wall carpets. There are various qualities of underlay. A quality underlay is a good investment.

Fig. 10-13   Special effects with carpeting. *Kohler*

Selection Criteria

If you are not certain which particular style and color of carpet will function best, here are some basic rules to help guide you in making a final choice:

1. To make a small room look larger: use medium and light colors rather than strong, bold colors. Use plain textures or sculptured designs rather than strong patterns.

2. To make a large room seem cozy: use strong warm tones and don't be afraid to use patterns.

3. To make a dark room seem brighter (perhaps one with northern exposure): use *hot* colors that reflect light more readily.

4. To make a room more restful: blues or greens are usually the solution. Of course, plain carpets convey a more restful impression than patterned ones.

5. To make a sunny room cooler: stay with the restful blue and green tones.

6. Patterns or tweeds show less daily soiling than most plain carpets for rooms that take heavy traffic.

7. Use small patterns in small rooms, large patterns in large rooms, or for dramatic effect.

8. Wall-to-wall carpeting will carry the color to the corners and push out the wall. Room-size rugs break up big expanses of floor.

9. Your best color choice will also depend to some extent on the type of room that is being carpeted. If the room is used extensively (e.g., a den or family room), take special care to use neutral, easy-to-look-at colors.

10. In rooms used less frequently, such as the bedroom or formal living room, the choice can be more daring. Often a vivid color will give the room a bold, exciting look.

11. Use accent rugs to tie furniture together into conversation groups, to brighten up a dim corner or hall, to dramatize a dining area by letting the shape of the rug (oval, round or rectangular) repeat the lines of the table. Or contrast shapes: round rugs for straight furniture, for example. Wherever you use them, here's an easy way to give a room that something special it lacks. Use carpeting also for special effects on walls or sculptured areas, as shown in Fig. 10-13.

Review Questions

1. Define the following terms: ceramic, terrazzo, parquet, random plank, resilient, subfloor, tile.
2. Complete exercises on pages 52 and 53 in the workbook.
3. For your scrapbook, collect pictures of floor coverings suitable for each room shown in Fig. 6-136.
4. Select floor coverings for a room or rooms of your own design.
5. Refer to Fig. 6-107. Specify the type of flooring you would design for each room in the plan. Indicate color, type, and size of each.
6. Name three general carpet sizes.
7. Name three types of wood flooring.
8. Name three basic types of floor covering.

WALLS

unit 11

Interior designers probably spend more time and effort in designing wall treatments than in any other facet of their work. Wall treatments set the mood or tone of a room and have the most influence on the remaining surface treatments. Walls are perpendicular to fields of vision and are, therefore, more observable than floors and ceilings. In designing wall treatments, the contemporary designer considers the total integration of the decor blending in not only the surface treatments of the walls, but also in the texture and color of other wall features such as windows, doors, arches, and fireplaces to create the desired total effect.

WALL COVERINGS

The texture of the walls has some influence on what you do. There are many wall textures: brick, stone, tile, plaster (rough and smooth), vinyl, Sheetrock, metal panels, wood (planks and paneling), and wall paper. Walls can be plastered (rough or smooth), painted, or papered. They can be made slick with shiny-surfaced wallpaper or they can be given a smooth matte finish without gloss or shine. They can be treated with fabrics or have murals painted or papered on them. What you can do with a wall is limited only by your imagination, budget, and the problem of maintenance.

The most commonly used wall coverings, the ones from which you will likely make your choices, are paint, wallpaper, and paneling.

Paint

Paint can brighten and improve the character of a room more quickly and inexpensively than any other wall covering. You can more closely match an exact color you want with paint.

Because paint is easily applied, finishing one's own walls can save the homeowner decorating costs. If a wall is in reasonably good condition, paint will give a smooth, uniform surface. If, however, there are stubborn blemishes, or if a perfectly smooth surface is not wanted paint will oblige. Stippled and spattered finishes will minimize scratches and spots. Texture effects can be obtained by using special paints and rollers or by going over the wet paint with crumpled paper, sponge, or brush.

Practically all of the paints used on interior walls are made from synthetic resins. Over half are water-thinned, latex paint. These rubber-base paints are easy to apply, fast-drying, durable, washable, and have little odor. Touch-up painting does not show. Latex paints are usually limited to flat and semigloss finishes.

Flat-finish paints are recommended for walls and ceilings, except in kitchens and bathrooms. There, semigloss or gloss finishes are recommended. Semigloss and gloss finishes are recommended for woodwork because they are easy to clean. Designing paint applications in patterns as shown in Fig. 11-1 provides variety and allows the designer to maximize the blending of color hues, and rhythm to achieve unity.

215

Fig. 11-1. Painting in patterns. *Rohm Haas Company*

Fig. 11-2. Floral patterns. *Wall Covering Industry Bureau*

Fig. 11-3. Toiles. *Wall Covering Industry Bureau*

Wallpaper

Wallpaper is another effective tool in the kit of the innovative decorator. Whether inexpensive or luxurious in quality, wallpaper can be used to set a mood—formal, gay, casual, sophisticated, conservative, daring. There is no quicker way to establish the feeling of a period than to use the "right" wallpaper.

Wallpaper offers many advantages as a wall covering. It can be used in any room in the house, can be applied by the householder, and is available in a wide variety of colors, patterns, prices, textures, and degrees of durability. Some types can be used to hide disfigured walls and camouflage architectural irregularities and defects. Wallpaper can make a room with little furniture look furnished and can draw attention away from furniture that lacks distinction.

Wallpapers are available in plain colors with varied textures and patterns large and small. There are flocked papers with raised fuzzy nap that look like textiles. There are marbleized and metallic papers and those which simulate the textures of brick, stone, bamboo, patent leather, etc. There are copies of period designs—Old French, English, early and colonial American. There are murals which can be used to reproduce a period or give the illusion of perspective in a small room.

Types of Patterns

The patterns used on wallpapers today are classified as *textures, geometrics, florals, damasks, toiles, paisleys, scenics, borders,* and *conversation pieces.*

Textures These are papers printed to have the appearance and feel of the rough surface of fabric, such as burlap or tweed.

Florals A floral pattern may be a small, neat pattern, an overall random pattern, or a large, bold pattern. Color plays an important part in any floral pattern, increasing or decreasing its naturalness, and making it airy or dense (Fig. 11-2). Since florals are not intended to be formal, the use of transparent inks that give a wet appearance can keep the flowers looking fresh.

Toiles A line-drawing type of scenic pattern. They can range from bucolic scenes, loosely put together, to classical allegories displayed in symmetrical frameworks. Recommended for traditional settings, as shown in Fig. 11-3.

Paisleys The cone, cypress tree, or leaf shapes identify this pattern. When the leaf shapes are enlarged, intricately meshed together and richly colored, they make a handsome, rather mysterious wall decoration. See Fig. 11-4.

Fig. 11-4. Paisleys. *Ici America, Incorporated*

Fig. 11-5. Damasks. *Wall Covering Industry Bureau*

Damasks. A large design of a scroll-type pattern that repeats regularly rather than at random, as shown in Fig. 11-5. Too conventionalized to be "florals," too fluid to be "geometrics," they combine architectural and natural elements in a way that makes them as close to all-purpose patterns as we will probably get. Recommended for formal settings.

Scenics A scenic paper is one that has repeating scenes. These may be of buildings, human figures, animals, foliage, and many other subjects. Popular scenics include such representations as landscapes, seascapes, and historical events.

Geometrics These are patterns based on angles and curves—abstractions without subject matter. For convenience, stripes, plaids, polka dots, and checks are sometimes classified as geometric, but their own names are better, being more descriptive.

Lattice, grille and tile are preferred over patterns which may qualify as being geometric but which have other, more distinctive decorative functions to be emphasized (Fig. 11-6A).

Borders A narrow strip of decorative wallpaper used as decorative border where wall and ceiling meet or around the doors and windows. They also are used to form frames around headboards, or cupboards, and to form a frame on a large wall. Soffitt borders are used in kitchens for that hard-to-decorate space above built-in cabinets. It is possible that the popularity of posters will revive the custom of "papering" rooms with reproductions of pictures, each surrounded by a "molding."

Murals

The terms *scenic* and *mural* are often used interchangeably.

A mural is a single complete scene without repeat, as shown in Fig. 11-6B. For ease in hanging, a mural may be made in two to eight or nine panels, which, when placed in position, form the composite picture.

Murals are designed for a specific wall space and are generally featured on one wall of a room with the balance of space painted or filled out with matching background paper. Serving the same role in decorating as a painting, murals generally are hung above mantles, dadoes, etc., and are intended to be viewed at eye level.

Wallpaper Types

In addition to the style of the pattern, some wallpapers are identified by terms that refer to the manufacturing process:

Fig. 11-6 A. Geometric patterns. *Bassett Furniture Industry*

Fig. 11-6 B. Mural patterns. *Canadian Wallpaper Manufacturers, Ltd.*

Embossed Paper Embossing is not a printing process, but a process of raising a design on the paper itself after the colored design has been printed. Paper is embossed by being passed between two rollers; one, the embossing roller, is of steel and carries the design in relief, and the other roller is of paper with the reversed image of the design.

Raised Printing Raised printing differs from embossing in that only the design is raised and the paper itself is not affected. This effect is achieved by printing the design with thickened colors.

Flocked Paper Flocked paper is made by sifting powdered rayon, nylon, or other synthetic material over a wet varnish design printed on the paper sheet. (Formerly, powdered wool was used for flocked papers.) This type of wallpaper produces a velvet effect. (Some of the oldest English papers still in existence, dating perhaps from the sixteenth century, are flocked papers. They were made to imitate some of the fine old Florentine and Genoese cut velvets.)

Washable Wallpapers Regular washable wallpapers are printed with a protein size, and a chemical is then applied to "fix" the colors. Because of the ease with which washable wallpapers can be cleaned with a dough-type cleaner, they are seldom washed except for removing stubborn spots around doors and light switches.

Some regular washable papers are also coated with a plastic film, which further improves their scrubbability. This process generally adds a slight gloss to the appearance of the paper which, however, is not objectionable for certain uses such as in bathrooms and kitchens. Other types of washable papers are printed with vinyl inks, which by their nature are waterproof.

Decorating with Wallpaper

The choice of a large pattern or a small pattern depends on the room. As a general rule, avoid large, bright, well-defined patterns in small rooms. Do use patterns with depth—they tend to push back the walls and add a sense of space. A large room will take the large, dramatic patterns. Or, if you prefer to give a sense of intimacy to a larger room, select a small, busy pattern.

One exception to the use of a large pattern in a large room is in the room that has broken wall space. In this case, scale the size of the pattern to the size of the wall spaces. Smaller patterns that are well connected, such as damasks, self-toned stripes, and all-over patterns, are preferable to definitely spaced, rhythmic designs interrupted by numerous windows and doors.

The direction of the pattern should be determined to some extent by the shape of the wall spaces. On tall, narrow wall spaces, use patterns with an up-and-down feel.

Wallpaper can help bring a long, narrow room into better proportion. Use a light shade of textured paper on side walls, and a dark or patterned paper on the end walls. Horizontal designs also widen narrow rooms. Grasscloths and subtle patterns with a horizontal impression accomplish this purpose. In a room with a too-low ceiling, use vertical stripes, or any pattern with a vertical motif.

In a bedroom with a high ceiling, a more intimate effect can be created by using a small overall floral paper on the ceiling and allowing it to extend part way down the wall, then painting the remainder of the area in a blending color.

For an attic room with sloping walls, a small, overall pattern, such as chintz, on both walls and ceiling is attractive. In early American or Provincial rooms—where the furniture is of maple, pine, or cherry—use neat, precise patterns, medallions, small scenes, provincials, chintz patterns, or pin stripes.

In formal nineteenth-century rooms, wide stripes and broad swag patterns, large scenic papers with historical or mythological subject matter, or marbleized papers are effective.

For very modern rooms, textured papers, plaids, and abstracts are suitable.

Special Decorative Effects One inexpensive way to treat a bare stretch of wall is to hang panels of colorful floral, scenic, or abstract paper over a plain background paper of harmonious color. Then frame the wallpaper panels with a harmonizing border or natural or painted wood molding.

Interest can be added to a bedroom by using a patterned paper on one wall only, usually the wall behind the bed. Or, if the headboard is in a recessed space, paper the entire recess with patterned paper.

Fig. 11-7. Wood-like plastic laminates. *United States Plywood Corporation*

Matching Fabrics By looking through the sample books, you will find that many wallpapers have matching fabrics, which can be used as draperies or slipcovers to coordinate the decorating scheme of a room very pleasingly.

Wood Paneling

The selection of the paneling normally depends on the type of room. Light-toned paneling is recommended for a room with limited natural light. It also makes the room look bigger. Dark-toned paneling looks better in bright rooms.

Some wood grains possess pronounced three-dimensional effects which create delightful perspectives in themselves and offer the illusion of greater space as well as attractive patterns. These advantages, along with the choices of light, medium, or dark woods, enable you to give just the right amount of emphasis to any given area.

Wood shakes were used mostly in the past for exterior construction. Now it has become popular as a decorating tool for interior design.

Hardwood Plywoods

These, once only available with fine domestic wood veneers, are now being made with less expensive face materials such as lauan—a Philippine mahogany. Wood-grain patterns and shades of more expensive domestic woods can also be simulated by printing them on the low-cost veneers.

Hardboard and Particle Board

New developments in panels have achieved the look, feel, and texture of real wood through the use of technological advances in stamping, printing, and embossing. A wide range of grain types and shades can also be printed on vinyl-clad hardboards which have fully washable surfaces that are impervious to household abuse.

Wood-like Plastic Laminates

These are not affected by moisture, making them ideal for use in pool or bath areas where other types of paneling are not practical. They are available in a variety of wood grains, solid or random grooving. See Fig. 11-7.

Solid Wood

Once available only in ¾″ thick panels, it is now offered in ⅜″ planks and panels designed for interior applications. This light-weight grade of solid wood is less expensive than the thicker planks yet looks the same and is easier to install.

Fabrics and Vinyl

Textiles have been used for wall coverings since the days they were needed to give warmth and color to rooms in stone-walled castles. Figure 11-8 shows the application of textiles as wall covering in a bedroom. Tapestries, embroideries, patterned fabrics of wool or linen, damasks, brocades, moiré silks, Chinese painted silks, cotton toiles, and painted East Indian cottons are a few of the fabrics which have been stretched on, draped over, or pasted to walls over the centuries.

Today's fabrics—felt, grasscloth, canvas, burlap, denim, and chintz—are often coated or impregnated with plastic. Plastic fabrics (usually vinyl) are increasingly popular. They may have printed designs or printed patterns. They can be made to look like linen, grasscloth, silk, damask, moiré, leather, wood paneling, or wallpaper. They are waterproof, resistant to dirt, stains or scuffs, and can be scrubbed repeatedly. They are not only durable but can be used to hide wall defects, even holding cracked plaster in place.

Vinyl wallcoverings are extremely popular for kitchens and bathrooms because they possess a degree of scrubbability no wallpaper can match. They make excellent vapor barriers and often are a cure for walls subject to cracking and peeling.

219

Fig. 11-8. Textiles used as wall covering. *Ethan Allen Traditional American Interiors*

Fig. 11-9. Interior use of brick. *Window Shade Manufacturers Assn.*

Fig. 11-10. Bookcases make a wall functional. *Home Planners, Inc.*

Ceramic and Plastic

Ceramic tiles have long been popular wall coverings in bathrooms and kitchens and around fireplaces. Now their use is spreading to living and family rooms, entrance halls, and foyers. Ceramic tiles are durable, easy to clean, resistant to water, stains, and fire. Beautiful and original designs can be achieved.

Vinyl tiles and panels can simulate brick, stone, leather, and wood. These easy to clean, durable, resilient wall coverings are widely used.

Brick, Stone, and Concrete

Although stone and brick are not new in the decorating of walls in the home, new manufacturing methods of producing thin, light-weight panels faced with brick, stone, or concrete have increased the buyer's selection of wall paneling. They are available in a variety of stone aggregates

(Fig. 11-9), textures, and colors and will greatly enhance the textural qualities of a room.

Leather

Leather is a most luxurious wall covering material, but maintenance does create a problem, and it is extremely high-priced. However, the synthetic leathers such as vinyl and polyurethane fabrics now approach the softness and fineness of leather and allows the designer great latitude in color and texture selection.

Functional Walls

In addition to covering walls with paint, wallpaper, paneling, fabrics, ceramics, or masonry, there are many functional wall treatment possibilities available, such as bookcases (Fig. 11-10), mirrored walls (Fig. 11-11), or window walls (Fig. 11-12).

Fig. 11-11. Effective use of mirrors in a bathroom decor. *Kohler Photo: Heinrich Blessing for Professional Builder*

Fig. 11-12. Effective use of window walls to capitalize on a view. *California Redwood Association*

Fig. 11-13 A. Well-proportioned windows as viewed from the exterior. *Scholz Homes, Inc.*

WINDOW TREATMENTS

Windows are an interior design feature which must also be considered in conjunction with the design of the exterior (Fig. 11-13A). Consequently, window functions such as light admission, ventilation, and view maximization must be considered from both the exterior and interior point of view. The effect on the proportions of a wall as shown in Figs. 11-13A and B, is also an important aesthetic consideration in selecting, placing, and/or decorating windows. Figure 11-13C shows the effect the lines of a window have on the proportional appearance of the same space.

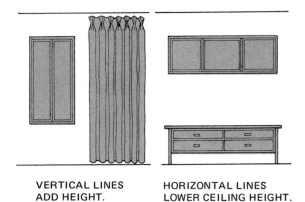

VERTICAL LINES
ADD HEIGHT.

HORIZONTAL LINES
LOWER CEILING HEIGHT.

Fig. 11-13 B. Window size and shape affects room proportions.

Admitting Light

It is desirable to try to obtain uniform daylight throughout the entire room. Factors influencing this are the size and location of windows, the amount of reflection of light by floors, walls, ceilings, and furnishings, and the direction which the window wall faces. Although most building codes recommend the glass area be not less than 10 percent of the room floor area, 20 percent would be more desirable. On brighter days the excess light can be controlled by blinds or drapes. Window drapes should be designed so that when in the open position, the entire glass area is exposed. Light colored walls, ceilings, and furniture also increase the light distribution.

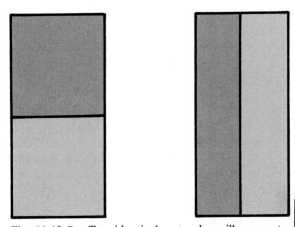

Fig. 11-13 C. Two identical rectangles will appear to change proportionally when subdivided differently.

221

Providing Ventilation

Since many homes do not have the necessary total home comfort requirements to keep windows closed at all times, many depend upon windows for ventilation.. The effectiveness of

good window ventilation depends upon which windows are opened, their location, and how far they are opened. Most building codes recommend a minimum of 5 percent of the floor area for ventilation area but 10 percent is more desirable.

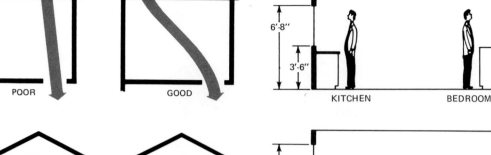

Fig. 11-14. Good and poor ventilation.

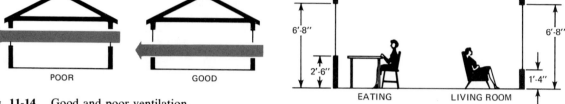

Fig. 11-15. Window viewing heights.

To control the air movement coming into the home, double hung, horizontal sliding, casement, and awning windows should be located, where possible, in the lower part of the wall. Windows in a room should be located so as to provide the best possible air movement (Fig. 11-14).

Providing a View

If there is an excellent view from a house take advantage of it by putting in a large picture window. If there is not a beautiful landscaped scheme, create one. Window walls can be used to extend indoor space outward. Outdoor living areas thus become an integral part of the house. The tops of all windows are normally the same height as outside doors, approximately 6'-8" (2033 mm) from the floor. The distance from the floor to the windowsill will depend upon room size and furniture arrangement. In rooms such as kitchens and bedrooms, where wall space is limited, the windowsill height varies from 3'-6" to 4' (1068 to 1220 mm), as shown in Fig. 11-15. This provides wall space below the windows for cabinet or furniture arrangement and at the same time provides an adequate view when people are standing or sitting.

In dining and living rooms the view from the windows should be observed from a sitting position. For adequate viewing the top of the sill should not be more than 2'-6" (763 mm) from the floor. Key window parts that affect design treatment are shown in Fig. 11-16.

222

Casing The part of a window that fits into the wall, usually covered by wide molding.

Frame or Sash The part holding the glass.

Sill Narrow "shelf" at the base.

Aprons That part of the casing below the sill.

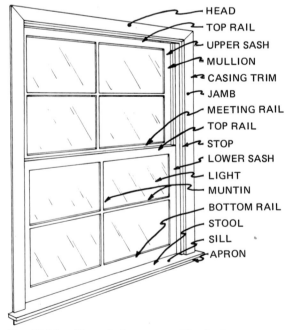

- HEAD
- TOP RAIL
- UPPER SASH
- MULLION
- CASING TRIM
- JAMB
- MEETING RAIL
- TOP RAIL
- STOP
- LOWER SASH
- LIGHT
- MUNTIN
- BOTTOM RAIL
- STOOL
- SILL
- APRON

Fig. 11-16. Key window parts. *Kirsch Company*

Window Styles

There are three basic types of windows used in home construction—sliding, swinging, and fixed. Within these types there are several varieties of design. All windows are available in wood, metal, or plastic. Wood frames do not transmit heat readily and as a result, do not become as cold as metal frames. Metal frames, being stronger, are not as bulky as wooden frames. Plastic frames are available in a variety of colors, slide smoothly, and do not rot or absorb moisture.

For years architects and builders have been repeating about 18 basic designs of windows in homes all over the country, in structures from the older style of home to the most contemporary. A clarification of a number of basic types of windows follows:

Slanting Window   Follows the line of a slanting roof. Simplest treatment: use traverse draperies, leave top uncurtained. Or have draperies custom-made to fit slant (Fig. 11-17A).

Clerestory   Shallow window set near ceiling for indoor privacy. Sometimes placed in slope of a beamed ceiling, in which case it is often left uncurtained (Fig. 11-17B).

Corner Windows   Any windows that come together at a corner. Best decorating effect is to treat windows as one (Fig. 11-17C).

Fixed-center, Double-hung Sides   One large, fixed pane, or fixed pane with movable sections. Make sure drapes are hung so as to allow opening to admit air at side (Fig. 11-17D).

Large, Fixed, Hopper Bottom   Usually a group of basic window units that form a vertical *wall* of windows. Can be treated as one wide window or as individual units (Fig. 11-17E).

In-swinging Casement   If it is not decorated properly, curtains and draperies may tangle with the window as it is opened (Fig. 11-17F).

Awning Type   Has wide, horizontal sashes that open outward to any angle. Unless it is awkwardly placed, it is an easy one to decorate (Fig. 11-17G).

Sliding Glass Doors   Often set into a wall construction, but sometimes part of a modern "glass wall." Make sure drapes draw away from opening (Fig. 11-17H).

Double-hung   Two sashes. Unless too high or too narrow, easy to decorate, using traverse draperies or café curtain treatment (Fig. 11-17I).

Jalousie Window   Narrow horizontal strips of glass that crank open to any desirable angle. A problem only when shape or location is unusual (Fig. 11-17J).

Fixed Arched Window   Any window arched at top. Easily treated with flexible aluminum rodding (Fig. 11-17K).

Ranch Windows   Most often a wide window, set high on the wall. Common to ranch-type and contemporary houses (Fig. 11-17L).

Bay   Three or more windows set at an angle to each other. You can use lots of imagination here, to make it a room's main decorative feature (Fig. 11-17M).

Glass-pane Door   Often in pairs, need special decorating to look their best, and to open easily. Just don't leave them bare (Fig. 11-17N).

Out-swinging Wood Frame   Opens outward by use of a crank, or operated by hand. Easily decorated in any of the standard ways (Fig. 11-17O).

Fixed Dormer Window   Usually a small window projecting from the roof in any alcove-like extension. This can use any of the usual treatments (Fig. 11-17P).

223

Double-hung or Multiple Windows   Pairs of windows or more than two, side by side. Usually treated as a single unit. Units slide up and down (Fig. 11-17Q).

Bow   Sometimes called a circular bay. The key to decorating this window lies in the selection of hardware (Fig. 11-17R).

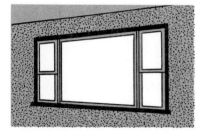

Fig. 11-17 *A*. Slanted window. *Kirsch Company*

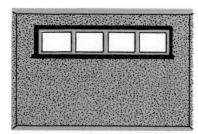

Fig. 11-17 *B*. Clerestory. *Kirsch Company*

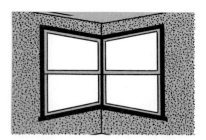

Fig. 11-17 *C*. Corner windows. *Kirsch Company*

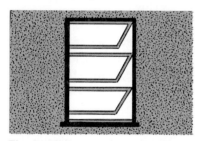

Fig. 11-17 *D*. Picture window. *Kirsch Company*

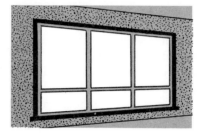

Fig. 11-17 *E*. Glass wall. *Kirsch Company*

Fig. 11-17 *F*. In-swinging casement. *Kirsch Company*

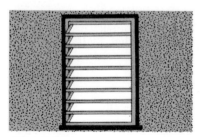

Fig. 11-17 *G*. Awning type. *Kirsch Company*

Fig. 11-17 *H*. Sliding glass doors. *Kirsch Company*

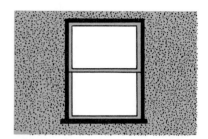

Fig. 11-17 *I*. Double hung. *Kirsch Company*

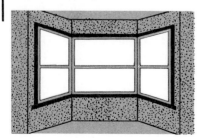

Fig. 11-17 *J*. Jalousie window. *Kirsch Company*

Fig. 11-17 *K*. Fixed arch window. *Kirsch Company*

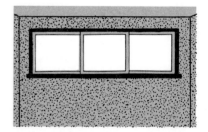

Fig. 11-17 *L*. Ranch windows. *Kirsch Company*

Fig. 11-17 *M*. Bay windows. *Kirsch Company*

Fig. 11-17 *N*. French glass pane door. *Kirsch Company*

Fig. 11-17 *O*. Outswinging wood frame. *Kirsch Company*

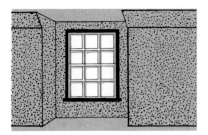

Fig. 11-17 P. Fixed dormer window. *Kirsch Company*

Fig. 11-17 Q. Double-hung window. *Kirsch Company*

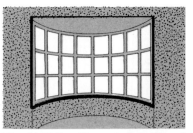

Fig. 11-17 R. Bow window. *Kirsch Company*

Draperies and Curtain Treatments

Form follows function is a fundamental rule of interior design. Consequently, light, view, and ventilation are of primary importance in designing window treatments. There are, however, many window treatment variations available to minimize the problems of view, ventilation, and light distribution. These include no covering, hanging plants, sheer treatments (glass, sheer curtains, and drapes), semicoverings (café curtains, Spanish grillwork, leaded glass), complete opaque coverings such as shades, and solid screens, as shown in Fig. 11-18. The view, from the inside out, must be considered in selecting window treatments, just as the view from the outside in

225

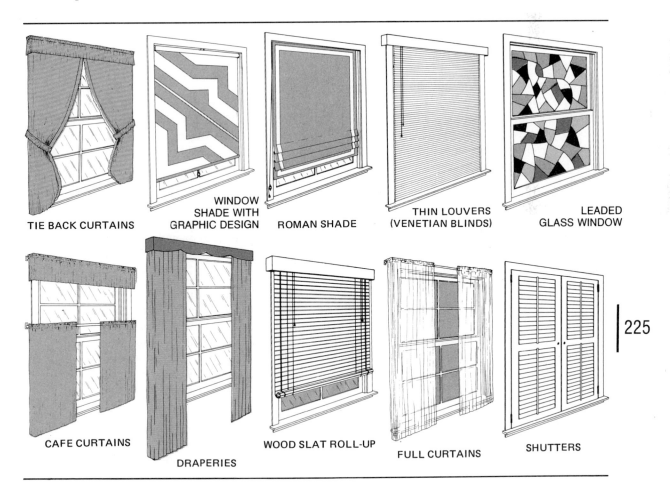

TIE BACK CURTAINS

WINDOW
SHADE WITH
GRAPHIC DESIGN

ROMAN SHADE

THIN LOUVERS
(VENETIAN BLINDS)

LEADED
GLASS WINDOW

CAFE CURTAINS

DRAPERIES

WOOD SLAT ROLL-UP

FULL CURTAINS

SHUTTERS

Fig. 11-18. Varieties of window treatments.

Fig. 11-19. Double-hung traverse. *Kirsch Company*

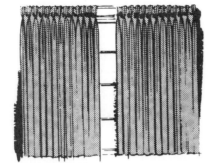

Fig. 11-20. Two-way draw traverse. *Kirsch Company*

Fig. 11-21. Swinging draw draperies. *Kirsch Company*

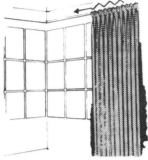

Fig. 11-22. One-way draw traverse. *Kirsch Company*

Fig. 11-23. Shirred glass curtains. *Kirsch Company*

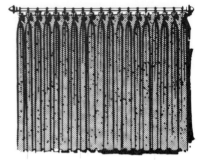

Fig. 11-24. Draw draperies on decorative rod. *Kirsch Company*

must be considered in selecting the placement of windows. The following drapery and curtain window treatments are suggested for various types of windows. However, the colors, fabrics, choice of rods, valances, and their embellishments make the choice of variations almost unlimited.

Double-hung Traverse
Under-draperies of a sheer or medium-weight fabric, and over-draperies (Fig. 11-19), usually of heavier fabric, both hung on traverse rods. Used for: glass walls; corner windows; a series of windows. Bays and curves can be treated with double custom rod sets. Combination brackets hold rods.

Two-way Draw Traverse
Hung from a traverse rod (Fig. 11-20), the drapes open from the center toward the outer edges of the window. Used alone; over shirred or traverse glass curtain; or with cafés. Can be used for most windows, from simple double-hung to walls of glass.

Swinging Draw Draperies
Used on French doors and on in-swinging casement windows (Fig. 11-21). Pleated traverse dra-

peries, with traverse rod mounted on frame, to swing right along with in-swinging French door or casement window when opened and closed. Two-way-draw rods can also be mounted beyond sides of doors.

One-way Draw Traverse
Hung from a one-way draw traverse rod (Fig. 11-22), to draw draperies all one way, from either side. Best for: walls of glass with little or no wall area on one side, or with a door opening at one end; side sections of bay windows; corner windows.

Shirred Glass Curtains
Stationary curtains, which can be in short or floor length, of any transparent or translucent fabric, shirred on a rod and hung next to glass (Fig. 11-23). Best for: double-hung, single, or paired windows: awning, jalousie, bay, bow, or corner windows; glass walls; or hung under draperies.

Draw Draperies on Decorative Rod
Regular pleated draperies, hung from a decorative brass traverse rod, with rings showing (Fig. 11-24). Like conventional two-way-draw traverse, can be used at most windows from standard

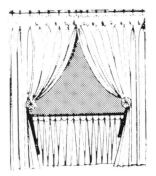

Fig. 11-25. Traverse with held-back side panels. *Kirsch Company*

Fig. 11-26. Decorative traverse with café. *Kirsch Company*

double-hung to picture windows and walls of glass.

Traverse with Held-back Side Panels

For a formal type of treatment—traverse draperies (Fig. 11-25) underneath, with side panels or full over-draperies usually in a contrasting color, tied back or hung straight. Effective at large picture windows; in bays and curves; multiple windows; standard single windows.

Decorative Traverse with Cafe

A high-fashion treatment for picture windows; bays; single or multiple standard windows; the tall, narrow window (Figs. 11-26 and 11-27). With over-draperies hung straight or swagged with decorative holdbacks or tiebacks, this offers real decorative impact.

Draw Draperies, Pleated Valance

Always an effective treatment, particularly in rooms of traditional feeling (Fig. 11-28). Good for giving continuity to a series of windows; and for

Fig. 11-27. Decorative traverse. *Kirsch Company*

picture windows, bays, and standard windows. With heading made exactly like pinch-pleated draperies, such a valance has the effect of "lowering" a too-tall window.

Café Curtains

A treatment now used on almost any type of window (Fig. 11-29). Short curtains or draperies in pairs or multiple tiers, with pleated, scalloped, or tubular-pleated tops. Hung by rings on any style or finish café rods.

Accordion-fold or Ripple-fold

Custom installations in which draperies, in large single pleats, front and back, snap onto carriers in a channeled rod, and when opened, stack back into less space than needed for draperies with

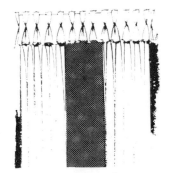

Fig. 11-28. Draw draperies, pleated valance. *Kirsch Company*

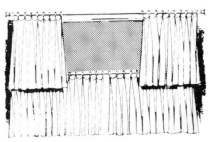

Fig. 11-29. Café curtains. *Kirsch Company*

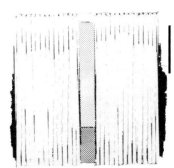

Fig. 11-30. Accordion fold. *Kirsch Company*

Fig. 11-31. Ruffled tiebacks. *Kirsch*

Fig. 11-32. Double windows treated as one. *Kirsch*

Fig. 11-33. Twin Priscilla curtains. *Kirsch*

Fig. 11-34. Swagged valance. *Kirsch*

conventional pinch-pleat headings (Fig. 11-30). Effective in modern rooms and offices.

Ruffled Tiebacks

Single or crisscrossed (called *Priscilla* as shown (Fig. 11-31)). Of sheer or medium-weight fabric, shirred on a single rod, with or without valance. Correct for: double-hung windows; picture windows; bays and dormer, especially in bedrooms, kitchens, baths.

Single, Double, and Multiple Windows

Most windows come as singles, or in pairs and multiples of singles, rather than as one large window. Because these present no opening and closing problems, they're the easiest of all types

to curtain or drape. And just because they are so easy, often they don't stimulate imaginative ideas. There are a number of different ways in which *ordinary* windows can be made to carry a big share of the overall decorative effect in a room. When double windows are close together, they are best treated as one wide window (Fig. 11-32). If curtained with tiebacks, treat each individually, but use a single pair of over-draperies.

Twin Priscilla curtains (Fig. 11-33) are mounted on a stationary rod with simple shirred curtains covering the lower half of the windows. The ruffled valance unites the two windows into one attractive element.

A swagged valance (Fig. 11-34) is another, more formal way to unify two windows. The swag is easy to make using festoon rings or a valance pleater. Cafés cover lower half of window.

For a pair of windows with wall space between, you can treat each window individually (Fig. 11-35). Unite them with a picture arrangement or piece of furniture. Use two curtain rods, one for each window.

A stationary drapery covers wall space between the windows (Fig. 11-36) and one pair of traverse draperies draws to meet it. Sheer curtains and a nicely pleated valance finish the treatment.

A full-width valance ties together these café-curtained standard windows, as shown in Fig. 11-37. All draperies draw simultaneously in a multiple draw. Café rods can be used on the lower part of the window.

Large Windows

Pleated curtains of a sheer fabric can be effectively used at a "viewless" stationary larger window (Fig. 11-38).

228

Fig. 11-35. Separated but matched window treatments. *Kirsch Company*

Fig. 11-36. Stationary drapery cover between windows. *Kirsch Company*

Fig. 11-37. Full valance ties multiple windows together. *Kirsch Company*

Fig. 11-38. Stationary sheer fabric. *Kirsch Company*

Fig. 11-39. Crisscross sheers. *Kirsch Company*

Fig. 11-40. Tier-on-tier treatment. *Kirsch Company*

Fig. 11-41. Sheer curtains under draperies. *Kirsch Company*

Fig. 11-42. Tieback draperies with café curtains. *Kirsch Company*

Fig. 11-43. One-way traverse for sliding doors. *Kirsch Company*

Fig. 11-44. Panels combined with cafés. *Kirsch Company*

If picture windows don't face an attractive vista, crisscross sheers, such as shown in Fig. 11-39, hung next to the glass will obscure the view yet admit light.

When a picture-window panel is below a stationary glass panel, use a tier-on-tier treatment as shown in Fig. 11-40. Use a traverse rod with a café rod at the bottom.

To diffuse direct sunlight use sheer curtains under draperies. Be sure they are the traverse kind, so they may be drawn back when not needed (Fig. 11-41).

Another treatment for larger windows: use tieback draperies and hang them over scalloped café curtains as done in Fig. 11-42.

If a sliding door closes near the corner of a room, a one-way traverse rod will pull the entire drapery to one side to leave the entrance-exit uncluttered. An application of this device is shown in Fig. 11-43.

Cafés create an interesting effect at a stationary picture window. Panels at top are pushed back to admit light; lower panels can be left closed if you want privacy. See Fig. 11-44.

For problem side windows use draw draperies which extend beyond windows, and cafés. Use decorative or regular traverse rods, wall or ceiling-mounted as shown in Fig. 11-45.

Accordion-fold is another handsome treatment for the "glass wall" or very large window. Used in both business offices and contemporary-style homes, as shown in Fig. 11-46.

Fig. 11-45. Double cafés. *Kirsch Company*

Fig. 11-46. Total wall accordia folds. *Kirsch Company*

Fig. 11-47. Combination of treatments. *Kirsch Company*

Fig. 11-48. Bay windows, single-drape treatment. *Kirsch Company*

Fig. 11-49. Bay window, multiple-drape treatment. *Kirsch Company*

Bay and Curved Windows

Planning the draping of bay or curved windows will take a bit of inventiveness, but treated well it can be one of the most inviting features of any decorative setting. Even if the outdoor view it exposes is not all that it could be, it still has tremendous potential, for the vista is easily played down. Most angle bays can use standard rods, but bows will need custom installation.

If the bay or curved "bow" window offers a magnificent view, let nature help in its decoration. A sheer or translucent material will cool the sun's rays while inviting the outdoor scenery to come in. If nighttime privacy is needed—or the color density of a heavier fabric is desired—traverse draperies can be used over the sheers, drawing back to each side.

The individual window of a conventional bay can be treated with separate curtains or draperies for each section—or with one wide pair for the entire group. But when treated individually, they should be unified by a single valance. See Fig. 11-47.

For either the bay or curved windows, curtains and draperies can come to the sill, apron, or floor; but if possible, they should match the length of other window treatments in the room. [Exception: the bay with the window seat should not dictate length of other draperies in the room (Fig. 11-48).]

In this treatment, one pair of draperies on a two-way traverse rod serves the center window. Another pair is divided, a single panel at each side, drawing toward the angle of the bay (Fig. 11-49).

In an early American living room, or a traditional bedroom, crisscross curtains provide a fresh bouffant look. In all but "out-sizes" these can be bought ready-made in many different materials (Fig. 11-50).

To minimize the scene outside, use semi-sheer draperies next to the glass, and "top-draw" draperies with a unifying valance (Fig. 11-51).

230

Fig. 11-50. Early American bay window treatment. *Kirsch Company*

Fig. 11-51. Combination sheer and opaque drapes. *Kirsch Company*

Fig. 11-52. Cafés under full drapes. *Kirsch Company*

Fig. 11-53. Maximum exposure of bay window. *Kirsch Company*

Fig. 11-54. Corner window treatment. *Kirsch Company*

Fig. 11-55. Unifying corner windows. *Kirsch Company*

Fig. 11-56. Casual corner-window treatment. *Kirsch Company*

Fig. 11-57. Full-length drawer for corner windows. *Kirsch Company*

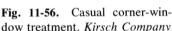

Fig. 11-58. Short corner-window treatment. *Kirsch Company*

To provide privacy, and also allow maximum light to enter, café rods for the curtains and a single curved traverse rod for over-draperies work extremely well (Fig. 11-52).

The graceful bow window, with its interesting wood muntins and mullions, is such a beauty in itself that the less it is "dressed up," the better. Simple traverse draperies are its best "costume" as shown in Fig. 11-53.

Corner Windows

Corner windows, like bays, are a decorating plus in any room, when played up by interesting drapery treatments.

If the corner window has a good view on only one side and the homeowner wishes to keep the other side closed, use separate traverse rods. Do the same if you wish to control sun striking each side at different times of the day.

If there's wall space in the corner, you may want to cover it. Use one-way traverse rods extending draperies beyond window frame, right into the corner. Or custom-order a traverse rod with extensions that fit the angle of the corner.

A graceful festoon valance turns this corner window into a center of interest. This is easy to create. As in Fig. 11-54, use holdbacks and two one-way traverse rods for draw curtains.

A unified effect is created by combining full traverse draperies and one wide matching valance, with sheer curtains underneath extending to apron, to block out unattractive views. Use a combination traverse and plain rod set and separate curtain rod for valance. See Fig. 11-55.

To create a casual effect at a corner window, use two tiers of café curtains as in the window in Fig. 11-56. This will give you all degrees of light and privacy you need. Use two café rods or wood poles for each window.

Floor-length draw draperies (Fig. 11-57) can be combined with one or more tiers of café curtains to give a highly decorative effect. The draperies, on traverse rods, will cover the cafés completely for evening privacy. Use two one-way traverse rods.

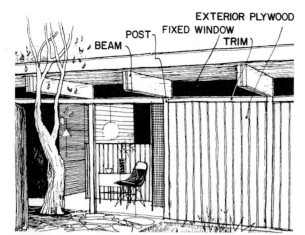

Fig. 11-59. High windows admit only light. *Masonite Corp.*

Rendering by George A. Parenti for the Masonite Corporation

Fig. 11-60. High-window treatment. *Kirsch Company*

Fig. 11-61. Extend traverse rod beyond windows to allow opening. *Kirsch Company*

Fig. 11-62. Sheers under opaque for nighttime privacy. *Kirsch Company*

Fig. 11-63. High-window Priscilla curtains. *Kirsch Company*

At a corner window over a counter, a built-in cabinet or desk, try short draperies. As in Fig. 11-58, these will control light at different times of the day. Use one-way traverse rods or two café rods with rings.

High Windows

Ranch windows (Fig. 11-59) are usually wide and set high on the wall. Clerestory windows are small, very shallow windows at ceiling height. Designed to allow more wall space for furniture placement, their treatment must be special. Clerestory windows set in the slope of a beamed ceiling often are not curtained at all; or if curtained, the fabric is the color of the wall. The following are treatments you might consider for these shallow windows.

A regular ranch window can be treated with a decorative traverse rod or, if the window opens in, sheer fabric onto sash rods top and bottom. See Fig. 11-60.

For the window with panels that swing into the room, extend rods beyond casing so draperies can be pulled back to allow window to open. Use a regular traverse rod, mounted beyond sides of window, as shown in Fig. 11-61.

If nighttime privacy is required, add traverse draperies over sheer café curtains. This allows control of light and air. Use traverse rod and café rod (Fig. 11-62).

Ready-made ruffled Priscilla curtains are adaptable for the "not-so-wide" ranch window

in bathroom, bedroom, kitchen, or dining area. Use double curtain rod. See Fig. 11-63.

Fig. 11-64. French-door treatment. *Kirsch Company*

Fig. 11-66. Drapes hung directly on French doors. *Kirsch Company*

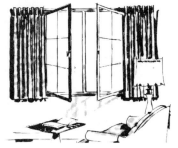

Fig. 11-68. Extensions allow windows to open. *Kirsch Company*

Fig. 11-65. Casement-window treatment. *Kirsch Company*

Fig. 11-67. Swinging traverse rod allows use of French doors. *Kirsch Company*

Fig. 11-69. Draperies hung on French-door traverse rod. *Kirsch Company*

French Doors and Casement Windows

You can use regular traverse draperies at in-swinging doors and casements; but be sure the rods are installed high enough to clear tops of frames and wide enough so that draperies will clear sides of windows or doors when opened.

A valance can be used at an in-swinging casement window if you mount the rod high enough so that bottom edge of the valance clears the window tops.

A fluffy effect is created with a curved valance attached to flexible eyelet rodding. Shirred curtains on a straight rod provide privacy. See Fig. 11-64. A properly mounted combination valance and traverse rod allows the windows to open and close without interference. The bottom of the valance must clear the bottom of the sash (Fig. 11-65).

Treat a group as shown in Fig. 11-66 as one unit, with shirred curtains and traversed draperies. Use sash rods for curtains; traverse rods for draperies.

Pull traverse draperies (Fig. 11-67) closed and you can still use the French doors. Rods swing right along with the door. Use swinging-door traverse rods.

Fig. 11-70. Swinging extension rods used with casement windows. *Kirsch Company*

An extension traverse rod carried beyond the edges of the window, mounted high enough to let the casement clear it, gives a beautiful and functional drapery treatment, as used in Fig. 11-68.

Draperies hung on a French door traverse rod over shirred curtains (Fig. 11-69) allow maximum use of a casement window for light and air.

At in-swinging casements (Fig. 11-70) stationary draperies can be hung on swinging extension rods. For more elegance, try swinging cranes.

Figure 11-71 shows another treatment using sash curtains shirred on round rodding at top and

 233

Fig. 11-71. Stationary sash curtains mounted permanently on window frame. *Kirsch Company*

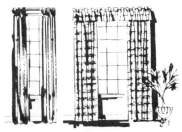

Fig. 11-72. Tall, narrow window treatment. *Kirsch Company*

bottom of glass panes, gathered in the center with big bow ties. Bows match draperies.

Tall, Narrow Windows

In Fig. 11-72 a tall, narrow window is shown before and after decorating. The width has been extended by rods that mount onto the walls at either side. Height has been "lowered" by a valance. In Fig. 11-73 height has been lowered with blinds.

Extend two sets of short, opaque fabric café curtains well beyond the casing of your narrow window and it appears wide and important. Use café rods as in Fig. 11-74.

Hanging draw draperies as done in Fig. 11-75 over draw curtains, again extending well beyond the casing, creates the illusion of extra width to the window. Use a double traverse rod.

This combination of draw draperies and café curtains, which is less formal, serves a double purpose: to give privacy when draperies are closed; semiprivacy when opened (Fig. 11-76).

Dormer Windows

For a room with a traditional air, café curtains (Fig. 11-77) or Priscilla curtains as used in Fig. 11-78 are the perfect way to decorate an arched dormer window.

Wide dormer windows present no problems in planning if treated as in Fig. 11-79. Draw draperies and a valance make a pleasing arrangement at such a window. Use a combination traverse and valance rod.

To make the best use of all available room space, put a desk or other piece of furniture into the area beneath the window, as seen in Fig. 11-80. Simple two-tiered café curtains are a good choice.

Fig. 11-73. Blind treatment of high, narrow windows. *Western Wood Products Association*

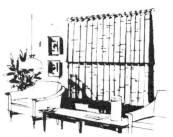

Fig. 11-74. Café treatment of high windows. *Kirsch Company*

Small Windows

Where there is not room to enlarge the apparent size of a small window, treat it simply, in a color to match the wall. Use café rods as shown in Figs. 11-81 and 11-82.

Small windows can be decorated to look larger. Draperies on extending rod draw back to the casing. Curtains are shirred on a rod mounted to the front edge of the windowsill—and cover bare walls. This has been done effectively in Fig. 11-83.

Another way to make a small window look bigger is to mount the adjustable curtain rod to the extender plates, which mount on casing and add between 9″ to 18″ (229 to 458 mm) on each side, as shown in Fig. 11-84.

234

Fig. 11-75. Extending drapes to the side of high, narrow windows. *Kirsch Company*

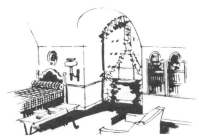

Fig. 11-76. Summer privacy treatment for high windows. *Kirsch Company*

Fig. 11-77. Dormer café curtains. *Kirsch Company*

Fig. 11-78. Dormer Priscilla curtains. *Kirsch Company*

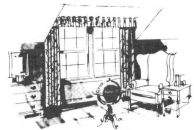

Fig. 11-79. Wide dormer combination. *Kirsch Company*

Fig. 11-80. Dormer double cafés behind desk. *Kirsch Company*

Fig. 11-81. Swinging cafés for small windows. *Kirsch Company*

Fig. 11-82. Separated cafés for small windows. *Kirsch Company*

Fig. 11-83. Small windows made to look larger. *Kirsch Company*

Fig. 11-84. Small window extension with curtain and side panels. *Kirsch Company*

SHAPED VALANCE

CASCADED VALANCE

SCALLOPED VALANCE

CASCADE AND JABOT
COMBINATION VALANCE

FESTOONED VALANCE

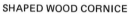

SHAPED WOOD CORNICE

PLEATED VALANCE

SQUARE WOOD CORNICE

RUFFLED VALANCE

SWAG VALANCE

SQUARE CUT VALANCE

Fig. 11-85. Cornices and valances. *Celanese Corporation*

Cornices, Valances, and Headings

The monotony of any drapery treatment can be relieved by the use of decorative headings, valances, or cornices appropriate to the style of the room. Figure 11-85 shows a variety of cornices and valances for this purpose. For very formal rooms, swags made up of festoons, jabots, and cascades are the best choice.

236

The semiformal room can have simple draped swags held by decorative hardware. This is the most popular type of valance for all rooms except Provincial or contemporary rooms. The swag valance can be used to beautiful advantage in almost any room.

Modern or contemporary decor is completed by tailored valances, headings, or cornices. A straight cornice is usually the best choice,

Fig. 11-86. Decorative corner cornice. *Armstrong Cork Company*

but if you like, an interesting cutout design can be equally good.

Be sure to keep the clean, crisp line that's right for modern furnishings. For Provincial or early American rooms you can choose pleated or ruffled styles. Each is equally right with the homespun charm of country furnishings.

Cornices

A cornice as shown in Fig. 11-86 is the horizontal, decorative feature used across the top of draperies. It extends from the ceiling and is normally 4″ to 6″ (102 to 152 mm) away from the wall. Cornices are popular where drapes cover a complete wall. They can be built in to match the walls or be designed as a decorative feature.

Valances

Valances (Fig. 11-87) are horizontal, decorative features used across the top of draperies. The top of the valance does not extend to the ceiling. Fabric valances may echo any popular form or assume a new shape. They may take their shape from the patterns of fabrics used, which may either match or contrast with draperies.

Fig. 11-87. Valance. *Clopay Corporation*

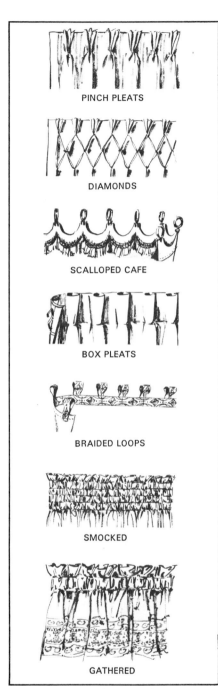

PINCH PLEATS

DIAMONDS

SCALLOPED CAFE

BOX PLEATS

BRAIDED LOOPS

SMOCKED

GATHERED

Fig. 11-88. Headings. *Graber Company*

Headings

Headings (Fig. 11-88) assemble the fullness of drapery fabric at the top of a window. Type of heading varies with window treatment. Sheers are often shirred, and café curtains often scalloped.

Fig. 11-89. Decorative shades. *Window Shade Manufacturers Assn.*

Fig. 11-90. Shades covering a variety of areas. *Window Shade Manufacturers Assn.*

Window Shades

Windows are available in many shapes and sizes. There are window walls and narrow ribbons of glass, bow and bay windows, double-hung and casements, single or multiple windows. Yet all, including skylights and studio windows, can be beautifully fitted with decorative shades as shown in Figs. 11-89 and 11-90.

Architectural as well as decorative problems can be solved by up-to-date installation methods and colorful new shade cloths.

There are a few guidelines to keep in mind. For example, when the wall pattern is the dominant theme of a room, it may be best to choose a shade in a color and texture that complements it. When the walls are plain, a pattern in a

Fig. 11-91. Wide windows treated with a single blind. *Window Shade Manufacturers Assn.*

laminated shade will spotlight the design point within the window frame. Shades also can be hung over storage shelves to hide clutter.

In choosing window shades, consider the following: How the room is used dictates whether a shade should be light-filtering or room-darkening.

Proper selection of window shades and installation methods can effectively control the view, light, privacy, and insulation from cold, heat, and noise. If the room is too sunny and bright or too dark and gloomy, select a shade to brighten a dull room or to tone down one that has too much glare.

If the windows are attractive, accent them; if unattractive, disguise them. Many installation methods for both categories aid the decorative theme. Work the design in this direction.

A window shade can match or contrast with walls, repeat the color of curtains or carpet, or supply a major color point in almost any tone and texture.

As light sources, windows are the eyes of the room and automatically attract attention. That is why the bench, chair, table, desk, or sofa in the foreground should harmonize with the window treatment, making a pleasing composition.

238

Today's shades can make an important decorative contribution as well as a functional one. They can offer a lively color note, and at the same time, modify or amplify the shape and size of windows that need correction.

Installation

The difference between an ordinary window and one that creates decorative excitement may easily

Fig. 11-92. Vertical shades. *Window Shade Manufacturers Assn.*

lie in the way the shades are mounted. They help to compensate for architectural defects, camouflage ungainly areas around a window, create the illusion of added height or width, update old-fashioned windows or create striking modern effects.

Before finalizing shade design or selection consider:

The small, awkward window often benefits from a lightly scaled treatment within the frame, sometimes with a shade valance.

Narrow windows—and rooms—can be made to look larger by the use of extra-wide shades that overlap the molding.

A pair of narrow, double-hung windows can be modernized by using one wide shade across both, preferably covering the moldings as well, thus unifying the area and ensuring a clean, contemporary line.

Wide windows (Fig. 11-91) can be treated as a single unit or divided into sections. One wide shade across a picture window or a shallow bay has a bold impact. Equally dramatic, in a different way, is a series of shades used to break up a broad glass area.

Window shades are not restricted to windows. An attractive, functional, and inexpensive room divider can be created with ceiling-hung or bottom-up shades.

Shades also need not be solid or horizontal. Figure 11-92 shows the application of vertical

Fig. 11-93. Combination drapes and shades. *Clopay Corporation*

Fig. 11-94. Folding shutters. *Ethan Allen*

shades to a window area. Figure 11-93 shows how drapes and shades can be used in combination.

Shutters

Shutters are designed as an architectural element to control light and air. They are available in a variety of styles: folding (Fig. 11-94), swinging (Fig. 11-95), sliding, or permanent, and are made of wood, plastic, or metal.

When used on the inside of the window they may be used as the only window decoration or may be used in combination with drapes or shades. See Fig. 11-96.

When placed on the outside of the window they provide the color and visual texture which will enhance the exterior. However, many outside shutters are mainly used for ornamental effect or as a decorative tool to make small windows look big or to tie windows together.

DOORS

The front door should be so designed that it becomes the focal point of the main entrance to the house. All outside doors should offer privacy and protection from weather and intruders.

Doors are of two types, paneled or flush, and may be installed to swing, slide, or fold. Both types can have windows.

Fig. 11-95. Swinging shutters. *Window Shade Manufacturers Assn.*

Fig. 11-96. Shutters used as exclusive window treatment. *Drexel Furniture*

Paneled doors (Fig. 11-97) are mainly used on traditional homes while flush doors are best suited on modern or contemporary homes.

Doors are constructed of wood, plastic, glass, or metal. The solid wood doors of the past were handsome but heavy. Today the majority of wood doors are of hollow-core construction, which makes them lighter, less expensive, and less likely to warp.

Door Styles

Swing Doors

By far the most popular door in home design today is the swing door. It is hinged on one side usually opening against a wall. Swing doors work well in pairs, but because of the swing space needed, this use is limited.

Fig. 11-98. Sliding doors. *PPG Industries*

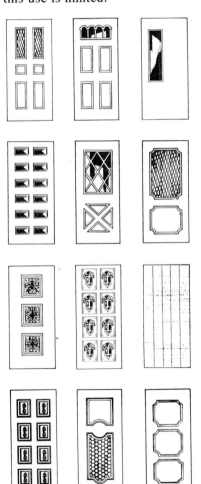

Fig. 11-97. Paneled-door designs. *Lakeshore Industries*

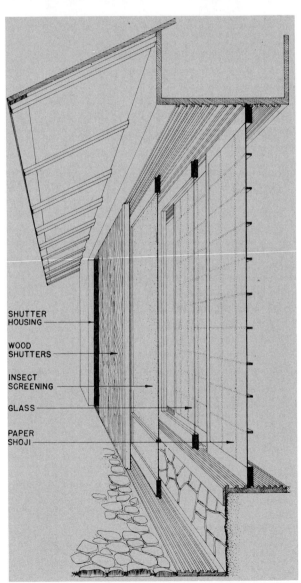

SHUTTER HOUSING

WOOD SHUTTERS

INSECT SCREENING

GLASS

PAPER SHOJI

Fig. 11-99. Typical shoji assembly. *House Beautiful*

240

Fig. 11-100. Folding doors. *United States Plywood Corporation*

Sliding Doors

These doors ride on an overhead track and are usually guided on bottom rails. Pocket and slide-by doors are made for places where space is a problem. They're perfect for dining rooms, bedrooms, and closets. Solid glass sliding doors or multipaneled French doors are ideally suited as outside doors which exit onto a patio or balcony. See Fig. 11-98.

Shoji Doors

Shown in Fig. 11-99 is another example of sliding doors that are extremely flexible in creating outside privacy areas.

Folding Doors

These doors are hinged and may be solid or louvered in design. Folding doors can separate one room from another without taking up much space. They can separate a kitchen from a dining room, or a living room from a dining room (Fig. 11-100).

They're great for closets, too, because they combine utility and elegance and are easy to open and close. Either way, they add something to a room.

Accordion Doors

The type of door shown in Fig. 11-101 is similar to a folding door but is smaller in width and usually constructed of a multifold fabric. Used in a manner similar to folding doors.

Fig. 11-101. Accordion doors. *Azrock Floor Products*

Fig. 11-102. Dutch doors. *Armstrong Cork Company*

241

Dutch Doors

Dutch doors are swing doors divided into a top and bottom section. It's charming. With the top half open, it's great for keeping small children in, and small animals out. It is ideally suited to homes of early American design, as it is used in Fig. 11-102.

Fig. 11-103. Double doors. *Georgia Pacific*

Fig. 11-105. Interior arches. *Ken Karp Photography*

Double Doors
Shown in Fig. 11-103 are double doors. Café double swing doors (Fig. 11-104) are also effective in providing semiprivacy.

Garage Doors
The number of decorative effects possible with garage doors is unlimited. You can keep them unadorned, to present a smooth, unbroken surface that blends with and extends your home. Or

Fig. 11-104. Café doors. *Birge Company*

you can decorate them in as many ways as you can imagine.

ARCHES

Arches and archways (Fig. 11-105) have always played an important role in home design. Since early Roman times they have been used to add grace, beauty, and structural charm to buildings. Today, however, they are used more as a decorative feature than a structural design.

Interior designers have replaced many doors with arches or see-through room dividers, such as beads or bamboo, to create the feeling of open space. Mediterranean home styles and furniture have also created a trend toward the use of arches in home designs.

FIREPLACES

Fireplaces function as heat-producing devices and as an aesthetic and integral part of the interior decor. Fireplaces are designed in three types: those constructed totally on the site, those using a manufactured firebox and flue system, and freestanding units. Fireplaces may also be classified by the type of fuel used: gas, or wood.

Fireplace Styles
The style of a fireplace is reflected in the size and shape of a firebox opening, the mantle (if

Fig. 11-106. A colonial fireplace. *Home Planners, Inc.*

Fig. 11-109. Fireplace open only to the front. *Home Planners, Inc.*

Fig. 11-107. Victorian fireplace.

any), the hearth (raised or floor-level), and the material, treatment, and color of the surrounding trim. Figure 11-106 shows a colonial fireplace which includes many of the identical molding patterns found in colonial furniture. Figure 11-107 shows a more formal Victorian-type fireplace utilizing Victorian wall panel treatments. Figure 11-108 shows a contemporary-design fireplace which is characterized by straight, uninterrupted lines and spaces, low or no hearth, and no mantle.

Fireplace Opening

Fireplace openings are classified into five basic types: (1) fireplaces, as shown in Fig. 11-109,

Fig. 11-108. Contemporary fireplace. *Home Planners, Inc.*

Fig. 11-110. Two-sided fireplace. *Home Planners, Inc.*

Fig. 11-112. See-through fireplace. *Canadian Housing Design Council*

open only to the front. These are one-sided fireplaces. (2) Fireplaces that open on two sides (Fig. 11-110), which are corner fireplaces. (3) Fireplaces that open on three sides (Fig. 11-111). (4) Fireplaces that open on two sides, front and back. These are referred to as "see-through" fireplaces (Fig. 11-112). (5) Fireplaces that are open on all sides, as illustrated in Fig. 11-113.

Material

Common brick is a popular fireplace material, though concrete block or natural stone may also

be used for the main construction. Firebrick or other refractory material must be used to line the firebox, and firebrick or flue tile should also comprise the inner course of the flue.

Location

Convenience, appearance, and the draft available both internally and externally (chimney), are prime considerations in fireplace location. Living rooms, recreation rooms, and family rooms are the most common fireplace locations, though

Fig. 11-111. Three-sided fireplace. *Home Planners, Inc.*

Fig. 11-113. Fireplace open on all sides. *Home Planners, Inc.*

Fig. 11-114. Freestanding fireplace. *Southern California Edison Company*

dining rooms and bedrooms are also frequent choices. Above all, put this important feature of the home in a prominent place, not in a seldom-used room or corner.

Structural support is of paramount consideration since great weight is involved. The fireplace and chimney must rest on a firm concrete footing. The design of your home, the "lay of the land," and the soil condition may limit your choice of location.

Costs can be cut on the installation of two fireplaces in a single home if they are constructed back to back or one above the other as in first-floor and basement rooms. The flues are thus built into the same chimney. A fireplace with openings in two adjoining rooms is also an interesting possibility.

Footings

Consult the local building code for footing size since these codes differ according to existing soil and moisture conditions in individual areas.

Warm-air Circulating Fireplaces

The "circulator" idea embodies a masonry fireplace and an effective "house warmer" in one preengineered, prebuilt metal fireplace unit.

Masonry is constructed around the unit. The result is a regular radiant fireplace and a circulator fireplace that sends warm air convection currents into the room—even into adjacent rooms—through a system of strategically located intake and outlet ducts and grills. These grills may be located at the front, side, or back of the fireplace directing the heat where it is most needed.

Prebuilt Fireplaces

However, the recent introduction of the all-metal, factory-built fireplace (Fig. 11-114) has changed the basic requirements of fireplace construction. With this preengineered and preproportioned unit, it is now possible—and quite advantageous—to build in a genuine, wood-burning fireplace without using a single brick, stone, concrete block, or ounce of mortar.

Multiple-wall construction of prebuilt fireplace units permit installation directly against wood flooring, studding, and joists. Air flowing in various directions between the walls of the metal components keeps the outer surfaces safely cool for this type of installation. This type of fireplace does not need a foundation because it is classified as a wood-burning stove.

Determine the location from house plans. If possible, select a location so that joists, trusses and rafters will not have to be cut where the chimney passes upward. Also select a location where the chimney top will suitably extend at least 2′ (610 mm) or more above the highest point of the roof within 10′ (3048 mm). This consideration applies also to any draft obstructions such as trees or other buildings.

These models may be placed directly on a combustible floor (Fig. 11-115) against a combustible wall, or raised on a wooden platform without clearance from combustible construction. Wood framing members may be placed directly against the side and back of the fireplace. Brick and other masonry materials are not needed for these installations; however, they may be used in a veneer finish if desired.

Gas Fireplaces

This type of fireplace offers maximum operating convenience and warm-air circulation. Concealed circulating fans keep air moving around the firebox and expel heated air into the room. The gas fireplace has an automatic pilot which is quickly turned off or on and the unit can also be thermostatically controlled. The gas log is realistic in appearance. Requiring neither heavy masonry and foundations nor front hearth, the gas fireplace rests on any type of flooring with no limitations on mantel size or trim.

Review Questions

1. Define the following terms: mural, embossed, flocked, bay, doublehung, clerestory, sash, sill, valance, corners, heading, traverse rod.

246
2. Complete exercises on pages 54–57 in the workbook.

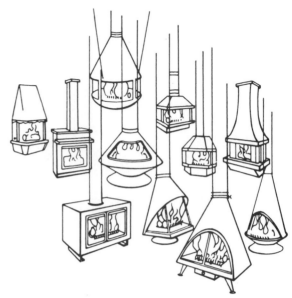

Fig. 11-115. Types of freestanding fireplaces. *Majestic American Standard*

3. For your scrapbook, find pictures of wall treatments of the type you would select for each room shown in Fig. 3-39.
4. Specify wall coverings, windows, doors, and draperies for a room of your own design.
5. Refer to Fig. 2-24. Specify the type of wall covering you would design for each wall. Refer to walls by room and compass direction. Indicate wall covering by color, type, and texture.
6. Prepare an interior elevation drawing of the north wall of the living room in Fig. 2-25. Design wall coverings and specify all materials by color, style, and texture.
7. Refer to Fig. 3-39. Specify windows and doors for the living and service areas. Refer to rooms and walls by compass direction.
8. Name three common types of wall coverings.
9. Name three functions of a window.
10. Name three basic types of windows.
11. Name two types of interior doors.
12. Name the three methods of door movement.

CEILINGS

Most conventional ceilings, as shown in Fig. 12-1, are simply a result of the enclosure of the roof. Ceilings are not utilized, as are the walls and floors; however, they can provide illumination, control temperature, and maximize the acoustical qualities of a room.

FLAT CEILINGS

Conventional flat ceilings are usually either plastered, sheetrocked, painted, or textured. Flat-ceilings, however, can be dropped with acoustical panels or translucent panels behind which lighting can be provided, as shown in Fig. 12-2. Flat ceilings can also be beamed and even heated if radiant heat is used (Fig. 12-3). The minimum height for flat ceilings from the floor to the ceiling is 8'0" (2438 mm).

Fig. 12-2. An example of a conventional flat translucent ceiling. *Southern California Edison*

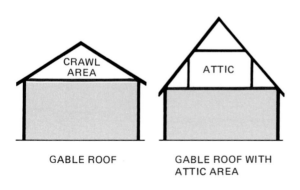

Fig. 12-1. Various conventional ceilings types.

Fig. 12-3. Resistance wires in a ceiling with radiant heat. *Electromode*

247

Fig. 12-4. Ceilings can be constructed at different levels. *Alan Gelbin, Architect*

Although flat ceilings are the most common, ceilings need not always be constructed in this manner. Different levels can be achieved, as shown in Fig. 12-4, to provide cove lighting and alleviate the monotonous single plane of a horizontal, flat ceiling.

Open Ceilings

The total ceiling surface can also be illuminated, or the ceiling can be treated as the underside of the roof (Fig. 12-5) in which beams are exposed add a greater feeling of space, air, and light circulation is achieved. Ceilings of this type are

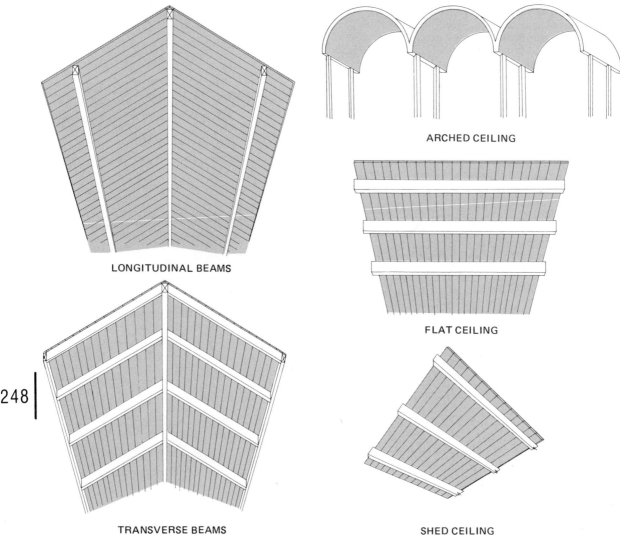

LONGITUDINAL BEAMS

ARCHED CEILING

FLAT CEILING

TRANSVERSE BEAMS

SHED CEILING

Fig. 12-5. Examples of ceilings as undersides of roofs.

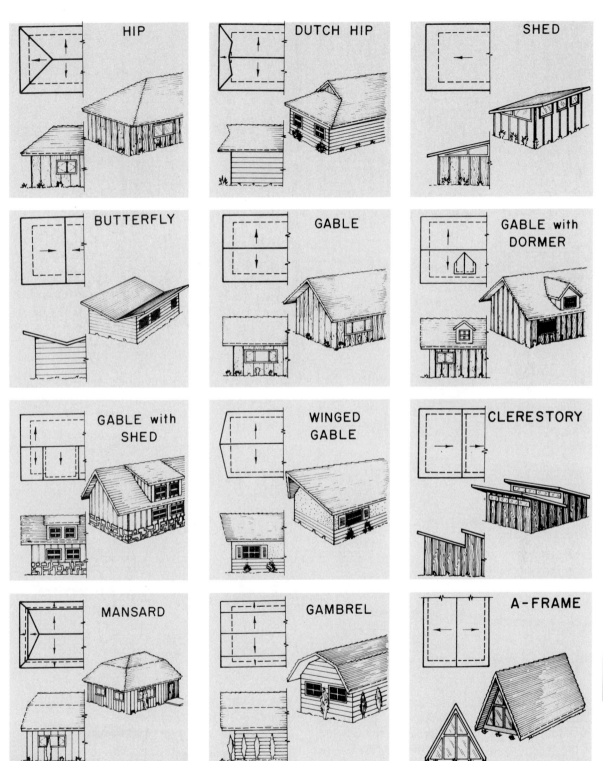

Fig. 12-6A. Roof and ceiling types.

directly related to the style of roof selected for the structure. Figure 12-6*A* shows typical roof styles used for most homes. Each style can be adapted to most types of floor plans. Figure 12-

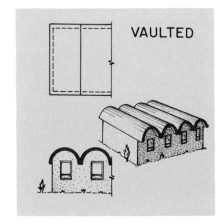
VAULTED

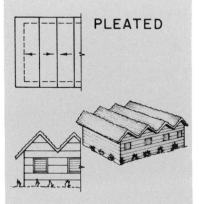
PLEATED

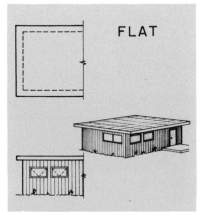
FLAT

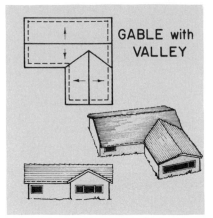
GABLE with VALLEY

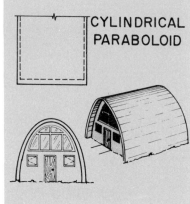
CYLINDRICAL PARABOLOID

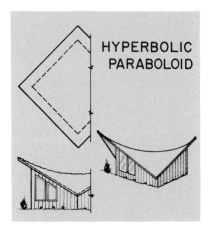
HYPERBOLIC PARABOLOID

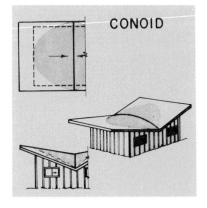
CONOID

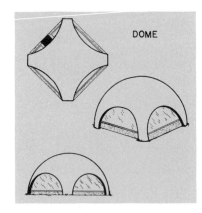
DOME

Fig. 12-6A. (*continued*)

6*B* shows the interior of a curved panel roof. Cathedral ceilings, as shown in Fig. 12-7, have the additional advantage of relating the outside of the structure to the inside through the use of continuous beams and roof lines through glassed wall areas.

A disadvantage of the open ceiling is the high rate of heat transfer. This type of ceiling is wasteful of energy.

Fig. 12-6B. A vaulted ceiling. *Georgia Pacific Corporation*

Fig. 12-7. Cathedral ceiling beams effect the appearance of the exterior. *Scholz Homes, Inc.*

Special Effects

In designing ceilings with massive beams or structural apparatus, the designer must keep the sense of room proportion under control. The larger the ceiling structure, the more ceiling height must be provided. Notice how the ceiling in Fig. 12-8 accomplishes this by providing open space without creating the feeling of enclosure.

In addition to the above ceiling types, more dramatic ceiling treatment effects can be achieved through such devices as fabric ceilings, translucent materials, or transparent skylights which allow sunlight to penetrate, create special moods, and provide lighting for internal or windowless rooms.

Elements of design can be applied in the following ways to create ceiling effects:

To raise a ceiling: Keep it light. Pale colors, either textures or small patterns, will make a ceiling recede. Use strong verticals on the walls. Stripes, or any patterns that definitely thrust upwards, will carry the eye with them. Place low furniture strategically, so that the space between the furniture and the ceiling will appear greater.

Fig. 12-8. Ceilings beams are used to create open space. *Potlatch Forest Products*

To lower a ceiling: Call attention to it (Fig. 12-9*A*). An eye-catching pattern, whether dark or bright in color, or beams, as shown in Fig. 12-9*B*, bring a ceiling nearer. Use horizontal patterns

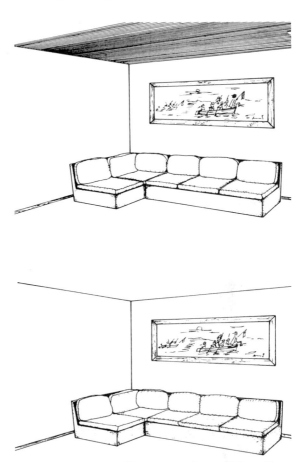

Fig. 12-9*A*. Dark ceilings appear lower; light ceilings appear higher.

Fig. 12-9*B*. Beams lower the effect of the ceiling. *Home Planners, Inc.*

251

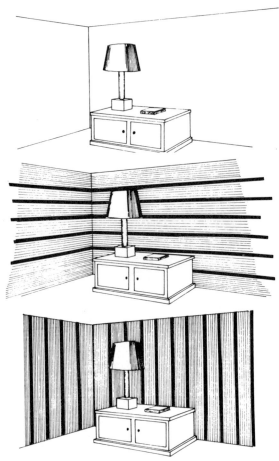

Fig. 12-9C. Horizontal wall patterns lower ceilings; vertical patterns raise ceilings.

on the walls as shown in Fig. 12-9C. Murals often serve the same purpose. Break the height of the wall with a dado or a chair rail, down below, and a moulding or border up above.

Regardless of the type, material, or special treatment, the design of ceilings must be consistent with all the elements of design utilized in floor and wall treatments and in the selection of furniture, equipment, lighting systems, and accessories.

Review Questions

1. Define the following terms: acoustical, translucent, radiant heat, cathedral ceiling, vaulted ceiling.
2. Complete the exercises on page 60 in the workbook.
3. For your scrapbook, collect examples of traditional ceiling treatments in a variety of materials and types.
4. Refer to Fig. 6-4. Describe the ceiling treatment you would select for each room by type, material, color, finish, and structural lighting.
5. List different types of ceiling treatments for maximum acoustical effect, lighting variations, cost efficiency, and rustic decor.

SECTION FOUR
FURNISHINGS AND EQUIPMENT

APPLIANCES unit 13

Appliance manufacturers once introduced a complete new line each January. Now major appliances are introduced any time there is a significant improvement in design. Occasionally there is a major breakthrough, but normally there are steady improvements in equipment design which follow clearly discernible trends. The informed designer will know when improvements in performance justify increases of expenditure.

SELECTION GUIDELINES

Regardless of the appliance (Fig. 13-1) (range, refrigerator, vacuum cleaner, washer, electric frying pan, or waffle baker), there are basic guidelines for selection:

• Will it contribute to more effective performance of tasks?

• Will it make the home safer? More livable? More enjoyable?
• Will it save energy, permit more creative activities, or both?
• In addition to its own cost, will the appliance result in sizable wiring, plumbing, delivery, and installation costs?
• Can you spare the necessary space?
• Will the appliance add objectionable heat, noise, or moisture?

There are many reputable manufacturers who produce quality products and whose service and warranty are beyond reproach. There are other manufacturers who do not enjoy this reputation. Selecting top-of-the-line models is not always a guarantee of satisfaction. If basic performance is all that is needed, then the bottom-of-the-line model may be satisfactory. Luxuries,

Fig. 13-1. A wide array of home appliances. *Westinghouse*

Fig. 13-2.   A freestanding range. *Hotpoint*

Fig. 13-3.   A built-in range. *Jane Hamilton-Merritt*

however, soon become necessities as new materials develop.

RANGES

Differences between electric and gas ranges continue to narrow both in sales and performance. Once gas was the faster of the fuels, now cooking speed is about the same. Once gas ranges alone had infinite heat adjustment; electric ranges alone had fixed-temperature settings. Now some electric ranges have infinite controls and some gas ranges have a few definite settings on their burners.

Freestanding Range

This is a one-piece model, as shown in Fig. 13-2, with surface elements and an oven with a broiler. It provides much flexibility in kitchen planning.

Three models are available: the conventional, which is found in most homes, the drop-in model which, when set between two cabinets, looks built-in, and the high-oven cabinet range. This range comes in two styles, one with the oven installed over the cooking units, and the other, with two ovens; one above the cooking units and one below.

Built-in range (Fig. 13-3)

Concealed-element Range

The range in Fig. 13-4 utilizes a smooth, single-sheet, glass-ceramic range top that shows no heating units or burner openings.

The only visible surface on top of the range is the smooth, flat sheet of glossy white glass-ceramic material. All electrical elements are sealed out of sight beneath the range top.

Heating elements beneath the smooth, glass-ceramic range top heat the surface. Each heating area is thermostatically controlled to maintain desired cooking speeds, and indicator lights show which areas are in use.

Another new range that is gaining in popularity has two ovens, an eye-level upper oven plus a larger lower oven, both with picture windows. With this range, baking and broiling can be done at the same time.

MICROWAVE OVEN

Microwave ovens come in sizes of approximately 20″ x 24″ x 24″ (508 × 610 × 610 mm). They usually sit on a countertop. Unlike most cooking appliances in which the food to be cooked is overwhelmed with heat, a microwave oven operates essentially at room temperatures. In fact, if anything, the food heats the oven.

The food load is shown positioned off the floor of the oven. This position permits some of the energy to be reflected from the oven floor

Fig. 13-4.   A concealed-element range. *Corning Glass Works*

Fig. 13-5. An upright freezer. *Jane Hamilton-Merritt*

Fig. 13-6. A built-in dishwasher. *General Electric*

into the food from below. If this were not done the bottom of the food would lag behind in cooking. It will be cooked unevenly.

REFRIGERATORS AND FREEZERS

The built-in furniture look, combined with an increased use of color, are trends in exterior refrigerator design. Combination refrigerator-freezers are the choice of 75 out of every 100 buyers. The long-term trends have been: more refrigerated capacity in less space; increased storage capacity for frozen foods; constantly improved conditions of temperature and humidity for different kinds of food; interior design that makes easy the orderly and convenient placement in the refrigerator of different kinds of food and food packages; automatic defrosting and improved ice cube storage.

Styles

Side-by-side freezer-refrigerators offer an upright freezer and a refrigerator side by side.

In a two-door refrigerator, the freezer can be located at the top or bottom. Zero-zone cold provides food storage for many months in the freezer.

The frozen-food compartment of a one-door refrigerator is not designed as a zero-degree freezer, and is suitable only for freezing ice cubes and storing frozen foods for one to three weeks. A compact refrigerator is a miniature of the one-door refrigerator.

In combination refrigerator-freezers the freezer compartment must reach 0° C to be truly effective. It has limited capacity but is ideal for a small family.

Chest freezers have a large food capacity and hold irregularly shaped foods. Because there is a minimum spillage of cold air when the freezer is opened, it is economical to operate.

Upright freezers require less floor space. Food freezes faster because of better air circulation. It is more convenient to fill. Frozen food is more accessible and the upright freezer can be integrated, like a refrigerator, into the decor, as shown in Fig. 13-5.

DISHWASHERS

Until recent years, the dishwasher had almost the slowest growth in the appliance industry. Now it is one of the three major appliances enjoying the fastest rate of growth.

The dishwasher should be installed beside the sink, to offer the optimum in convenience and to minimize plumbing connections. The closer the dishwasher is to the dining area, the easier and faster you can load it.

Built-in

The undercounter type (Fig. 13-6) that is permanently connected to water lines, drain pipe, and an electric circuit is very popular with people who are building or remodeling their kitchens. The dishwasher is integrated with the cabinets, giving a unified look to the kitchen. You can even get a front panel of the same wood as your cabinets.

Portable

This requires no installation and is ready to go to work as soon as you snap its hoses to the kitchen faucet and plug it into a wall outlet. Roll it to the table for loading or unloading. Push it out of the way for storage when not in use—even to another room. If you move to another house or apartment, you can take your portable dishwasher with you. Choose a top-opening regular portable, or front-opening convertible.

Freestanding

Similar to the built-in undercounter type, it is designed to go into a vacant space, usually at the end of a row of cabinets. It comes with a countertop made of maple wood, laminated plastic, or porcelain, and a panel for the exposed side or sides.

Convertible

This front-loading portable dishwasher is ideal for people who are planning to move or remodel later. It can be used as a portable immediately. Later you can remove its casters and have it installed as an undercounter or freestanding model.

Dishwasher-sink

Sink top and bowl, cabinet, faucets and dishwasher, all in one compact unit.

FOOD DISPOSERS

There are two types of waste disposers, the electric food waste disposer which takes care chiefly of food wastes, and the gas incinerator which disposes of burnable trash as well as food wastes.

There are two types of electric disposers; the continuous-feed with a wall switch, and the batch-feed where the tight-fitting rotating lid acts as the starting switch. Continuing trends in design include: improved shredding and cutting devices; quieter operation; greater durability, jamproof operation; various styling; sizes, shapes and fittings designed to permit installation in both new and old sinks.

Gas incinerators, available in both indoor and outdoor models, consume both wet and dry wastes. They will not handle metal, glass, or ceramic materials. Newer models are wind and weatherproof and do not discharge smoke, odor, fly ash, or other products of combustion.

TRASH COMPACTOR

This appliance has been designed to compact a week's worth of trash for the average family in a neat small bag. The unit eliminates daily trips to the garbage can. In fact, it may eliminate the need for them completely. The bulk of trash will be reduced to a four-to-one ratio.

WATER PURIFIERS

Water scientists have designed a purifier that can turn salty or brackish water into fresh water and transform ordinary city or private well supplies into water of high quality and purity. It is for home or apartment use. Water can now be better than it has ever been before thanks to the introduction of a compact household water purifier that works on a principle similar to human cells, to reject contaminants.

WASHERS AND DRYERS

Modern washers and dryers are usually positioned in tandem side by side as shown in Fig. 13-7, or stacked. Keeping the units in close

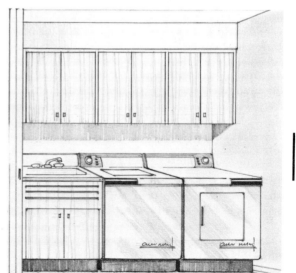

Fig. 13-7. A side by side washer and dryer. *General Electric*

257

proximity eliminates the need for intermediate space since most clothes are transferred directly from the washer to the dryer. As covered in Unit 7, the washing and drying function covers most of the laundry function.

The compact units (Fig. 13-8) are ideal for home areas generally thought too small for standard laundry equipment—in or near bedrooms, bathrooms, or even some closets. Both the washer and dryer operate on a standard three-pronged ground electrical outlet and each has a capacity of about half that of standard-size appliances.

Washers

Because nonautomatic washers use less water than automatics and cost less to buy and maintain, there will probably always be a market for this type of washer. However, they are not engineered to do the best possible job on small loads, woolens, wash-and-wear, durable press, or delicate fabrics.

Styles

Washers differ in their washing action and are classified accordingly:

Agitation Type   An agitator in the center moves back and forth or up and down, circulating the clothes through the water. The lid is in the top, and articles may be added during the cycle.

Tumbler Type   The whole drum revolves, lifting the clothes out of the water and dropping them in again. The door in the front, permits the top to be used for counter work space. If floor space is limited, this type may be stacked with a dryer.

Dryers

258   Some models require venting to the outer wall; others can be located anywhere since venting is not necessary. Thus the need for venting determines or restricts the placement of dryers.

WATER-SOFTENING EQUIPMENT

Water hardness is caused by limestone and other similar rocks (hardness minerals) which are dissolved by water. These hardness minerals have

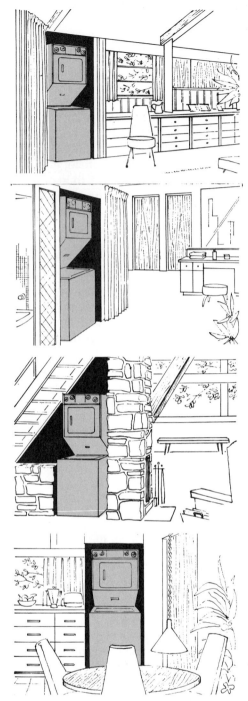

Fig. 13-8.   Possible locations for a compact washer and dryer. *Frigidaire*

one thing in common: They all contain one or both of the hardness elements, calcium and magnesium. These substances constitute water hardness and occur in significant amounts in more than 85 percent of the water supplies of the United States and Canada.

FOOD PREPARATION APPLIANCES

Portables used for food preparation are generally laborsavers. The mixer, blender, food grinder, ice crusher, ice-cream freezer, can opener, and juice extractor are all designed to do mechanical tasks which would require varying amounts of human energy. Appliances do many of these tasks better as well as more easily.

The interior designer of kitchens must not only provide storage space for these appliances but must also provide working space for their use. Figure 13-9 shows a storage and working center for an integrated system of food preparation appliances.

Review Questions

1. Define the following terms: self-cleaning oven, warranty, programmed cooking control, Teflon-coated, osmosis, blender, water softener.
2. Complete the workbook exercises on pages 59–60.
3. For your scrapbook, collect two examples of each appliance covered in this unit.
4. Refer to Fig. 6-119. Describe the type of appliance you would specify for this residence and list the features you would specify for each.
5. List three types of refrigerators, sinks, ovens, ranges.

Fig. 13-9. A food preparation appliance center. *Rauson*

FURNITURE

Furniture, the living equipment of a dwelling, more than any other design feature reflects and affects the life-style of the inhabitants. Furniture is classified by its use (dining, living, storage, recreation), kind (table, chair, seat, chest, cabinet), material (wood, plastic, metal, glass, stone, bamboo), and/or embellishment (carved, covered, stained, upholstered, stamped, painted). The combination of these characteristics and the configuration of arrangements are infinite, and reflect the art and creativity of the designer.

CONSISTENCY

Furniture must not only perform the prescribed function, but it must do so within the framework of architectural consistency. That is, a colonial structure should be furnished with related furniture. The same degree of consistency should be achieved with traditional and contemporary furniture, as shown in Fig. 14-1. Furniture should also be consistent in style within the decor; that is, don't mix styles such as modern or period, as shown in Fig. 14-2.

INVENTORY

After analyzing furniture needs as outlined in Unit 2, list the furniture that exists in each room that may be usable within functional and architectural style consistency standards. Next list

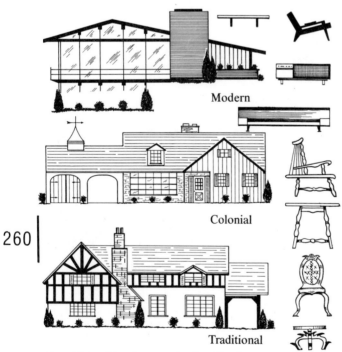

Modern

Colonial

Traditional

Fig. 14-1. Furniture style should relate to architectural style.

260

Fig. 14-2. Furniture styles should not be mixed.

NUMBER	ITEM	MIN PRICE		MAX PRICE
1	Couch	1500		2000
2	End Tables (200 ea)	400	(500 ea)	1000
1	Coffee Table	150		400
1	Lounge Chair	500		700
1	Chaise Lounge	600		800
1	TV	300		500
2	Bookcase (300 ea)	600	(400 ea)	800
4	Planters (100 ea)	400	(200 ea)	800
1	Stereo System	1000		2500
2	Table Lamps (50 ea)	100	(100 ea)	200
2	Floor Lamps (100 ea)	200	(200 ea)	400
Totals		**5750**		**10,100**

Fig. 14-3. As example of a furniture budget.

furniture needed to complete the design. If budget is a factor, and it usually is, separate the list on a minimum-maximum cost basis as shown in Fig. 14-3.

FURNITURE BUDGET

The amount of money available for furnishings varies and must be determined on an individual basis. The income, size of house, size of family, stage in family cycle plus values and goals and other financial commitments influence the furnishings budget. For furnishing new residences an amount equal to one-fourth the cost of the house or an amount equal to one-half of one year's income can be invested in furnishings, as a rule of thumb. If income fluctuates, use an average income determined over a period of years.

FUNCTIONAL REQUIREMENTS

Functional furniture is furniture that serves its intended use. Remember: form follows function, not vice versa. To be truly functional, furniture must be sized for all occupants and support the total lifestyle of all occupants including hobby, entertainment, relaxation, service, and sleeping activities. Furniture that *only* "looks good" and is not comfortable or lifestyle supportive has only form, not function.

In addition to lifestyle considerations preference for an open or closed plan and the use of

built-ins (Fig. 14-4) greatly affect the selection of furniture, the design of furniture, or both.

Dual-function Furniture

Where space is limited "convertible" furniture can be used effectively to eliminate overcrowd-

Fig. 14-4. Functional built-in furniture. *Royal System Incorporated*

261

Fig. 14-5A. Convertible couch. © *Michael Weisbrot and Family*

Fig. 14-5B. Converting the couch. © *Michael Weisbrot and Family*

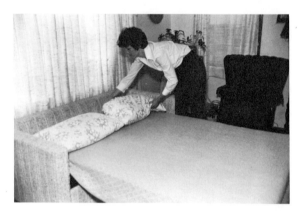

Fig. 14-5C. Converted bed. © *Michael Weisbrot and Family*

ing. But do not compromise the principles of good design in selecting dual-purpose furniture. Figures 14-5A, B, and C show the dual application of a convertible couch-bed.

Another technique for conserving space by rearranging furniture for specific purposes is the use of modular units, as shown in Figs. 14-6A and B. These units can be used to convert a couch to separate chairs as the function demands.

Functional Relationships

Each piece of furniture must not only be functional in comfort and lifestyle support, but must also be functionally consistent in size to other pieces of related furniture. For example, end tables should be the same height as couch or chair arms by which they are used. Coffee tables

Fig. 14-6A. A modular couch configuration.

Fig. 14-6B. Another use of a modular couch configuration. *Gould, Incorporated*

Fig. 14-7. Storage facilities in modular units. *Thomasville Furniture Industries*

must be related in height to the couch seat height and dining chairs must correctly relate in seat height to table height. Likewise, bedside tables should be at a usable level to the bed surface.

Storage Function

Furniture that either doubles as a storage facility or that converts for storage use is extremely effective in reducing clutter in small areas. Modular units (Fig. 14-7) that can be arranged, stacked, or added to fit otherwise dead space solves many storage problems.

FURNITURE ARRANGEMENTS

As covered in Unit 2, and as shown in Fig. 14-8, prepare furniture templates to the same scale as the floor plans. If no floor plan is available, draw rooms to scale. Use graph paper or make your

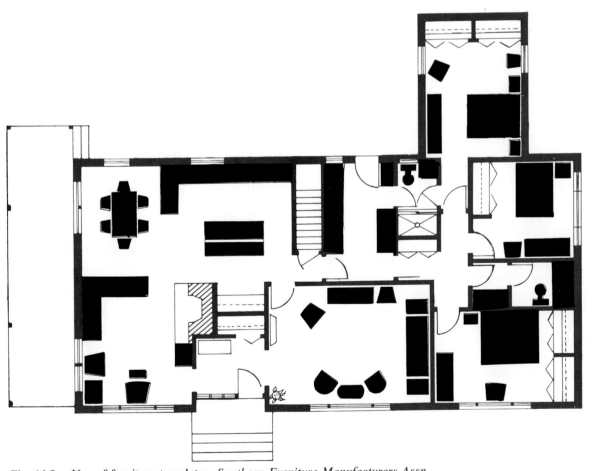

Fig. 14-8. Use of furniture templates. *Southern Furniture Manufacturers Assn.*

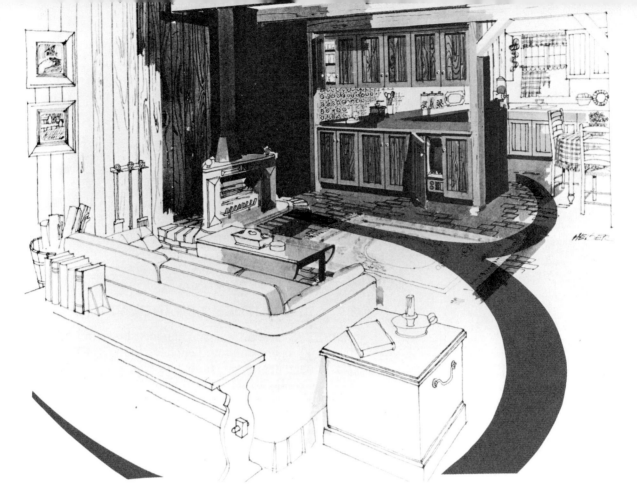

Fig. 14-9. Plan traffic patterns around furniture placement. *Georgia Pacific*

own drawing to a scale of ¼″ = 1′-0″. Be sure to indicate all architectural features, such as doors, windows, offsets, and electrical outlets. Draw each piece of furniture to scale and cut out.

Floor space is already organized to some extent by the partitions and architectural features of your house. Your task is to further organize this space to suit the activities that will take place in each room.

Move the furniture around on the paper until you have an arrangement that suits you. This approach will enable you to know exactly what pieces of furniture you need, where they can be placed, and what size they need to be.

Place large and basic pieces of furniture first. Add any existing furniture. Then it is easy to decide what pieces you need to complete each room.

Remember that rooms have three dimensions and that sometimes an arrangement which looks good on flat paper is not balanced properly when the height of the furniture is considered.

To check this, the wall and furniture elevations can be drawn to scale.

Guidelines for Arranging

Patterns of living vary, and so there are no hard-and-fast rules that apply to all situations. However, there are some basic guidelines that will help you in furniture placement:

Keep traffic lanes open. The paths that people take when walking through a room form the traffic pattern. Place major conversation groups so that they are not disturbed by traffic. If doors are so placed that traffic must bisect the room, you may be able to arrange a main group and a second smaller group.

It is sometimes possible to arrange furniture to redirect traffic and to make the room more usable and interesting.

Allow ample space for people to move easily within the room and to use the furniture with convenience, as shown in Fig. 14-9.

Fig. 14-10. Place large pieces against walls to conserve space. *Marlite*

Place large pieces close to and parallel to the wall. They will take up less floor space and conform to the lines of the room (Fig. 14-10).

Each room should have a center of interest or focal point. This can be a fireplace, a window area, an important piece of furniture, or an outstanding accessory. The way furniture is arranged can also dramatize your choice (Fig. 14-11).

Group together the pieces that are used together. Furniture groupings play a major role in a room's capacity to adapt to different situations. Much of today's furniture is designed to be versatile—it can be shifted into many configurations, as shown in Fig. 14-12, depending on

Fig. 14-12. Different arrangements for the same space.

Fig. 14-11. A couch used as the focal point. *Domani*

265

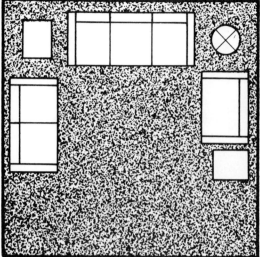

Fig. 14-13. Alternative arrangements. (See above and left.) *Thayer Coggin, Incorporated*

the needs of the occupants. Figure 14-13 also shows several alternative arrangements for the same number of furniture pieces.

Group furniture according to the way it will be used. The conversation group (Fig. 14-14) is usually the starting point in a living area; the eating group, in the dining room; and the sleeping group, in the bedroom. Once these basic arrange-

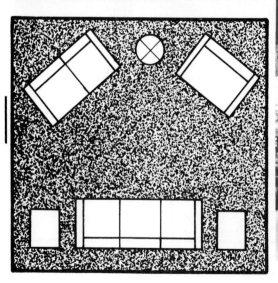

Fig. 14-14. Conversation grouping. *Kohler*

ments are carefully worked out, other groupings can be arranged. Arrangement can determine function. Furniture can often function as a divider or partition between different areas. Bookcases, cabinets, and chests are often finished on back and front so they can be seen from all sides. Much of today's modular furniture can be stacked and added according to need and use.

Standing screens, shutters, and shades are often used to make furniture groupings more effective. The modular furniture shown in Figs. 14-15A and B can be adjusted for a wide variety of functions by adjusting the arrangement.

Harmony of scale, line, and color contributes more to unity than choice of specific furniture styles. Almost any style of furniture can be combined if the pieces have a common unity of character or form. In the final analysis, color is the element that may determine the success of the combination.

The total room should reflect thoughtful use of the elements of good design. Tying lines together is important. Not all surfaces should be the same height, but some uniformity does contribute to the feeling of harmony. Furniture lines should have a pleasing relationship to the architectural features, such as doors, mantels, and windows. Arrangement of furniture also helps to

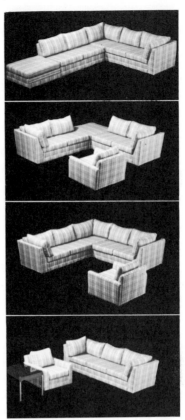

Fig. 14-15A. Modular furniture alternatives. *Simpson Sears, Ltd.*

Fig. 14-15B. Connected assembly of modular units.

267

Fig. 14-16. Furniture unity through rectangular shape. *Potlatch Corp.*

Fig. 14-18. A formally balanced furniture arrangement. *Kevlyn, Incorporated*

carry out the general feeling or character you wish to achieve. The furniture in Fig. 14-16 is related harmoniously through the unity of rectangular shape.

Create a spacious look. When rooms are small, your problem is to make them seem as large as possible. Items of furniture should be kept to a minimum. Lightweight pieces with slender legs and open arms give a feeling of spaciousness. Arrange furniture close to the walls and corners to leave maximum floor space open, as shown in Fig. 14-17. Avoid too many small accessories. A large mirror carefully placed can help increase the apparent size of a room.

Good Design Arrangement

Balance
Heavy pieces of furniture and dominant colors must be distributed harmoniously. Groupings within the room should also balance. A combination of formal and informal balance is usually pleasing. Figure 14-18 shows a formally balanced furniture arrangement and Fig. 14-19 shows an informal arrangement.

Scale and Proportion
Each piece of furniture should be proportioned to suit the room, the space it will occupy in the

Fig. 14-17. Tight wall placement can save floor space. *Georgia Pacific*

Fig. 14-19. An informal furniture arrangement. *Beylerlan, Ltd.*

Fig. 14-20. Furniture with a high degree of line unity. *Chromcraft, Incorporated*

room, and the other furniture. This does not always mean one should select large furniture for large rooms and small furniture for small rooms. For example, a full-length sofa in a small room looks more spacious than would three or four separate chairs. Poor proportion in a room can often be improved by the way furniture is arranged. A long, narrow room, for instance, will appear better proportioned if heavier furniture is placed at the ends.

Contrast or Emphasis

Eye appeal is achieved by use of variety in shape, size, color, and texture. Some high and some low furniture adds interest. Likewise, a combination of some straight and some curved lines is more pleasing than either one alone.

Unity

Proper application of the principles of design should result in a blending effect—a feeling that each part belongs to the whole. Color and line provide a high degree of unity to the furniture shown in Fig. 14-20.

PERIODS AND STYLES

Throughout the ages furniture designs have represented a way of life. Whether an authentic antique, a reproduction, an adaptation, or this year's modern, furniture tells a story about people and their cultures.

The best designs of each era have lived, been copied, modified, and used again and again. Today there is furniture of good design in every discernible style and period, in every price range.

Due to differences in interpretation, terms relating to styles are often confusing. Style refers to the use of design characteristics. Period designates the period of history (or time) when these characteristics were popularized. However, these terms are used interchangeably in the furniture world.

Design characteristics help identify furniture of the various periods. These characteristics are copied or adapted by designers and manufacturers in creating today's styles.

Do not confuse style with type. *Furniture type* refers to a particular set of characteristics which relate to the functional use of the furniture. For example the *types* of beds shown in Fig. 14-21 can be designed and manufactured in a number of different styles although some types do become associated with a particular style. For example, since there were no water beds during the development of period styles, this type of bed is normally associated with contemporary design.

Each manufacturer identifies their products with descriptive names which may also be confusing to the consumer. However, there are three broad areas which the furniture world uses in

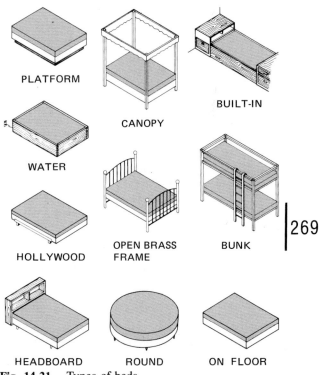

Fig. 14-21. Types of beds.

269

Fig. 14-22. Traditional furniture. *Kimball Furniture Company*

classifying furniture styles: traditional, Provincial, and contemporary.

Traditional (Fig. 14-22) includes those styles with design characteristics typical of master artisans of past generations. The term's period and style usually refer to either an original or a reproduction which contains enough of its characteristics to make its origin clear. Much of the traditional furniture was first designed for royal courts and nobility. Through the years it has been associated with elegance and formality.

The court styles of each country were copied in simplified versions for the masses. This furniture is referred to as *Provincial, country,* or *rural.* The French and Italian Provincial and early American are typical examples of this style.

Contemporary furniture includes a broad group of designs that are adapted for modern methods of production and present-day living. Contemporary furniture is furniture designed without reference to the past and is characterized by smooth, or straight, simple lines and the use of a wide variety of materials. Much of it is small in scale, light in appearance, versatile in use, and easy to maintain. Figure 14-23 shows contemporary furniture which utilizes plastic molding, an art form and technology not available during the development of period furniture.

270

Development of Furniture Styles

Styles of furniture have developed gradually over a long period of time and have reached different areas of the world at widely spaced intervals. The forces that influence the way people live also influence their furnishings.

Fig. 14-23. Contemporary furniture.

Economic status, artistic development, religion, politics, technology, communications, the climate, and available materials have affected the development of the furniture of each era and country.

Current furniture designs usually date back to about the fifteenth century. However, ideas and motifs are often borrowed from the ancient Greeks, Romans, and Egyptians.

As the nations of Europe developed, their peoples began to erect large buildings, chiefly castles, churches, and monasteries. Architecture became an important mode of expression and architectural details were applied to furniture. By the thirteenth and fourteenth centuries the Gothic style flourished and furniture followed the same theme. Furniture was large and heavy with extensive carving. It was characterized by architectural detail, pointed arches, and religious motifs.

The Renaissance which began in Italy during the fourteenth century and reached its height

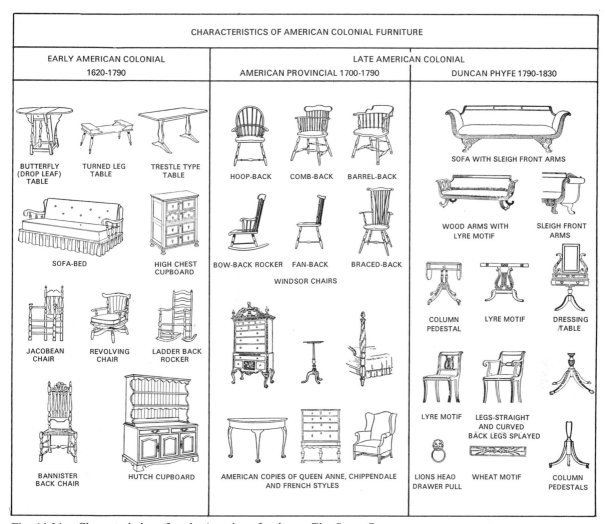

Fig. 14-24. Characteristics of early American furniture. *The Seng Company*

during the last half of the sixteenth century spread to each country in Europe and stimulated an era of cultural development.

Furniture designs reflected the new interest in the arts by becoming more refined in form and more graceful in proportion. The techniques of ornamentation followed the development of an appreciation of the artistic.

Following the Renaissance, the decorative arts flourished in France; then in England and surrounding countries. The early settlers of America were predominantly English but there were also Dutch, Scandinavian, German, French, and Spanish settlers. They brought with them furniture and ideas from their homelands. American furniture styles are a blending of these many influences.

Early American

Early American is the name given to adaptations of furniture used by the first settlers in the colonies, particularly the pioneers who moved westward from New England. Figure 14-24 shows the basic characteristics of early American furniture.

Wood Furniture

Maple is the most popular wood for early American wood furniture. Scrolls and scallops appear

271

Fig. 14-25. Early American wood furniture. *Keller Manufacturing Company*

on bases and tops of cabinets and chests. Edges are rounded and there are no sharp corners, suggesting they were worn over the years, as shown in Fig. 14-25.

Antique brass is often used for hardware, and antique brass back plates used for drawer pulls often have designs derived from nature, such as butterflies.

Upholstered
Sofas and chairs have high backs, to which are generally attached pillows, filled with a soft cushioning material.

A box-pleated skirt across the front and around the sides is often used. It can also be gathered or shirred.

A good way to recognize early American styling of today is by the upholstered wings which extend from the top of the back down to the arm.

Decorative wood, usually with a maple finish, is found on many early American pieces. It may appear as a wood "knuckle" at the front of the arm or as a decorative trim on the face of the wing or arm.

Ranch Styles
Ranch furniture is an informal, provincial style. Simple and rustic in design, it simulates frontier artistry. Decorative motifs and hardware are in

272

the ranch and Western spirit with color themes and finishes suggested by the hues of the desert foliage.

Wood furniture
Wooden seats are flat, not hollowed, and decorative cushions are frequently used. Legs are usually square-cornered and tapered but occasionally are turned. Oak, redwood, maple, pine, birch, and other native woods are customarily employed. (Fig. 14-26).

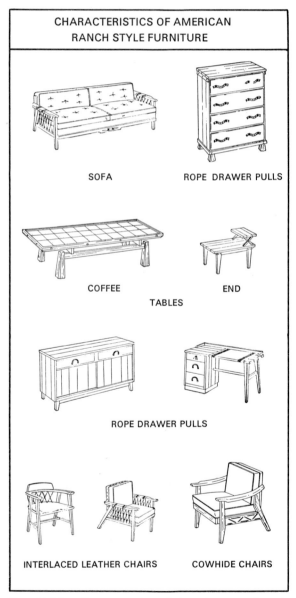

Fig. 14-26. Characteristics of American ranch-style furniture. *The Seng Company*

Fig. 14-27. Upholstered ranch-type furniture. *Ethan Allen Traditional American Interiors*

Upholstered

Use of leather, interlaced plastic cord, or rawhide help maintain the Western pioneer atmosphere, as shown in Fig. 14-27.

Traditional

Literally defined, traditional furniture should mean all styles with an historical heritage. However, because many styles are sold under the name of the country of design origin, *traditional* has come to refer to designs inspired by seventeenth- and eighteenth-century English designers or as exemplified by the designers or royalty: Queen Anne, Louis XV, Chippendale (Fig. 14-28*A*), Adams, Hepplewhite, and Sheraton (Fig. 14-28*B*).

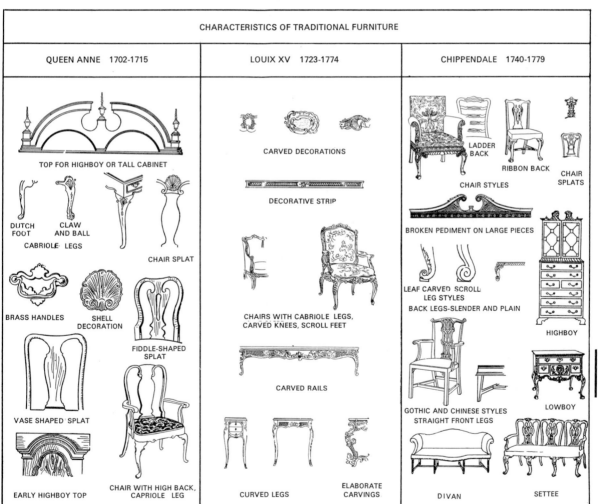

Fig. 14-28*A*. Characteristics of traditional furniture. *The Seng Company*

273

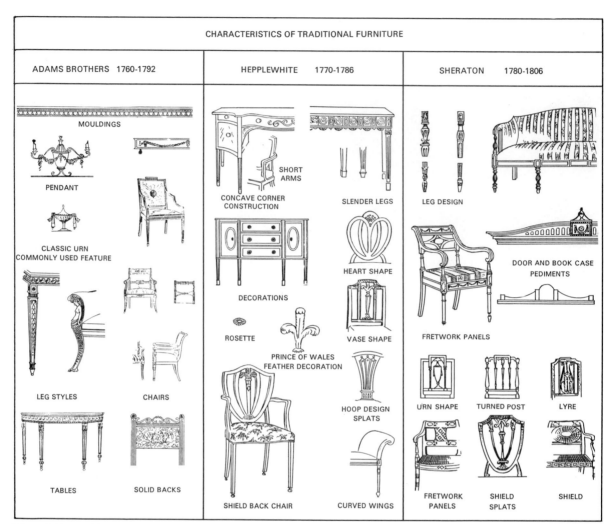

CHARACTERISTICS OF TRADITIONAL FURNITURE

ADAMS BROTHERS 1760-1792 — HEPPLEWHITE 1770-1786 — SHERATON 1780-1806

MOULDINGS
PENDANT
CLASSIC URN COMMONLY USED FEATURE
LEG STYLES
CHAIRS
TABLES
SOLID BACKS

CONCAVE CORNER CONSTRUCTION
SHORT ARMS
SLENDER LEGS
DECORATIONS
ROSETTE
PRINCE OF WALES FEATHER DECORATION
HEART SHAPE
VASE SHAPE
HOOP DESIGN SPLATS
SHIELD BACK CHAIR
CURVED WINGS

LEG DESIGN
DOOR AND BOOK CASE PEDIMENTS
FRETWORK PANELS
URN SHAPE
TURNED POST
LYRE
FRETWORK PANELS
SHIELD SPLATS
SHIELD

Fig. 14-28*B*. Characteristics of traditional furniture. *The Seng Company*

Upholstered

The majority of traditional furniture today is upholstered, as in Fig. 14-29.

A softly rolled arm, reminiscent of Chippendale and Sheraton, is frequently used. A squarer "Lawson" arm or soft "cap" arm is also used on traditional styles.

Backs are softly tufted with an open- or closed-diamond effect, and the sofas and chairs have a straight, trim, formal skirt with neat, inverted pleats. This skirt can be plain or scalloped.

There is a refined, quiet formality associated with traditional upholstered furniture styling of today.

However, unlike English designs of the seventeenth and eighteenth centuries, today's traditional sofas and chairs emphasize comfort.

274

Deep, coiled springs and foam-softened arms and backs are now important in traditional furniture designs.

Wood Furniture

Traditional designs in dining room and bedroom furniture are frequently adaptations of eighteenth-century English designs, from the Georgian period. Motifs from such designers as Hepplewhite, Sheraton, and Chippendale are often used.

The earlier Queen Anne period is also an important influence on today's traditional furniture, as is furniture from the French Empire and American Federal periods, which were both of classic design inspiration. Figure 14-30 shows a summary of characteristics used to identify various traditional styles.

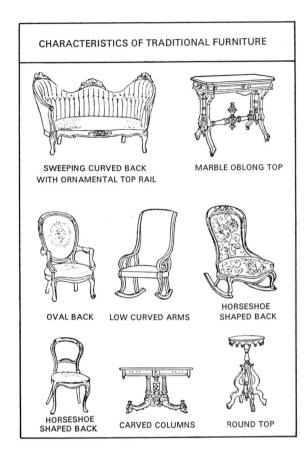

Fig. 14-29. Characteristics of traditional upholstered furniture. *The Seng Company*

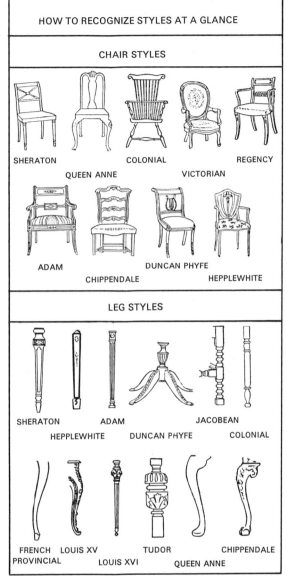

Fig. 14-30. Identification of traditional styles. *The Seng Company*

French Provincial

Louis XVI and his predecessors on the throne of France employed full-time artisans to create the elaborate furniture for the palaces of Versailles and the Louvre.

Copying the fashions of the court was very popular in the eighteenth century, and it followed that court furniture was adapted for use in the provinces, as was the manner of dress.

However, local artisans made simpler versions of the court designs and, as a result, created a new furniture style. See Fig. 14-31. They retained the curving lines and cabriole leg but eliminated the elaborate carvings.

Upholstered

Curved lines, usually a scroll, appear along the top of the back and base of the sofa. Fruitwood-finished wood follows the flowing shape of the base and flows into the cabriole leg. French Provincial sofas never have a skirt, but do have a high, shaped leg. A small pad arm is a feature often seen.

Wood Furniture

Both white and fruitwood finishes are used. Again, there is much use made of curving lines and scallops, along with elaborate ornate drawer handles.

French Provincial bedroom and dining room furniture is graceful and lends itself to formal decorating schemes.

Fig. 14-31. Characteristics of French Provincial furniture—1650–1900. *The Seng Company*

Italian Provincial

This style originated in much the same way as French Provincial. There was a desire on the part of the people to copy the Baroque decorative furnishings from the Renaissance palaces of Florence, Rome, and Venice, and to imitate the style of living of nobility.

The furniture we call *Italian Provincial* is derived from a later period of design, when there was a return to the classic Greek and Roman lines.

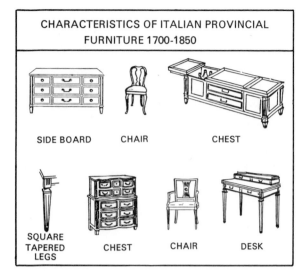

Fig. 14-32. Characteristics of Italian Provincial furniture—1700–1850. *The Seng Company*

Upholstered

Straight, simple lines are found, and there are often square, loose cushions used against the backs of sofas and chairs.

Usually, a square, carved post is the front leg and runs straight to the top of the arms. This post shows a classical influence with its carved designs and routings, features often seen on Greek and Roman pillars.

Italian Provincial sofas and chairs are never skirted and make extensive use of exposed wood trim, which is often walnut or fruitwood.

Wood Furniture

It has the same motif of straight lines and fluted posts. Decorative use is made of ornamental metal drawer pulls. Cherry, walnut, and lighter tones of fruitwood are often used, as shown in Fig. 14-32.

Mediterranean

A furniture style (Fig. 14-33) was developed from the cultures of the countries on the Mediterranean Sea.

It evolved from many influences, from the Renaissance palaces of Italy to the Moorish designs of Spain and North Africa.

Upholstered

Sofas and chairs in this design theme have decorative effects in the form of wood trim, highly

CHARACTERISTICS OF MEDITERRANEAN FURNITURE

DEEP MOLDINGS LOW LOOK

CHAIR

HIGH BACK CHAIR

TURNED SPINDLE SOFA

TRESTLE TABLE

ORNAMENTAL FRETS AND GUILLOCHES

OCTAGONAL TABLE

TRESTLE TABLE

CONSOLE

OCTAGONAL TABLE

Fig. 14-33. Characteristics of Mediterranean furniture. *The Seng Company*

Fig. 14-34. Contemporary scaling of Mediterranean designs. *Fox Manufacturing Company*

Fig. 14-35. Contemporary molded furniture. *Chromcraft, Incorporated*

carved. This detail can appear on the outside of an arm or in decorative carvings along the back of the sofa or chair.

Wood Furniture

It is a decorative type of furniture with deep moldings and carved detailing. Chests and dressers have a sculptured appearance. There is considerable use of turned spindles. Metal hardware is often filigree and an important design feature. While the overall lines are generally straight, the ornamental details have elaborate shapes.

Mediterranean designs are massive in appearance, and emphasize ornamentation, as seen in Fig. 14-34. Yet today's designs are scaled for smaller homes.

Contemporary

All the above furniture styles had strong ties with the past. Modern furniture represents a break with the past, and a departure from historical designs and classical shapes.

Modern furniture (Fig. 14-35) reflects the needs and technologies of today. It is furniture which is created with new materials such as plastic, glass, and metal, as well as with beautiful woods and fabrics.

The mood of modern architecture employs many of the same design elements, such as cubes

277

Cube-emphasizing furniture. *Thayer Coggin, Incorporated*

Fig. 14-36B. Rectangular emphasis in wall-hung furniture. *Lewis Reens*

Fig. 14-36C. Use of circles and arts in furniture design. *James Lansing Company*

278

Fig. 14-36D. Furniture emphasizing clean, unbroken contour lines. *Knoll Associates*

(Fig. 14-36A) rectangles (Fig. 14-36B), and curves (Fig. 14-36C).

In 1919 Walter Gropius founded the Bauhaus School in Germany. It was dedicated to a new form of industrial design expression, one which would be creative and fresh and would not rely on the past.

From this school came the movement which has now influenced furniture design throughout Europe, moving from Scandinavia to the United States.

Modern furniture can be recognized by an absence of ornamentation. Lines are clean and unbroken (Fig. 14-36D) whether they are straight or curved. The legs on sofas, chairs, and wood pieces are higher than other styles.

The design freedom has resulted in many functional new ideas never known in furniture. Multipurpose pieces, modular components for storage, and slim but highly comfortable seating pieces are all the result of the modern trend.

Precise artistry and careful tailoring are other "trademarks" of good modern furniture design.

Modern furniture design is in a constant state of development. It will never reach its peak as long as there are new materials, new problems, and new methods of manufacture to challenge the designers. Figure 14-36A shows the application and blend of metal and fabric into a stark straight-line design.

Newer contemporary sofas and chairs can be recognized by a visual softness and loose-back cushions with a billowy comfortable look. The

Fig. 14-37. Contemporary furniture with a built-in yet soft, comfortable look. *Scholz Homes, Inc.*

profile of the furniture is an important design feature, as shown in Fig. 14-37.

Scandinavian

Scandinavian renditions possess severe, but flowing, silhouettes and an almost total absence of ornamental flourishes, as seen in Fig. 14-38.

Wood furniture

Styles are in plain, straight grain woods (walnut, teak) in simple curves and roundings, with tapered feet and flat turnings. Legs are square-tapered or round-tapered.

Fig. 14-38. Scandinavian furniture. *Armstrong Cork Company*

Fig. 14-39. Oriental furniture. *Thomasville Furniture Industries*

Upholstered

Woven fibers of plain design are used widely in chair seats and modern plastics are evident.

Oriental

Fine Oriental furniture (Fig. 14-39) is usually diminutive in size, simple in form, with luxurious undertones. It mixes well to predominate or accent traditional or contemporary furniture. Partitions, *shoji screens,* and windows covered with translucent paper with oriental designs are consistent with Oriental furniture.

BUYING FURNITURE

Wood furniture is usually referred to as *case goods.* This category of furniture includes chests, dressers, tables, headboards, desks, and similar items. Recognizing good quality in case goods requires a knowledge of different woods and wood finishes as well as good construction features. Figure 14-40 shows construction details to look for in purchasing quality furniture.

While wood has always been and still is the favorite, metals, glass, plastic, and other materials are being used in making today's furniture. Often, interesting effects are achieved by a combination of materials.

Woods

Quality, availability, and cost usually determine how various woods are used in making furniture.

Botanically, woods are classified either as hard or soft.

Hardwood trees have a natural beauty of grain that makes them desirable for fine quality furniture. As a group, hardwoods are stronger and less likely to dent than the softwoods; they also hold screws more securely. Popular hardwoods for furniture construction include walnut, mahogany, birch, cherry, maple, gum, pecan, and oak.

Softwood trees have soft areas which do not accept natural finishes well for furniture use. The most often used softwoods are redwood, pine, cypress, and cedar.

Wood is composed mainly of cellulose in the form of long fibers or cells. The arrangement of these fibers influences the strength of the wood, and the ability to absorb paints, stains, and finishes. As new fibers are formed during the growth of the tree, the grain pattern develops. The various species of woods have different types of fibers that affect texture. For example, birch and maple have a fine grain; oak has a coarse or "open" grain.

A cross section of a tree trunk shows fibers arranged in "annual rings." When the fiber arrangement is distorted, twisted, or curled, the

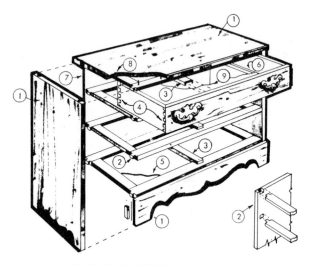

1. SELECTED HARDWOODS
2. MORTISE AND TENON JOINTS
3. HEAVY DUTY DRAWER GUIDES
4. DRAWERS-DOVETAILED JOINTS
5. DUST PANELS BETWEEN DRAWERS
6. DURABLE DRAWER BOTTOMS
7. BACKS RECESSED INTO ENDS
8. WELL MOUNTED TOP AND SIDES
9. DRAWER INTERIORS SANDED AND SEALED

Fig. 14-40. Furniture construction details. *Southern Furniture Manufacturers Assn.*

Fig. 14-41. A flat-grain pattern. *Thomasville Furniture Industries*

Fig. 14-42. A crotch-grain pattern.

grain patterns may be enhanced. Examples of this are the crotch figures, knots, and burls. The way the trunk is cut also influences the grain pattern of the wood. Figure 14-41 shows a flat-grain pattern and Fig. 14-42 shows a crotch-grain pattern.

Solid and Veneered Woods

Either solid, veneered, or a combination of both can be used in making furniture of varying qualities.

"Solid" construction of all wood parts, including case and table tops, end panels, drawer fronts, and headboard panels, are made of whole wood, usually the same species. There may be some surface decoration such as inlay. Most of the solid furniture on the market is early American and colonial style furniture with some Scandinavian and eighteenth-century traditional pieces.

A majority of the furniture manufactured today makes use of plywood construction. The top layer, or face veneer, is cut from wood selected for beauty of grain, color, and texture. The other layers are made of wood that is strong and stable but less costly. The center, or core, is usually thicker than the others and can be either solid or chipcore. All layers are glued with synthetic resins that provide a secure bond. Improved methods of gluing and alternating grains provide strength, both crosswise and lengthwise, and therefore maximum strength in construction. Plywood is used as the base in much of the finest furniture. Rare and exotic woods are often used for the exposed surfaces.

281

Popular Furniture Woods

The history of furniture reflects the availability and use of various woods in making fine furniture. At the present time designers are using a wide variety of woods. The woods are chosen for their colors, textures, and grains, all of which become an integral part of the furniture design.

Oak

Because of its availability and its hard, durable qualities, oak has been widely used for both architectural design and furniture since medieval days. Many species of the oak tree grow in North America, Asia, Europe, and Africa. About 50 varieties are native to the United States. The white and red oak are best known.

Oak has a characteristic coarse "open grain." This makes it especially suited to special color effects and finishes. The natural color varies from light yellow to a deep amber.

Maple

Maple wood is close-grained, hard, strong, and durable. It shapes easily and has high resistance to splitting. Its fine texture has a natural smoothness; its color range is from almost white to reddish brown.

The grain of maple is normally straight but the wavy, curly, and bird's-eye grain patterns are beautiful variations.

Birch

The general characteristics of birch are similar to maple. Since it is durable and relatively low in cost, it is often used in plywood construction and for structural parts of furniture.

The color is light golden brown, but it can be bleached or stained to resemble other woods.

Fruitwoods

Since there is no *one* fruitwood, this term is often misunderstood. The term covers the group of woods coming from trees that bear fruits. The most common are cherry, apple, and pear. Other woods are often given a fruitwood finish. This finish is a light brown tone to simulate that used in making French Provincial furniture.

Cherry

Cherry is the most widely used in the fruitwoods. It has a natural reddish color. The grain is close and suited to a variety of finishes, but the grain pattern is less distinctive than that of some of the other hardwoods.

Due to the waste in cutting, cherry wood is expensive. Apple and pear woods are rare and used chiefly for trim and inlay work on fine furniture. Both are light in color and have fine smooth grain.

Teak

Teak wood is imported from India, Burma, and surrounding areas. It is a moderately hard wood with a natural color that ranges from light to dark brown with fine black streaks.

Since it works easily, it has been a favorite with furniture designers over the years.

Rosewood

The color gradations from light to dark reddish brown make this an interesting wood. In modern furniture the finish is chosen to capitalize on the dark streaks often found in rosewood. It is an imported wood from Brazil and India.

Mahogany

Master artisans of the past often preferred mahogany because of its strength, beautiful grain, and workability. Genuine mahogany grows in tropical regions of Central America, the West Indies, South America, and Africa. Luan, known as *Philippine mahogany,* and the primavera, known as *white mahogany,* are both used in making furniture but are not true mahoganies.

Natural mahogany varies in color from a light golden brown to a deeper brown with a reddish cast. Today's finish is often chosen to enhance the natural light brown color. Or the wood is bleached and finished a lighter tone.

Walnut

The popularity of walnut for fine furniture is due primarily to its natural beauty. It is a hardwood with high strength that can withstand stress and strain. It has a medium grain and can be finished in a variety of ways.

The different species vary in color range. The native American walnut, or "black walnut," ranges in tone from light to dark rich brown. It is named for the color of the nut shells. Butternut, often called "white walnut," is lighter in color. The crotch, burl, and stump wood produce a wide variety of beautiful grain patterns.

Gum

This is a native wood that is readily available and relatively inexpensive. However, it must be seasoned properly under controlled conditions or it will split and warp. It has a close smooth grain that is easy to work with. It can be finished to resemble walnut, mahogany, and other woods.

Gum is often used for framework and solid parts, such as posts and legs.

Ash

White ash is the most common variety used in furniture construction. It is a hard, strong wood with a grain very much like oak. Ash is used mostly in frames and unexposed parts. The natural color varies from white to light brown.

Poplar

Several types grow in eastern and southern states. They range in color from white through yellow to light brown. The woods are easy to work, lightweight, and take well to paints and finishes.

Pine

Pine is a softwood and is not widely used in furniture construction. It is used in certain styles of inexpensive furniture and in making unpainted furniture.

The Finish

Many types of finishes are used today. Woods are often given an entirely new look through their finish. For example, we usually think of mahogany as a dark reddish wood. With one of the new finishes it can be a soft brown color resembling walnut or fruitwood. Woods may be bleached and stained, made dark or light, and given a glossy or dull finish. Finishes are applied to wood furniture

- To produce or develop color
- To seal the pores, to prevent moisture movement, and to provide a smooth even surface
- To protect the wood
- To decorate the surface

Fine wood finishes require a series of processes that cannot be hurried. Many manufacturers maintain that a lively patina can be developed only by the time-consuming hand method. Naturally, the number of operations and cost of labor affect retail cost.

Plastics have been developed to match wood grain and are being used by many manufacturers. Improved printing or engraving wood

techniques have also made these processes gain in consumer acceptance. Each season finds these finishes being used on better furniture.

You should inspect any finish under good lighting conditions. It should be smooth and free from rough spots. Some finishes are resistant to heat, alcohol, water, and other types of wear.

Labels concerning finishes are extremely important. Don't be misled by the label that reads "Walnut finish," or any other kind of wood finish. It means that the piece of wood has been finished to look like walnut and does not refer to the type of wood. Manufacturers develop their own finishes and name them for customer appeal.

Buying Metal, Plastic, and Glass

Several other materials are in various stages of development and are being used to simulate, complement, or replace wood.

Among those growing rapidly in use and quality are the synthetics. For some time, they have been skillfully used to provide scuff-proof, wear-resistant tops for tables, chests, and other pieces of furniture. In addition, they are molded into items of furniture, such as a chair or table; into parts, such as legs or drawer fronts; or into intricate decorative designs. Both the laminates and molded plastics can be finished to look like beautiful woods, marble, and fabric.

Because plastics are light in weight, durable, easily maintained, and comparatively inexpensive they are likely to play an increasingly important role in furniture production. Many manufacturers have combined plastics, woods, and metals together to form furniture of interesting design.

Metal in furniture may be chrome-plated or anodized. Among the finishes are bronze, copper, and wrought iron black.

The metals are strong, durable materials suitable for indoor as well as outdoor furniture. Modern designers have found many interesting ways to combine metals with wood.

See-through materials, such as glass and plexiglass, are also being used in new and interesting ways.

Buying Upholstered Furniture

Today's upholstered furniture comes in a wide variety of styles, sizes, qualities, and prices as

283

COMMON TYPES OF UPHOLSTERED FURNITURE

CROWN OR CAMELBACK   CHARLES OF LONDON   FIRESIDE

CHESTERFIELD   LAWSON   LAWSON

TUXEDO   CHARLES OF LONDON   TUB

OCCASIONAL OPEN ARM   CLOSED ARM   FANBACK   CLUB

WING STANDARD AND TUFTED   BARRELL   BANK OF ENGLAND

COCKFIGHT   COGSWELL   CORNER   SHELL

Fig. 14-43. Types of upholstered furniture. *The Seng Company*

284

shown in Fig. 14-43. The choice of style is determined by the general atmosphere you wish to create.

Consider the size of the house, floor space, and the persons who will be using the furniture when determining the size of pieces.

Quality in upholstered furniture is difficult to judge. There are some features you can see and test carefully. However, much of what you do not see affects the quality of upholstered furniture. This means you must rely upon the

integrity of the manufacturer and the dealer, although some information is included on the label.

The quality of the materials and skill used to create the outside is an indication of the general quality on the inside. Since the outside part is exposed to daily scrutiny, there are some features you should check carefully. Good tailoring is an indication of skillful work throughout. The fabric should be cut and placed so that the weave or grain line will look even. This means that the crosswise threads will run parallel to the bottom edge of the frame; the lengthwise threads will be perpendicular to the base of the frame.

Decoration

In general you can expect better quality in furniture that has little or no decoration. If furniture has good line, good proportion, and is of good quality (unless authenic period), decoration is not necessary. However, some styles of furniture require embellishment. Veneer is often used as a form of decoration. Carving, marquetry, and inlay are expensive and are seldom found in low-cost furniture. Low-quality imitations are quickly detected.

Upholstery Fabrics

You may purchase a piece of furniture already covered but more often you will select a style and then have a choice of upholstery fabrics. Your choice of fabric may completely change the general appearance of the piece of furniture. The fabrics used for the same piece of furniture can vary considerably in quality and price.

Upholstery fabric should be strong and closely woven. Pull in both lengthwise and crosswise to see that the threads do not shift. Or scratch the fabric with your fingernail to see if there are threads that will catch or pull easily.

Most upholstery has a backing finish which is rubber, a synthetic rubber, or one of the newer foam products. This helps make the upholstery remain smooth and firm over the padding. It also makes it easier for the upholsterer to handle.

Learn about the fiber content as fiber has certain characteristics that help determine wear. Fabrics sold by the yard must be labeled according to fiber content. This does not apply to furniture that is already upholstered. However, a reliable dealer can get this information for you.

You cannot tell about the fastness of color by appearance. This information also should be on a label. One of the most critical tests for upholstery is whether or not the fabric is colorfast to light.

Finishes are available to add spot and stain resistance to all fabrics regardless of fiber content. Some protect against water-borne stains; some protect against water and oily stains. They also give increased resistance to wear. If a fabric has been treated for spot and stain resistance, this information is usually included on the label. Permanent mothproofing prevents moth damage to wools and wool blends.

All of the classic types of fabric are made for upholstery use—tapestry, damask, brocade, homespun, bouclé, frieze, and plush as well as velvet, tweeds, and chintz. Each of these fabrics is made in a number of different fibers or combination of fibers. Many of the newer fabrics are described by textures, color combinations, or the country of origin.

Hems and Pleats   Hems and pleats should be even and hang straight. Check grain line carefully.

Pattern   Fabric patterns, whether large or small, should be centered and carefully placed. The placement of pattern, particularly bold patterns, on the back, cushion, front, and arms should be placed to best advantage.

Welting   The cording or welting should be smooth, straight, and firmly stitched.

Cushions   Cushions should fit snugly into seat corners and with adjoining cushions. Reversible cushions will help distribute wear.

Use of Fabric   In better-quality furniture the areas under the cushions and across the back are of the same quality fabric as that used for the more exposed areas.

Decorative Detail   Tufting, trapunto, buttons, and other decorative details add to the cost of furniture. They give the individuality one expects in the more expensive and high-quality furniture.

Selecting Appropriate Colors and Fabrics for Furniture Styles

Early American   Colorful prints in fresh, bright colors are very effective. A glazed chintz or textured fabric printed with scenic designs is very popular. Prints may be drawings of old shop signs, nautical themes, or colonial homes of the period. The large floral pattern of a country garden also complements the informal early American style. Quilted prints provide a luxurious appearance.

The colors should be strong and clear, whether in a print or on tweeds which are also very popular.

Traditional   The fabric for this style should have an elegant appearance. Satins, either plain or textured, are good. Soft floral prints, in which the flowers are formal in arrangement, enhance the traditional sofa or chair. Quilted prints, particularly where the quilt stitching follows the outline of the floral pattern, add richness.

Other good traditional fabrics are damask, velvet, brocade, matelassé, and satin.

Traditional styling can take either pastel colors or stronger shades. All colors are good, particularly warm green, blue, gold, and red.

French Provincial   The use of pattern is very important on this style. The pattern can range from a very small print to a large etched scenic design. A "toile" print showing French country scenes is a popular choice.

The floral prints suitable on French Provincial are less formal in design than used on traditional.

All of the prints can be quilted and give a look of elegance to the fabric.

Nubby country tweeds are popular with this style also.

Colors can be robust or soft. Popular are the medium tones such as a delph blue.

Italian Provincial   Velvet, cut velvet, damask, or satins are all effective with this style.

The classical heritage of the style is reflected in the choice of fabrics. The Greek acanthus leaf is often used on the damask fabrics.

Rich Renaissance colors are most attractive. The bold tones of red, deep green, and gold add beauty to the furniture style.

285

Contemporary Both flat textured fabrics and nubby tweeds are good with modern furniture.

Fresh bright prints, which can be modern floral designs or an abstract pattern, are increasing in popularity.

Modern upholstered furniture lends itself to strong, clear colors with depth.

The bright, fresh colors are used both in plain fabrics and prints.

Important colors in modern decor today are vivid blue, olive, lemon, and even bright red.

The nubby, heavy tweeds can be used in subtle shades such as a salt-and-pepper combination.

Leather

Leather is an excellent, though expensive, upholstery material. Improvements have made leather softer, thus making beautiful tailoring detail easier. Leathers are available in a wide range of colors and textures. Leather upholstery combined with wood is a distinguishing feature of the Ames chair shown in Fig. 14-44.

Vinyl Plastics

There are many qualities of vinyl plastic. Some look like leather, some like fabric, and some have a fabric backing.

Low-quality vinyl tears at the corners and splits at the seams. It also has low resistance to stains and fading. However, vinyl is easily cleaned. It is waterproof but difficult to repair once it breaks.

Review Questions

1. Define the following furniture terms: modular, period, flat grain, case goods, period, contemporary, colonial, traditional, hardwood, veneer.

Fig. 14-44. The Ames chair utilizes leather effectively. *Knape Manufacturing Company*

2. For your scrapbook find examples of period, colonial, and traditional furniture.
3. Complete exercises on pages 61–64 in the workbook.
4. List three types of furniture compatible with Tudor architecture.
5. List three styles of furniture compatible with colonial architecture.
6. List six dark furniture hardwoods.
7. Sketch furniture suitable for the plan shown in Fig. 1-24 A.
8. Sketch furniture compatible with the plan shown in Fig. 1-21 A.
9. Describe the difference between *furniture period* and *furniture style*.
10. List six features to look for in purchasing furniture.

ACCESSORIES

unit 15

The total interior design job is not complete until every item contributing to that design is placed in a room. The floor plan may show information relating to wall covering and ceiling treatments, but the design is not unified until such accessory items as clocks, screens, pillows, mirrors, books, plants, and pictures are added. Accessories such as these can add the necessary line, form, and color ingredients to a room. They can occupy needed space, provide light and shadow variations, and contribute material variety to a room. Accessories can help provide balance, rhythm, and emphasis to an otherwise uninteresting decor. Accessories can help balance proportions and provide unity and variety perhaps not achieved through the use of furniture, wall, ceiling, and floor treatments. In short, the choice and arrangement of accessories in a room can, through the use of the elements of design, complete the total decor through the application of the principles of design.

Accessories may be purely decorative such as pictures, plants, and flowers, or be functional, such as screens, pillows, candles, mirrors, and books. But regardless of the function, accessories should be used to complement the design and not dominate it. Figure 15-1A shows the relationship between accessories and other interior design components. Too few accessories can result in a stark, nonfunctioning room. Accessories should be the most personal items in a decor, reflecting the personality, tastes, and even background of the occupants. The accessories in Fig. 15-1B reflect the interests and taste of the occupants, and also reinforce the colonial decor. In this case, accessories take on more meaning than simple ornaments: they contribute to the enrichment of a room by reflecting the personality of the occupants.

Fashion as reflected in the use of accessories changes constantly. When game hunting was popular, walls were covered with trophies of the hunt. In Victorian times, people filled their homes with collections of reflections and memories of the immediate past. Today, the use of accessories is an individual affair and varies greatly depending on the background and interests of the occupants. Usually, personal interests, tastes, and backgrounds are reflected, not only in the use of accessories, but also in the entire interior decor and in the selection of the basic achitectural style. For this reason, accessories and all furnishings are usually consistent with the architectural style of the structure.

Add functional accessories first, since they are required. Add decorative or nonfunctional accessories last. Quite often, once functional accessories are added, there is less need for purely decorative accessories, since functional accessories play both roles.

WALL ACCESSORIES

Functional wall accessories include shelving, mirrors, cabinets, and clocks. Purely decorative wall accessories include pictures, collages, mirrors, plaques, sconces, etc. In the process of designing the interior, usually some architectural feature has been added to a wall. Windows, doors, fireplaces, and offsets fall into this category. The selection and placement of wall accessories must be designed around these existing

ROOM PLANNING GUIDE

PERIOD TYPE	ASSOCIATED STYLES	WALLS & CEILINGS	FLOOR COVERINGS		DRAPERIES			UPHOLSTERY FABRICS
			HARD SURFACE	CARPETING	FABRIC	COLORS	DESIGN	
SPANISH RENAISSANCE	Italian Renaissance Early English Louis XIV	Rough plaster Painted Ceilings, same or beamed	Hardwood Tiles Linoleum in tile pattern.	Spanish or Oriental rugs	Velvet, damask, crewel work, India prints, printed and emb. linen.	Rich, vigorous colors; red, green and gold	Bold patterns in classic and heraldic designs, also arabesques	Leather Tapestry Velvet Linen Brocatelle
EARLY COLONIAL	All Early English styles William and Mary Queen Anne wing chair	Oak panels Rough plaster with oak trim Pargetry ceilings	Hardwood flooring or planks. Linoleum in jaspe pattern.	Braided or hooked rugs	Crewel embroideries, hand-blocked linen. Silk and worsted damask, velvet, brocade.	Full-bodied crimson, green, and yellow.	Large bold patterns: tree branch, fruits, flowers, oak leaf, animals, heraldic.	Tapestry Leather Needlework Velvet Brocade
LATE COLONIAL	Late Georgian Chippendale Queen Anne Duncan Phyfe French Provincial	Smooth plaster light trim Wall paper, scenic and Chinese designs. Paneling Ceiling, plaster	Dark hardwood flooring. Linoleum in plain or jaspe patterns.	Hooked, braided, Oriental rugs. Domestic rugs or carpet, plain, two-toned or patterned.	Toile de Jouy, damask, chintz, organdy, cretonne.	All colors, but more subdued than in early period.	Scenic birds, animals, and floral.	Haircloth Mohair Rep Linen Chintz Velours
MODERN	Swedish modern Chinese Chippendale	Painted solid colors. Stripe figured, plain papers, Combinations of above.	Hardwood parquetry Linoleum in modern pattern.	Carpeting Rugs in solid colors. Geometric patterns.	Textured and novelty weaves. All fabrics.	All colors, bright to pastel	Solid colors Modern designs Stripes	All fabrics Novelty weaves Plastics
FRENCH PROVINCIAL	18th Century American Colonial, Federal Biedermeier	Smooth plaster Wallpaper in scenic or geometric designs.	Hardwood parquetry	Aubussons Homespun carpet. Small pattern Orientals.	Chintz Cretonne Blocked linen, velvet	Subdued colors. Pastel shades	Screen prints Block print.	Solid colors Textured weaves Tapestry
VICTORIAN	Colonial Wm. and Mary Queen Anne	Larger pattern paper.	Hardwood	Carpeting in large patterns. Orientals.	Velvet Brocades Damask	Turkey red. Other rich colors.	Solid colors Formal patterns.	Haircloth Needlework

Fig. 15-1A. Room planning guide. *The Seng Company*

Fig. 15-1B. Accessories reflect the occupants' tastes. *Drexel Furniture*

architectural features, otherwise the entire balance, proportion, and unity of the wall will be sacrificed. For this reason, the texture and color of the wall as well as the placement of furniture and other design features must be completed before the accessory design is started. However, remember that accessories should not be treated as an afterthought. They should be incorporated into the total design affecting the original color and texture of the floor, ceiling, and walls.

In designing a wall treatment, first prepare a wall elevation sketch on cross-sectional paper complete with architectural features and furniture placement. The remaining space represents the challenge for wall accessory design. Next, make overlay sketches of various alternatives, beginning first with consideration of functional accessories such as bookshelves and cabinets. If functional accessories are not needed on a particular wall, begin successive sketches of decorative accessories such as paintings, mirrors, and so forth. Figure 15-2 shows a wall sketch in preparation for accessory design.

Fig. 15-2. Wall sketch used for accessory planning. *Georgia Pacific*

Fig. 15-3. Accessory grouping. *Nettle Creek Industries*

difficult to arrange in this respect. However, breaking the wall down into a series of groupings while keeping in mind the basic principles of balance, emphasis, proportion, and unity is the best approach. Developing a high degree of unity as shown in Fig. 15-3 is the key to good wall grouping design.

Horizontal groupings are ideal over mantels, couches, buffets, chests, or similar architectural features. Vertical arrangements as shown in Fig. 15-4 are best suited for narrow strips of walls. Random groupings are more asymmetrical and suited to square or rectangular surfaces, as shown in Fig. 15-5.

Fig. 15-4. Vertical accessory arrangement. *Syroco*

Fig. 15-5. Asymmetrical random grouping. *Syroco*

Groupings

In designing the treatment for any wall it is wise to think in terms of groupings of accessories. In every grouping one focal point should dominate. Large uninterrupted blank walls without windows, doors, or architectural features are most

Fig. 15-6. Built-in shelves.

Shelves

Shelving is a most versatile and extremely functional wall treatment method. Not only are shelves a functional accessory, but the objects placed on shelves can vary greatly to provide almost limitless variety. Prebuilt shelves and built-in shelves are available in a wide range of sizes and shapes. This makes it possible to fill almost exactly the amount of space necessary.

Shelves can either be built in as shown in Fig. 15-6, assembled from modular units, or purchased as individual shelves. Regardless of which type is used, sketches should be made of the wall elevation, with alternative configurations complete with anticipated shelf content, before deciding on the most appropriate type of shelf. In designing shelves, remember to allow sufficient vertical height for easy access and to eliminate the crammed appearance. In placing objects on shelves, do so with the principles of design in mind, especially balance and variety.

In designing shelves remember to incorporate effective lighting techniques. Shelving is available in wood, metal, glass, and plastic, but must be selected to be consistent in color and texture with the remainder of the decor.

Pictures

Pictures are probably one of the most frequently used decorating accessories for walls, since

Fig. 15-7. Pictures supply focal points. *Bassett Furniture Industries*

Fig. 15-8. Related groupings of pictures. *Syroco*

291

they're available in all shapes and sizes, colors, and themes, and can be used singularly as a focal point (Fig. 15-7), or in groupings with other related objects, as shown in Fig. 15-8. The variety of subject matter in pictures is even greater than the styles and types of pictures available. Detailed (busy) pictures are best displayed on plain walls, and vice versa. In grouping pictures, pay particular attention to the principles of unity and

Fig. 15-9. Unity and variety practiced in grouping.

Fig. 15-10. Individual, functional mirror accessory. *Scholz Homes, Inc.*

variety. These principles of design are exemplified in the arrangement shown in Fig. 15-9.

In positioning pictures, don't place them too high out of eye contact, or too low, obstructing the use of the space. Remember that vertically aligned pictures or groups make a room look higher, while horizontally oriented pictures or groups make a room look wider.

Apply the same principles of selection and positioning of paintings to photographs, collages, posters, etchings, lithographs, maps, plaques, or sconces.

Picture frames must be selected to coincide with the scale, texture, and color of the picture. Smaller pictures require narrow frames, and, of course, larger pictures can accommodate wider frames. The color of the frame should harmonize with the picture and also with the other colors and tones used in the room. Mattes are sometimes more effective than frames, especially if the picture is relatively small, since a mat can widen the size of the space occupied. Mattes are also very effective in providing the transition from a patterned background to the picture. Other pictures, such as posters, need no frame if their size and subject matter supply sufficient identity.

292

Fig. 15-11. Decorative mirrors. *Syroco*

Mirrors

Mirrors may be either functional or decorative, and may be either individual, as shown in Fig. 15-10, or arranged in decorative clusters, as shown in Fig. 15-11. Mirrors may be used to open up a room, that is, make it seem larger, by placing a mirror near a window, or at right angles to a corner. Functional mirrors include those built into bath, dressing, or powder rooms, and freestanding mirrors located in bedrooms or dressing rooms. Decorative mirrors are more frequently used in the living area, to create an expansion of space.

Fig. 15-12. Traditional built-in wall cabinets. *Benjamin Moore Company*

Wall Cabinets and Racks

Wall cabinets are either built in, as shown in Fig. 15-12, or purchased as preconstructed modular units, as shown in Fig. 15-13. The choice is dependent on the amount of space available and how closely a commercially manufactured unit will fit the space and the decor. Remember that including cabinets that completely fill a floor-to-ceiling space diminishes the size of the room. Consequently, some variation of cabinet and shelf space usually is more appealing than solid cabinet storage facilities.

Clocks

Figure 15-14 shows a clock accessory consistent in style with the remainder of the decor. Since clocks are available in such a wide variety of styles, the selection of this functional accessory should be carefully undertaken to ensure that the style is consistent with the architectural decor.

FLOOR ACCESSORIES

Floor accessories such as statuary, screens, plants, and floor pillows occupy space in relation to furniture but should be assigned last and should not compete with basic furniture. Floor accessories either perform a function, fill in an awkward space in the floor pattern, or provide a focal point of emphasis.

Fig. 15-13. Modular wall unit. *Haas Cabinet Company*

Fig. 15-14. Clock accessories should be consistent in style. *Thomas Industries, Incorporated*

Statuary

Statuary is nonfunctional but may be used to fill unused blank spaces or provide a point of em-

293

Fig. 15-15. Statuary must relate to the remainder of the furniture.

Fig. 15-16. Plants can create a center of focus. *Scholz Homes, Inc.*

phasis. Selection of floor statuary should be carefully made with particular attention to the role of emphasis and proportion to the total decor, especially furniture. Notice how the statuary in Fig. 15-15 relates to the remainder of the furnishings.

Screens

The popularity of the open plan has caused a rebirth in the use of screens as room dividers. In this capacity, screens are functional accessories, breaking visual contact from one area to another. But screens may also be used to mask an unattractive feature. Screens are available in panels of three, four, and five units hinged together. Panels are covered with fabric, wallpaper, or paint, and are made of sheer silk, rice paper, clear translucent glass, plastics, tapestry, brocades, leather, shutters, bamboo poles, plywood, and fabric. The material chosen for screens should be consistent with the material used as wall treatment for the remainder of the room.

Pillows

Pillows are both functional and decorative accessories. They can add color and shape to a

room, and can also be used as auxiliary furniture. Pillows in both categories are available in many sizes and shapes (circular, square, triangular, and rectangular) and in many textural materials. Floor pillows can be used to break up symmetrical lines of furniture, or to provide additional lounging facilities.

Plants

Although inanimate objects such as tables, chairs, rugs, and pictures are used primarily by interior designers, plants are used as well. Plants are living things, and people relate to them in that manner. Consequently, plants provide a welcome organic relief to the sterility of many interiors. Modern architecture is partly responsible for the revival of the use of indoor plants. The soft flowing lines and color of plants and their everchanging nature add contrast to the straight lines and sometimes boring consistency of many modern interiors. Plants are available in a wide variety of sizes, shapes, and colors, although, of course, green predominates. They can be used as a point of emphasis, or to camouflage or minimize unsightly room features. Plant areas should create an area of emphasis, as shown in Fig. 15-16, while individual plants, as shown in Fig. 15-17,

Fig. 15-17. Use of individual plants. *Scholz Homes, Inc.*

are used to blend parts of the decor together or to fill in dead areas. The area shown in Fig. 15-16 can also be seen partially in Fig. 15-17.

Some factors to consider in the selection of plants in the interior design process include:

Plants do not live forever, and will need to be replaced from time to time. Plants selected some time ago may grow too large and become out of scale or proportion. Using these in other locations creates a need for recycling or rotation of plans for plants.

Plants have different needs. In using several varieties, make sure the light conditions are compatible to all plants in the grouping. Most flowering plants require sunlight or artificial lighting. Leafy plants do not require much sun. Plants that thrive on humidity should be used in high-humidity areas, such as bathrooms.

Plants do require some attention—do not plan them for areas that do not receive regular maintenance attention.

TABLE ACCESSORIES

Accessories placed on tabletops are important to the total decor by either complementing or clashing with the color, light, or material patterns of the room. Flowers and table plants, fruit bowls, candles, tableware, and table statuary provide the interior designer with the opportunity to reinforce all of the elements of design used in the room decor. Tabletop objects must be selected and arranged to relate to the total background and space of their surroundings. First consider the appropriateness of the selection of the item, and next, the positioning. The selection must be made with particular attention to form, color, and space, and the position must ensure effective balance, rhythm, emphasis, proportion, and unity with the decor.

Flowers

Although plants must be chosen and positioned in respect to their need for sunlight and humidity, cut flowers, which live only a few days, can be selected only for their contribution to the form, space, and color of the decor. Flower arranging is an art form that uses all of the elements and principles of design. In creating a flower arrangement that complements an interior design, first decide on the shape and color of the floral arrangement. Then select a combination of flowers that live up to these requirements, as shown in Fig. 15-18.

Candles

Candles and candlesticks not only provide an aesthetic accessory in both color and form, but also add to the soft lighting characteristic of a room for nighttime use. Thus, candles not only

Fig. 15-18. Flower arrangement consistent with decor. *General Electric*

Fig. 15-19. Plan to use candles both in daytime and nighttime settings. *Scholz Homes, Inc.*

are functional at night but contribute to the decorative daytime decor, as shown in Fig. 15-19. Notice the atrium in Fig. 15-19 is the same as the one shown in Fig. 15-17.

Art Objects

Art objects or table statuary can provide the needed balance and diminish the starkness of tabletop surfaces.

Tableware Accessories

The selection and design of tableware accessories are integral parts of any interior design since the line, form, color, and material used in table settings must be consistent with the overall decor. In fact, a tabletop treatment in the dining room or family kitchen may provide the major point of emphasis and unity. Tableware components include flatware, dinnerware, glassware, and table coverings.

Flatware

Flatware is purchased in place settings and is available in many different materials. Silverware, (sterling silver), is the finest grade of flatware. Silverplate, stainless steel, and pewter are the common types of metal flatware. Flatware is also

available in china, wood, ivory, pearl, bone, and plastic. A wide variety of colors are available which enable the interior designer to completely coordinate a color arrangement not only in the table setting but with the entire decor. In addition to color, the flatware should be chosen to be consistent with the general lines of the design. Flatware with simple, plain lines relate best to modern interior design, while more ornate pieces of flatware are used with period decors.

Dinnerware

Dinnerware is available in a wide array of materials, colors, and designs, and are purchased in service sets. Chinaware made of the finest white clay is highly durable, consistent in tone and color, semitranslucent, and quite expensive. It is manufactured in ornate and simple designs which enable it to be used in a wide variety of interior settings.

Earthenware is dinnerware manufactured from slightly heavier and coarser clay. Earthenware is opaque, porous, somewhat inconsistent in color, and tends to chip and crack more than fine china. Earthenware resembles pottery but is extremely adaptable to colorful patterns and designs. It is often painted before being fired, thus providing the designer with great flexibility in providing repetition and variety in color, material, and form.

Plastic dinnerware is extremely popular and practical, since it is virtually indestructible and can withstand high temperatures for long periods of time. Its surface appearance, however, does deteriorate with prolonged use. It is available in a wide variety of decorator colors, most of them solid. When combined with background surfaces that are complementary in color, form, and line, this type of dinnerware can be extremely effective and is very practical in display situations.

In selecting dinnerware, look carefully at the silhouette and match the silhouette form to the major form and lines of the table and room. Particularly, check the outline of cups and shapes of handles and ensure that these elements are balanced with the total design.

In purchasing dinnerware, investigate whether the design is available in open stock, that is, on a piece-by-piece basis. If it is not, then the maximum place setting should be purchased at one time to ensure it can still be used for the maximum number of dinners and after any pieces are broken.

Glassware

Because of its transparent, neutral characteristics, glassware must be selected with particular emphasis on line and form consistency with the table setting. Color is sometimes a factor when tinted glasses are used. Glassware with simple contours are consistent with most contemporary designs, while glassware with more ornate lines and decorations are associated with period and colonial decors.

Table Backgrounds

Table surfaces can remain exposed or covered with tablecloths or place mats, as shown in Fig. 15-20. Surfaces can, and often should, remain uncovered if the color, or wood grain of the surface is in harmony with the total scheme of the room. Tablecloths should be selected to extend beyond the edge of the table approximately 6″ to 8″ (152 to 203 mm). They are available in rectangular, square, oval, and round shapes, and any wide variety of sizes. In more formal arrangements, the overhang sometimes extends from 12″ to 16″ (304 to 406 mm). The more traditional the decor, the more ornate the table covering. In addition to covering the table surface, a tablecloth protects the table surface and lessens noise. Tablecloths provide a total background to dinnerware and flatware and can be used effectively as a unifying factor in the design.

Individual place mats are effective in less formal settings and are also available in rectangular, round, and oval shapes. Place mats are effective as interior design elements for display purposes because sizes need not precisely coincide with table dimensions and can be used in a wide variety of colors to change the nature of the decor. Mats must be chosen in sizes large enough to hold the dinnerware, flatware, and glassware for each place setting. Remember that much of the table surface will show when mats are used; consequently, the mat color and texture must blend with the table surface.

Napkins provide a designer with an additional opportunity to repeat and emphasize elements of the interior design through the coordination of color and form. Napkins, usually 144

Fig. 15-20. Three types of table backgrounds. (top) *Sterling Silversmiths* (middle) *Lennox, Incorporated* (bottom) *The Gotham Company*

in² (0.09 m²), can be folded in many different shapes. For formal settings, fabric napkins folded in the oblong fold are preferred, while informal

Fig. 15-21. A formal setting. *Oneida, Ltd.*

settings can utilize paper napkins without sacrificing the spirit of the decor. Napkin holders are also effective in adding consistency to the setting by repeating the style features of flatware.

Formality

Formal settings, as shown in Fig. 15-21, include tablecloths, cloth napkins, fine china, crystal glassware, a centerpiece, and a full complement of flatware. Informal settings often use blank tabletops or placements, earthenware or plastic dinnerware, and paper napkins, and all elements possess a heavier texture.

Backgrounds

The color scheme of the table setting, perhaps of the total room, can be determined and controlled by the table background color. The background color must harmonize with the flatware, dinnerware, napkins, and, of course, color scheme of the remainder of the room.

Patterned backgrounds and decorations are extremely effective in reinforcing lines and space relationships. However, care must be taken not to create inconsistent lines with the dinnerware and flatware. Solid dinnerware can be placed against a patterned background and vice versa,

298

but remember that one element should always dominate either the background or the dinnerware. Don't make them compete.

HOUSEHOLD LINEN

Although chosen primarily for functional characteristics, household linen such as sheets, pillowcases, blankets, etc., should be chosen for their consistency in color, line, and form relationships to the remainder of the decor. Bath and kitchen linens, towels, washcloths, etc., can be used as effective accessories in reinforcing and possibly even dominating the color scheme of these rooms.

Review Questions

1. Define the following terms: accessory, grouping, prebuilt, modular, matting, statuary, flatware, earthenware, fashion.
2. Complete the exercises in the workbook on pp. 67–69.
3. For your scrapbook, find accessories in magazines for each room in a home with a colonial, traditional, and contemporary decor.
4. From magazine and newspaper illustrations, select examples of horizontal, vertical, and random placement of accessories for your scrapbook.
5. From magazines and newspapers, select examples of formal and informal use of accessories for your scrapbook.
6. Sketch a living-room wall elevation. Show the wall with a symmetrical arrangement and with an asymmetrical arrangement of accessories.
7. Refer to Fig. 6-2. Select and sketch the outline of furniture and accessories on this plan. Use one color for furniture and another color for accessories. List and describe each accessory you selected for each room. Sketch major accessories that are not otherwise describable on the plan.
8. List six functional accessories.
9. List six nonfunctional accessories.

LIGHTING

Electricity is the major source of energy for buildings. Electricity cooks, washes, cleans, heats, air-conditions, lights, preserves, and entertains. Good interior decors can be ruined, or mediocre ones saved, by the way the lighting system is planned. Planning for adequate and effective lighting involves consideration of three elements: the eyes, the object, and the light (Fig. 16-1). Planning to light the home involves three questions: How much light is needed? What is the best quality of light? How should this light be distributed?

Quality lighting is important for several reasons. It adds comfort. Good lighting reduces eyestrain, which is a major cause of fatigue. Lighting also affects the length of time that close work (reading, writing, sewing) can be effectively pursued. Good lighting enhances the interior by creating moods to match the decor. Lighting can also be used to emphasize decorative features in the decor. Careful consideration must be given to lighting for safety inside and outside the home. Inside the home, adequate lighting in hallways, stairways, and closets prevents accidents. Small night-lights are valuable in children's rooms and bathrooms. Lighting outside the home on walkways and at entrances provides safety, convenience, and security in addition to the decorative effect achieved.

RULES FOR GOOD LIGHTING

Here are four rules for providing effective lighting:

Provide Sufficient Light   There are several ways to increase the amount of light: (1) Don't over-shield the light source. Provide just enough shading to eliminate glare. (2) Provide adequate (but not excessive) wattage bulbs in fixtures and lamps; however, the wattage should not exceed the amount for which the fixture was designed. (3) Lighten the colors used on ceilings, walls,

floors, and furnishings to produce more light from the same wattage. Because dark colors absorb light, a change to lighter colors can make a significant difference in intensity.

Insufficient wattage causes dim and dismal impressions while an overabundance of general wattage can create a sterile atmosphere. Provide adequate but minimal general lighting and add local lighting of greater intensity where necessary. This eliminates creating an entire room of light to accommodate a maximum light area. For example, in a restaurant or dining room, general lighting can be quite low and table light added to provide local illumination. This creates a more pleasing atmosphere, yet provides functional levels of light where needed.

Avoid Glare   Direct and reflected glare causes eyestrain and discomfort. Direct glare results from unshielded bulbs and from improperly

THE EYES   THE LIGHT SOURCE

THE TASK

Fig. 16-1. Lighting needs vary according to three factors.

Fig. 16-2. Uses of incandescent lighting. *Consoweld Corporation*

placed lighting. Portable lamps should be arranged so that the light source is not visible to anyone in the room. Reflected glare is probably a more common problem. Light that is reflected from shiny surfaces such as the glossy pages of a magazine, a mirror, a highly polished surface, or the television picture tube causes discomfort. This can be corrected by moving either the light source or the shiny surface. Shield the light source enough to reduce glare but not enough to reduce lighting efficiency.

Avoid Excessive Contrasts An excessive contrast in amounts of light results when one area of a room is darker than another. This can be corrected by the addition of general lighting and by selecting reading lamps that direct some light up to the ceiling as well as down on the reading material. Discomfort results if one spot or area of a room is lighted and the remainder of the room is in semi-darkness.

Avoid Shadows Shadows result when a person or object is placed between the light source and the seeing task. For tasks such as writing and sewing, the source of light for a right-handed person should be on the left and for a left-handed person it should be on the right. Shadows can also be a problem on kitchen counters. The use of additional light sources decreases shadows.

Provide sufficient, well-located light switches. Sufficient light switches, properly placed, allow a person to enter or leave any room without walking through darkness. This can be achieved by placing switches near every entrance.

TYPES OF LIGHT

Candles and oil and natural gas lamps were once the major sources of light. Today's major source of light in the home comes from the incandescent and the fluorescent lamps, while candles are used to provide soft mood special effects.

Incandescent Lighting

The use of incandescent lamps is shown in Fig. 16-2. A filament inside the bulb provides a small, concentrated glow of light when an electric current heats the filament to the glowing point. Following are some of the many types of incandescent bulbs:

Inside-frosted bulbs to spread out the light
White bulbs for softer light for exposed bulbs
Silver-bowl bulbs that direct the light upward
Outdoor projector bulbs for spotlight or floodlight
Colored bulbs for decorative effects.
Sunlamp bulbs for sun tanning.
Infrared bulbs for instant heat
Reflector bulbs that are used to display a spot or floodlight
Outdoor yellow bulbs that do not attract insects
Night-light bulbs

Fluorescent Lighting

Fluorescent lamps (Fig. 16-3) give an unbroken line of light, a uniform, glareless light which is ideal for large working areas. Fluorescent lamps give more light per watt than incandescent lamps and last as much as seven times longer. In the

Fig. 16-3. An example of fluorescent lighting.

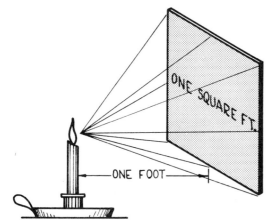

Fig. 16-4. One footcandle is equal to the amount of light falling on one square foot of surface, one foot away.

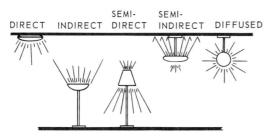

Fig. 16-5. Methods of light dispersement.

fluorescent lamp, current flows through mercury vapor and activates the light-giving properties of the coating inside the tube.

LIGHT MEASUREMENTS

You can read in bright sunlight or in a dimly lit room because your eyes are adaptable to varying intensities of light. However, you must be given enough time to adjust slowly to different light levels. Sudden extreme changes of light cause great discomfort.

Light is measured in customary units called *footcandles* (fc). A footcandle is equal to the amount of light a candle throws on an object one foot away (Fig. 16-4). Ten footcandles equal the amount of light that ten candles throw on a surface one foot away. A 75-W (watt) bulb provides 30 fc of light at a distance of 3 ft. It provides 20 fc at a distance of 6 ft.

In the metric system the standard unit of illumination is the lux (lx). One lux is equal to 0.093 footcandles. To convert footcandles to lux, multiply by 10.764.

On a clear summer day the sun delivers 10,000 fc (107,650 lx) of light to the earth. This is found at the beaches and in open fields. In the shade of a tree there will be 1000 fc (10,764 lx). In the shade on an open porch there will be 500 fc (5382 lx). Inside the house a few feet from the window there will be 200 fc (2153 lx); and in the center of the house, 10 fc (108 lx).

Accepted light levels for various living activities are as follows:

10 to 20 fc (108 to 215 lx): Casual visual tasks, card playing, making conversation, watching television, listening to music

20 to 30 fc (215 to 323 lx): easy reading, sewing, knitting, house cleaning

30 to 50 fc (323 to 539 lx): reading newspapers, doing kitchen and laundry work, typing

50 to 70 fc (539 to 753 lx): prolonged reading, machine sewing, pursuing hobbies, doing homework

70 to 200 fc (753 to 2153 lx): prolonged detailed tasks such as fine sewing, reading fine print, drafting

DISPERSEMENT OF LIGHT

After the necessary amount of light is established the method of spreading, or dispersing, the light through the rooms must be determined.

There are five types of lighting dispersement (Fig. 16-5): direct, indirect, semidirect, semi-indirect, and diffused. Direct light shines directly on an object from the light source. Indirect light is reflected from large surfaces. Semidirect light shines mainly down as direct light, but a small portion of it is directed upward as indirect light. Diffused light is spread evenly in all directions.

All objects absorb and reflect light. Some white surfaces reflect 94 percent of the light. Some black surfaces reflect 2 percent of the light. The rest of the light is absorbed. The proper amount of reflectance is obtained by the color and type of finish. The amounts of reflectance that are recommended are from 60 to 90 percent for the ceiling, from 35 to 60 percent for the walls, and from 15 to 35 percent for the floor.

All surfaces in a room will act as a secondary source of light when the light is reflected. Glare can be eliminated from this secondary source of

301

Fig. 16-6. Use of a skylight. *Potlach Corp.*

light by having a dull, or matte, finish on surfaces and by avoiding strong beams of light and strong contrasts of light. Eliminating excessive glare is essential in designing adequate lighting.

LIGHTING METHODS

Good lighting in a home depends upon three methods. *General lighting* spreads an even, low-level light throughout a room. *Specific (local) lighting* directs light to an area used for a specific visual task. *Decorative lighting* makes use of lights to develop different moods and to accent objects for interest.

General Lighting

General lighting is achieved by direct or indirect methods of light dispersement. In addition to artificial general light sources, skylights, as shown in Fig. 16-6, can be used to admit light during the day. If the skylight is covered with translucent panels, it can contain an artificial light source, usually fluorescent, for nighttime use (Fig. 16-7). General light can also be produced by many portable lamps, ceiling fixtures, or long lengths of lights on the walls (Fig. 16-8). In the living and sleeping areas, the intensity of general lighting should be between 5 and 10 fc (54 to 108 lx) A higher level of general lighting should be used in the service area and bathrooms.

302

Specific Lighting

Specific (local) lighting (Fig. 16-9) for a particular visual task is directed into the area in which the

Fig. 16-7. Use of translucent panels. *Elger Corp.*

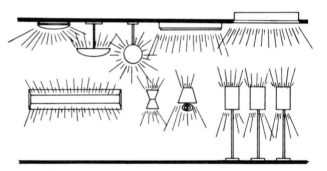

Fig. 16-8. Types of general lighting.

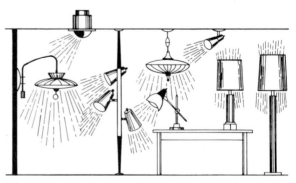

Fig. 16-9. Types of specific lighting.

task will be done. The specific light in a room will add to the general lighting level. Figure 16-10 shows the use of specific lighting in a den.

Fig. 16-10. Specific lighting.

Decorative Lighting

Decorative lighting (Fig. 16-11) is used for atmosphere and interest when activities do not require much light. Bright lights are stimulating; low levels of lighting are quieting. Decorative lighting strives for ususual effects. Some of these can be obtained with candlelight, lights behind draperies, lights under planters, lights in the bottoms of ponds, controlled lights with a dimmer switch, and different types of cover materials over floor lights and spotlights.

STRUCTURAL LIGHTING

Structural lighting is the term used to describe light sources built into the structure.

Because structural lighting is built right into walls and ceilings, it can be designed to blend with any motif or color scheme.

One of the major functions of structural lighting is to lighten and enhance walls and ceilings.

The walls are the background of the home landscape. Pale, well-lighted walls appear to recede. Hence, wall lighting extends the visual area, increasing the apparent space.

With structural lighting, colors of wall coverings and draperies become more vivid and windows have daytime value after dark. Because the major source of light is directed on the entire wall surface instead of a small fixture or lamp, the resulting room lighting is soft and relatively shadow-free. This "horizontal" lighting molds forms and features in a more flattering way than

Fig. 16-11. Decorative lighting. *Westinghouse*

MOUNTING HEIGHTS FOR STRUCTURAL LIGHTING	
LOCATION	**MOUNTING HEIGHT**
KITCHEN RANGE	58 in from floor
SINGLE BED	52 in from floor
DOUBLE BED	52 in from floor
EXTRA WIDE BED OR TWINS WITH SINGLE HEADBOARD	52 in from floor
LOUNGE FURNITURE	55 in or more from floor
BUFFETS	60 in from floor
DESK	15 to 18 in from desk top
MIRROR OR PICTURE GROUPING	Mount diredtly at top edge of mirror or above picture grouping

Fig. 16-12. Mounting heights for structural lighting. *General Electric*

light from above or below. Figure 16-12 shows specifications for structural lighting.

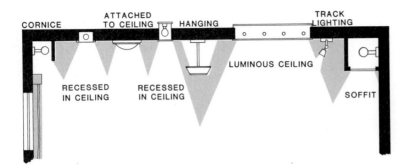

Fig. 16-13. Types of ceiling fixtures.

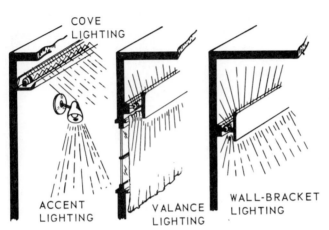

Fig. 16-14. Types of wall fixtures.

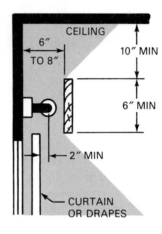

Fig. 16-15. An example of valance lighting.

Structural fixtures are either built into ceilings, as shown in Fig. 16-13, or walls, as shown in Fig. 16-14.

Valance

A valance is a covering over a long source of light over a window. Its light illuminates the wall and draperies for the spacious effect that daylight gives a room. The lighted valance is always connected with the window. It usually directs light both upward over the ceiling and downward over the wall and drapery.

Valance faceboards (Fig. 16-15) can be simple and unobtrusive, or they can be as decorative and ornate as the decor demands. A wide variety of faceboard materials are available that can be trimmed with moldings—scalloped, notched, perforated, papered, upholstered, or painted. Faceboards should have a minimum width of 6″ (152 mm) and seldom should be wider than 10″ (254 mm).

304

The most critical dimension of a valance is the spacing between the fluorescent lamp and the front surface of the drapery material. There must be at least 2″ (51 mm) between the center of the lamp and the front face of the drapery material. This ensures that the draperies will be more uniformly lighted from top to bottom. Draperies hung near the tops of their pleats hang straighter, causing less interference with the light.

The inside of the faceboard should be located about 6½″ (165 mm) from the wall. If bulky draperies, or a double track, are used, the faceboard might need to be extended to a distance 8″ (203 mm) or more from the wall.

A 10″ (254 mm) space between the top of the valance faceboard and the finished ceiling is recommended. Valances that are closer than this to the ceiling will trap light near the ceiling and produce a "hot streak" of light. If there is less space than this available, the valance should either be closed at the top, or the fluorescent cornice should be used. To assure a wide spread

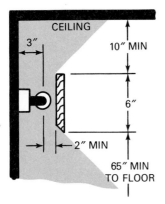

HIGH WALL BRACKET

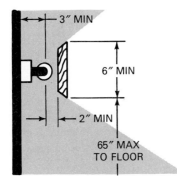

LOW WALL BRACKET

Fig. 16-16. Wall brackets.

Fig. 16-17. High wall-brackets. *Window Shade Manufacturers Assn.*

Fig. 16-18. Low wall-brackets. *General Electric*

of light on the ceiling, the fluorescent channel and lamp should be mounted close to the top of the faceboard.

Wall Brackets

A wall bracket (Fig. 16-16) balances the light of a valance. It gives an upward and downward wash of light difficult to obtain on an inner wall. The wall bracket is probably the single most useful structural lighting device. It can be used in any room. There are two kinds of wall brackets: high and low. The construction differs depending on whether the bracket is to be used high on the wall for general lighting, or lower on the wall for specific-task lighting.

High Wall Brackets

A high wall bracket (Fig. 16-17) is a valance on a wall rather than over a window. It is used as a source of general lighting for a room. Quite often it will be used to balance the illumination from a matching valance at an opposite window.

Low Wall Brackets

The low wall bracket is a working light commonly used where specific seeing tasks are performed close to a wall. They are used to highlight fireplaces and pictures, and to provide functional lighting over desks, sofas, etc. Figure 16-18 gives

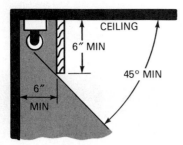

Fig. 16-19. Cornice lighting.

height location for low wall brackets and the type of lamp that should be used.

Cornice Lighting

The lighted cornice (Fig. 16-19) is positioned on the ceiling at the junction between the wall and ceiling. All of its light is directed downward to light the wall surface below. For this reason, the lighting effect produced is a dramatic one. It emphasizes wall textures and wall coverings, and will light pictures and other wall hangings. Also, because the wall is emphasized, the cornice gives an impression of greater ceiling height. Cornices are, therefore, ideally suited for low-ceiling rooms.

Soffit Lighting

The underside of any architectural member is known as a *soffit*. Often these spaces can provide a housing for light sources. Suitable soffits for lighting can be formed in furred-down areas over

kitchen sinks and work areas, furred-down areas over bathroom mirrors, undersides of pass-throughs, niches, and beams. There are basically two uses for lighted soffits: to direct light downward onto a horizontal plane, and to direct light outward to a vertical surface (such as a face in front of a mirror). Figure 16-20 shows soffit construction data.

When a soffit is used to light a horizontal surface below it, the fluorescent channels should be equipped with polished aluminum reflectors. Reflectors will more than double the useful light output of the soffit if the bottom is closed with louvers or a material that does not diffuse the light to any extent.

In living areas, the soffit has a more acceptable appearance if a lightly etched or configurated glass or plastic is used. To further reduce the brightness as viewed from seated positions in the room, the inside back vertical surface of the soffit can be surfaced with a dark matte finish.

For mirror lighting the soffit over the bath or dressing room mirror scatters light outward to light a person's face. For this reason, the soffit is usually made shallower and wider to let more light escape. The bottom is covered with a highly diffusing glass or plastic.

LUMINOUS CEILING PANELS

The comfortable lighting effects and the sensation of spaciousness created by luminous ceilings (Fig. 16-21) make them natural for applications in kitchens, bathrooms, entryways, recreation rooms, and even dining areas.

SOFFIT CONSTRUCTION DATA				
		CAVITY DIMENSIONS		
LOCATION	USE	DEPTH	WIDTH	LENGTH
KITCHEN	Over sink or work center	8″ to 12″	12″	38″ Min.
BATH OR DRESSING ROOM	Over large mirror	8″	18″ to 24″	Length of mirror
LIVING AREA	Over piano, desk, sofa, or other seeing area	10″	Fit space available 12″ Min.	Fit space available 50″ Min.

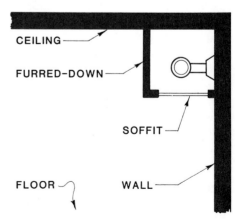

Fig. 16-20. Soffit construction data. *General Electric*

Fig. 16-21. Luminous ceiling panels. *Armstrong Cork Company*

Many manufacturers make packaged luminous ceiling assemblies. The design of luminous ceilings varies with the room size, room proportion, and intended use. Usually these ceilings are only applicable in rooms with high ceilings where

the plastic diffusers can be dropped 10″ to 12″ (254 to 305 mm).

An entire ceiling, however, need not be luminous to be effective and attractive. A simple method of luminous ceiling panel construction is to utilize the space between ceiling joists. This space is an ideal location for fluorescent lighting equipment if the ends are boxed in and a plastic diffuser suspended below.

A number of cavities may be joined together to create a large luminous panel, or they may be used in single strips or pairs over critical viewing areas.

LAMPS

Lamps provide light needed for a seeing task. The bottom of the shade must be below the level of the eyes doing the visual task (Fig. 16-22A). The source of light for a lamp should be a short distance at one side of the work area.

Because portable lamps are often designed to serve several different purposes, it is important to consider both how the lamp will be used and where it will be placed before selecting. Consider whether the lamp will be used primarily for casual reading, studying, sewing, doing make-up, television viewing, or another task. Consider if the lamp should be located on the floor, on an end

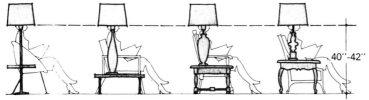

TYPICAL HEIGHTS OF LAMPS AND TABLES FOR SHADE AT EYE LEVEL

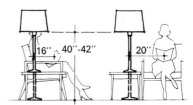

PLACEMENT DIMENSIONS FOR SHADE
AT EYE LEVEL

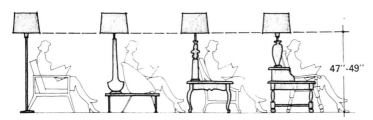

TYPICAL HEIGHTS OF LAMPS AND TABLES FOR SHADE
ABOVE EYE LEVEL

307

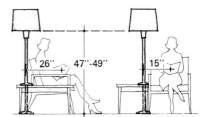

PLACEMENT DIMENSIONS FOR SHADE
ABOVE EYE LEVEL

Fig. 16-22 A. Placement of table and floor lamps. *Agricultural Engineering Research Div., U.S. Dept. of Agriculture*

Fig. 16-22 *B*. Examples of portable plug-in lamps.

table, on a dresser, or on a desk. Figure 16-22*B* shows basic types of portable lamps. If the lamp is to be placed on an end table, the height of the tabletop must be considered.

To avoid contrast between a light and a dark area of a room it is generally advisable to select a portable lamp which provides some general lighting to the room. Therefore, the top of the shade should be open unless other lighting fixtures and lamps provide sufficient general lighting.

Another consideration in selecting portable lamps is the lamp's capacity to provide some means of diffusing the light. A glass or plastic diffusing bowl or diffusing disc helps spread the light so that it does not appear as a bright spot behind the lampshade.

The lampshade helps to further diffuse the light and to direct it. Off-white or white linings provide good diffusion without absorbing the light. The shape and size of the shade serves to direct the optimum proportion of light upward for general lighting and downward to the seeing task.

Three-way bulbs are frequently used to add flexibility to the purposes the lamp can serve.

308 GENERAL LIGHTING

Living Room and Family Room

The living room (Fig. 16-23) requires a low level of general lighting but should have specific lighting for areas used for reading and other close visual tasks. Decorative lighting should also be utilized where appropriate in the living room.

Functional Lighting

Portable lamps, table and floor, housing 3-way 50/100/150-W bulbs, or a minimum of one standard 150-W bulb, are recommended for seeing tasks, such as reading, sewing, etc.

The height of table lamps should be related to the tables on which they are placed. The bottom of the lamp shade should be approximately 42" to 44" (1067 to 1118 mm) from the floor, or at eye level of a person seated next to it.

Floor lamps should be placed to the side, either right or left, and slightly behind the user, so that light comes over the shoulder and onto the reading material. Because the lamp is slightly to the rear of the chair, height is less critical—the user cannot look up and see the exposed bulb under the shade.

Lampshades should usually be semitranslucent, allowing light through the sides as well as top and bottom. However, opaque shades are sometimes desirable because of the color scheme of the room.

If opaque shades are used, they should have a light lining inside the shade to help direct the light out at the top and bottom.

Wall-mounted lamps and brackets beside or behind the user also provide suitable reading light provided that the light source or sources are well shielded.

Fig. 16-23. Living area lighting. *Armstrong Cork Company*

Reading light may be provided by ceiling fixtures, recessed or surface-mounted, installed directly overhead.

Reading lights of any type, portable or ceiling, should never be used alone. Always provide a comfortable level of general lighting in the room to break down contrasts between the lighted task and the surroundings. High-intensity lamps produce a concentration of light in a confined area without any spread. Use them only for supplementary lighting for close-work seeing tasks. Another use might be on bookshelves to accent a piece of art.

For TV viewing make sure that there is light somewhere in the room. Never watch TV in the dark. Turn on table lamps or fixtures for a soft level of comfortable light in the room. To avoid any annoying reflections from the TV screen, use lights that are not directly in line with the TV.

Decorative Lighting

There are many techniques which can be used to emphasize and enhance furnishings and other possessions. The living room is usually the room in which guests are entertained and where the owners may wish to provide attractive light accents.

Consider lighting: walls on which paintings are arranged in groupings or singly; draperies; fireplaces; and bookshelves. Two techniques can be used to light vertical surfaces: wall washing and glazing.

Wall washing is used to create an even wash of light on paintings, bookshelves, or draperies, approximately 24″ (610 mm) out from the wall and 24″ on center.

Grazing is used to emphasize texture, for example, in brick or stone fireplace walls and draperies, using down lights, ceiling-recessed, or surface-mounted fixtures. The light is located close to the vertical surface, approximately 6″ to 8″ (152 to 203 mm) out from the wall and 10″ (254 mm) apart.

Dining Room

The dining area (Fig. 16-24) requires a low level of general lighting, with local lighting over the dining table.

Fig. 16-24. Dining area lighting. *Scholz Homes, Inc.*

Functional Lighting

The table is the most important area to consider. Frequently, a chandelier or other decorative pendant type of fixture is selected as the sole source of light for the table, and sometimes the entire room. Chandeliers serve merely as "the frosting on the cake." They distribute light in every direction but do not, with few exceptions, provide focal light for the tabletop. In addition to the chandelier, consider using two or more recessed devices to accent the table.

Decorative Lighting

Provide a pleasant environment in which to dine by lighting vertical surface areas—draperies and paintings—or accent the buffet with down-lights for food service. China cabinets may be lighted from inside. The dining room chandelier should be dimmer-controlled. By dimming the fixture and other accent lighting in the room, the mood can be controlled.

Remember that light directed onto the tabletop will be reflected onto the faces of the diners, therefore exercise care in the choice of the color of tablecloths or place mats.

Fig. 16-25. Bedroom lighting. *Westinghouse*

Bedroom

The bedroom (Fig. 16-25) requires a low level of general lighting but should have specific lighting (for reading in bed) and on both sides of the dressing-table mirror. The dressing area requires a high level of general lighting. Children's bedrooms require a high level of general lighting. Closets should have a fixture placed high at the front.

Functional Lighting

Many people enjoy reading in bed and there are several lighting solutions which can be employed:

Two portable lamps placed on end tables on either side of the bed with 3-way 50/100/150-W bulbs. The lower edge of the lampshade should be at eye level of the user. The base of the lamp shade should be in line with the user's shoulder.

Wall lamps or adjustable pendant fixtures. The lower edge of the shade should be at eye level or if a stationary unit is used, locate the lower edge of the shade 30″ (762 mm) above the mattress and slightly behind the reader.

Fluorescent wall brackets. For a single bed use one 30-W tube; for a double bed, use one 40-W tube; and for king-size or twin beds, use two 30- or two 40-W tubes as a single unit. The lower edge of the bracket should be 30″ (762 mm) above

the mattress; or if the bed has a storage headboard, 48″ (1219 mm) above the mattress.

Decorative Lighting

Consider lighting vertical surfaces in the bedroom as in the living area with dimmer control from a central location near the bed.

Study Area

A study lamp provides the right amount of light and the right kind of distribution of light, as shown in Fig. 16-26. It houses an inside-frosted bulb. Other alternatives are:

Table lamp with a base 15″ (381 mm) in height measured to the bottom of the shade, housing one 100-W bulb or a 3-way 50/100/150-W bulb. Place the center of the lampshade 15″ (381 mm) to the left of the work center (or right, if the person is left-handed) and 12″ (305 mm) back from the front edge of the desk.

A fluorescent-lighted shelf mounted on the wall, 15″ to 18″ (381 to 457 mm) above the desk top to the bottom of the unit. Mount one 30- or 40-W tube at the front edge of the shelf, which should be about 9″ to 12″ (229 to 305 mm) back from the front edge shield of the desk. The inside of the front shield of the unit should be painted matte white.

A pair of ceiling or wall-mounted fixtures. Center the fixtures 36″ (914 mm) apart and not more than 17″ (432 mm) back from the front edge of the desk.

Fig. 16-26. Den and study lighting. *Armstrong Cork Company*

Fig. 16-27 A. Bathroom general lighting. *Eljer*

Fig. 16-27 B. Bathroom local lighting. *Kohler*

Bathroom

The bathroom (Figs. 16-27 *A* and *B*) requires a high level of general lighting from ceiling fixtures. The shower and water closet, if compartmentalized, should have a recessed, vaporproof light.

For personal grooming, shaving, and applying make-up it is recommended that, if possible, fixtures be installed on either side of the mirror; also a ceiling fixture should be located over the head of the user.

Plan for a night-light, either separately switched, dimmer-controlled wall bracket, or fixture, or a plug-in type of 7-W night-light.

Other considerations might be given to using sunlamps with a timer device and to heat lamps in special fixtures for cool winter mornings.

Traffic Areas

Traffic areas require a high level of general lighting for safety and convenience. The lighting of a foyer (Fig. 16-28) and the outside entrance (Fig. 16-29) must not only be functional at all hours but should be designed for maximum visual effect. That is, the lighting must be at the correct level to create an inviting yet warm atmosphere. Entrance lighting should be controllable from a remote source and at the point of entry. A delay switch will allow the occupant to leave the premises under light but not permit the entry lights to use energy for more than the time needed.

Fig. 16-28. Foyer lighting. *Scholz Homes, Inc.*

Fig. 16-29. Entrance lighting. *Thomas Industries, Inc.*

Fig. 16-30. Traffic area lighting. *Armstrong Cork Company*

Fig. 16-31. Kitchen lighting. *General Electric*

Halls and traffic corridors (Fig. 16-30) through rooms must be adequately lit with controls on both entry and exit sides of the area.

Garages

The major areas where light is needed in a garage are on each side of the car or between cars, especially over the front and rear.

Closets

Either incandescent bulbs or fluorescent tubes are suitable. The source should be located out of normal view, generally to the front of the closet and above the door.

Fig. 16-32. Lighting of art objects. *Armstrong Cork Company*

Kitchen

The kitchen (Fig. 16-31) requires a high level of general lighting from ceiling fixtures. Specific lighting for all work areas—range, sink, tables, and counters—is also recommended. In addition to general lighting there must be an adequate number of convenience outlets at the counters and one for the refrigerator. Special outlets are also needed for the electric range, clock, exhaust fan, and dishwasher. For permanent lighting there should be a main ceiling light, one light over the sink, and another light over the eating area.

DECORATIVE LIGHTING

Art objects used for decorative effects should be intimately related with light to bring these elements of design into focus, as shown in Fig. 16-32.

When lighting art treasures do not rely on general room illumination alone. Select appropriate lighting devices to enhance line, form, texture, and color of the art. Light sources may be concealed in the corners of a cabinet. Small art objects placed in a lighted breakfront or on open shelves come to life during the evening hours.

Larger freestanding objects can be treated individually. When lighting sculpture, the desired effects—distance, three-dimensional form, deep shadow, silhouette, contour—dictate the number and positioning of light sources and the type of equipment to be used. It is desirable to create

Fig. 16-33. Outdoor decorative lighting. *General Electric*

interplays of light and shadow and to emphasize texture. Suitable equipment for lighting sculpture includes adjustable devices housing flood or spot bulbs and individual framing projectors. Back lighting will place the sculpture in silhouette.

Wall-mounted carvings, metal sculpture, and tapestries may be lighted by recessed or surface-mounted devices to accent the art or wash the art and surrounding wall area with light.

It is recommended that equipment used for lighting art objects be controlled by dimmers for flexibility in lighting levels. Frequently the most pleasing and subtle results are obtained when the level of illumination is dimmed down to an almost subtle indistinguishable level.

OUTDOOR LIGHTING

Exciting new dimensions can be added by lighting the areas surrounding the home to enhance their intrinsic charm, beauty, and utility at night, as shown in Fig. 16-33. Extending imaginative patterns of indoor illumination to outdoor areas—gardens, patios, pools, work and play spots—not only is consistent with good, overall planning but opens up new vistas for increased enjoyment and safety.

Well-planned residential outdoor lighting creates a total home environment combining maximum aesthetic appeal with efficiency. It makes the home and its surrounding grounds complementary and endows the entire living area with a distinctive aura of unity and completeness in all seasons. It reveals the beauty of gardens, trees, and foliage, expands the hospitality and comfort of patios and porches, stretches the hours for outdoor recreation or work, and provides sure seeing to safeguard everyone against accident.

While the exterior environment is visually dominant during daytime hours, lighting takes over at night and the interior spaces become the primary focal points of interest. The use of glass as a structural building material contributes much to the development of this relationship.

One of the most complementary features of any home exterior is the garden. To achieve the greatest pleasure from gardens, they should be extensions of interior living spaces wherever practicable.

313

Spatial relationships of home to grounds are among the first considerations in lighting the various elements and features of gardens, patios, walkways, and other areas surrounding or adjacent to the home. The surrounding grounds of a home differ from its interior spaces primarily because their boundaries are defined but not confined. Literally, the sky is the limit in planning an exterior lighting scheme. In considering spatial relationships, one or more sides of the grounds or outdoor living areas may be closed by a wall, hedge, fence, or by the side of a building. Tree tops or lattices covered with foliage can be used to form a "natural" ceiling. In any event, exterior-lighted areas and lighting levels must always be in scale with the areas and their uses. Large areas, for example, can be floodlit at night purely for recreational use. But floodlighting a garden merely to disperse the darkness defeats the artistic use of light to create charm, glamour, and to captivate visual associations.

Be careful to avoid placing furniture in lounge areas in direct light. This can result in light shining directly into someone's eyes.

Outdoor Lighting Techniques

Silhouetting Exterior objects having interesting line and form are frequently best lighted so they are seen in silhouette, either a dark object against a lighted background or a luminous material against darkness. The first method is to light wall, fence, or shrubbery behind the object with very little light on the front. Silhouetting objects against darkness is achieved by beaming light through translucent materials like certain types of leaves and other foliage.

Grazing Light Grazing light can be used to great advantage in emphasizing the textural qualities of tree bark, hedges, masonry, fences, and many other outdoor objects.

Modeling Depth and three-dimensional character can be given to exterior objects at night by lighting them from several directions. A large tree, for example, can be modeled by casting light upon it from many directions, thereby emphasizing various aspects of its form. More light

from one side than the other accentuates the effect. A smaller tree can be lighted from just two sides with a spotlight from one side and a floodlight 90° away.

Highlighting Highlighting usually refers to downlighting for patios and other outdoor living areas or for small flower beds that require special focal emphasis. Lighting equipment can be mounted high in trees and aimed down to light a garden area, or mushroom-type fixtures can be spiked in the ground to emphasize certain parts of a garden.

Shadow Patterns Shadows can be used advantageously to create broken or solid patterns and to introduce the excitement of movement such as that from tree branches or foliage. The object which casts the shadows—house, plant, ornament, or other—doesn't have to be visible. The elongated shadows of a group of poplars or a row of hollyhocks, for example, can convey the suggestion of another area, with imagination creating the remainder of a visual impression for the viewer.

Tinted Light Tinted light is used primarily for emphasis—to bring out the color in flowers, shrubbery, and special objects. Generally, light of the same color as the object to be lighted is a good choice for heightening its color.

Fitting Lighting to the Subject

Trees and Shrubs Gardens, trees, and foliage all have different features which must be considered individually in any good plan for night lighting. To make certain the lighting fits the subjects, they should be carefully analyzed to determine their exact form, texture, and reflectance characteristics.

Flowers Flowers require lighting at night since they frequently trace the basic design of the garden or surrounding grounds of a home. Flower beds take many forms and vary in their relationship to architecture, home interior, and grounds. Flowers are colorless at night without adequate lighting.

Fig. 16-34. Outdoor statuary lighting. *General Electric*

Lawns and Ground Covers The intermediate area should never be left in darkness because gardens and foliage beyond will appear to be "floating," creating an unpleasant visual impression. Floodlights mounted on the house—at least 12' to 20' (3.7 to 6.1 m) above the ground—can be used to light this area.

Garden Steps and Paths Steps and paths in the garden must be treated in a much more subtle fashion than the utilitarian lighting used at entrances of the home. Equipment can be mounted high on buildings or in trees. Local lighting should provide sufficient illumination for safety.

Statuary In many cases, a garden is planned around statues (Fig. 16-34) as the prime focal point and light can transform an interesting piece of sculpture into the home's feature attraction after dark. Owing to the inherent brightness and sheen of some forms of statuary—like polished marble—the light source must be carefully related to the light reflectance characteristics of the material. The size of the statuary must also be considered.

Statues are usually more natural looking when lighted from above, as in daytime. Most statuary is also more interesting if lighted from at least two sides, creating the modeling effect which develops depth and gives it a three-dimensional character.

Swimming Pools Whether a home swimming pool is small or large, outdoor lighting is absolutely essential for the creation of after-dark atmosphere and safety. The pool can become a large light source much like a gigantic fluorescent bulb lighting tree branches that extend within its range. Light from the pool can provide the emphasis that will unify the exterior decor at night.

Ponds and Fountains A wealth of exciting design opportunities exist in lighting small garden ponds. A lighted pond can be far more enchanting at night than during the day and a jet-type fountain in the pond lends just that much more glamour to the nocturnal scene.

Patios and Porches Group activities for family and friends become as pleasurable outdoors as in the home when imaginative lighting treatment is given to patios, porches, and similar adjacent living areas. Lighting of this type must be suited to the varying demands of visual activities.

Entrance Ways and Walks No home outdoor lighting plan can ever be considered complete without attention given to illuminating entrance ways, walks, and driveways. Such lighting not only enhances the exterior appearance of the home but also contributes measurably to the safety of the family and visitors.

Good selection and placement of lighting equipment depends on three basic considerations: architectural suitability (the "fit" of the fixtures to the general exterior arrangement); minimum glare; and a light distribution pattern that permits clear seeing along all entrance ways, walks, and driveways as well as recognition of callers.

A wide range of exterior fixtures for wall, ceiling, or post mounting is available in all architectural styles.

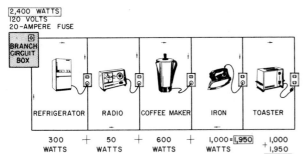

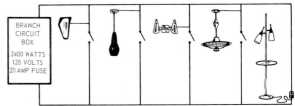

Fig. 16-36. Lighting circuits.

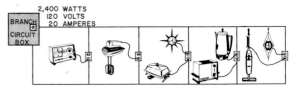

Fig. 16-37. Small-appliance circuits.

Fig. 16-35. Total wattage determines the capacity of circuits.

WIRING CIRCUITS

The electrical energy is brought to the home by the service entrance wires. The size of the service entrance wires determines the amount of electricity that can enter the wiring system safely. The heavy service wires are connected to the watt-hour meter then to the service entrance equipment, with the same heavy wire. At the service entrance equipment is a distribution panel that sends the electricity throughout the house with branch circuits.

Between the meter and the branch circuit box is a main fuse or circuit breaker. If too much current is drawn from the outside source and heats the wires, the fuse will burn out. If there is a circuit breaker instead of a fuse, it will trip itself and open the circuit. In addition to the protection of the main source of power, each branch circuit is protected with fuses. Branch circuits become hot when too many appliances draw too much current. The fuse then blows or the circuit breaker trips.

Branch Circuits

Each branch circuit delivers electricity to one or more outlets. It is necessary to divide the electricity that enters the house into branch circuits so that one line will not have to carry all the energy. If the whole house were on one circuit, a short circuit or an overloading would leave the entire house without power.

To determine the size of service entrance wires needed, the designer should know how much current will be needed. In the older-style home, a 60-A (ampere) electric service was suf-

ficient. Today the size should be selected from the following guidance list for homes:

A service of 100 A: appliance circuits, lighting circuits, electric cooking, electric water heater, electric laundry. 100 A at 120 V (volts) = 12,000 W (watts). 100 A at 240 V = 24,000 W.

A service of 150 A: appliance circuits, lighting circuits, electric cooking, electric water heater, electric laundry, electric heating, air conditioning for a small home. 150 A at 120 V = 18,000 W. 150 A at 240 V = 36,000 W.

A service of 200 A: appliance circuits, lighting circuits, electric cooking, electric water heater, electric laundry, electric heating, air conditioning for a large home. 200 A at 120 V = 24,000 W. 200 A at 240 V = 48,000 W.

To plan the size of a branch circuit, add all the wattages of the appliances to be placed on the circuit. The total wattage determines the size of the wire and fuses or circuit breakers (Fig. 16-35). A 120-V circuit has one fuse. A 240-V circuit has two fuses.

The branch circuits are divided into three groups.

Lighting circuits (Fig. 16-36) provide for the lighting outlets in the home. Multiple lights in one room should be on different circuits. If one fuse blows, the room will not be in total darkness. Use a No. 12 wire with a 20-A fuse for 2400 W for lighting circuits. Lighting requires about 6000 W of power. Have a minimum of four 15-A fuse circuits for 1800 W each or three 20-A fuse circuits for 2400 W each.

Small-appliance circuits serve only convenience outlets (Fig. 16-37). Use No. 12 wire with

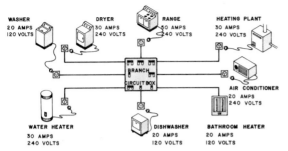

Fig. 16-38. Individual circuits.

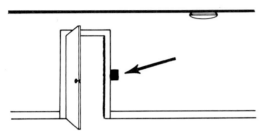

Fig. 16-39. Locate switches convenient to the door.

a 20-A fuse for 2400 W on each circuit. For more power, use a double-branch circuit with three wires and two fuses for 240 V. With a 20-A fuse, this circuit will safely carry up to 4800 W.

Individual circuits serve one piece of electrical equipment (Fig. 16-38). Appliances that require individual circuits are the electric range, automatic heating units, water heater, clothes dryer, air conditioner, built-in electric heater, shop bench, and large motor-driven appliances such as washers, disposals, and dish washers. When a motor starts, it needs an extra surge of power. This is called the *starting load*.

Allow extra circuits and outlets for future addition of appliances. Well-planned wiring gives more power throughout the home for appliances, and makes the lighting more efficient.

Planning with Electricity

Wiring methods are controlled by building codes. The job of wiring is performed by licensed electricians. However, the wiring plans for a building are prepared by the architect. But interior designers must be able to plan the interior to conform with basic electrical principles. For large structures a consulting electrical contractor may

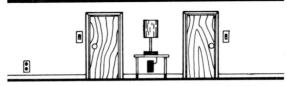

Fig. 16-40. Wall spaces between doors should have a convenience outlet.

aid in the preparation of the final plans. Electrical plans must include information concerning the type and location of all switches, fixtures, and controls.

Basic Planning Rules

Basic rules to follow when planning the electrical system are listed below.

1. The main source of light in a room should be controlled by a wall switch located on the latch side of the room's entrance. It should not be necessary to walk into a dark room to find the light switch (Fig. 16-39).
2. Electrical outlets (except in the kitchen) should average one for every 6' (1.8 m) of wall space.
3. Electrical outlets in kitchens should average one for every 4' (1.2 m) of wall space.
4. Walls between doors should have an outlet, regardless of the size of the wall space (Fig. 16-40).
5. Each room should have in the ceiling or wall a light outlet that will be a major source of light for the whole room (Fig. 16-41).
6. Each room should have adequate lighting for all visual tasks.
7. Each room should have at least one easy-to-reach outlet for the vacuum cleaner or other appliances which are often used.
8. Not all the lights in one room should be on the same circuit.

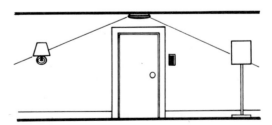

Fig. 16-41. The switch by the door should control the main source of light.

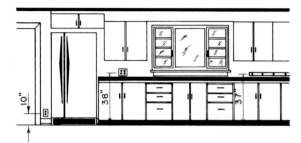

Fig. 16-42. The heights of all outlets should be noted on wall elevations or in specifications.

9. List the height of all outlets in the house (Fig. 16-42) on the plans.

Switch Location

Switches should be located according to the following guides.

1. Plan what switches are needed for all lights and electrical equipment. Toggle switches are available in several different types: single-pole, double-pole, three-way, and four-way.
2. Show location and height of switches.
3. Select the type of switches, type of switch-plate cover, and type of finish.
4. If there are only lamps in a room, the entry switch should control the outlet into which the lamps are plugged.
5. Lights for stairways and halls must be controlled from both ends (Fig. 16-43).
6. Bedroom lights should be controlled from bedsides and entrances with a three-way switch.
7. Outside lights must be controlled with a three-way switch from the garage and from the exit of the house.
8. Basement lights should be controlled by a switch and a pilot light in the house at the head of the basement stairs (Fig. 16-44).
9. Install wall switches in preference to pull-string switches in closets.
10. Describe all special controls to be used.

Special Controls

Special controls make appliances and lighting systems more efficient. Some special controls for electrical equipment include the following:

Mercury switches are silent, shockproof, easy to wire and install, and last longer than a regular toggle switch.

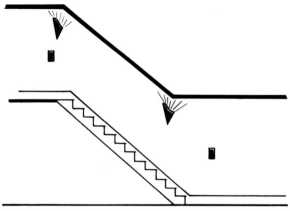

Fig. 16-43. Three-way switches should be used on stairway lights.

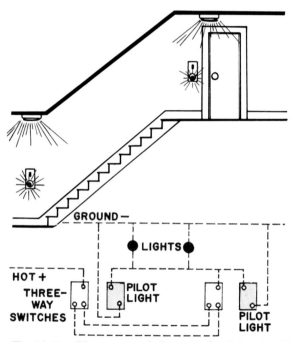

Fig. 16-44. Three-way switches and pilot lights should be used on basement stairs.

Automatic cycle controls, as on washers, can be installed on appliances to make them perform their functions on a time cycle.

Photoelectric cells control switching at a wave of the hand.

Automatic controls adjust heating and cooling systems.

Clock thermostats adjust heating units for day and night.

Aquastats keep water heated to selected temperatures.

Dimmers control intensity of light.

Time switches control lights or watering systems.

Safety alarms activate a bell when a circuit on a door or window is broken.

Master switches control switching throughout the home from one location.

Low-voltage switching systems provide economical long runs.

The low-voltage method of switching offers convenience and flexibility. A relay isolates all switches from the 120-V system. The voltage from the switch to the appliance is only 24 V. At the appliance a magnet-controlled switch opens the full 120 V to the appliance. The magnet-controlled switch is more commonly called a *touch switch*. The low, 24-V system permits long runs of inexpensive wiring that is easy to install and safe to use. This makes it ideal for master-control switching from one location in the house.

Electrical Outlets

There are several types of electrical outlets. The convenience outlet is the plug-in, receptacle type. It is available in single, double, triple, or strip outlets.

Lighting outlets are for the connection of lampholders, surface-mounted fixtures, flush or recessed fixtures, and all other types of lighting fixtures.

The special-purpose outlet is the connection point of a circuit for one special piece of equipment.

The wires that hook up the whole electric system are installed during the construction of the building, in the walls, floors, and ceilings. In a finished house, the entire system is hidden. The conventional wiring system used for outlets, lights, and small appliances consists of a black wire (the hot wire) and a white wire (the neutral or common wire). A third, green, wire is a grounding wire. For large appliances the wiring consists of a black wire and a red wire both of which are hot wires, and a white wire. All three wires connect through a switch to the appliance.

If the wire is too long or too small, there will be a voltage drop because of the wire's resistance. Another cause of voltage drop is the drawing of too much current from the branch circuit. This will cause heating appliances such as toasters, irons, and electric heaters to work inefficiently. Motor-driven appliances will overwork and possibly burn out.

Electrical Working Drawings

Complete electrical plans will ensure the installation of electrical equipment and wiring exactly as planned. If electrical plans are incomplete and sketchy, the completeness of the installation is largely dependent upon the judgment of the electrician. The designer should not rely upon the electrician to design the electrical system, only to install it.

After the basic floor plan is drawn, the designer should determine the exact position of all appliances and lighting fixtures on the plan, as shown in Fig. 16-45. The exact position of

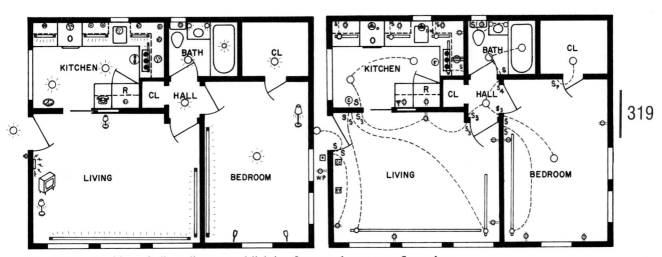

Fig. 16-45. Position of all appliances and lighting fixtures shown on a floor plan.

NAME	ABBREV	SYMBOL	ELEVATION	PICTORIAL
SINGLE-POLE SWITCH	S	$+S$		
THREE-WAY SWITCH	S_3	$+S_3$		
AUTOMATIC DOOR SWITCH	S_D	S_D		
TWO SWITCHES	SS	$+S+S$		
DUPLEX OUTLET	DUP OUT			
SINGLE OUTLET	S OUT	1		
SPECIAL-PURPOSE OUTLET 110 VOLTAGE	SP PUR OUT	X X		
LIGHTING OUTLET — CEILING	LT OUT CLG	$\bigcirc$		

NAME	ABBREV	SYMBOL	ELEVATION	PICTORIAL
LIGHTING OUTLET – WALL	LT OUT WALL			
FLOOD LIGHT	FL			
WALL BRACKET LIGHT WITH SWITCH	WL BRK LT/S			
LIGHTING FLOURESCENT	LT FLUOR			
BELL	BL			
INTERCOMMUNI-CATION PANEL	INTERCOM			
TELEPHONE OUTLET	TEL OUT			
DIMMER SWITCH	DM SW			

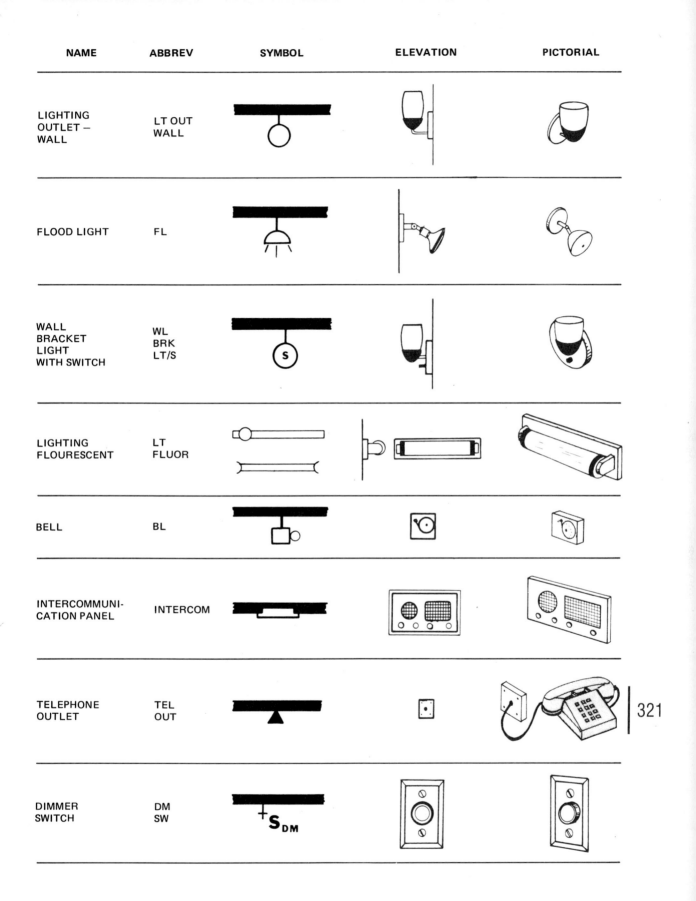

321

Fig. 16-47. A dotted line connects the switch with the fixture control.

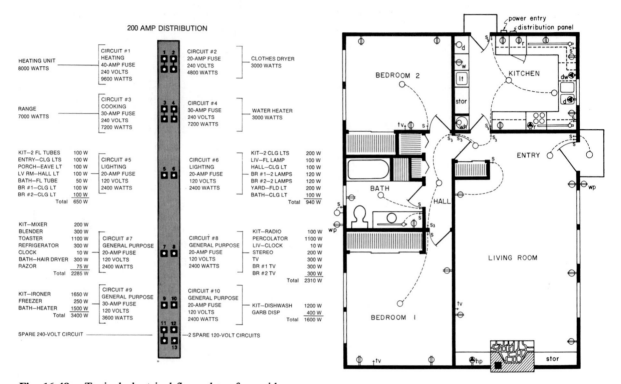

200 AMP DISTRIBUTION

HEATING UNIT 8000 WATTS	CIRCUIT #1 HEATING 40-AMP FUSE 240 VOLTS 9600 WATTS	CIRCUIT #2 20-AMP FUSE 240 VOLTS 4800 WATTS	CLOTHES DRYER 3000 WATTS
RANGE 7000 WATTS	CIRCUIT #3 COOKING 30-AMP FUSE 240 VOLTS 7200 WATTS	CIRCUIT #4 30-AMP FUSE 240 VOLTS 7200 WATTS	WATER HEATER 3000 WATTS

KIT—2 FL TUBES 100 W
ENTRY—CLG LTS 100 W
PORCH—EAVE LT 100 W
LV RM—HALL LT 100 W
BATH—FL TUBE 50 W
BR #1—CLG LT 100 W
BR #2—CLG LT 100 W
Total 650 W

CIRCUIT #5
LIGHTING
20-AMP FUSE
120 VOLTS
2400 WATTS

CIRCUIT #6
LIGHTING
20-AMP FUSE
120 VOLTS
2400 WATTS

KIT—2 CLG LTS 200 W
LIV—FL LAMP 100 W
HALL—CLG LT 100 W
BR #1—2 LAMPS 120 W
BR #2—2 LAMPS 120 W
YARD—FLD LT 200 W
BATH—CLG LT 100 W
Total 940 W

KIT—MIXER 200 W
BLENDER 300 W
TOASTER 1100 W
REFRIGERATOR 300 W
CLOCK 10 W
BATH—HAIR DRYER 300 W
RAZOR 75 W
Total 2285 W

CIRCUIT #7
GENERAL PURPOSE
20-AMP FUSE
120 VOLTS
2400 WATTS

CIRCUIT #8
GENERAL PURPOSE
20-AMP FUSE
120 VOLTS
2400 WATTS

KIT—RADIO 100 W
PERCOLATOR 1100 W
LIV—CLOCK 10 W
STEREO 200 W
TV 300 W
BR #1 TV 300 W
BR #2 TV 300 W
Total 2310 W

KIT—IRONER 1650 W
FREEZER 250 W
BATH—HEATER 1500 W
Total 3400 W

CIRCUIT #9
GENERAL PURPOSE
30-AMP FUSE
120 VOLTS
3600 WATTS

CIRCUIT #10
GENERAL PURPOSE
20-AMP FUSE
120 VOLTS
2400 WATTS

KIT—DISHWASH 1200 W
GARB DISP 400 W
Total 1600 W

SPARE 240-VOLT CIRCUIT ———— 2 SPARE 120-VOLT CIRCUITS

Fig. 16-48. Typical electrical floor plan of a residence.

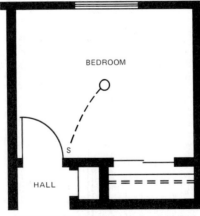

LOCATION OF A CEILING LIGHT AND SWITCH

Fig. 16-49 A. Bedroom wiring diagram.

322

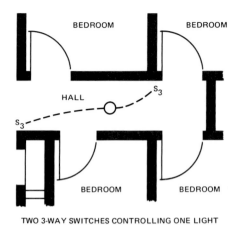

TWO 3-WAY SWITCHES CONTROLLING ONE LIGHT

Fig. 16-49 B. Hall wiring diagram.

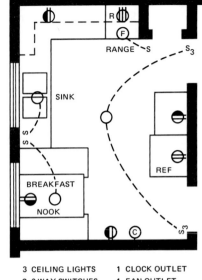

3 CEILING LIGHTS   1 CLOCK OUTLET
2 3-WAY SWITCHES   1 FAN OUTLET
5 CONVENIENCE OUTLETS
3 STANDARD SWITCHES
1 RANGE OUTLET (3 WIRE)

Fig. 16-49 C. Kitchen wiring diagram.

switches and outlets to accommodate these appliances and fixtures should be determined. Next, the electrical symbols representing the switches, outlets, and electrical devices (Fig. 16-46) should be drawn on the floor plan. A line is then drawn from each switch to the connecting fixture (Fig. 16-47). The exact position of each wire is determined by the electrician. The designer indicates only the position of the fixture, the switch, and the connecting line.

Figure 16-48 shows a typical electrical plan of a residence. The circuits for this plan are also shown.

Figures 16-49A through 16-49D show some typical wiring diagrams of various rooms in the home. Refer to the symbols shown to identify the various symbols. You will notice how much more involved the electric appliances for the kitchen and laundry are than those in the other rooms in the house. Notice also the use of three-way and four-way switches in halls and other traffic areas to provide flexibility and control.

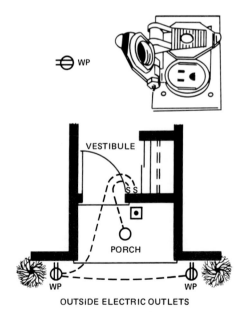

OUTSIDE ELECTRIC OUTLETS

Fig. 16-49 D. Entrance area wiring diagram.

Review Questions

1. Define the following terms: silhouette, structural, fluorescent, incandescent, valance, glazing, soffit, luminous, circuit, wattage, diffuse, indirect, circuit breaker, aquastat, outlet, dimmer, jack.
2. Complete the workbook exercises on pp. 70–72.
3. For your scrapbook, find examples and label uses of general lighting, structural lighting, local lighting, and decorative lighting.
4. Complete a wiring plan for a floor plan of your own design.

323

5. Develop a lighting plan for the floor plan shown in Fig. 19-1B. Show each symbol and position of all fixtures.

6. Design a lighting plan for the floor plan shown in Fig. 16-50.

7. List the styles of furnishing that would be appropriate for the lighting fixtures shown in Fig. 16-36.

8. List the structural lighting installations you would design into the plan as shown in Fig. 8-19.

9. Name four appliances that require special-purpose outlets.

10. Name the three general classifications of lighting.

11. What are the five methods used to disperse light?

12. Describe the purpose of three-way switches as shown in Fig. 16-44.

13. Refer to the floor plan shown in Fig. 16-50. Visit a lighting store or lighting department and select fixtures for each room in this plan.

14. Prepare a wiring plan for your own home.

15. Describe how a four-way switch is used.

16. Make a sketch of the electrical symbols (page 16-48). Sketch one appliance or fixture for each symbol.

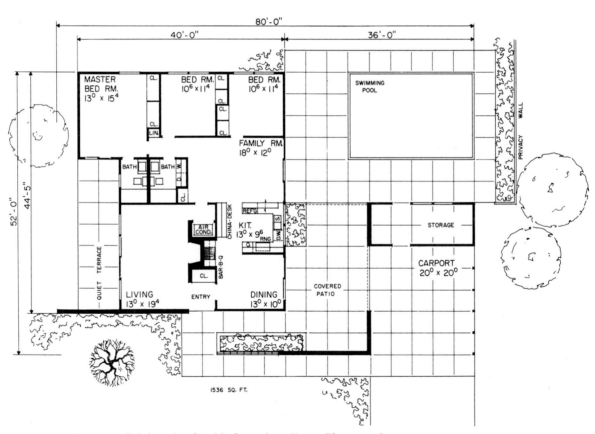

Fig. 16-50. Prepare a lighting plan for this floor plan. *Home Planners, Inc.*

Presenting interior design ideas and concepts is a communication skill which must be mastered by every interior designer. Visual and verbal communications bridge the gap between what the client wants and what the designer envisions. The more effective the communication, the more both the client and the designer will understand about the other's needs and ideas. To make this communication effective, the successful interior designer uses line drawings, sketches, formal renderings, photographs, material samples, models, and full-size displays. The size of the project and the budget determine the number and type of media used for presentation. For example, presentation of a prototype hotel room may involve all of the above media and may be presented to a relatively large group by the designer. On the other hand, a residential proposal may be presented in floor-plan, elevation, or pictorial-sketch form by the designer on a one-to-one basis with the client.

PRESENTATION DRAWINGS

Floor Plans

Although architectural floor plans suffice for establishing interior design layout, they're often inadequate for presentation purposes. Adding depth, color coding, shadowing, and material texture, as shown in the floor plan in Fig. 17-1, is often used effectively to present a more realistic picture. Floor plans of this type are often prepared as overlays to the basic floor plan in order to preserve the original plan.

Interior Wall Elevations

Interior wall elevations that show only the outline of features, fixtures, furniture, and accessories are an accurate tool for the designer's use, but

326

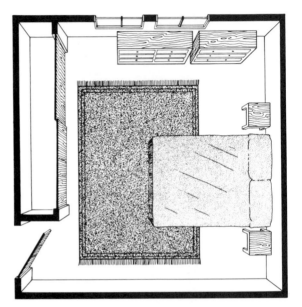

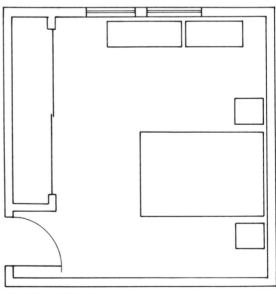

Fig. 17-1. Presentation floor plan.

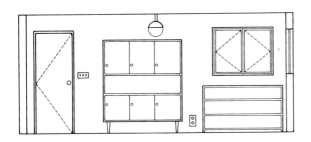

Fig. 17-2. Wall elevation presentation drawing.

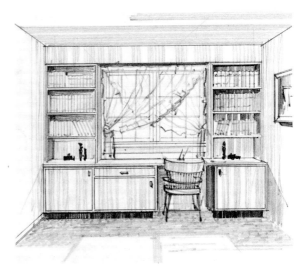

Fig. 17-3. Pictorial presentation technique. *Home Planners, Inc.*

like the architectural floor plan, these wall elevations don't provide the communication link needed for presentation work. Adding additional color and texture plus providing depth and shadow lines, as shown in Fig. 17-2, makes a wall elevation appear more realistic. Converting a wall elevation to a simple one-point perspective, as shown in Fig. 17-3, will often provide the needed pictorial quality. More complex wall elevations such as the one shown in Fig. 17-4 may

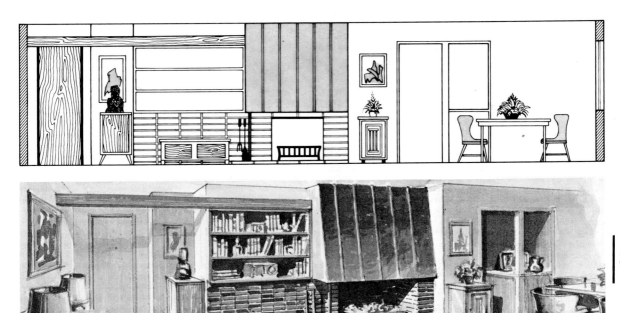

Fig. 17-4. Pictorial conversion of a wall elevation. *Home Planners, Inc.*

Fig. 17-5. Line drawing with wash added for presentation. *Georgia Pacific.*

Fig. 17-6. Use of an overlay to show alternative furniture styles. *Home Planners, Inc.*

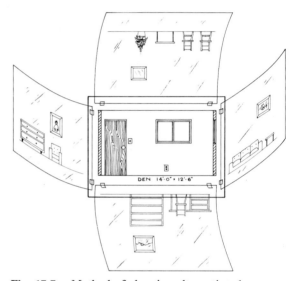

Fig. 17-7. Method of showing alternative decors.

require a more elaborate pictorial drawing for presentation purposes.

Pictorial line sketches, as shown in Fig. 17-5, or pictorial line drawings can be converted to presentation drawings by adding watercolor wash applications using the proposed color scheme directly over the line drawing.

Presenting Design Alternatives

Presentation drawings are not only used to present final designs for approval but also to present design alternatives before the total design is finalized. These alternatives range from total concept to furniture placement, accessory arrangement, or color schemes. To present alternative design features, either separate drawings must be prepared for each alternative or overlays used on a constant-base drawing. Figure 17-6 shows use of an overlay to show alternative furniture styles, and Fig. 17-7 shows four alternative wall decors each on a separate overlay keyed to an interior wall elevation. This same technique can be used to show design alternatives when applied to a photograph of an existing area. Black-and-white photographs, if underdeveloped on the light side, can also be used to show alternative color schemes directly on the photographic paper.

If several alternative color schemes are being considered, a clear acetate overlay with color added can be used for each proposed scheme. Dry markers which are quick drying and waterproof may be also used in the same manner.

SAMPLE BOARDS

Floor plans, wall elevations, pictorial sketches, and even full-color renderings cannot completely and accurately describe the actual color and texture of all elements of the design. Actual samples are needed to show these features on draperies, wall surfaces, paint, wood grain, carpeting, tile, and fabrics.

The client often wants to see more furniture construction and accessory detail than is possible to show in renderings. For this reason a collage

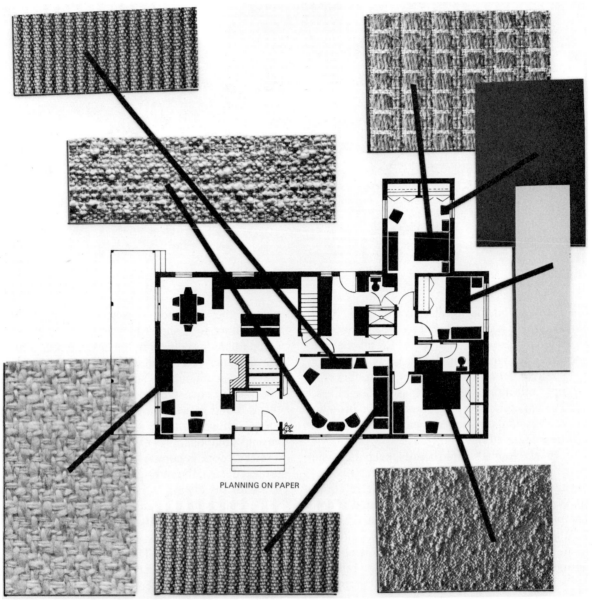

PLANNING ON PAPER

Fig. 17-8. Sample board collage. *Southern Furniture Manufacturer's Association and North Carolina State University and Scalamandré*

of sample materials and/or pictures of furniture, appliances, and accessories is prepared to allow the client to see and feel the physical characteristics of the materials. A typical sample board collage is shown in Fig. 17-8.

Sample boards may be constructed on mat board sheets using a window method in which the mat boards are cut and the material is placed behind the opening. Or, the materials can be attached to the mat board with glue or rubber cement. The color of the mat board should be neutral to eliminate competition with the materials. Each item should be labeled and the lettering should be unobtrusive and constant. A separate sample board should be prepared for each room or integrated area, keeping the size of the components in relative size to their impact on the total design. For example, don't include a small sample of wall-to-wall carpeting and a large sample of a table napkin. Include consistent title block information on each board indicating the room, assigned phase, client, and designer. Keep

Fig. 17-9. Typical manufacturer's showroom setting of furniture. *DMI Furniture Company*

the boards within manageable size; 11″ × 17″ (279 × 431 mm) is a common sample board size but larger boards up to 3′ × 5′ (1 × 1.5 m) may be necessary for larger complex projects.

Where actual samples are not possible (for example, furniture, design, masonry samples, appliances), either the total object can be brought to the presentation site, or a picture of the item can be integrated into the collage.

In developing sample boards, keep the basic elements of design constantly in mind but remember that the line, form, and space relationships can only be observed in the actual room. Sample boards, therefore, should focus on color relationships, light and tone qualities, and material textures. Apply the basic principles of design to the composition of the collage but pay particular attention to developing good emphasis and balance.

ROOM DISPLAYS

Several types of room displays are used by the interior designer: the manufacturer's showroom, the comprehensive room displays, the architectural center, and actual prototype room displays.

The manufacturer's showroom, either separate or located in a merchandise mart, is primarily used to show the designer and/or the client the actual furniture fixture, rug, or other component in its real form. However, the client should have a good grasp of the design before visiting the showroom. Forseeing an item such as furniture in a showroom setting is not at all comparable to seeing it in the environment which the designer has created. Figure 17-9 shows a typical manufacturer's showroom.

Comprehensive room displays, such as those found in department stores, approximate room settings but the choice of styles in the various components is extremely restrictive. Unless the room is somewhat compatible with the project design, the setting can create false impressions for the client.

Architectural centers are excellent sources of investigating materials such as masonry, paneling, flooring, fireplaces, windows, and bath and kitchen components. The designer uses these centers to select materials and also to show the client what may not be possible on a sample board. Seeing several inches of paneling on a sample board provides an impression of the color and texture, but seeing an entire wall of paneling has much greater impact.

Actual prototypes (full-size rooms) are relatively rare in interior design work. However, where the design is to be duplicated, for example, in the design of a large hotel-motel complex or tract homes, a full-size room is sometimes constructed and furnished to enable the client to see the actual finished room. In some office design situations, the office is usually used on an experimental basis. Feedback from the users is used by the interior designer to revise and refine the design to the client's needs.

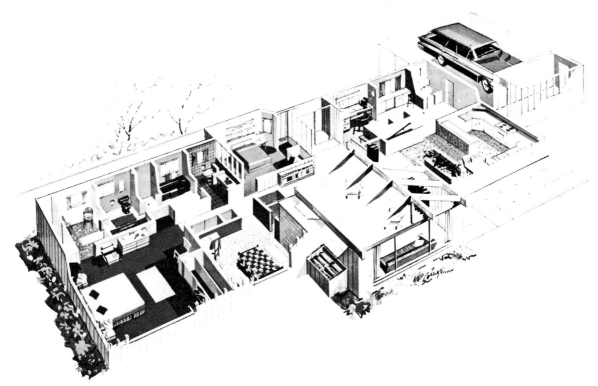

Fig. 17-10.   Full residential model.

MODELS

With the exception of the full-size prototypes, a three-dimensional room model is the most effective means of truly describing the volume of an area. Since models are extremely expensive to produce, they are usually restricted to large commercial projects. Residence models as shown in Fig. 17-10 are quite rare. However, to describe the volume of a room to a client, often a box model (four sides) or a two-wall model, as shown in Fig. 17-11, are sometimes prepared.

The most expensive and time-consuming aspect of model building involves the construction of special architectural features, furniture, and fixtures. For this reason, often block (representative) furniture or doll house furniture, available at hobby shops, is used to fill the space even though it might not precisely match the actual item specified. Using stock model mate-

Fig. 17-11.   Two-wall model.

PART	MODEL MATERIALS	METHODS OF CONSTRUCTION
WALLS	Soft wood; cardboard	Cut wall to exact dimensions of elevations. Allow for overlapping of joints at corners. Have wall thicknesses to scale.
ROOFS	Thin, stiff cardboard; paint-colored sand; sandpaper; wood pieces	Cut out roof patterns and assembly. For sand or gravel roof, paint with slow-drying enamel the color of roof. Sprinkle on sand. For shingle roof, cut sandpaper or thin wood pieces, and glue on as if laying shingle roof.
BRICK & STONE	Commercially printed paper	Glue paper in place; cut grooves in wood, and paint color of bricks or stones.
WOOD PANELING	Commercially printed paper; 1/32" veneer wood	Glue paper in place; with veneer wood, rule on black lines for strip effect, and glue in place. Mahogany veneer equals redwood.
STUCCO	Plaster of Paris	Mix and dab on with brush.
WINDOWS & DOORS	Preformed plastic; wood strips and clear plastic	Purchase ready-made windows to scale in model store; or frame openings with wood strips and glue in clear plastic for windows or wood panel for door.
FLOORS	Flocked carpet; commercially printed paper; 1/32" veneer wood	Paint area with slow-drying colored enamel, and apply flock, removing excess when dry. With paper, glue in place. With veneer, rule on black lines for strip effect, and glue in place.
FURNITURE	Cardboard, nails, flock, wood, clay	Fashion furniture to scale. Paint and flock to give effect of material.
SITE AREAS	Wood slab, wire screen, paper mâché	Build up hilly areas with sticks and wire. Place paper mâché over wire.
GRASS	Green enamel paint and flock	Paint grass area. Apply flock, removing excess when dry.
TREES & BUSHES	Sponge; lichen	Grind up sponges and paint different shades of green. Use small pieces for bushes. Glue small pieces to tree twigs for trees. Lichen may be purchased in model stores and used in the same manner as sponges.
AUTOS & PEOPLE	Toys and miniatures	If time permits, carve from soft wood.

Fig. 17-12. Materials used on architectural models.

332

rials for building components and furniture and equipment as shown in Fig. 17-12 saves much time and expense. If an entire residence is to be constructed, a scale of ¼" or ½" to a foot is recommended. However, for separate rooms a scale of ¾" = 1'-0 or 1" = 1'-0 is recommended.

In preparing room models, first draw the floor plan to the scale selected for the model (Fig. 17-13A). Glue the drawing directly to a baseboard, either ¼" plywood or foamboard, as shown in Fig. 17-13B.

Next, from cardboard or foamboard, cut out the four outside walls, two if a two-wall model is being constructed. Cut out holes for windows and doors. Do the same for any room dividers or partitions, as shown in Fig. 17-13C.

Next add wall covering materials since it is easier to add the materials before the walls are erected. Glue door and window frames and other construction features, including accessories and lighting, directly onto the walls. Glue the walls to the base using rubber cement or quick-drying

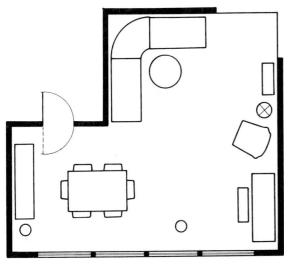

Fig. 17-13 A. Floor plan prepared for base of model.

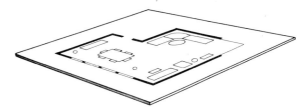

Fig. 17-13 B. Floor plan attached to base.

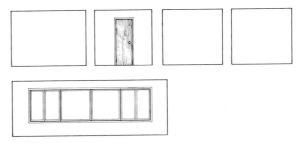

Fig. 17-13 C. Model walls.

glue. Add in floor covering features and any built-in furniture. Then add movable furniture and accessories, as shown in Fig. 17-13D.

Review Questions

1. Define the following terms: collage, prototype, sample boards, showroom, box model, two-wall model.
2. Complete workbook exercises on pp. 73–78.
3. Collect photos from magazines and newspapers of interior models for your scrapbook.
4. Construct a box model of a living area of your own design. Construct a two-wall model of an interior of your own design.
5. Prepare a presentation rendering of an interior of your own design.
6. Trace the pictorial drawings shown in Fig. 16-26. Add additional features and color to the drawing for presentation purposes.
7. Create a sample board showing the materials you would design for the interior of the living area of the plan shown in Fig. 17-13.
8. Trace the elevation showing in Fig. 17-4A. Add shading and surface textures to the drawing for illustration purposes.
9. Trace the plan shown in Fig. 6-4. Add furniture and color the floor plan for presentation purposes.
10. Construct a model of the interior of a home of your own design.

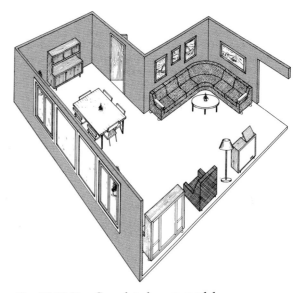

Fig. 17-13 D. Completed room model.

11. Construct a three-wall model of an interior of your own design.
12. Construct a model of the plan shown in Fig. 6-4.
13. By use of overlays, show alternative decors for a room of your own design.
14. By means of overlays, show alternative decors for the wall shown in Fig. 17-2.
15. Construct a box model of the dining room of your own design.
16. Construct a box model of a master-bedroom suite of your own design.

LEGAL AND FINANCIAL PLANNING unit 18

Plans and drawings are documents prepared to ensure that the project will be constructed as planned. However, it is impossible to show on the drawings all details pertaining to the construction of the job and describe conditions that relate to that work. Additional information is needed which pertains to specific components and materials to be used and specifications to be followed to ensure the work is constructed precisely as designed. Additional legal insurance is needed to ensure that the finished work conforms to established codes and that the contractual obligations between the designer, builder, and client are clearly established and maintained.

LEGAL CONSIDERATIONS

Documents needed to fulfill these requirements include schedules, specifications, building codes, contracts, and bids. *Contracts* legally outline and describe the roles and responsibilities of all parties involved in a project. *Bids* represent a legal commitment to produce the specified building or parts of the building at a predetermined price and within a specified period of time.

Contracts

Contracts define and affix responsibility for various aspects of construction to the designer, builder or contractor, and the owner or purchaser. Legal documents define agreements reached between the designer, builder, and owner. This agreement indicates the fees to be paid the designer and builder and the general conditions under which the project is undertaken.

Contracts include fees and fee schedules, performance bond, labor and materials bonds, payments, time schedules, estimates, general conditions, and supplementary conditions. Schedules, specifications, and working drawings are also indexed to the contracts so that they become legal adjuncts to the contract.

Contracts describe responsibilities for relevant financial changes which may be affected by time schedules or unavoidable delays, such as acts of God and strikes. Performance bond is offered by the contractor and guarantees that the partners will perform their responsibilities as builder according to the conditions of the contract.

Labor and materials bonds posted by the contractor guarantee that invoices for materials, supplies, and services of subcontractors will be paid by the major contractors (prime contractor) according to the terms of the contract.

Payment schedules are an important part of any contract. Payments are directly related to completion of various phases of the work, such as acceptance of the bid, beginning of work, completion of working phases of construction, and final approval by building inspector.

Licensed subcontractors are specified and required on most jobs. Indications of licensing requirements are usually included in construction contracts. Supervision of the labor force of temporary workers in each specific area and the use of licensed electricians and licensed plumbers are also specified in contracts.

Bids

Contractors receive invitations to bid by mail, through newspaper advertisements, or through

334

private resources such as McGraw-Hill Dodge reports. Bid forms are very specific in indicating the availability of documents, when the documents can be examined, provision for the resolution of questions, approval for submission of materials, specific dates for bids submission, and the form for preparing bids. The bid form includes specific instructions to the bidders, price of the bid, substitution, restrictions, and involvements of subcontractors.

The bid form is a letter which is sent from the bidder to the party responsible for issuing the construction bid. This may be the architect, general contractor, or owner. The letter covers the following points: verification of receipt of all drawings and documents, specific length of time bid will be held open, price quotation for the entire project or stipulation of the part being bid, and a listing of substitute materials or components if any item varies from specified requirements. When the bidder signs this bid form, he or she agrees to abide by all of the conditions of the bid, including the price, time, quality of work, materials as specified in the contract documents, and drawings.

FINANCIAL PLANNING

It is not enough to be able to design creative and functional interiors. The designer must be able to establish fees and compensation plans while producing acceptable levels of compensation for profit and growth. Beyond this the designer must control budgets, manage purchases, and successfully collect and account for revenue. A number of professional consultants can help in these tasks. Whether an interior designer works independently, with an association, with a partner, or forms a corporation, professional assistance is needed from an accountant, banker, legal counsel, insurance advisor, and a wide variety of technical advisors.

Fees and Compensation

Interior designers work with a variety of methods which provide compensation for services depending on whether the contract includes the conceptualization of the design, installation and purchasing of all equipment, travel expenses, or consultation services in relation to builders and architects.

Flat-fee Basis This fee only covers charges for the designer's time and does not include any charges for materials, equipment, labor, or installation.

Flat Fee plus Percentage of Total Costs This type of arrangement protects the designer from escalating projects. The designer is paid a flat fee on an original estimate for the total job. If the budget or actual expenditures for the total job increase beyond the estimated total, then the designer's fee increases proportionately. This percentage may vary from 10 to 25 percent.

Per Diem Fee This is a variation of the fixed-fee base but calculated on the number of days the designer spends on a job. Although the estimate is on a per diem basis, the billing is normally converted to an hourly basis. This protects the designer when the nature of the job is somewhat nebulous and may or may not involve considerable time in travel, consultation, and architectural coordination.

Retail Base In this system the merchandise supplied to the client is billed at the list price which is normally 70 to 100 percent of the manufacturer's net price. This is the most profitable method of remuneration for a designer. This system is used extensively where the cost of materials greatly exceeds the amount of design time for the project. The profit in this case comes not from the amount of time or creativity applied to the job but from the differential between the list and net price of the merchandise.

Cost-plus System In using this method, the designer agrees with the client that he will be reimbursed for services by marking up the cost of all materials between 20 and 30 percent. This is the least popular method for financial reimbursement for designers.

The advisability of using any of these compensation methods should be determined only after thorough investigation of the nature of the client, availability of materials, need for special design items, nature and physical conditions of the site, ease or complexity of delivery, timing of the project, and the need to utilize additional technical consultants. The amount of design time anticipated, and the projected budget for labor and materials must also be considered.

335

Budgets

Budgets are developed by interior designers to determine if indeed the job is sufficiently profitable to undertake and/or to ensure that once established, the anticipated revenue will be forthcoming. Once a design has been approved and a floor plan keyed, a designer's worksheet should be prepared for each room. This worksheet should include the following information pertaining to each item to be purchased:

- Key number
- Quantity
- Manufacture and model number
- Name of item
- Color, finish and/or material
- Cost
- Unit and total
- Estimate and final costs
- Selling price
- Estimate and final costs
- Purchase order
- Number and date

By controlling the budget on each item, the designer controls the total budget for all materials. It shows the designer how far he can go in making substitutions, provides a basis for discussion with clients, and establishes sources of purchasing materials.

Once the budget is established, materials must be ordered through purchase orders which should include:

- Order number
- Ship-to address
- Billing address
- Date to be shipped
- Method of shipment
- Quantity
- Description of each item
- Price
- Receipt signature
- Receipt date

336

Budgets must also be controlled for each item by the use of inventory management forms which should include:

- Order number
- Source
- Name of item

- Purchase price
- Selling price
- Invoice number and date
- Discount (if any)
- Payment date and amount

Billing

Billing procedures should be set up in the original contract and adhered to religiously by all parties. The contract should include billing terms including credit limits, allowances, and adjustments, stipulations for return of merchandise, and stipulations for changes in the plans request. Billing may be done by period or by establishing a fund from which the designer draws for the payment of labor and materials. Some budgets are established so that billing is done on the basis of the percentage of the job completed. That is, a percentage of the budget may represent a deposit and another percentage may be payable upon completion of a major portion of the project and the last payment made upon delivery or installation. The billing system must be established to ensure adequate cash flow to cover the designer's overhead costs, such as labor and real estate expenses, and minimize or eliminate unreimbursed investment in materials and supplies.

Review Questions

1. Define the following terms: document, code, bid, contract, deed, bond, estimates, retail base, prime contractor, subcontractor.
2. Complete the workbook problems on page 79.
3. Complete a bid letter including price, quotations, and fee schedule for your own design.
4. Complete a bid letter for an interior design you would create for the living area in Fig. 17-8.
5. List other professionals from which an interior designer may receive technical assistance.
6. Describe several acts of God by legal definition.
7. Describe four types of interior design fee schedules. Indicate the advantage of each.
8. Name the four phases of a normal payment schedule.

SCHEDULES, CODES, AND SPECIFICATIONS unit 19

The plans and drawings of an interior are documents prepared to ensure that the project will be constructed as planned. However, it is sometimes difficult or impossible to show on the drawings all details pertaining to construction. All features not shown on a drawing should be listed in a schedule or in the specifications.

A *schedule* is a chart of materials and products. Total interior designs include a window, door, interior-finish, furniture, accessory, appliance, and fixture schedule. Schedules are also prepared for electrical and plumbing fixtures.

Specifications are lists of details and products to be included in the building. Specifications may be rather brief descriptions of the materials needed, or they may be complete specifications which list the size, manufacturer, grade, color, style, and price of each item of material to be ordered.

SCHEDULES

Furniture and Accessory Schedules

Only the location and amount of space occupied can be shown conveniently for each piece of furniture or accessory on a floor plan. If additional information is added such as color, materials, and dimensions, the floor plan can become extremely cluttered and difficult to read. For this reason, furniture and accessory schedules are

prepared. The schedule includes all pertinent information relating to each item, as shown in Fig. 19-1A. Each item is numbered and these numbers placed on the appropriate item on the floor plan, as shown in Fig. 19-1B. This system allows the designer and client to record and find both the locations and significant specifications of each item. Pictures of major pieces are also sometimes keyed or attached to the schedule.

Fixture and Appliance Schedule

To ensure that appliances and fixtures will blend with the decor of each room, a separate schedule is prepared (Fig. 19-2). Similar schedules are sometimes prepared for built-in components. By preparing schedules of this kind, the designer can control every aspect of the overall design, including colors, materials, and styles.

Schedules not only are useful in designing and ensuring that the finishing is completed as planned, but also are valuable as aids in ordering manufactured items and in controlling budgets.

Door and Window Schedules

Door and window schedules conserve time and space on a drawing. Rather than include all the information about a door or window on the drawing, a key number or letter is attached to

SYM	ITEM	ROOM	LEN.	WID.	HT.	MATERIAL	COLOR	QUAN.	MANUFAC.	CAT #	COST	REMARKS
1	Drapes	Bedroom	11'	—	7'	Cotton blend	Brown	1 set	Sears	CD 101	$75.00	Lined
2	Drapes	Mbr	12'	—	7'	Cotton blend	Yellow	1 set	Sears	CD 107	$85.00	Lined
3	Drapes	Den	7'	—	7'	Cotton blend	Yellow	1 set	Sears	CD 106	$65.00	Lined
4	Drapes	Living/Dining	24'	—	7'	Acrylic	Brown pat.	1 set	Sears	CD 203	150.00	Lined
5	Chair	Mbr/Den	18"	18"	18"	Plastic	Brown	4	ID Furn. Co.	X117	45.00ea	
6	Chair	Din/Kit	18"	18"	18"	Oak	Natural	9	"	L217	65.00ea	Natural oil finish
7	China cab	Dining	6'	18"	5'-6"	Oak	"	1	Danish Furn. Co.	13712	650.00	" " "
8	Piano Bench	Living	33"	10"	18"	Mahogany	Brn stain	1	Music Co. Inc.	23L19	50.00	Piano finish
9	Piano	Living	5'-6"	2'-0"	5'-6"	"	" "	1	" " "	P17731	1750.00	" "
10	Up. wing ch.	Living	33"	30"	20"	Leather	Natural	1	Danish Furn. Co.	18973	575.00	
11	Fl lamp	Living	14" dia	—	4'-6"	Metal/cloth	Tan	1	" " "	37111	85.00	
12	Stereo	Living	30"	11"	4'-0"	Teak	Brown	1	"	60701	450.00	
13	Sofa/sec.	Living	14'	30"	18"	Velveteen	Red	3 pcs	" " "	42107	1200.00	
14	Coffee tbl	Living	30" dia	—	15"	Teak	Natural	1	" "	77310	110.00	Natural oil finish
15	Television	Den	21"	18"	30"	21" color	Brown	1	Sony	XL19	675.00	
16	Coffee tbl	Den	48"	15"	15"	Oak	Natural	1	Danish Furn. Co.	78325	80.00	Natural oil finish
17	Sofa	Den	6'-6"	30"	18"	Cotton blend	Tan	1	" " "	59781	800.00	
18	Fl lamp	Mbr/Br/Den	15" dia	—	5'-0"	Wood/cloth	Brown	3	" " "	66362	75.00ea	
19	Fl lamp	Den	12" dia	—	4'-6"	Wood/plastic	Yellow	1	" " "	65731	50.00	
20	Desk	Mbr/Den	39"	18"	29"	Oak	Natural	2	" " "	47772	225.00ea	Natural oil finish
21	Night stand	Mbr/Br	18"	15"	24"	Oak	Natural	3	" " "	64991	45.00ea	" "
22	Tbl lamp	Mbr	9" dia	—	30"	Wood/plastic	Brown	2	" " "	65820	35.00ea	
23	Pull bed	Mbr	6'-9"	46"	20"	Standard	—	1				
24	Dresser	Mbr	39"	20"	48"	Oak	Natural	1				
25	Dresser	Br	48"	20"	52"	Oak	Natural	1				
26	Twin bed	Br	6'-9"	42"	20"	Standard	—	1				
27	Planter	Mbr/Liv/Den/Por	10" dia	—	12"	Terra cotta	Brown	4				
28	Table	Kitchen	36"	22"	30"	Teak	Natural	1				
29	Table	Dining	5'-0"	3'-3"	30"	"	Natural	1				

Fig. 19-1 *A*. Furniture accessory schedule.

MANUFAC.	CAT. #	COST	REMARKS
Acme Bed Co.	AC12	235.00	Box spring/mad/frame
Danish Furn. Co.	37452	125.00	Dbl dresser
'' '' ''	37471	200.00	Triple ''
Acme Bed Co.	AC08	190.00	Box spring/mat/frame
Flowers Inc.	23FP	10.00 ea	
Danish Furn. Co.	17832	110.00	Natural oil finish
'' '' ''	17876	235.00	'' '' ''

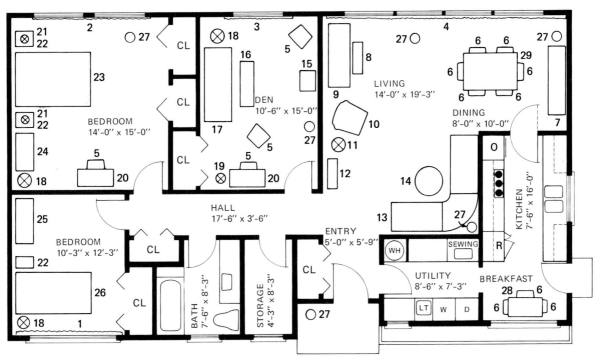

Fig. 19-1 B. Key numbered floor plan.

FIXTURE AND APPLIANCE SCHEDULES

APPLIANCE SCHEDULE

ROOM	APPLIANCE	TYPE	SIZE	COLOR	MANUFACTURER	MODEL NO.
KITCHEN	Electric stove	Cook top	4 Burner	Yellow	Ideale Appliances	341 MG
KITCHEN	Electric oven	Built-in	30" × 24" × 24"	Yellow	Zeidler Oven Mfg.	27 Mg
SERVICE	Hot-water heater	Gas	50 Gal	White	Oratz Water Htr.	249 KG

FIXTURE SCHEDULE

ROOM	FIXTURE	TYPE	MATERIAL	MANUFACTURER	MODEL NUMBER
LIVING	2 Electric lights	Hanging	Brass reflectors	Hot Spark Ltd.	1037 IG
BEDROOM 1	2 Spot lights	Wall bracket	Flexible neck—aluminum	Gurian & Barris Inc.	1426 SG
BATHS 1 & 2	2 Electric lights	Wall bracket	Aluminum—water resistant	Marks Electrical Co.	2432 DG

Fig. 19-2. Fixture and appliance schedules.

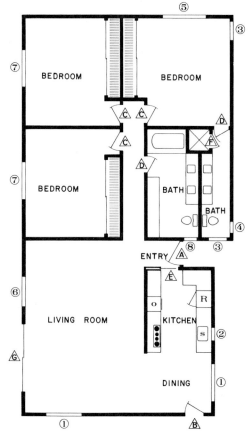

Fig. 19-3. Use of door and window key numbers on floor plan.

each door and window (Fig. 19-3). This symbol (number or letter) is then keyed to the door and window schedule, which includes the width, height, material, type, quantity, and other general information about each window or door (Fig. 19-4). Window schedules eliminate space-consuming notes on drawings. In addition to the information shown in chart form on the door and window schedule, the door or window design is often drawn separately, and indexed to the schedule. Unless an interior wall elevation is prepared for every wall in the house, it is impossible to determine the style of interior doors from the floor-plan drawing. Figure 19-5 shows drawings of interior door styles which may be indexed to the door schedule.

Window styles are normally depicted on the elevation drawing and complete information included in the window schedule. However, to conserve time many architectural drafters draw a separate window detail and show only the window's outline and the schedule key for that window on the elevation drawing.

Finish and Materials Schedules

Finish Schedule

To describe the type of finish—enamel, paint, and stain—and the amount of gloss and color of

340

THE KEY SYMBOL IS INDEXED TO A DOOR AND WINDOW SCHEDULE

DOOR SCHEDULE

SYM-BOL	WIDTH	HEIGHT	THICK-NESS	MATERIAL	TYPE	SCREEN	QUAN-TITY	THRESH-OLD	REMARKS	MANUFACTURER
A	3'-0"	7'-0"	1¾"	Wood—Ash	Slab core	No	1	Oak	Outdoor varnish	A. D. & D. Door, Inc.
B	2'-6"	7'-0"	1¾"	Wood—Ash	Slab core	Yes	1	Oak	Oil stain	A. D. & D. Door, Inc.
C	2'-3"	6'-8"	1⅜"	Wood—Oak	Hollow core	No	3	None	Oil stain	A. D. & D. Door, Inc.
D	2'-0"	6'-8"	1⅜"	Wood—Ash	Hollow core	No	2	None	Oil stain	A. D. & D. Door, Inc.
E	2'-3"	6'-8"	1¼"	Wood—Fir	Plywood	No	1	None	Sliding door	A. D. & D. Door, Inc.
F	1'-9"	5'-6"	½"	Glass & metal	Shower door	No	1	None	Frosted glass	A. D. & D. Door, Inc.
G	4'-6"	6'-6"	½"	Glass & metal	Sliding	Yes	2	Metal	1 sliding screen	A. D. & D. Door, Inc.

WINDOW SCHEDULE

SYMBOL	WIDTH	HEIGHT	MATERIAL	TYPE	SCREEN	QUANTITY	REMARKS	MANUFACTURER	CATALOG NUMBER
1	5'-0"	4'-0"	Aluminum	Stationary	No	2		A & B Glass Co.	18BW
2	2'-9"	3'-0"	Aluminum	Louver	Yes	1		A & B Glass Co.	23JW
3	2'-6"	3'-0"	Wood	Double Hung	Yes	2	4 Lites—2 High	A & B Glass Co.	141PW
4	1'-6"	1'-6"	Aluminum	Louver	Yes	1		Hampton Glass Co.	972 BW
5	6'-0"	3'-6"	Aluminum	Louvered Sides	Yes	1		Hampton Glass Co.	417CW
6	4'-0"	6'-6"	Aluminum	Stationary	No	1		H & W Window Co.	57DH
7	5'-0"	3'-6"	Aluminum	Sliding	Yes	2	Frosted Glass	H & W Window Co.	22DH
8	1'-9"	3'-0"	Aluminum	Awing	Yes	1		H & W Window Co.	1711JB

Fig. 19-4. Key symbol index to a door and window schedule.

Fig. 19-5. Door designs indexed to floor plan keys.

each finish for each room would require an exhaustive list with many duplications. A finishing schedule is a chart which enables the designer to condense all this information. The interior-finish schedule shown in Fig. 19-6 includes, in the horizontal column, the parts of each room and the type of finish to be applied. In the vertical column is information pertaining to the application of the finish and the room to which it is to be applied. The exact color classification has been noted in the appropriate intersecting block. The last column, headed ''Remarks,'' is used for making notes about the finish application.

Materials Schedule

To ensure that all floor, wall, and ceiling coverings blend well with the overall decor in each room, an interior-finish schedule can be prepared. All the possible materials for each part of the room should be listed in the horizontal column. The rooms are listed in the vertical column. The appropriate block can be checked for the suitable material for the ceiling, wall, wainscoting, base, and floor of each room (Fig. 19-7). When a schedule is prepared in this manner, it is easy to read and facilitates checking the color scheme of each room and of the overall decor. This kind of schedule condenses pages of unrelated material lists for each room into one chart, thus enabling the designer to see at a glance all the material that should be ordered for each room.

SPECIFICATIONS

Specifications are written instructions describing the basic requirements for constructing a build-

INTERIOR FINISHING SCHEDULE

ROOMS	FLOOR VARNISH	UNFINISHED	WAXES	CEILING: ENAMEL GLOSS	ENAMEL SEMIGLOSS	ENAMEL FLAT	FLAT LATEX	STAIN	WALL: ENAMEL GLASS	ENAMEL SEMIGLOSS	ENAMEL FLAT	FLAT LATEX	STAIN	BASE: ENAMEL GLOSS	ENAMEL SEMIGLOSS	ENAMEL FLAT	FLAT LATEX	STAIN	TRIM: ENAMEL GLOSS	ENAMEL SEMIGLOSS	FLAT LATEX	ENAMEL FLAT	STAIN	REMARKS
ENTRY		✓					OFF WHT					OFF WHT			OFF WHT					OFF WHT				OIL STAIN
HALL		✓					LT BRN			TAN		DRK BRN			DRK BRN					DRK BRN				OIL STAIN
BEDROOM 1	✓						OFF WHT					OFF WHT				GREY				GREY				ONE COAT PRIMER & SEALER —PAINTED SURFACE
BEDROOM 2	✓						OFF WHT					LT YEL				YEL					YEL			ONE COAT PRIMER & SEALER —PAINTED SURFACE
BEDROOM 3			✓				OFF WHT					LT BRN				DRK BRN							TAN	ONE COAT PRIMER & SEALER —PAINTED SURFACE
BATH 1			WHT			WHT						LT BLUE				LT BLUE								WATER-RESISTANT FINISHES
BATH 2			WHT			WHT						LT BLUE				LT BLUE								WATER-RESISTANT FINISHES
CLOSETS	✓					BRN					BRN					BRN					BRN			
KITCHEN			✓	WHT			YEL					YEL				YEL								
DINING			✓			TAN	YEL					YEL				YEL								OIL STAIN
LIVING	✓					TAN						LT BRN				LT BRN						LT BRN		OIL STAIN

Fig. 19-6. Interior finishing schedule.

341

INTERIOR MATERIALS SCHEDULE

ROOMS	FLOOR										CEILING				WALL			WAINSCOT						BASE				REMARKS
	ASPHALT TILE	CERAMIC TILE	CORK TILE	LINOLEUM TILE	WOOD STRIP—OAK	WOODS SOS—OAK	PLYWOOD PANEL	CARPETING	SLATE	DIATO	PLASTER	WOOD PANEL	ACOUSTICAL TILE	EXPOSED BEAM	PLASTER	WOOD PANEL	WALL PAPER	WOOD	CERAMIC TILE	PAPER	ASPHALT TILE	STONE VENEER	LINOLEUM	WOOD	RUBBER	TILE—CERAMIC	ASPHALT	
ENTRY									√	√	√				√									√				TERAZZO COVERING
HALL	√										√				√						√			√				
BEDROOM 1				√								√	√		√			√								√		MAHOGANY WAINSCOT
BEDROOM 2				√								√	√		√		√	√								√		MAHOGANY WAINSCOT
BEDROOM 3							√	√				√			√											√		SEE OWNER FOR GRADE CARPET
BATH 1		√									√				√			√								√		WATER-SEAL-TILE EDGES
BATH 2	√										√				√			√								√		WATER-SEAL-TILE EDGES
KITCHEN				√								√	√								√	√						
DINING				√								√	√	√						√	√							
LIVING							√	√				√			√						√	√						SEE OWNER FOR GRADE CARPET

Fig. 19-7. Interior materials schedule.

ing. Specifications describe sizes, kinds, and quality of building materials. The methods of construction, fabrication, or installation are also spelled out explicitly. Specifically they tell the contractor, "These are the materials you must use, and this is how you must use them, and these are the conditions under which you undertake this job." Specifications guarantee the purchaser that the contractor will deliver the building when it is finished exactly as specified.

Information that cannot be conveniently included in the drawings, such as the legal responsibilities, methods of purchasing materials, and insurance requirements, is included in the specifications. In order to make an accurate construction estimate, contractors refer to the material lists that are included in the specifications.

Specifications help ensure that the building will be constructed according to standards that the building laws require. Specifications are used frequently by banks and federal agencies in appraising the market value of a building.

The following specifications outline shows the major divisions and subdivisions of a typical set of specifications. This outline does not include the exact size and kind of material included under each category, as these would vary with each building. You will notice that the sequence of the outline roughly approximates the sequence of actual construction.

Specifications Outline

Client's name and address
Contractor's name and address
Designer's name and address
Location of structure

1. General information
List of all drawings, specifications, legal documents
Allowances of money for special orders, such as wallpaper, carpeting, fixtures
Completion date
Contractor's bid
List of manufactured items bought for the job
Guarantees for all manufactured items

2. Legal responsibilities—contractor
Good workmanship
Adherence to plans and specifications
Fulfillment of building laws
Purchase of materials
Hiring and paying all workers
Obtaining and paying for all permits
Providing owner with certificate of passed inspection
Responsibility for correction of errors
Responsibility for complete cleanup
Furnish all tools and equipment
Providing personal supervision

342

Having a supervisor on the job at all times
Providing a written guarantee of work

3. Legal responsibilities—client
Carrying fire insurance during construction
Paying utilities during construction
Specifying method of payment

Carpentry
Required types of wood grades
Maximum amount of moisture in wood
List of construction members, sizes, and
    amount of wood needed
Special woods, mill work

Floors
Type, size, and finish of floor
Floor coverings

Doors and windows
Sizes
Material
Type
Quantity
Manufacturer and model number
Window or door trims
Frames for screens
Amount of window space per room
Amount of openable window space per room
Types of glass and mirrors
Types of sashes
Window and door frames
Weather stripping and caulking

Lath and plaster
Type, size, and amount of lath needed
Type, size, and amount of wire mesh, felt,
    paper, and nails
Types of interior and exterior plaster
Instructions of manufacturer for mixing and
    applying
Number of coats
Finishing between coats
Drying time

Dry walls
Wall covering—types, sizes, manufacturer's
    model number

Electrical needs
Electrical outlets and their locations
Electrical switches and their locations
Wall brackets and their locations
Ceiling outlets and their locations

Signed certificate that electrical work has
    passed the building inspection
Guarantee for all parts
List of all electrical parts with name, type,
    size, color, model number, and lamp wat-
    tage
Locations for television outlet and aerial,
    telephone outlet, main switches, panel
    board, circuits, and meter
Size of wire used for wiring
Number of circuits

Plumbing
List of fixtures with make, color, style, manu-
    facturer, and catalog number
List of type and size of plumbing lines—gas,
    water, and waste
Vent pipes and sizes
Inspection slips on plumbing
Guarantees for plumbing
Instructions for installing and connecting
    pipelines

Heating and air conditioning
List of all equipment with make, style, color,
    manufacturer's name, catalog number
Guarantee for all equipment
Signed equipment inspection certificate
List and location of all sheet-metal work for
    heat ducts
List of fuels, outlets, exhausts, and registers
Types of insulation
Location for heating and air-conditioning
    units

Stone and brickwork
List and location of all stone and brickwork
    (fireplace, chimney, retaining walls)
Concrete and mortar mix
Reinforcing steel
Kind, size, and name of manufacturer of any
    synthetic stone

Built-ins
List of all built-ins to be constructed on the
    job
Dimensions

Kinds of materials
List of all manufactured objects to be built
    in
Model number
Make
Color

343

Catalog number
Manufacturer

Ceramic tile
List of types, sizes, colors, manufacturers,
    catalog numbers
Mortar mix

Painting
List of paints to be used—type, color, manu-
    facturer's name, catalog number
Preparation of painted surface
Number of coats and preparation of each
Instructions for stained surfaces or special
    finishes (type of finish, color, manufac-
    turer, and catalog number)

Finish hardware
List of hardware—type, make, material,
    color, manufacturer's name, catalog num-
    ber

BUILDING CODES

A building code is a collection of laws that outlines the restrictions necessary to maintain minimum standards established by building and health departments of communities. These codes (laws) help control design, construction, materials, maintenance, location of structures, use of structures, number of occupants, quality of materials, and use of materials. To stay within the law, designers and builders must observe the local building codes.

Before any structure is built, altered, or repaired, a building permit must be obtained from the municipality building department. This permit ensures the appearance of an inspector to inspect the work. Inspections are made of plans, grading of land, excavations, foundations, forms, carpentry, plumbing, heating, ventilating, and electrical work.

344

To be effective, codes must be updated continually to keep pace with new types of construction materials; otherwise, the use of antiquated materials and methods is perpetuated by outdated building codes.

Building codes vary in different communities because of geographical differences. Each municipality formulates its own building-code requirements. Building codes are necessary to ensure not only that substandard or unsafe buildings are not erected but that unattractive or architecturally inconsistent buildings are not built in an area. Building codes also help regulate the kinds of structures that can be built in specific areas by zoning.

Zones are usually classified as residential, commercial, or industrial. Building codes also contain regulations pertaining to building permits, fees, inspection requirements, drawings required, property location, and general legal implications connected with the building.

Size restrictions are a vital part of every code. Some of the most common items included in building codes include room sizes, ceiling heights, window areas, foundations, retaining walls, concrete mix, and girders.

The type and composition of foundations are outlined specifically in building codes, as are the sizes and spacing of girders, posts, and joists. The size of door and window openings related to the size of the lintel and the weight of support required of that lintel are also spelled out in building codes. Roof types, pitches, size of materials, and spacing of rafters, especially in cold climates where snow loads are prevalent, are rigidly controlled through building codes.

The maximum amount of load permissible for each kind of structure is always listed in the building codes. Live loads, which include the weight of any movable object on floors, roofs, or ceilings, and dead loads, the weight of the building itself that must be supported, are rigidly controlled through specifying the size and type of materials that are used in foundations to support these loads. The size and spacing of materials in walls that support roof loads are also specified. Maximum loads in pounds per square foot as related to the pitch of the roof are specified in building codes.

Review Questions

1. Define the following terms: schedule, specifications, code, minimum standards, building permit, fixture schedule, finish schedule.
2. Complete the exercises in the workbook on page 80.
3. Prepare a finishing schedule of an interior design of your own.
4. Prepare a finishing schedule for the remodeling of your own home.

5. Design floor, wall, and ceiling treatments for the living area shown in Fig. 19-8. Develop and complete a finishing schedule for the project.

6. Prepare an appliance schedule for the appliances you would use in Fig. 17-8. Indicate the appliance name, type, size, color.

7. Prepare a window schedule for the floor plan shown in Fig. 19-8.

8. Prepare a door schedule for the floor plan shown in Fig. 19-8.

9. Prepare an appliance schedule for the floor plan shown in Fig. 19-8.

10. Prepare an accessory schedule for the floor plan shown in Fig. 19-8.

11. Prepare a painting schedule for the floor plan shown in Fig. 19-8.

12. Prepare a fixture schedule for the floor plan shown in Fig. 17-8.

13. Prepare a drawing of the windows you would design for Fig. 17-10. Develop a window schedule indexed to these styles.

14. Prepare a drawing for the doors you would design for Fig. 17-10. Prepare a door schedule indexed to these styles. Sketch a floor plan and key-number the plan to the completed schedule.

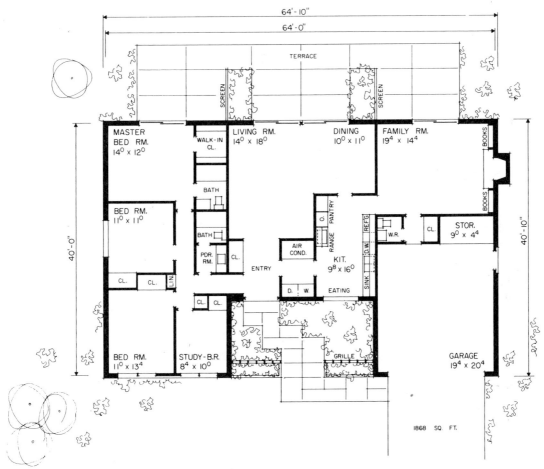

Fig. 19-8. Prepare an appliance; accessories; pantry and fixtures; and door and window schedule for this plan. *Home Planners, Inc.*

GLOSSARY

Abstract design Stylized form created without total reference to the actual physical shape of an object or a natural form.

Abstract of title A summary of all deeds, wills, and legal actions to show ownership.

Accessories Items added to the design that are not an integral part of the structure or the major furnishings.

Acoustical materials Natural or manufactured items that diminish noise within a room or prevent it from passing through walls.

Acoustics Study of the production, transmittal, and control of sound.

Adobe construction Walls constructed of sun-dried units of adobe soil, usually found in the southwestern United States.

Aesthetic Accepted standards of beauty and taste.

Air conditioner An apparatus that can heat, cool, clean, and circulate air.

Air duct A pipe usually made of sheet metal that conducts air to rooms from a central source.

Air trap A U-shaped pipe filled with water and located beneath plumbing fixtures to form a seal against the passage of gases and odors.

Air-dried lumber Lumber that is dried in the open air rather than in a kiln.

Alabaster Smooth white masonry.

Alcove A recessed space connected at the side of a larger room.

Alteration A change in, or addition to, an existing building.

Amortize Spreading payments over a period of time.

Analogous color A color harmony that combines colors adjacent on the color wheel.

Antique An object created more than one hundred years ago.

348

Apartment A suite of rooms or a multifamily unit in a housing complex.

Apex Topmost point in a design.

Appliqué A design or markings added to another surface.

Appraisal Formal evaluation of property's worth.

Apron A horizontal molding strip directly under a windowsill.

—**APRON**

Arcade A series of arches supported by a row of columns.

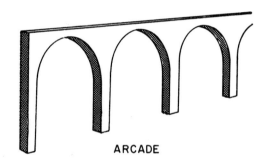

ARCADE

Arch A curved structure that will support itself and the weight above its curved opening by mutual pressure.

ARCH

Architect A person who plans and designs buildings and oversees their construction.

Areawall A wall surrounding an areaway to admit light and air to a basement.

Areaway A recessed area below grade around the foundation to allow light and ventilation into a basement window or doorway.

Asbestos A soft, fibrous, fireproof mineral fiber used in fireproofing building materials.

Asbestos board A fire-resistant sheet made from asbestos fiber and portland cement.

Ash pit The area below the hearth of a fireplace in which the ashes collect.

Ashlar A facing of squared stones.

Asphalt tile Synthetic composition material used as a floor surface.

Assessed value A value set by government assessors to determine tax assessments.

Asymmetrical Balanced design in which two sides are equal but not identical.

Atrium An open court within a building.

Attic The space between the roof and the ceiling.

Awning window An outswinging window hinged at the top.

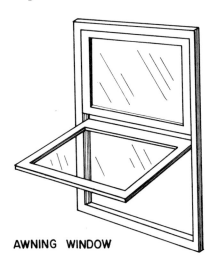

AWNING WINDOW

Awnings Projecting overhangs that provide protection for windows.

Back hearth The part of the hearth inside the fireplace.

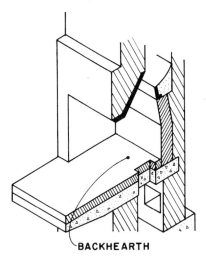

BACKHEARTH

Baffle A partial barrier against a flow of wind or sound.

Balance Equilibrium in design.

Balcony A deck projecting from the wall of a building above the ground.

BALCONY

Ball and claw foot Furniture legs depicting a claw grasping a ball.

Baluster The vertical support for a handrail.

Balustrade A series of balusters or posts connected by a rail, generally used for porches and balconies.

Banister A hand rail.

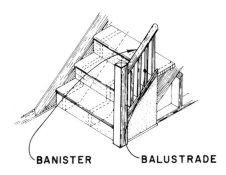

BANISTER   BALUSTRADE

349

Baroque An elaborate and ornamental style of art and architecture characteristic of 17th-century Europe.

Base The finish of a room at the junction of the walls and floor.

Base course The lowest part of masonry construction.

Base molding Any molding used on the bottom of an object or room.

Base shoe A molding used next to the floor in interior baseboards.

Baseboard The finish board covering the interior wall where the wall and floor meet.

Baseline A located line for reference control purposes.

Basement The lowest story of a building, partially or entirely below ground.

Basket weave A weave using large threads of equal size, in which the weft crosses over alternate warp threads.

Bas-relief A sculpted surface raised from the background material.

Batt A blanket insulation material usually made of mineral fibers and designed to be installed between framing members.

Batten A narrow strip of board used to cover cracks between the boards in board and batten siding.

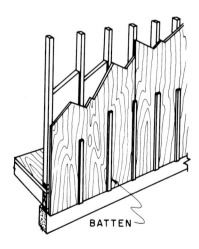

BATTEN

Bay The space between columns or vertical supports.

Bay window A window projecting out from the wall of a building to form a recess in the room.

Bead An ornamental molding comprised of a series of spherical forms in line.

Beam A horizontal structural member that carries a load.

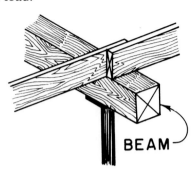

BEAM

Beam ceiling A ceiling in which the ceiling beams are exposed to view.

Bearing wall or partition A wall supporting any vertical load other than its own weight.

Bevel The edge of any surface that is not at right angles to the major surface.

Bevel siding Shingles or other siding board thicker on one edge than the other. The thick edge overlaps the thin edge of the next board.

Bib A threaded faucet to which a hose can be attached.

Bill of material A parts list of material accompanying a structural drawing.

Birdseye grain Wood surface characterized by small circular markings, found mostly in maple.

Blanket insulation Insulation in rolled-sheet form, often backed by treated paper which forms a vapor barrier.

Bleach Removing original color or whitening of a surface or material.

Blocking Small wood framing members that fill the spaces between the floor and ceiling joists to add stiffness to the floors and ceiling.

Blueprint An architectural drawing used by workers as a building plan. The original drawing is transferred to a sensitized paper that turns blue with white lines when printed.

Board and batten Wall construction consisting of wide vertical boards whose joints are covered with narrow vertical strips known as battens.

Board measure A system of lumber measurement based on a board-foot. One board-foot is the equivalent of 1 foot square by 1 inch thick.

Bow window A bay window which appears as an unbroken curved surface.

Breakfront A bookcase or cabinet with a center that projects forward from the sides.

Breezeway A roofed walkway with open sides connecting the house and garage. If it is large enough it can be used as a patio.

Broadloom A woven carpet more than three feet wide.

Brocade A type of weave that resembles embroidery.

Broker An agent in buying and selling property.

BTU Abbreviation for British thermal unit, a standard unit for measuring heat gain or loss.

Buffet Furniture for storing dining accessories, usually with a surface from which food can be served.

Building code A collection of legal requirements designed to maintain building standards to protect the safety, health, and general welfare of people who work and live in them.

Building paper A heavy, waterproof paper used over sheathing and subfloors to prevent passage of air and water.

Building permit A permit issued by a municipal government authorizing the construction of a building or structure.

Built-up beam A beam constructed of smaller members fastened together.

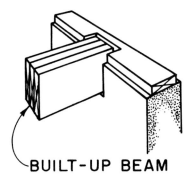

BUILT-UP BEAM

Bural Irregular grained wood surfaces caused by limb intersections.

Butt joint The point at which one surface meets another at right angles to form a common bond.

Butterfly roof A roof with two sides sloping down toward the interior of the house.

Butterfly table Early American drop-leaf table.

BX cable Armored electric cable wrapped in rubber and protected by a flexible steel covering.

Cabinetwork Finished woodwork made by a cabinetmaker.

Cabriole Furniture leg in the form of an animal's leg.

Cafes Curtains which cover the top portion of a window surface.

Camber An upward curve.

Canopy A projection over windows and doors which protects them from the weather.

Cantilever A projecting member supported only at one end.

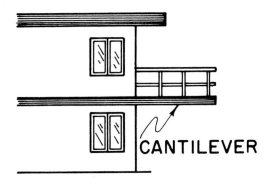

CANTILEVER

Capital The top decorative motif of a column.

Carport An automobile shelter not fully enclosed.

Carriage The horizontal part of the stringers of a stair that supports the treads.

Case furniture Furniture used for any type of storage.

Casement window A hinged window that opens out, usually made of metal.

CASEMENT
WINDOW

Casing A metal or wooden member around door and window openings to give a finished appearance.

Caster Wheels fastened to furniture.

Cathedral window Windows which follow a sloping roof line.

Caulking Waterproof material used to seal cracks.

Cavity wall A hollow wall usually made of two brick walls built a few inches apart, joined with brick or metal ties.

Cedar shingles Roofing and siding shingles made from western red cedar.

Cellulose A synthetic material.

Cement A masonry adhesive material purchased in the form of pulverized powder. Any substance used in its soft state to join other materials together and which afterward dries and hardens.

Central heating A single source of heat which is distributed by pipes of ducts.

Ceramics Clay shaped in various useful or decorative forms and fired in a kiln to produce a hard surface.

Certificate of title A document given to the home buyer with the deed, stating that the title to the property named in the deed is clearly established.

Chaise lounge An elongated chair which can support a person in a reclining position.

Chalk line A string that is heavily chalked, held tight, then plucked to make a straight guideline against boards or other surfaces.

Chandelier Lighting fixture suspended from ceiling.

Chase A vertical space within a building for ducts, pipes, or wires.

352

Chasing Ornamental metalwork created by indenting the surface.

Checks Splits or cracks in a board, ordinarily caused by excessive rapid drying.

Chimney A vertical flue that extends above the roof and carries smoke and gases outside.

Chintz Plain woven fabric finished with a lustrous glaze.

Chromo A term referring to color intensity.

Cinder block A building block made of cement and cinder.

Circuit The path of an electric current. The closed loop of wire in which an electric current can flow.

Circuit breaker A device used to open and close an electric circuit.

Clapboard A horizontal board, thicker on one side than the other, used to overlap an adjacent board to make house siding.

Classic Established standard of excellence.

Clearance A clear space; a passageway.

CLEARANCE

Clerestory An outside wall with windows that rises above an adjoining roof. A set of high windows often above a roof line.

CLERESTORY

Clinch A fastening achieved by bending and flattening the protruding end of a nail.

Clip A small connecting angle used for fastening various parts of a structure.

Closed plan A floor plan that compartmentalizes internal space by isolating each room with walls and doors.

Cobbler's bench Bench used by shoemakers, often replicated as a coffee table.

Collage An artistic composition combining many items in one layered pattern.

Colonial Furniture and accessories designs from the American colonial period.

Column In architecture: a circular supporting member, perpendicular to its load; in engineering: a vertical structural member supporting loads acting on or near and in the direction of its longitudinal axis.

Commode A low chest.

Common wall A wall that serves two dwelling units.

Complementary color One of a pair of colors opposite each other on the color wheel.

Composition The arrangement of separate elements in a properly proportioned design.

Concrete A combination of cement, sand, and gravel mixed with water.

Concrete block Precast-hollow or solid blocks of concrete.

Condemn To legally declare unfit for use.

Condensation The formation of frost or drops of water on inside walls when warm vapor inside a room meets a cold wall or window.

Conductor In architecture a drain pipe leading from the roof. In electricity any material that permits the passage of an electric current.

Conduit A channel built to convey water or other fluids; a drain or sewer. In electrical work, a channel that carries wires for protection and for safety.

Console A table designed to fit against a wall.

Construction loan A mortgage loan that is used to pay for labor and materials necessary for construction of a house. Money is usually advanced to the builder as construction progresses and is repaid when the house is completed and sold.

Continuous beam A beam that has three or more supports.

Contractor A person offering to build for a specified sum of money.

Convector A heat-transfer surface that uses convection currents to transfer heat.

Convenience outlet Electrical device into which portable lighting and electrical appliances are plugged.

Conventional Design characteristics of the present.

Cool colors Colors that are close to blue on the color wheel.

Corbel A projection in a masonry wall made by setting courses beyond the lower ones.

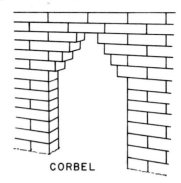

CORBEL

Corner bead A metal molding built into plaster corners to prevent the accidental breaking off of the plaster.

Cornice The part of a roof that projects out from the wall.

Cornice lighting Structural, continuous, indirect-lighting placed on a wall just below the ceiling line.

Counterflashing A flashing used under the regular flashing.

Course A continuous row of stone or brick of uniform height.

Court A open space surrounded partially or entirely by a building.

Cove Concave surface molding.

Cove lighting Structural lighting that is recessed in the upper part of a wall against the ceiling.

Crawl space The shallow space below the floor of a house which is built above the ground. It is surrounded by a foundation wall.

Crossbatch Lines drawn closely together at a 40° angle to show a sectional cut

Crown molding The top molding of any design.

Cull Building material rejected as below standard grade.

Curb A very low wall.

Cure To allow concrete to dry slowly by keeping it moist to allow maximum strength.

Curtain wall An exterior wall that provides no structural support.

Dado A joint in which one surface is plowed to receive the other.

Damp course A layer of water-proof material.

Damper A movable plate which regulates the draft of a stove, fireplace, or furnace.

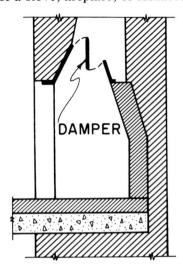

Dead load All the weight in a structure made up of immovable materials. See also Loads.

Deadening Construction intended to prevent the passage of sound.

Decay The disintegration of wood through the action of fungi.

Decorative design Design without function.

Deed A legal document indicating ownership of property.

Dehumidify To reduce the moisture content in the air.

Density The number of people living in a calculated area of land such as a square mile or square kilometer.

Depreciation Loss of value.

Detail To provide specific instructions to accompany a drawing, dimensions, notes, or specifications.

354

Diameter The distance across the center of a circle.

Diffused light Light that is spread evenly over a surface.

Dimension building material Building material that has been precut to specific sizes.

Dimension line A line with arrowheads at either end to show the distance between two points.

Direct light Light that shines directly on a surface without interruption.

Disposal A sink device which grinds waste prior to removal through sewer pipes.

Dome A hemispherical roof form.

Doorstop The strips on the doorjambs against which the door closes.

Dormer A structure that projects from a sloping roof to accommodate a window.

Double glazing A pane construction consisting of two pieces of glass with air space in between and sealed to provide insulation.

Double header A type of construction in which two or more timbers are joined for strength.

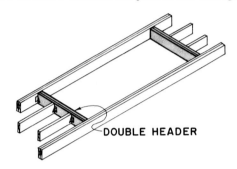

Double hung A construction feature of a window in which top and bottom sashes are each capable of movement up and down.

DOUBLE HUNG

Dovetail A joint with interlocking wedges used mostly for drawer fronts.

Dowel A round length of wood or metal.

Dowel joint A small length of dowel used to reinforce a butt joint.

Drain A pipe for carrying waste water.

Draperies Material used to cover windows.

Draw curtain A curtain that may be drawn by means of cords and pulleys.

Dressed lumber Lumber machined and smoothed at the mill. Usually ½ inch less than nominal (rough) size.

Drop ceiling A ceiling constructed below the level of the original ceiling.

Dry-wall construction An interior wall covering other than plaster, usually referred to as gypsumboard surfacing.

Ducts Sheet-metal conductors for warm- and cold-air distribution.

Dutch doors Doors in which the top and bottom halves open and close separately.

Earthenware A coarse grade of ceramic fired at a low temperature.

Efflorescence The effect of whitish powder forming on the surface of bricks or stone walls due to evaporation of moisture containing salts.

Eggshell finish A semigloss finish.

Elbow An L-shaped pipe fitting.

Electroplating The metal coating with a thin surface composed of more valuable metal.

Elements of design The tools of the designer—color, line, form, texture, material, light, and space.

Elevation The drawings of the front, side, or rear face of a building.

Ell An extension or wing of a building at right angles to the main section.

Embellish To add decoration.

Embossing Stamping or hammering on a surface to create a design.

Enamel Paint with a considerable amount of varnish, producing a hard, glossy surface.

Equity The interest in or value of real estate the owner has in excess of the mortgage indebtedness.

Escutcheon A metal fitting or plate to which door hardware, keyholes, and knobs are attached.

Etchings Prints made from metal plates which have been tolled or acid burned.

Fabrication Work done on parts of a structure at the factory before delivery to the building site.

Facade The face or front elevation of a building.

Face brick A brick used on the outside face of a wall.

Facing A finish material used to cover another material.

Fascia A horizontal, flat molding; a vertical board nailed on the ends of rafters, forming part of the cornice.

Fatigue A weakening of structural members.

Fenestration The arrangement of windows in a building.

Fiber Material capable of being formed into fabric.

Fiberboard Chemically bonded building material comprised of fibrous material and binders.

Filigree Intricate ornamental openwork in lacework patterns.

Filled insulation A loose insulating material poured from bags or blown by machines into walls.

Fillet A concave molding.

Finial The top ornament of an object.

Finish lumber Dressed wood used for building trim.

Firebrick An especially hard, heat-resistant brick that is used in fireplaces.

Fireclay A grade of clay that can withstand a large quantity of heat, used for firebrick.

Fire door A door that will resist fire.

Fire partition A barrier designed to restrict the spread of fire.

Fire stop Obstruction across air passages in buildings to prevent the spread of hot gases and flames; a horizontal blocking between wall studs.

Fixed light A permanently sealed window.

Fixture A piece of electric or plumbing equipment.

Flagging Cut stone, slate, or marble used for floors.

Flagstone A flat stone used for floors, steps, walks, or walls.

Flashing The material used for, and the process of making watertight, the roof intersections and other exposed places on the outside of a house.

Flat roof A roof with just enough pitch to let water drain.

Floating Spreading plaster, stucco, or cement on walls by means of a tool called a float.

Flocking A surface covering with velvet-type powdered wool.

Floor plan The top view of a building at a specified floor level. A floor plan includes all vertical details at or above windowsill levels.

Floor plug An electrical outlet flush with the floor.

Flue The opening in a chimney through which smoke passes.

Flue lining Terra cotta pipe used for the inner lining of chimneys.

Flush surface A continuous surface without an angle.

Fluorescent light The illumination created in a glass tube when an electrical current activates mercury and argon vapors.

Flutes Parallel concave grooves used to ornament a surface.

Footcandle The amount of light produced on a surface one foot from a light source.

Form Three-dimensional matter.

Formal balance Symmetry in design.

French provincial A furniture style based on design in the seventeenth and eighteenth century French provinces, as adapted for the general population.

Frieze The flat board of cornice trim that is fastened to the wall.

Frost line The depth into which frost penetrates the soil.

Fumigate To destroy harmful insect or animal life with fumes.

Furring Narrow strips of board nailed on walls and ceilings to form a straight surface, for the purpose of attaching wallboards or ceiling tile.

Fuse A strip of soft metal inserted in an electric circuit which is designed to melt and open the circuit should the current exceed a predetermined value.

Gable The triangular end of an exterior wall above the eaves.

Gable roof A roof that slopes from two sides only.

Galvanize A lead and zinc bath treatment used to prevent metal from rusting.

Gambrel roof A symmetrical roof with two different pitches or slopes on each side.

Garret An attic.

Gateleg table A drop-leaf table.

General lighting Lighting which illuminates large areas.

Geodesic dome A vault created by a series of joined triangular structures.

Geometric designs Patterns derived from combinations of circles, ovals, squares, triangles, rectangles, octagons, hexagons, and pentagons in precise, mathematical formations.

Gingerbread Showy, but unsubstantial, referring to an excessive ornamental style found in Victorian-type designs.

Girder A horizontal beam that supports floor joists.

Glass block Glass molded in brick form.

Glass curtains Draperies made from fiberglass material.

Glaze A glossy, protective coating.

Glazing The fitting of glass in windows or doors.

Golden rectangle A rectangle whose proportions have a ratio of 2 to 3.

Gothic Formal architecture of the 11th through 15th centuries.

Grade The level of the ground around a building.

Grain Color variations in wood, resulting from a tree's summer and winter growth.

Graining The artificial creation of grain patterns on a surface.

Granite Extremely hard rock crystalized from quartz to mica.

Graphic symbols Symbolic representations used in drawing to simplify the presentation of complicated items.

Green lumber Timber that still contains moisture or sap.

Grills Surfaces with open spaces designed to allow the passage of light, heat, and air.

Grout A thin cement mortar used for leveling and filling masonry holes.

Gypsum board A fiberboard made of plaster with a covering of paper, used for interior walls.

Half timber A frame construction of heavy timbers in which the spaces are filled in with masonry.

Hardwood Wood from trees that grow slowly and develop hard, close densities.

Harmony The sense of order among the elements of design.

Hassock A cushioned footstool.

Head The upper frame on a door or window.

Header The horizontal supporting member above an opening, for example, a lintel; one or more pieces of lumber supporting the ends of joists, used in framing the openings of stairs and chimneys.

Headroom The clear space between the floor line and ceiling, as in a stairway.

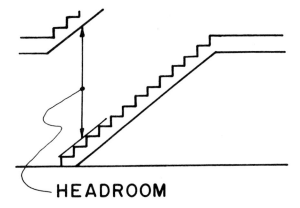

HEADROOM

Hearth That part of the floor directly in front of the fireplace and the floor inside the fireplace on which the fire is built. It is made of fire-resistant masonry.

Hellenistic Referring to Greek origin.

Hemp An Asiatic fiber.

Highboy A tall chest.

Hip roof A roof with four sloping sides.

Hooked rug A floor covering created by hooking strips of cloth through a canvas backing.

Horseshoe arch An arch created when the curve is continued past the horizontal diameter on both sides.

Hue The basic name of a color, such as red, blue, or yellow.

Humidifier A mechanical device that controls the amount of water vapor to be added to the atmosphere.

Humidistat An instrument used for measuring and controlling moisture in the air.

Humidity The moisture content in the air.

Hutch A chest or cabinet.

I beam A steel beam with an I-shaped cross-section.

I-BEAM

Incandescent lighting Illumination created in a closed bulb by means of heating a filament.

Incised A term referring to the pattern produced by carving or cutting the inlay ornamentation of one material into another.

Indigenous A term referring to materials that are native to an area.

Indirect lighting Artificial illumination that is reflected from walls or ceilings and perceived without eye contact with the source.

Informal balance Asymmetry in design.

Insulating board Any board suitable for insulating purposes, usually manufactured board made from vegetable fibers, such as fiberboard.

Insulation Materials for obstructing the passage of sound, heat, or cold from one surface to another.

Intensity The strength of a color hue.

Interest The amount of money paid as a percentage of the amount borrowed.

Interior trim General term for all the finish molding, casing, baseboard, etc.

Intermediate colors See **Tertiary colors.**

Jacquard weave A complex weave used to create elaborate carpet and textile designs.

Jalousie A type of window consisting of a number of long, thin, hinged panels.

JALOUSIE

Jamb The sides of a doorway or window opening.

Joinery Woodworking skills.

Joints The meeting of two separate pieces of material for a common bond.

Joist A horizontal structural member that supports the floor system or ceiling system.

Kalamein door A fireproof door with a metal covering.

Kapok Natural fiber used for the manufacture of cushion fillings.

Keystone The top, wedge-shaped stone of an arch.

KEYSTONE

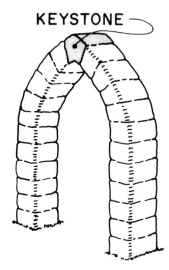

Kiln A heating chamber for drying lumber.

Knee wall A low wall resulting from one-and-one-half–story construction.

Knitted fabrics Material created by the process of interlooping continuous yarn.

Knotty pine Pine panelling with knots left intact and sealed.

Lally column A steel column used as a support for girders and beams.

Laminated beam A beam made by bonding together several layers of material.

Laminates Sheets that have been formed by bonding with other sheets.

Lamination The bonding of material in layers with glue and heat to produce a stronger material.

Landing A platform in a flight of steps.

Lap joint A joint produced by lapping two pieces of material.

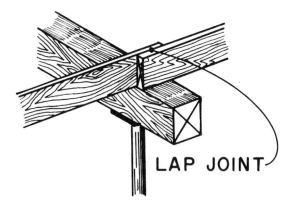

LAP JOINT

Lath (metal) Sheet-metal screening used as a base for plastering.

Lath (wood) A wooden strip nailed to studding and joists, to which plaster is applied.

Lattice A grille or openwork made by crossing strips of wood or metal.

Lavatory A washbasin or a room equipped with a washbasin.

Layout The sketch of a floor plan.

Lease A document describing the legal assignment of property from one party to another.

Leasee The party to whom property is assigned for a period of time.

Leasor The property controller who assigns property to another for a period of time.

Leather Fabric created from animal hides.

Ledger A wood strip nailed to the lower side of a girder to provide a bearing surface for joists.

Lien A legal claim on a property, which may be exercised in default of payment of a debt.

Light meter An instrument used to measure light intensity.

Light window The small panes of glass in a window.

Line One element of design using a single line without enclosing and creating dimensional form.

Lineal foot A measurement of one foot along a straight line.

Lintel A horizontal piece of wood, stone, or steel placed across the top of door and window openings in order to bear the weight of the walls above the opening.

Loads *Live load:* the total of all moving and variable loads that may be placed upon a building; *dead load:* the weight of all permanent, stationary construction including a building.

Load-bearing walls Walls that support weight from above as well as their own weight.

Loft The extension of an internal balcony or upper commercial building floor.

Loggia A roofed, open passage along the front or side of a building. It is often at an upper level, and frequently has a series of columns on either or both sides.

Louver A set of fixed or movable slats adjusted to provide both shelter and ventilation.

LOUVER

Lowboy A low chest of drawers.

Luminous A term that describes material through which light passes.

Lux The metric unit of light measure.

Mansard roof A roof with two slopes on each side, with the lower slope much steeper than the upper.

Mantel A shelf over a fireplace.

Marble Limestone with a highly polished appearance.

Marbling The effect of veining a surface in a marblelike pattern.

Market price The cost that property can be sold for at a given time.

Market value The amount that property is worth at a given time.

Marquetry Patterns created by inserting metal or contrasting woods into wood surfaces.

Masonry Anything built with stone, brick, tiles, or concrete.

Matte A dull surface.

Medium The material used in the creation of a design.

Meeting rail The horizontal rails on a double-hung sash that fit together when the window is closed.

Member A single piece in a structure that is complete in itself.

Metal tie A strip of metal used to fasten construction members together.

Metal wall ties Strips of corrugated metal used to tie a brick veneer wall to framework.

Mildew A mold on wood caused by fungi.

Millwork The finish woodwork in a building, such as cabinets and trim.

Mineral wool An insulating material made into a fibrous form from mineral slag.

Miter The corner intersection in which angles of each piece are equal.

Modular construction Construction in which the size of the building and the building materials are based on a common unit of measure.

Mohair A heavy-pile upholstery material.

Moire The effect created when objects reflect light in varying wavy patterns as the light and the angle of sight change.

Moisture barrier A material such as specially treated paper that retards the passage of vapor or moisture into walls and prevents condensation within the walls.

Monochrome The use of a single color in a scheme.

Monolithic A term describing concrete construction that is poured and cast in one structural mass without joints.

Montage A composition created by combining many parts.

Mortar A mixture of cement, sand, and water used by a mason as a bonding agent for binding bricks and stone.

Mortgage A pledging of property, conditional on payment of the debt in full.

Mortgagee The lender of money to the mortgagor.

Mortgagor The owner who mortgages property in return for a loan.

Mosaic Small colored tile, glass, stone, or similar material arranged on an adhesive ground to produce a decorative surface.

Motif A recurring and consistent design theme.

Mud room A small room or entranceway where one can remove muddy overshoes and wet garments before entering other rooms.

Mullion A vertical bar in a window separating two windows.

MULLION

Muntin A small bar separating the glass lights in a window.

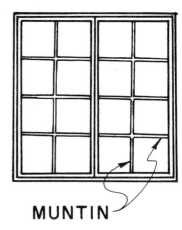

MUNTIN

Natural Derived from nature, as opposed to artificially created.

Neoclassical A term referring to the revival of classical design with contemporary style or materials.

Neutral Without emphasis, able to blend in with many things.

Newel A post supporting the handrail at the top or bottom of a stairway.

Niche A recessed space.

Noise Unwanted sound.

Nominal dimensions Dimensions for finished lumber in which the stated dimension is usually larger than the actual dimension. These dimensions are usually larger by an amount required to smooth a board.

Nonbearing wall A dividing wall that does not support a vertical load other than its own weight.

Nonferrous metal Metal containing no iron, such as copper, brass, and aluminum.

Nosing The rounded edge of a stair tread.

Obscure glass Sheet glass that is made translucent instead of transparent.

Off-white Pure white with the slight addition of a hue.

On-center A term referring to measurement from the center of one member to the center of another (noted oc).

Opaque A term that describes material through which light cannot pass.

Open plan A floor plan organized with minimum interior partitions.

Open-ended mortgage A mortgage that permits the remaining amount of the loan to be increased, for such reason as for improvements, by mutual agreement of the lender and borrower without rewriting the mortgage.

Optical balance The achieving of a balanced appearance without using the exact dimensions of balance; a slight, desirable optical illusion created in the design.

Orientation The relationship of design components to one factor, such as their relationship to sun-solar orientation.

Ornamented Decorated.

Ottoman A low, cushioned seat.

Outlet Any kind of electrical box allowing current to be drawn from the electrical system for lighting or appliances.

Overhang The horizontal distance that a roof projects beyond a wall.

Pane A framed sheet of window glass.

Panel A two-dimensional surface.

Pargework Decorative plaster.

Parging A thin coat of plaster applied to masonry surfaces for smoothing purposes.

Parquet flooring Flooring, usually of wood, laid in an alternating or inlaid pattern to form various designs.

Partition An interior wall that separates two rooms.

Party wall Between two adjoining buildings, a wall which both owners share, such as a common wall between row houses.

Pastel Colors with light tints.

Patio An open court.

Pedestal A supporting base.

Pendant A hanging ornament.

Penny The term for the length of a nail, abbreviated *d* (for example 16d).

Penthouse A dwelling located on the top floor of a building.

Period furniture Furniture manufactured in a style associated directly with a specific period of history.

Periphery The entire outside edge of an object.

Perspective The art of drawing an object on a plane surface to look as it would in a three-dimensional form, i.e., an object drawn as it would appear to the eye.

Pewter A tin and lead alloy with a gray appearance, originally used as a substitute for silver.

Picture window A single-pane large window without mullions or muntins.

Pigment A substance from which colored paints are derived.

Pilaster A portion of a square column, usually set within or against a wall for the purpose of strengthening the wall; a decorative column attached to a wall.

Pile Carpets or textiles constructed with upright loops.

Pillar A column used for supporting parts of a structure.

Pinnacle The projecting or ornamental cap on the high point of a roof.

Plan A horizontal, graphic representational section of a building, showing the walls, doors, windows, stairs, chimneys, and surrounding objects, like walks and landscape.

Planks Material 2 or 3 in (50 or 75 mm) thick and more than 4 in (100 mm) wide, such as joists, flooring, and the like.

Plaster A mortarlike composition used for covering walls and ceilings, generally made of portland cement mixed with sand and water.

Plaster ground A nailer strip included in plaster walls to act as a gauge for the thickness of plaster and to give a nailing support for finish trim around openings and near the base of a wall.

Plasterboard A board made of plastering material covered on both sides with heavy paper. Also called gypsum board, it is often used instead of plaster.

Plastic Artificial, malleable material.

Plate glass A high-quality sheet of glass used in large windows.

Plenum system A method of heating or air conditioning in which air is forced through a chamber connected to distributing ducts.

Plow To cut a groove running in the same direction as the grain of the wood.

Plumb A term describing an object when it is in true vertical position, as determined by a plumb bob.

Plywood A piece of wood made of three or more layers of veneer joined with glue and usually laid with the grain of adjoining plies at right angles.

Polychrome The use of many colors in a design.

Porch A covered area attached to the entrance of a house.

Portico The covering of an entrance area supported by columns; a roof supported by columns, whether attached to a building or wholly by itself.

Portland cement An extremely hard hydraulic cement formed by burning silica, lime, and alumina together and then grinding up the mixture.

Post A perpendicular supporting member.

Post and beam construction Wall construction consisting of posts rather than studs.

Precast A term describing concrete shapes that have been made separately before being used in a structure.

Prefabricated A term referring to components that are built at a factory and assembled on the site.

Primary coat The first coat of paint.

Primary colors Red, yellow, and blue—the colors that cannot be created by mixing other colors.

Principal The original amount of money loaned.

Principles of design Guidelines for the use of the elements of design.

Proportion The relationship of the amount of one design element to all others.

Quad An enclosed court.

Quarry tile A machine-made, unglazed tile.

Quarter-round A convex molding, a quarter of a circle.

Quilted fabrics Fabrics that have been sewn together with another fabric, with filler material between the two layers.

Quoins Large squared stones set in the corners of a masonry building for appearance.

Radial balance Symmetry around a given point.

Radiant heating A system using heating elements in the floors, ceilings, or walls to radiate heat into the room.

Rafters Structural members used to frame a roof. Several types are: common, hip, jack, valley, and cripple.

Rail Vertical strips.

Random plank Wood planks of varying widths.

Realtor A real estate broker who is a member of a local chapter of the National Association of Real Estate Boards.

Receding color Colors that appear to move away from the viewer.

Register The open end of a duct in a room for warm or cool air.

Reinforced concrete Concrete in which steel bars or webbing has been embedded for strength.

Relief An area created by rising surfaces.

Remodel To rebuild.

Rendering The art of shading or coloring a drawing.

Replica A reproduction of an original.

Restoration Rebuilding a structure so that it will appear in its original form.

Restrictions Limitations on the use of real estate as set by law or contained in a deed.

Retaining wall A wall used to hold back an earth embankment.

Rheostat An instrument for regulating electric current.

Rhythm The sense of movement in a design.

Rise The vertical height of a roof.

Riser The vertical board in a stairway between two treads.

Rock wool An insulating material that looks like wool but is composed of such substances as granite or silica.

Rocker A chair with curved supports.

Roll shades Window shades that roll up and down on a cylinder.

Roman shades Window shades that raise in accordian folds.

Rough floor The subfloor on which the finished floor is laid.

Rough hardware All the hardware used in a house, such as nails and bolts, that is not visible in the completed house.

Rough lumber Lumber as it comes from the saw.

Rough opening Any unfinished opening in the framing of a building.

Roughing in Putting up the skeleton of a building.

Rubble Masonry in irregularly shaped, rough form.

Run Stonework having irregularly shaped units and no indication of systematic course work; the horizontal distance covered by a flight of stairs; the length of a rafter.

Sand finish A final plaster coat; a skim coat.

Sap All the fluids in a tree.

Sash The movable framework in which window panes are set.

Scab A small wood member, fastened on the outside face, that is used to join other members.

Schedule A list of parts or details.

Sconce Wall brackets that hold candles or light bulbs.

Scratch coat The first coat of plaster, which is scratched to provide a good bond for the next coat.

Screed A guide for the correct thickness of plaster or concrete to be placed on surfaces.

Scroll Decorative spiral lines.

Scuttle A small opening in a ceiling used to provide access to an attic or roof.

Seasoning The drying out of green lumber, either in an oven or kiln or by exposure to air.

Second mortgage A mortgage made by a home buyer to raise money for a down payment required under the first mortgage.

Secondary colors Colors produced by combining two primary colors.

Secretary A tall desk with shelves and drawers for storage, and a surface for writing.

Section The drawing of an object that is cut to show the interior; a panel construction used in walls, floors, ceilings, or roofs.

Shade Color that contains a percentage of black.

Shakes Thick, hand-cut shingles.

Shed roof A flat roof slanting in one direction.

Shim A piece of material used to level or fill in the space between two surfaces.

Shingles Thin pieces of wood or other materials that overlap each other in covering a roof. The number and kind needed depend on the steepness of the roof slope and other factors. Kinds of shingles include tile shingles, slate shingles, asbestos-cement shingles, and asphalt shingles.

Shiplap Boards with lapped joints along their edges.

Shirring The gathering of textiles into folds.

Shoe mold The small mold against the baseboard at the floor.

Shutters External solid window covers.

Siding The outside boards of an exterior wall.

Silhouette The outline of an object without internal detail.

Sill The horizontal exterior member below a window or door opening; the wood member placed directly on top of the foundation wall in wood-frame construction.

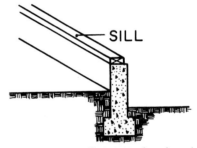

Skeleton construction Construction in which the frame carries all the weight.

Skylight An opening in the roof for admitting light.

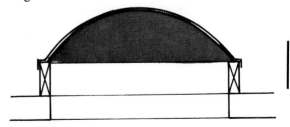

SKYLIGHT

Slab foundation A reinforced concrete floor and foundation system.

Sleepers Strips of wood, usually 2 x 2's, laid over a slab floor to which finished wood is nailed.

363

Sliding windows Windows that open and close by sliding horizontally.

Smoke chamber The portion of a chimney flue located directly over the fireplace.

Soffit The underside of a projecting architectural detail.

Soffit lighting Structural lighting attached near the ceiling line.

Softwood Low-density wood that can be easily cut and used for general construction but not for fine furniture.

Soil stack The main verticle pipe that receives waste from all fixtures.

Solar heat Heat from the sun's rays.

Sole The horizontal framing member directly under the studs.

Spacing The distance between structural members.

Spackle To cover wallboard joints with plaster.

Span The distance between structural supports.

Specification The written or printed direction regarding the details of a building or other construction.

Spike A large, heavy nail.

Splice The joining of two similar members in a straight line.

Split-level A building with floors that intersect two other floors at different levels.

Stack A vertical pipe.

Stained glass Colored glass.

Steel-framing Skeleton framing with structural steel beams.

Steening Brickwork without mortar.

Stencil A method of printing by brushing paint through a precut pattern.

Stile A vertical member of a door, window, or panel.

Stipple To apply paint in a dot form by means of a brush or a coarse spray.

Stock Common sizes of building materials and equipment available from most commercial industries.

Stool An inside windowsill.

Stop A small strip used to hold a door or window sash in place.

364

Storm door or window An extra door or extra window placed outside an ordinary door or window for added protection against the cold.

Stretcher The horizontal member that connects furniture legs.

Stringer The sides of a flight of stairs; the supporting member cut to receive the treads and risers.

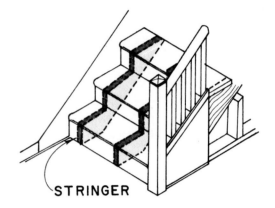

STRINGER

Structural lighting Lighting fixtures that are an integral part of a building.

Stucco Any of various plasters used for covering walls, especially an exterior wall covering in which cement is used.

Studs Upright beams in the framework of a building, usually referred to as 2 x 4's and spaced at 16 in from center to center.

Studio A one-room apartment.

Subfloor A rough flooring surface laid directly on floor joists and covered with finished floor materials.

SUBFLOOR

Sump A pit in a basement floor to collect water, into which a sump pump is placed to remove the water through sewer pipes.

Surfaced lumber Timber that is dressed by running it through a planer.

Swag Draping in a loop effect.

Symmetrical balance A phrase that describes designs in which both halves are identical.

Synthetic Made of artificial materials

Tapestry A heavy fabric with designs or scenes woven directly into the material.

Tempered A term referring to thoroughly mixed cement or mortar.

Terra cotta Low-fired red-brown clay.

Terrazzo A floor surface material made from crushed marble and cement.

Tertiary colors Colors made by combining a primary and a secondary color.

Tester The framework over a four-poster bed.

Textile A fiber for making cloth.

Texture The tactile surface quality of a material.

Thermal conductor A substance capable of transmitting heat.

Thermostat A device for automatically controlling the supply of heat.

Threshold The beveled piece of stone, wood, or metal over which a door swings. It is sometimes called a carpet strip or a saddle.

Throat A passage directly above a fireplace opening where a damper is set.

Tie A structural member used to bind others together.

Tile Thin slabs used for covering large, flat areas like walls, ceilings, roofs, and floors.

Tilt top A tabletop hinged to enable part of the top to be moved vertically.

Timber Lumber with a cross section larger than 4 by 6 in (100 by 150 mm) for posts, fills, and girders.

Tint A color made by adding white to its hue.

Toenail To drive nails at an angle.

Tolerance The acceptable variance of dimensions from a standard size.

Tongue A projection on the edge of wood that joins with a similarly shaped groove.

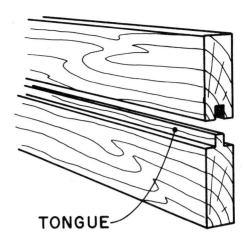

TONGUE

Tongue and groove A wood joint in which two of wood are connected by inserting the tongue of one into the groove of the other.

Total run The sum of all the tread widths in a stair.

Traditional A term referring to established criteria in period design.

Traffic lanes Planned routes through which people move.

Translucent A term describing material that transmits light but not images.

Transom A small window over a door.

Transparent A term describing see-through material.

Tread The step or horizontal member of a stair.

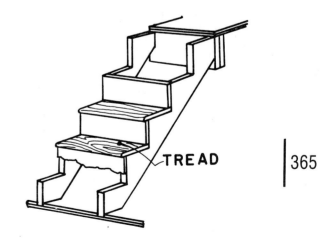

TREAD

Truss A triangularly shaped unit for supporting roof leads over long spans.

Tweed Fabric containing two or more woven colors.

Undressed lumber Timber that is not squared or finished smoothly.

Unfinished furniture Furniture that has not been sealed, painted, lacquered, or stained.

Unit construction Construction that includes two or more preassembled walls, together with floor and ceiling construction, ready for shipment to the building site.

Unity The effect of designs in which the parts interrelate, creating an integrated whole.

Upholstery The fabric covering of furniture.

Valance A horizontal member used over the top of a drapery system.

Valance lighting Structural lighting used over windows.

Valley The internal angle formed by the two slopes of a roof.

Value (color) The amount of black or white in a color.

Valve A device for regulating the flow of material in a pipe.

Vapor barrier A watertight material used to prevent the passage of moisture or water vapor into and through walls.

Vault A series of connected arches.

Veneer A thin covering of valuable material over a less expensive material.

Venetian blinds Window shades made from horizontal slats connected with vertical tapes.

Vent A screened opening for ventilation.

Vent pipes Small ventilating pipes extending from each fixture of a plumbing system to the vent stack.

Vent stack The upper portion of a soil or waste stack above the highest fixture.

Ventilation The process of supplying and removing air by natural or mechanical means to or from any space.

Vestibule A small lobby or entrance room.

Vinyl A synthetic material used in fabrics and floor coverings.

Vitreous Pertaining to a composition of materials that resembles glass.

Volume The amount of space, measured in cubic units, occupied by an object.

Wainscot The facing for the lower part of an interior wall.

Wallboard Wood pulp, gypsum, or similar materials made into large, rigid sheets that may be fastened to the frame of a building to provide a surface finish.

Warm colors Colors that border on the red side of the color wheel.

Warp Any change from a true or plane surface. Warping includes such instances as bows, crooks, cups, and twists.

Warranty A written guarantee of performance.

Wash The slant upon a sill, capping, etc., to allow the water to run off.

Waste stack A vertical pipe in a plumbing system that carries the discharge from any fixture.

Waterproof Material or construction that prevents the passage of water.

Watt A unit of electrical energy.

Weathering The mechanical or chemical disintegration and discoloration of the surface of exterior building materials.

Weatherstrip A strip of metal or fabric fastened along the edges of windows and doors to reduce drafts and heat loss.

Weaving The interlocking of two or more yarns to create textiles.

Weep hole An opening at the bottom of a wall to allow the drainage of water.

Well opening A floor opening for a stairway.

Wood grain The dark and light patterns of wood.

Work area The part of a dwelling used to maintain and provide services such as cooking, cleaning, storage, and maintenance.

Work triangle The triangular pattern created by connecting the three basic areas in a kitchen—storage, cleaning and preparation, and cooking.

Yarn Twisted fibers in long strands.

Yoke An angled crossbar.

Zoning Building restrictions as to size, location, and type of structures to be erected in specific areas.

INDEX

368

372